To hear
Best health

Lost In The Sand

by Shanna Ahmad

A novel based on true events.

shannaahmad@hotmail.com

This book is dedicated to,

All the victims of genocide.

The thousands of children still suffering the effects
of chemical warfare.
Effects that have no cure.

To all those who have lost their lives attempting to
bring peace to Iraq.

To the brave soldiers of the coalition and the many
peace loving citizens of my country in their ongoing
attempts to bring peace and stability to the land of
my birth.

prologue

Children screamed in agony as the falling yellow mist burned eyes and faces after looking skywards at the odd happenings over the village. Mothers hearing the appalling cries of their children, attempted to shield them from the mist by covering them with their own bodies. Yet the act of rushing to aid the little ones caused them to draw the mist deep into their lungs. Instantly eyes, throats, and lungs burned in excruciating pain. Screaming became impossible. The men of the village, who had been sitting talking when the aircraft appeared overhead, rushed to aid their families. They too succumbed to the mist sprayed over the village and fell dying, grotesquely contorted.

In just a few minutes not a single human, animal, neither bird, nor insect within the village remained alive. The story of their lives is written in the sand, to be read by no one. Two children, Najat, a village girl of seven, and Shwan, a shepherd boy of nine summers, looked down onto the village of Zalan from their vantage point high up in the grazing lands above the settlement in Northern Iraq. They were the only witnesses and survivors of that mass killing.

The following relates the story of Najat's survival during the Iraqi Ba'ath Regime's attempts at genocide of the Iraqi Kurdish people. It also recounts the brutal torture she endured in Saddam Hussein's atrocious prisons in her quest to help bring freedom and some semblance of peace to her beloved country.

chapter one

Barely conscious from the latest beating, I felt myself being pulled by my arms with my feet dragging along the rough concrete passage. The guards hurled me into my kennel-like cell. I heard the sound of the slamming door and boots receding down the passage. I lay still on the cold floor having insufficient strength to crawl to the disgusting feces and blood stained pad that served as a mattress. In an odd way, the coldness of the floor soothed my tortured body.

Eventually, I managed to crawl to the pad and lay face down, breathing in the foulness of it. Lying on my back was not an option. The torturers had reduced it to a bleeding mass of ridges created by the repeated beatings from my shoulders down to the soles of my feet.

I had a distinct feeling that my death was imminent unless I kept control over my will to survive. I knew I must concentrate on something other than my present situation. I forced myself to think of my parents and my earliest recollections of them. I turned my memories into a mental reliving of my life thus far.

My mother, Nassrean, delivered me into this world in a mud built house in the village of Zalan in the Kurdish region of Iraq. My parents named me Najat. I was their only child and they doted on me. I had been born with dark round eyes. I remember so well my father, Kaka Hamma, gazing into them as I sat by his side while mother prepared our meals. He would pull my cheek and ask,

"Have you been a good little girl today, Najat?" I would nod at him shaking my black hair, and he would smile the brightest of smiles. Even though our family, like the others in Zalan, had little money to spend on luxuries, Father would occasionally bring home some candy in his pocket. He bought it from the vendor who came with a truck from far beyond the mountains. Each week he brought candies and foods not available in Zalan to the village.

"See what I have found in my coat, Najat," he would say with a look of mock surprise.

Father wore traditional Kurdish clothing: long baggy pants, woolen jacket, and bulky headwear. He had a dark beard and worked with several other men on vegetable farms. At other times he took a position as shepherd and sheep shearer. Father was often called upon to slaughter a sheep or goat and received meat as payment. As I recall, he worked relatively long hours. However, he always had a little time to spend with me as we sat around our stove eating the good things mother gave us before going to bed. His hands, arms, and face were weathered from working outdoors in both the searing summer sun and the winter winds icy winds that swept down from the high snow-capped ridges above our village of about thirty houses and several livestock shelters.

Mother, like the other wives and mothers in Zalan, wore traditional Kurdish garments. She had long jet-black hair which hung well below her shoulders when it wasn't tied up and tucked under her headwear. Her eyes, like my father's, were dark. Her hands and face were wrinkled from laboring in the hot, dry atmosphere that cloaked Zalan in the summer months. She worked within the four walls of our small house with the exception of tending our garden. On washing day she and the other women went with their youngsters down to the river with bundles of laundry and bars of hard soap. There remain fond memories of those days. For us children it was like a carnival. We played games like tag, and the girls played a game remarkably like the English game of Ring Around the Rosie. We shouted and laughed. Then on warm days we splashed in the water, pretending to do laundry like our mothers.

I harbor no recollection of either of my parents ever being angry with me. We were poor, but having known no other way of life, I never felt poor. Sitting on the floor to dine was a Kurdish tradition and normal for the residents of Zalan. My family had plenty to eat and warm woolen blankets to sleep in and sheepskins to lie upon. But we had very little of the material things people in other countries consider essential. We did have love and plenty of it. My parents loved each other, and together they loved me, and I flourished in the glow of their love.

I suppose I must have been about four or five years old when I began to really notice things around me. I had seen the high peaks above Zalan many times, but now I saw them in a new way. They were no longer just big hills. Now the mountains became objects of great beauty in both the summer and winter seasons. I marveled at the expanse of small farms; they stretched from the base of the mountains on each side of the valley, creating a patchwork of various green colors. The grazing land which appeared in varying shades of brown climbed up the hillsides. I remember too the soothing sounds of a shepherd's flute drifting down from the hills that echoed through the day.

I remember winters, wrapped warmly against the cold, playing in the light snow that fell onto Zalan and the surrounding hills. I recall too, my summers playing games with friends with marks for hopscotch scored into the ground under the shade of trees within the village. We often played in the shallow pools in the river when the sun became unbearably hot. Our parents always had fears for us. Playing in the water and swimming was not part of the Kurdish tradition for females.

I recall springtime as a special time. The melting snow brought vibrant life to our valley. With a child's song on my lips I would go out to pick wildflowers for my mother. The ones she liked best consisted of red blossoms on tall stalks called "gullala swra".

"Oh, Najat, they are so lovely, my good girl," she would always say. However I remember every springtime also had a downside. When the frost receded, the dirt streets in the village became soft with wet mud which clung tenaciously to my shoes on the way home from school. It was a daily chore to keep the mud out of the house, and mother always came to my rescue and cleaned off my shoes with a pail of water.

"Najat, my precious one," she would say, "try to walk close to the houses where the ground is dryer."

Zalan had a small school which we children attended from a very early age. It had only one room with a single window and a blackboard on the opposite wall. The furnishings were plain wooden desks and benches. Our teachers came from far away cities and were highly respected for their knowledge and ability to teach us reading, writing, and arithmetic. My generation was among the first to receive any schooling. My parents and the others in the village were for the most part illiterate. Our village had no electricity, so at home we had an open stove for heating and cooking and there mother would also dry my shoes. At bedtime by candle light, mother would tell me stories that she had learned from her mother about characters who lived in unfamiliar places beyond our valley. Even at such a young age I knew there were exotic and dangerous lands beyond the surrounding hills. It was about this time I first heard some of the village men speaking about an enemy lurking beyond our protective mountains who did evil things. I had no real understanding of what they said and my father discouraged me from asking questions about it.

"You are much too young to hear of such things, my beautiful child, but I want you to be alert and if you see soldiers or Peshmarga, (Freedom Fighters) come quickly back to the house," he would tell me.

In the spring of that fifth year of my life when the new baby lambs were almost weaned, I met Shwan, a shepherd boy. In the morning and during the day Shwan took care of his father's flock, driving them up into the hills to graze and brought them back each evening. He played a flute as he ambled along behind the flock. His wooden flute was a home-made instrument. He had mastered only a few rudimentary, off key tunes. The sound fascinated me, and the haunting notes were always the first thing that came to my mind whenever I thought of Zalan, and I drew closer to hear the boy play.

Shwan wore clothing that would best be described as rags. He was a typical boy with a grubby face and runny nose. His dark hair had been shaved, the stubble covering his head contrasted against his lighter eyebrows. His cheeks were a bright red from constantly being outdoors in the sun and wind, and the kllash on his feet suffered from neglect. At first Shwan made it abundantly clear that he didn't want a girl hanging round he threw pebbles at me.

"Play me a tune" I shouted at him. He responded by hurling another stone. I didn't think it was his intention to hit me, but it did. The sharp stone struck me on the right side of my neck; I fell down and began to bleed. The shepherd boy ran to me in distress thinking he had done me a major injury. When he leaned over me, he wiped his nose into a handkerchief, and then wiped my wound with the same cloth.

"Hold the cloth against the wound," he said in a concerned voice. I resisted his hap- hazard attempt at first aid and pushed away his hand containing the obnoxious handkerchief.

"Why are you so mean? I only wanted to hear you play," I cried out. Flushed with guilt and possibly fearing his father's discipline, he catered to my demands.

"I will play a few tunes for you, but they are for your ears only. My name is Shwan. What is yours?"

He played several tunes for me as we waited for my wound to stop bleeding. Then together we followed the grazing sheep. On that day we formed a friendship that was to last through our childhood years into adulthood.

Shwan no longer attended the village school. It was his lot in life to help his father by taking care of his family's sheep while his father worked in the vegetable fields. Therefore, it was only on days when there were no classes that I was able to accompany him as he took the sheep to pasture on the hill sides. Mother, knowing that her daughter would come to no harm while accompanying the shepherd boy and his flock, would often wrap some food in a scarf. Shwan and I would share it when the sun reached its zenith.

"Race you home!" I would shout at Shwan when the time came to take the sheep back to the village.

"You know I can't race you, Najat. I have to bring the flock home," he would shout back in false annoyance.

The next two years were among the happiest I can remember. I loved school, and I was an eager student. On the days I accompanied Shwan up into the foothills, I marveled at the beauty of my valley and the peaks above it. I looked for rare wildflowers and watched in wonderment how quickly the lambs grew into wooly sheep. I smelled the clean air drifting down from the mountain's crests, and I developed a deep abiding love of my country.

One afternoon in Zalan, a wedding had been planned. Two young people were to begin their lives together, and the women of Zalan were busy making preparations of special foods for the celebrations. A wedding involved almost all members of our community. A feast would be held under the shade trees close to the school. There would be dancing and the singing of songs. The men would sit and chatter about work and the state of things in the outside of Zalan, and the women would fuss about the bride, offering their own special advice. The children would fill their tummies with the sweet foods from the large selection laid out on large cloths under the shade trees.

The haunting sounds of Shwan's flute in the distance caused me to realize I did not wish to be at the ceremonial events. Instead I longed for the freedom of the cool mountain air far away from the dust which would soon fill the air stirred up by the villagers. My mother's constant watching eye caught me in a not so subtle attempt to escape as I stuffed sweets into my scarf for Shwan and I to share. Mother told me my father in all likelihood would disapprove my leaving the village. She, however, was more worried about the dangers of playing in the water. She said, "You will always be a free spirit Najat. Off you go, my beautiful child." So off I went.

Shwan had just freed the sheep from the safety of their paddock. Driving them before us, we started the slow, even climb to the grazing lands in the foothills. Not a single cloud marred the blue sky and by noon the land was parched and baking hot.

"There is a large pond a little higher up than where I normally pasture the sheep, Najat. I will drive the sheep there to drink." He herded the sheep up the hill in his usual ritual of calling out to them in his monotone voice. I picked up a stick and mimicked all his actions. We arrived at the pond just as the afternoon heat had begun to peak. Lush grass surrounded the pond which was shaded by large pomegranate trees whose ripe fruit spoiled on the ground. Shwan removed his shirt and footwear and jumped into the water splashing and flinging water at me.

"Come in. It's not too deep," he called.

"No. My mother warned me about playing in the water, she said I might drown!" I shouted back.

Shwan laughed at me. "Look, it's not even up to my chest." I stepped in, being cautious in case it was too deep for me. Then I felt soft mud squeezing between my toes. I became instantly afraid and shrieked as I clambered out of the water. Shwan said, "You are afraid. You are a big baby, Najat." His words enraged me. I stiffened my spine and glared at him.

"I am not afraid. The mud between my toes felt funny that's all!" Continuing to laugh, Shwan mocked, "Prove it."

Glaring at him I stepped back into the pond and walked across the muddy bottom until the water reached my chest. I quickly forgot my annoyance with Shwan as the water brought sweet relief from the heat. Without warning a roaring sound like nothing I had ever heard before filled the air around us. Vibrations caused ripples on the pond surface and it seemed the ground beneath us shook. I glanced at Shwan for an explanation but because of the incredible noise, I saw that only his lips moved as he pointed upward. An airplane passed overhead, so large and close it seemed that I could reach out and touch it. I feared that the aircraft would hit us, but it swept past us in a shallow dive to the valley below. The sheep panicked at this ear shattering event and scattered, fleeing down the hillside towards the safety of their paddock in Zalan.

We climbed out of the pond and stood on the bank watching the plane turn, flying directly over the village. Suddenly a yellow cloud began to spew from its underside. The hazy cloud drifted gently down over Zalan. With an increasing roar the aircraft began climbing, circling over the village and then flew off over the mountain peaks as silence returned. Our village could hardly be discerned through the thick haze settling down over it.

I began to cry and begged Shwan to explain what was happening. He gestured for me to hush my crying.

"How can I know what that noisy beast was, and what it was doing?" A mountain breeze caressed my face and as we gazed down toward Zalan we saw that the same breeze had begun to cause the yellow cloud to move, it climbed towards us. We did not move from our vantage point at the pond. I wanted only to see my home down below. Shwan scanned the hillside for the sheep. The breeze quickened, and the thinning cloud was soon upon us. There was an immediate sensation of irritation on my skin and my eyes began to burn. It felt as if I were too close to an open fire. I screamed at Shwan but I saw that he too suffered the same things. He grabbed my hand.

"Quick, come with me." He jerked my arm violently and pulled me back into the pond. The thick, wind driven cloud now enveloped us. Shwan pulled me to the deepest part and with a scream he pulled me down under the water. Once I was over my initial shock I opened my eyes and saw him looking at me. My first thought was to get to the surface for air, but he held me down pointing at the yellow mist crossing the pond surface above. I struggled free, desperate for air. I broke the surface and instantly felt as though a thousand bee stings had hit my face. In my quest for air I gulped down some of the noxious cloud just before Shwan pulled me under again. My mouth, throat and lungs screamed for some fresh, clean air and I gagged, but continued to hold me under, not allowing me to come up to the top again. I though I might die. Shwan watched through the water and held me until the cloud had passed. Then the pair of us exploded out of the water to suck in our first breaths. A film of a yellow substance covered the pond. It began to burn so we hurried to get out and rushed down the hillside not seeing clearly. Shwan with his limited vision tripped over one of his sheep. It lay dead with its mouth gaping wide open.

"My sheep! My sheep! What has happened to my sheep?" he cried out in distress. We passed many of the other sheep lying dead as we ran down to the village. I ran to the place where I had last left my mother. I found her on the ground not moving. I could not see my father anywhere close by. Pulling on mother's dress I shouted,

"Wake up. Wake up Mother!" I begged her to answer. "Why are you sleeping, Mother? Why won't you wake up?" I wrapped my hand around her finger and pulled with all my strength. I looked beside me and saw a mother holding her baby leaning against a wall with blank eyes staring at me. They frightened me and I renewed my efforts to awaken my mother.

"Mother, wake up. Please get them to stop staring at me! Wake up, Mother, wake up!" But the only sounds in Zalan were my own distressed pleas. I lay down beside my mother and put my arms over her waiting for her to awaken. Eventually her skin grew cold and her eyes had the same blank gaze as the woman and child. I heard a voice; Shwan spoke my name. He took my hand. His hand intensified the burning sensation on my skin. He helped me up from my mother's side and led me to our house. He closed the door behind us, letting the door and walls shield us from the appalling scene on Zalan's narrow streets. We were terrified by the haunting and horrific day. When night arrived we lay feet to feet on the bed trying to sleep. We found it difficult to fall asleep among the field of dead and with the appalling silence outside. I had the feeling that if I closed my eyes I would be hunted through the night.

"Try to sleep if you can, Najat, and we will decide what to do in the morning."

"I am very frightened, Shwan. I do not know what I should do."

"I will take care of you, Najat. It seems as though we only have each other now, and I will do my best to see that you come to no harm. Try to sleep."

"I don't think I will be able to, my face and arms hurt."

Despite my grief at losing my parents and the pain each time my skin touched something, I must have fallen asleep for the rustling sound of the canvas door opening woke me. It was early, but yet it was bright and hot. Shwan, too, had wakened and stood outside the door looking down the street. I joined him and stared in awe at the school and the big shade tree.

"We must go back to see if they have wakened, Shwan."

"I don't think they will have, Najat. I am sure they were all dead, not just sleeping."

"Shwan, I want to go. You don't know. You're wrong, don't lie to me."

We did go back to the shade tree. Once there, what I thought was a nightmare became a morbid reality. We found that the villagers were all dead. Their bodies had begun to bloat, and the skin had begun to fall from exposed flesh. I found my mother again. Now she looked dreadful. Her eyes had turned a whitish gray like the eyes of a blind dog, and her body had swollen to twice its size. In the dust beside her body I saw a glint of something shiny. It was the coin necklace that she always wore around her neck. I picked it up and placed it in my pocket.

"I don't want to leave Zalan, Shwan," I wailed in my distress.

"There is nothing to stay here for now. Najat, we might as well leave right away. The next village is called Sarkan. I have been there twice with my father; it is a day's walk from here. He warned me that while we walked through the mountains to stay away from the road in case we ran into army men.

We left Zalan when the sun had reached the highest point in the sky and were it not for Shwan's encouragement I think I might have died on that awful journey. Many times I wanted to give up and lie down but Shwan made us keep walking until darkness fell. Exhausted, we finally slept under some trees a little way from the road. At first light we began walking again. I felt I had nothing to live for, but Shwan cajoled and even yelled at me to keep going despite my hunger, skin burns, and sore feet. Tiredness wracked my body, hunger tore at my belly and grief wracked my mind. After what seemed an eternity, I saw the houses of Sarkan down in the valley below us.

"We are nearly there, Najat. We must keep going until we find someone to help us."

"But we do not know anyone here, Shwan," I wailed.

"Try to be strong, Najat. Someone will help us," he

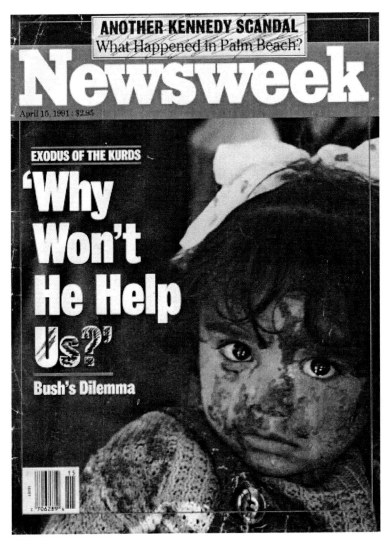

Kurdish child asks for America to stop Saddam Hussein's chemical weapons from suffocating and burning us.

answered confidently.

I walked the last mile into Sarkan in utter agony. My feet were rubbed raw inside my shoes. My hunger was terribly hard to bear and the first layer of skin on our faces and hands were peeling off in ugly flakes. The new skin below had been burned by the incessant sun. My tongue and throat were parched for lack of water, and I could barely croak, let alone speak.

"Very soon we will be able to find a drink of water, Najat," Shwan said in encouragement for my lagging spirits. I did not answer him, but soon we came across a water trough for animals.

I clearly recall putting my face deep into the water and gulping it down as fast as I could. I drank until my stomach was filled. Then I splashed the soothing liquid over the burns on my skin. I took off my shoes and washed and cooled my sore feet while Shwan did the same. When we had rested and taken our fill of water, we sat scanning the village as the occupants began their daily routines. Shwan seemed to be concentrating on a truck that was being loaded, and I trusted that he had a plan to take care of us. Eventually he spoke,

"Najat, when the truck is loaded and ready to go we are going to get aboard and ride. I have a feeling it is bound for Sulaymania. It is a large city where we stand a better chance at getting help than here in this village."

We walked up and stood near the vehicle. When the driver got in to leave and the engine started, we moved close behind the truck. When it began to move we chased it. Shwan leapt onto the bumper and heaved himself in. I struggled to keep up as the speed increased. Then Shwan leaned out, grabbed my hand, and pulled me in. We settled down among the sacks of produce and with my head on his lap we both fell asleep.

We slept all the way to Sulaymania, which is located near the north-east border of Iraq. The sound of the slowing truck awoke us as it entered the Mayanaka, the open air produce market: Shwan grabbed me.

"Come, Najat, we have to get out now!" We left the truck and Shwan appeared to set off with a purpose. "We should be able to find some food here," Shwan told me. I found it a little easier to walk now that I had soothed my feet. The music and noise from the marketplace fascinated me. Never having been anywhere in my life but Zalan, I almost forgot my tiredness as I observed the hustle and bustle of a city market. There were smells of foods I had never experienced before, bolts of bright coloured cloth, jewelry, and all manner of clothing. Most of all I was amazed at the numbers of people walking about. Never before had I seen more than twenty or so people in one place at a time.

The stores and buildings surrounding the market were tall, well built structures, so unlike the drab brown mud houses of Zalan. They held hardware such as colorful dishes, bedding, pots and pans and farming tools. Others contained ornaments in pretty colors with flowers painted on them. Still others contained sweets and pastries.

"Sit here and wait for me. I will try to get us something to eat," Shwan advised. I did as he bid, for I was so tired argument would have been foolish. I sat on the sidewalk in front of a store and watched the people pass by.

I saw a smartly dressed woman holding the hand of a child about my age. The child was also very well dressed in fine cloth with a face scrubbed shiny and clean. It was at that moment I realized how different I looked with my homespun garments coated in the dust of travel, my shoes scuffed and worn. My hair had not been brushed or combed since my mother dressed me for the wedding. Chunks of loose skin hung from my face which I had been unable to wash since leaving Zalan on the morning of the wedding. The realization of how I looked added to my feelings of utter dejection.

"Here, Najat," Shwan said as he appeared beside me and stuffed a small piece of pannear, cheese, into my swollen hand. "Eat it quickly before anyone sees you. I have taken it from a stall when the man wasn't looking."

"But that is stealing, Shwan. I can't eat this."

"Yes, you can. We have no money. This is the way we may have to live from now on until we get help." Shwan left me again. This time he was gone for a long time. As evening approached, many of the throngs of people left. I began to think he had abandoned me in this strange place. fear overtook me and I could not control the painful tears that rolled down my cheeks. A dark shadow came over me and I looked up. A woman towered above me. She was dressed in a flowing black abaya covering her from head to toe with just her face and hands visible. She held a basket containing some of the foods I had seen on the market stalls. In a small way she frightened me, but her face seemed friendly and her eyes spelled caring and compassion. In a soft voice she asked,

"Why are you crying, little girl? Have you lost your mother? Are you waiting for her to find you?" The fear and the struggle for survival, plus the loss of all that was familiar to me, became too much to bear. Knowing that someone in this strange new place cared, I burst into unashamed tears and wailed,

"My mother and father are dead and I am alone. My friend Shwan brought me here but now he too has gone."

"What happened to your face child? Why is it burned?"

"It was the yellow cloud," I replied.

"Come with me child. What is your name?"

"I am Najat from Zalan. Everyone there including the sheep are dead. I think it was the yellow cloud that killed them." The kind lady led me to a mosque where she spoke to a man wearing long black robes. He had a flowing white beard and a turban of white silk adorned his head.

"Can you tell me what happened from the beginning, child?" he asked. Between my tears I spoke of everything that had happened during the last few days. He appeared to have a better understanding of the yellow cloud than I did. He spoke privately with the lady. Then she kissed his hand and led me away.

"I am taking you to my house, Najat. I will give you food, clean you up and give you a warm place to sleep."

"What about my friend, Shwan. What will happen to him?"

"The mullah will put out the word to look for him and he too will be taken care of when he is found. Don't worry, your friend Shwan will be alright."

The lady walked quite quickly. She put her basket of food under her abaya as I struggled to keep up with her. Then the thought struck me. Did this woman want to transform me into a slave girl like in the stories my parents used to tell me? I became stricken with fear What would become of me?

chapter two

My first instinct was to run to escape from the woman in black and try to find Shwan. It was at the moment I planned to run, that the woman spoke to me in a soft comforting voice,

"I have two children of my own, Najat. My youngest child is called Shilan. She will be so pleased to have a new sister. I have a son named Rebwar. He is just a little older than you. My goodness, Najat, I have not told you my name. I am Shafika". The woman's kindly voice allayed my fears when I realized that she was a mother, a kind mother similar to my own.

The thought of my own mother caused the tears to flow again. Knowing I should never feel her arms around me and feel her sweet kisses ever again caused me to sob. Shafika heard me and ceased walking. Then she swept me up into her arms the way my mother used to do. I remember thinking she must be a very strong woman, for despite my seven years and my large size, she carried me like an infant. I lay in her arms as she walked through many narrow streets with long stretches of concrete walls and brightly coloured doors until finally she paused outside a bright blue door and put me down.

"We are home, Najat," she announced. I followed her into the cooking and eating room. "Sit, child, and I will bring you some food and drink." I was so ravenous from my long fast that I have no recollection of what I ate or drank on that first night. When my appetite had been sated, she took and bathed me and gave me clean clothes to wear. Then she applied a soothing salve to my face, arms, and hands. She anointed my feet with a soft cream before placing me in a bed with multi-coloured, embroidered bedding. Within minutes I fell into an exhausted sleep.

I awoke to the sound of giggling close by my bed. When I opened my eyes, a boy and girl stood looking at me. I stared at them with my eyes still sticky and blurred from sleep.

"You slept a long time, Najat. I am Shilan and this is my brother Rebwar. Mother said she found you at the Mayanaka and brought you home to live with us. There is food waiting for our morning meal, and mother sent us to see if you were awake."

"Yes, I am awake now, Shilan."

"Why is your face a funny color, Najat?"

"It was burned by a yellow cloud."

"I have never seen a yellow cloud. Where did it come from?"

"It came from a big airplane that came over the mountains."

"Oh." My explanation seemed to satisfy Shilan for she asked no further questions. I followed her and

Rebwar to the eating room where Shafika had a meal waiting for us all.

"The children's father has already left for work, Najat. He looked in on you before he left."

So began my first day with my new family. At such a tender age I was unaware that my new mother and father, like my real parents, were an oddity in this part of Iraq. They did not have large families like most of the Kurdish people. My position in the family as a daughter and sister was accepted without reservation. However, it took me much longer to adjust and accept my new surroundings. Everyone around me was a stranger and I was a stranger to them. I hid behind the shadow of my fear and the loss that I couldn't understand.

Some nights when the house was quiet, I had recurring nightmares of seeing my parents and the villagers dead all around me, then finding myself wandering all alone in the wilderness. I would awaken from them with my heart beating wildly, soaked in perspiration. When I was able to calm down I wept quietly and secretly into my pillow for my mother and father. I would feel a strange hollowness in my chest that would remain forever.

The vision of the past would overwhelm me each time I handled my mother's necklace, bringing back the emotional memories of her. It brought to mind the last moments we shared together before the day of the yellow cloud. I would recall the clear skies and the fresh mountain air of that morning when I said goodbye to Mother and left for the hills with Shwan and the sheep. I knew until my dying day I would never forget her or my father. The memory of Shwan's laughter never left me. I drew comfort from a sound that only I could hear. The memory of the haunting sound of his flute lulled me into sleep.

Having come from a small mountain village I found

myself woefully ignorant of the ways of city children, and I bore the brunt of their taunting and childish cruelty.

In retrospect the cruelty meted out by the children was a mirror image of what they saw daily on the streets of Goeza, which was the name of our neighborhood. Many of the games they played were based on witnessing the sadistic actions of the Ba'ath regime's army personnel. The topic of conversation at gatherings and mealtimes was always about the savage treatment of ordinary civilians. Having become hardened to it, even the children spoke of the brutality in a blasé tone.

In my lonely moments I often thought about Shwan and wondered where he was living and what he was doing. Sometimes at night I would dream that Shwan would come to the house for me and take me back to Zalan. It was just a dream and I would awaken and find the tears of joy turning into tears of lost and empty sadness.

Despite being hurled headlong into an adult world that I could not understand, I had the logic of a child and I used it to try to understand the reasons for my tragic loss. I did not know how to express my anger towards those responsible for my situation which caused me to internalize it. As a result I appeared to be a shy and quiet girl to adults and a stupid mountain valley girl to the neighborhood children. Most days I could not face going out to play in the streets with them. My fear of the outside had the effect of making my new home a prison.

I would open the door and peep through the crack wanting the sounds that the outside offered, but my insecurities brought me back into the shadows. My new mother and father were wise enough to let me quietly adjust and learn so that Rebwar and Shilan would understand and not see me as different from them.

One morning a bright light illuminated my darkened

world. As I peeped out of the house door I worked up the courage to venture outside again to see what things were going on in the street, I saw a girl staring inquisitively at me. I knew she lived next door to us for I had previously seen her coming and going there. I also knew her name from hearing her mother calling loudly, "Shanna! Come in to eat. The meal is ready!"

I had previously noticed the girl had a look of ease about her as she played with other children on the street. Shanna seemed somewhat different to the other girls she associated with. She wore hand-me-down clothing from her seven older sisters. On this day she wore a mud-stained dress and her knees were skinned from rough play. Shanna exuded an air of complete confidence as our gazes met. Without realizing it at that time, it was her disregard and lack of judgment of me that became the seed of our friendship. We were different, but I perceived it mattered nothing to her, this gave me the confidence to ignore my fear and open the door wider. I placed my foot on the doorstep and Shanna walked right up to me, ignoring the stares of the other children.

I think Shanna was a little older than I, but the instant rapport between us made the difference a non issue. She smiled. My heart raced, for I felt I had found a kindred soul. I took her extended hand and she led me into the world of the Sulaymania streets. Shanna became my protector and my mentor. I bathed in her smiles and laughter. She led me to share in her imaginary world. It was an idyllic world where we played together, oblivious to the daily violence and brutality surrounding us. I learned how to laugh again, to regain my interrupted childhood. I learned at her hand how to deal with the jibes and insults of the more audacious children. Shafika enrolled me in a school close by. It was nothing like the little school in Zalan. I did well and the teachers were pleased with my progress. Outside the classroom things were different; I was deemed a misfit by the other students.

Sulaymania, at that time, was a city under siege. A siege was imposed by the Ba'ath political party. Normal life for the citizens consisted of constant turmoil. At six p.m. a curfew emptied the streets and all the electrical systems were shut down. Fear and terror reigned during the hours of darkness. The chilled night air reeked of human blood and spent gunpowder. Dawn would find human bodies littering the streets, the bodies of those who dared to flout the curfew. Inside the homes of citizens, families sat in darkness whispering fear-filled at the constant sound of gunfire. At times the sound of feet running across the house roofs panicked the inhabitants. Were they the feet of miscreants, or the sound of military forces in a manhunt? Some families spent many hours in prayer hoping for divine intervention during the carnage.

During the hours of darkness, Kurdish fighters picked off soldiers in an attempt to free the nation from the Ba'ath party's iron grip. Then the dawn raids by their forces would begin. The soldiers entered any house that they wanted to conduct searches. They were looking for any evidence of any written materials which could be construed as a threat to the Ba'ath regime. They searched the houses from top to bottom looking for concealed freedom fighters or forbidden weapons. The discovery of anything the soldiers felt was a risk to the regime incurred an instant death sentence. Most often this was carried out in front of the house with bystanders witnessing the act. I remember the first time I was witnessed a young man being pulled out of a neighboring house and shot in the head. The memory of the fear still clings to my heart. I could not hold back my fear and clung to my mother's hand and hid my face behind her back. I was much too afraid to take a second look. Slowly I moved my head and peeked at the man lying in the road with his blood spilling onto the gravel. The vision made me vomit and later caused me to have a fever. After seeing this scene repeated several times I became hardened to it a survival tactic, just like the other children.

Any books discovered having any political content were also considered to be a threat to the regime and resulted in instant death without trial. We children too lived in fear and held onto our mother's abayas and watched in horror as the killings were carried out. However, I am sad to say that we became so hardened to the violence as a means of survival that we stood around the bodies until they had been cleared away.

Our parents did not try to ease our fears of the carnage around us. Rather, they allowed us to learn from it in the effort to survive and not spend our childhood whimpering in the dark. We learned the hard way how to get by in a country with only minimal humanity displayed by our leaders. I learned how to play the children's political games such as government spies or pretended to be a Kurdish freedom fighter.

The freedom fighters were big and powerful men in our minds at that age. They dressed in traditional Kurdish garb as mountain fighters. They wore wide leather ammunition straps across their bodies and carried rifles. A system of whistles indicated when it was safe for them to emerge from hiding and be fed and rested at the homes of supporters.

Occasionally a quiet day occurred in the neighborhood when the army terrorized the citizens in a different part of Sulaymania. The loudest noise on the street would be my father's rusty dump truck as the engine clanked into life at the start of his work day. Moments later the sound of the call to morning prayers drifted across the rooftops from the minaret of the nearby mosque. Perhaps a donkey cart with iron rimmed wheels bringing in fruits and vegetables from the Mayanaka market would shatter the calm morning air. The man driving the cart might stop and sell to patrons who came out of their homes to barter and bargain in loud voices. The vendor protested vociferously that he would starve if he sold his produce to them at such a low price.

I remember one such morning when the donkey cart paused outside our house as Shafika made a purchase of green vegetables. I stroked the donkey's long, doleful face with his sad almost tearful eyes. He was such a small donkey for such a large cart and so I asked," Why do you make him pull such a heavy load day after day, Sir? He is such a small, helpless donkey. I hope one day you will set him free." I also remember Shafika saying, "it is a noble sentiment you have expressed, Najat, but as you see in the world around you, there is little appreciation for human life and values. So you will understand there is none at all for the donkey and his ilk. Come into the house, children, and we will have breakfast." Every day the breakfast was exactly the same. We had hot, fresh bread; cheese; yogurt; and a cup of hot, sweet tea. After breakfast Shanna and I, along with my sister Shilan, sat on the doorstep watching the goings on in the street with wary eyes.

Mothers carrying shopping baskets hurried furtively along the streets to the market, speaking in hushed voices about the latest atrocities perpetrated by the Ba'ath Party's forces. The light, unconcerned voices of children at play softened the grim atmosphere of our street.

Malla Sabiha strode up to our door with a hungry looking and scruffy boy at her heels. She was the tallest woman I had ever seen. Her complexion was a darker shade than most of Sulaymania's residents, contrasting with her long white uncovered hair. Her eyes had a piercing gaze that always held my attention. The long blue dress she wore was dust stained at the hem from walking the graveled streets, as were her rubber sandals. Malla Sabiha read passages from the Koran for coins; she suggested that her readings brought good luck and health to the donor. I remember Mother would bargain with Malla in order that she would sing three or four passages for the price of two.

In our Kurdish culture the local cemetery has great importance. On Friday of each week some of the women would take their children to pray for the souls of those killed by the gassings and murders at the hands of the Regime and for family members long departed. I remember Mother taking me to the cemetery along with Shilan and Rebwar. She took us to a tomb as big as our bedroom. It was the resting place of a long departed Sheik atop the graveyard hill. I recall it must have been built many years ago sparing no expense. The entire structure encircled by grapevines. A few people gathered around offering their prayers as wisps of Buzurd, (incense) drifted among the worshippers. Mother admonished us for we accidentally stepped on long forgotten graves as we made our way down the hill.

"It is a bad thing to step on the graves; you may waken up the dead."

Upon hearing it my mind immediately went to my real mother. Perhaps if I went back to Zalan and walked on her grave she might awaken and be my mother again. But just as quickly I realized my real mother did not have a grave to awaken from.

As we entered the tomb at the entrance gates the modern day Sheik welcomed us by nodding his head. He lived in a small house at the bottom of the cemetery hill. I heard mother pray out loud,

"Please, God, allow my children to grow up and not

be killed or made to disappear without a trace, and please bring peace to our country by taking the Ba'ath violent regime away." She would place a few coins in the box by the door and we would all walk home.

Some afternoons Mother would have us dress up in our best clothes in order to take us to visit Shilan and Rebwar's aunts and uncles. Shilan and I wore identical outfits including freshly shined shoes along with white socks. Occasionally she would allow Shanna to accompany us provided she too dressed up. Being an active tomboy, Shanna found it difficult to sit quietly like a young lady and fidgeted constantly in the tall chair. Mother would glare at her to no avail; Shanna could not keep still and waited excitedly for the food which our aunt had prepared. She would serve sweet pastries and fresh fruit along with fizzy beverages for the children and tea for herself and mother. After the visit she often hired a horse and cart to take us all back home. For the most part we children found these visits quite boring. Gratefully with the change of seasons the visits lessened in frequency.

I recall springtime as a special time at this period in my life. The spring rains brought new life bursting from the soil and flowers abounded. Warm, sunny days allowed us to play outside in light clothing. There was always a spring picnic. There were other picnics during the year mostly held on Thursdays and Fridays but the spring picnic was always special. The festivities started on March twenty-first, the Kurdish New Year's Day, where the women traditionally dressed in vibrant colors and wore bright jewelry. There would be music and dancing in the style passed down through the generations. We children joined in the celebrations joyfully; child and adult alike forgetting for a short while the oppressive regime we lived under.

My father worked long hours with his rusty dump

truck carrying all manner of goods to different towns. We did not see him often but he always made sure he attended the spring picnic. At dawn we would all be ready and began to load the truck with Mother's special foods and all the supplies for the day. Shanna's parents were always invited and rode in the cab with Mother and Father while we children rode in the dump box behind with all the supplies and a bevy of stray children from our street. We could barely control our excitement as we stood on tiptoe trying to look over the top of the dump box. Through the rear window I could see inside the cab, the four adults piled together as Father drove. Crowds of people walking were making their way to the picnic grounds, and Father honked his horn at them, and they all waved back building the excitement for the picnic to begin.

Upon our noisy arrival at the riverside picnic grounds, families jostled to find the best places to sit either on the riverbank or close to the waterfalls and the music had already started. When all the supplies were unpacked and we children had been lifted down from the truck the dancing began.

Within our culture unmarried men and women traditionally do not physically touch each other outside of marriage but on the day of the spring picnic the taboo is temporarily ignored during the dancing. For spring or picnic days the females wore revealing clothing highly decorated with embroidery and accented with jewelry. Plunging necklines exposed cleavage only tolerated on this spring picnic day. Men and women often had their long flowing sleeves tied together by their children during the nonstop dancing. Flirtations abounded and inhibitions were put aside. It was often on these special days that young lovers tended to find each other.

Restrictions placed on children also were abandoned for the day, and we joined in the dancing, trying to

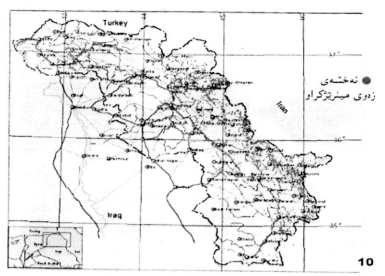

The map of Northern Iraq (Kurdish Territory.) The dots indicate mined areas leaving virtually no un-mined lands.

Some of the many types of land mines buried all over Northern Iraq.

emulate the adults. We played all manner of games and ate the special foods our mothers had prepared the previous day.

Then we began to chase each other as we played "Hide and Seek" behind several trees. In our play we forgot how far we had run from our families. Shanna, as usual, was ahead of the crowd with the boys while I often stopped to catch my breath, at the same time giving little Shilan a much needed rest. Shanna's older sister, along with three boys, yelled as they sat on their heels.

"Come see what we have found." We walked faster to get to them, and Shanna lay down on the gravel as the sound of an explosion shattered the still air. Gravel and body parts were flung asunder.

All the parents came running looking for the children yelling at them. "Watch where you are stepping! There are land mines in this area!" My father was hysterically shaking me, for my sister Shilan was not to be seen. He yelled at me and said,

"Why did you go so far away? Didn't I tell you to stay put? Where is Shilan? Where is my baby? You are bad luck to our family." It was the only time he punished me. He slapped my face very hard, and I remember the sting of it to this very day. He began running around yelling,

"Shilan! Shilan!" at the top of his voice. Eventually he found her among a group of dazed and wounded children. Shanna's parents were hysterical, wailing loudly in grief as they collected up pieces of their eldest daughter, Bahras, in a blanket and brought her back to my father's truck. Her mother clutched the remains of the little body close to her own. With tears streaming down her face, she beseeched God to tell her what awful thing she may have done to have been punished this way. As we rode home in the dump box she wailed out loud for God to destroy the evil Ba'ath politicians so they would know and understand how she felt.

What had begun as a wonderful day ended in tragedy. The men and boys waited outside our house for the bodies to be prepared, while the women were left to deal with the aftermath of the blast. The dead and mangled bodies of the victims were laid out on a sort of board or table in Shanna's back yard and the women washed away the dirt and blood as we younger girls watched. The dead, three young boys and Bahras, were then wrapped in white linen. Afterwards the father, of the children and some other men came and carried them off to the graveyard. The normally joyous spring picnic ended in sadness and anger. Parents reiterated to their children the dangers of straying into areas that the regime had land-mined and to walk only on known paths.

Once the grieving for the four children had subsided, life returned to a dubious sense of normal for a city under siege. Despite the uncertainty of our life expectancy we still maintained our strict education. Shilan and I were in the same class in a school that looked remarkably like the surrounding houses except much larger with numerous windows. Our schoolroom had a large blackboard and rickety, wooden desks. In one corner stood a smoky oil stove that over time had blackened the walls and ceiling. We girls wore school uniforms but in the winter months we had to wear our coats over them as we sat in class.

Our teacher commanded total attention. She stood and towered above the class, a figure of total authority who drilled into us a sense of discipline and focus. My friend, Shanna, often brought the teacher's wrath upon herself with her silly antics and rejection of authority. This would result in her being singled out in the schoolyard roll-call by the principal. Madam Parwen, or as we secretly called her "Kalla Yash" (which means black turkey) was a rather large woman. She had a stern face to complement her stern attitude. According to local gossip, Madam Parwen had never been asked to marry. Her sour looks had discouraged possible suitors and she had to live with the shame in our culture of being an unmarried woman.

She would call out the names of the brightest students and my name was often among them, and then we received a round of applause from the other children. Then she would call out what she termed the stupid pupils and the slow learners.

Madam Parwen's punishment for the errant children was to make them stand on one leg while dispensing blows to the hands with a long ruler. The rewards for the bright students were a wide, red ribbon which Shanna and I often received.

When the spring had turned to early summer, Shanna and I took to sleeping on the flat house roof, much to the dismay of our mothers. On quiet nights we would look at the twinkling stars and foolishly try to count them. On the not so peaceful nights we would watch the tracer bullets screaming across the sky or lean over the eave to watch the clandestine activities on the street below. Mother would yell at us to get under our bedrolls when the bullets were flying, but we rarely did preferring to watch the free light show overhead.

At daylight we would watch men carrying dead bodies to the graveyard. From our vantage point we could tell where they were buried in the cemetery. In our culture we were told that after the bodies had been buried, if they were good people they would turn into angels; if they were bad they became ghosts. Sometimes the bigger boys dug up the bodies while we girls kept watch to see if it really happened. We had become so hardened to death and corpses on a daily basis that doing what we did seemed more like a childish prank.

One day we were caught in the act by the sheik pacing in his graveyard domain. The word of our irreverent deed spread rapidly into the community. In their admonishments our parents instructed us that the body has to lie for forty days before the transformation takes place, and the spirit of the departed still lived among us. If he had been a good person, good luck would befall upon us. Were he otherwise, his spirit would haunt us forever. We girls never joined in the excavations again, but some of the bolder boys did.

Shanna, Shilan, and I sat on the roof edge with our legs dangling over, watching the passersby below in the street. A parade of men carrying a coffin approached. As we wiggled to get a better look, Shilan fell, landing on the lid of the passing coffin. It broke her fall. The pallbearers dropped the coffin in terror and ran while the others broke into uproarious laughter and yelled,

"come back. There is nothing to fear! It's just a little girl who fell off the roof." I had my own kind of panic; I had to tell my mother that Shilan had fallen from the roof. Fortunately she was unhurt and some said it was the spirit of the deceased that protected her from injury. After that incident, Shilan was considered to be an especially blessed person and because of it I did not get punished for allowing her to fall.

chapter three

The sound of pitiful screams hurled my memory away. I found myself in the agonizing present, breathing in the stale air of my cell mixed with the other smells that permeated the prison. They were the screams of a man coming from the torture room at the end of the passage. My mind stiffened at the thoughts of what the guards were doing to him. After an interminable length of time the screams subsided. I could only hope the victim had died and now was free from his agony. Once again I forced my mind to take me from this place of horror and retreat back into itself.

I had reached the age of thirteen years when Saddam Hussein brutally and forcefully made his entry into the Ba'ath Party. Radio and television were filled with his voice and image twenty four hours each day. It was a monumental propaganda campaign. He promised that all Kurdish families would receive free land, more wages, and better working conditions. Many buildings would be erected for the poor. The markets would be overloaded with food and goods; there would be a vibrant economy and a much better life for everyone. As a result the Kurdish freedom fighters laid down their arms to await the good times under Saddam.

Unfortunately for the Kurdish peoples the good times were just a myth and by the time I had reached the age of fifteen there were even less jobs available, less food, and virtually no building going on. Iraq had become a complex military state. The war raged between Saddam's army and Iran. Tanks and army trucks and a multitude of uniformed soldiers passed through Sulaymania every day. The sound of roaring vehicle engines, explosions, and aircraft became the dominant sound within the city. Saddam's army established a number of bases in the larger cities to the north of the country, including Sulaymania, under the guise of protecting our people from Shia Muslims of Iran. Meanwhile the mountain villages were still under the control of the Kurdish freedom fighters. I recall none of our people wanted a war, but the barrage of propaganda led us to believe that neither did we want to live under the thumb of the fanatical religious Iranians. Neither did the women of Iraq wish to lose the freedoms they enjoyed and be ruled by Muslim religious doctrine.

A soldier who knew my family came to visit our house. He informed us on the role of the military and the war zone. He told us the names of the weapons they were using including the bombs and the names of the aircraft and how they were told that every Iraqi soldier was a hero to Saddam.

As the residents of Sulaymania shared opinions among themselves, we discovered the best and worst of the situation we found ourselves in. Some felt that Saddam's army was really protecting us from the Iranians while others expressed the opinion that Saddam was a trickster, a coyote who had taken over power to destroy. Still others wished out loud that this was just a bad dream and the situation in our country would not endure more than six months.

Saddam's war was not going as well as he expected. The women of Iraq were forced to give their rings and jewelry to his war effort and men were conscripted to the front line on penalty of death for non-compliance. Whatever previous law had existed, Saddam them null and void. He and his cohorts made their own laws as it suited them.

Within Kurdistan there no longer was a concerted effort to defeat Saddam's army; instead, opposing groups within the country fought his forces independently. With no unified force against him, Saddam's military meted out atrocities to any they considered to be a threat or non supportive of their aims. Murder, immolations and sudden and permanent disappearances became the order of the day coupled with the bulldozing of homes. The daily business of Iraq had become anarchy. Great numbers of our people fled to cross the border into surrounding countries reaching out for help and offering the only thing we had left our identity as Kurds.

Saddam retaliated at the Kurd's resistance to his doctrine. He effectively closed the northern end of our country, severing electricity, food, and water supplies. This lack of basic human needs turned many of the people against each other in the quest for survival. We were as caged rats in a desperate situation and some citizens gave death resulting evidence against fellow citizens to gain sustenance and survival for their own children.

I remember with great clarity those terrible days.

They are branded into my brain with the hot irons of human suffering and degradation. Though but a child still, I knew all this was wrong. I did not know why this was happening to us but I was determined to find out.

I continued attending school, along with taking English courses in summer break, and at age fifteen I began to study the history and heritage of my people. I studied every document I could lay my hands on searching for the answers to the peculiar dynamics of our nation. The more I learned the less I really knew of a resolution to our problems. I studied voraciously a number of books on the western world. I read the books I could find about their freedoms. I also read the works of Russian scholars. The very possession of these works was a sentence of death had I been caught with them.

I began to secretly write down my thoughts based upon my new knowledge. Despite my young age I found that adults paid attention when I entered a conversation presenting a point of view they had heard before from others older than I. It had occurred to many of us that religion was being used as an excuse for invasions upon others, a weapon used for killing, and the accumulation of wealth.

My young mind slowly processed this huge amount of information and eventually changed my thinking. My feelings on religion led me to believe there was a correlation between religion and oppression, many of them rigid and restrictive with their own particular set of rules, leading me to the conclusion that these groups function with a power structure of oppressor and oppressed. The knowledge I gained allowed me to see things differently and observe the world in a new light. I thought, (I suppose rather naively,) that my knowledge might make a difference to my beloved country and what I might do as a single individual to protect the next generation. I did come to recognize that most Kurds, as a nation, were not religious fanatics or a warlike people.

When I reached the age of sixteen, Shanna and I had remained constant companions and shared our ideas and ideals. Together we joined an underground group known as an educated group that grew inside of theYa-keti which was one of the two groups of freedom fighters in the north led by Jalal-Talabani. We believed our generation needed a different way of thinking. The idea appealed to both of us. We felt that we understood the problems in our country much better than our parents who had grown up under a different set of beliefs. Mussakaffen stated that through ideas and education we could possibly break the cycle of war and violence perpetrated upon us by the Ba'ath regime.

By not understanding, our parent's generation had lived with corruption, violence, and political oppression. Mussakaffen believed that we might be able to change their thinking. As a group we did not support either the Kurdish freedom fighters or the Ba'ath regime.

Communism began to infiltrate our country causing a threat to the freedom fighters. The concepts of this new political idea became confused with the ideas of Mussakaffen. Consequently, we were judged in the same way; both views claiming that western values and ideology were attempting to replace our long standing religious beliefs and culture. They suggested that were such ideas adopted, it would lead to decadence. Women would become as chattels to be used sexually by any man. They would obtain too much freedom and an incurable virus would inundate our entire society.

In the face of all this misinformation and misunderstanding, Mussakaffen did not waver in our ideas and aims. Our articles were often prohibited from being published in our secret underground papers and in meetings we lived in fear of being informed upon by those who disagreed with our views.

I remember the first meeting, Shanna, and I attended. "Will you come to the underground meeting with me, Shanna? I know it is risky but I would be able to get permission from Mother if you were to accompany me."

"You know it means we will be killed if we are caught there, Najat."

"Yes I know. But if we genuinely believe in what we are doing we should go despite the risks."

"Very well, I will take the risk with you. What will your mother say?"

"I don't know. I can't possibly tell her. To learn of my involvement in such matters would jeopardize her life and safety."

The clandestine meeting was held in the basement of the hospital. We waited outside the gates with the people visiting patients so as not to arouse any suspicion. When we were allowed to enter, the meeting attendees filtered off a few at a time to the large basement meeting room. The air was hot and the people fanned their faces with books and sheets of writing paper as they spoke and exchanged ideas. With Shanna at my side, I listened to snatches of conversation and felt very much out of place realizing that I did not know as much about the situation in our country as I thought I did. My knowledge had come mostly from books and hearsay, many of the professionals in the room had a much deeper knowledge than I, based upon experiences and inside knowledge of the Ba'ath regime.

A man with a huge neck banged on the front desk bringing silence to the room. Calm and intelligent debate ensued with hands going up to ask questions. The questions were answered without political rhetoric or undue patriotism. I learned much at this meeting and resolved to attend as many others as I could. The meetings were held weekly and there I made a number of friends who were attending university. I also met doctors, lawyers, university professors, and writers all of them politically active. My friend Shanna found the meetings utterly boring.

"I don't want to come with you to these stupid meetings any more, Najat. So please don't ask me," she said one night. Shanna now dressed well and flirted openly, so unlike the tomboy girl I had grown up with and thus we slowly drifted apart.

Over the next two years I attended the meetings regularly. I learned much about political activity and the differing ways of thinking within the different groups. In a way I felt I had been brainwashed up to now. With my new-found knowledge I felt it would be much better to achieve our aims through education and by building bridges with the western world. In my opinion, it was a much better solution than patriotic freedom fighters running round in the mountains trying to protect territory, language, and ancient customs without equality for our women and spreading false doctrine. So the meetings were often a constant battle of words between the old and new thinkers.

At one meeting, Shanna having nothing else to do accompanied me. The meeting room at the hospital filled to overflowing. The air was stifling and sweat poured from our foreheads. The air was so bad I felt I would faint or fall asleep, so I said,

"Shanna, come on. Let's get out of here." As we struggled to leave and get out into the fresh air Shanna said, "well it's about time, Najat. Two years of coming to this boring place and you finally decide to get out." I held myself back from commenting upon her constant behavior of flirting with young men, for our friendship was too long and deep to destroy it with an unkind word.

I stood up ready to leave, when I heard a voice from the rear of the hall. I glanced at the source and saw a young man similar in age to myself with a vaguely familiar face. His black hair was neatly groomed and contrasted against his white collarless shirt. With dark piercing eyes he looked straight ahead at the moderator, Dr. Marwen. In a voice sounding strangely familiar and yet not recognizable, he spoke,

"My name is Shwan. We only progress along with technology and international trade. Under the present administration our country has become isolated. This is what has happened to us in Iraq."

His name and familiarity distracted my train of thought and concentration and I could not help but wonder if he was the Shwan I knew from long ago. I knew now I could not leave the meeting no matter how uncomfortable I felt until I had spoken with this man. Shanna pulled at me as I sat down again. Dr. Marwen responded to Shwan's statement,

"Perhaps we can correct this. Now that Western technologies are accelerating the progress of our country, our nation will advance." Shwan replied,

"I believe what you are saying and writing is damaging and confusing to people who have been threatened by statements of liberation." I became lost in the subject as I listened intently to Shwan and Dr. Marwen in informed debate. I discovered that Shwan and I shared the same views on solutions to the crisis in our country. It was very obvious to me that this man, Shwan, had studied hard and long just as I had. He had become an accomplished orator and stated his case with calm conviction. I could hardly wait for the meeting to end so I could speak with him and find out if it really was the Shwan I had known as a child, although the young man didn't look like the Shwan I remembered.

I tried to formulate a political question for him so he would notice me, but in my nervous state I could not think of one, but I kept turning round to look at him and I believe he noticed me. As the meeting ended, Shanna and I moved toward the door behind the crowd. I walked directly to him, as my mother had said I have a free nature and we walked outside into the cool air with Shanna following. Looking at me Shwan said,

"I have noticed you here before. How long have you been coming to the meetings?" I knew he did not recognize me. After all I had reached womanhood and at our parting I had been just a slip of a girl.

"You do not recognize me, Shwan? We have been separated for so long." He looked at me closely,

"What do you mean separated?" I lifted my hair and showed him the small scar on my neck where his thrown rock had hit me and he got a better view of the coin necklace that had been my real mother's. I watched his face as recognition flooded his mind. "Is it really you, Najat? You look well and all grown up." We both began to laugh feeling as much pain as joy at our reunion.

"The memory of the sound of your flute has always given me comfort through the worst of my nightmares."

"The guilt of leaving you behind at the Mayanaka has kept me awake for many long nights, Najat."

"I never forgot you either, Shwan. For many days I worried and wondered about you and if you were well treated and happy."

As we stood inside the hospital gates I felt Shwan's fingers feel for mine. I took them gratefully and memories of him holding my hand at the worst time in my life flooded into my mind. My eyes filled with tears and he saw them in the fading light. We looked at each other and began to laugh again at the joy of a lost friendship regained.

Afraid of being spotted walking alone with a male, Shanna discreetly walked alongside me as Shwan told me his story.

"The Mullah took me to the mosque where Mullah Grewen punished me for stealing by beating my hands until they were badly bruised. Then he put me to work scrubbing the sheik's tomb. It took me months to complete the job. He took me into his home to raise me along with his own four sons and gave me the family surname "Grewen." He arranged for me to go to school. Of course I was years behind the other children in my education, I was nine years of age and was placed with the five year olds. The Mullah also had two daughters but they did not attend school as he believed that educating girls conflicted with the teachings of Mohammed. Now tell me about you, Najat." Then I told him my story

"I am twenty years old now; Najat and I will be starting at Baghdad University in a few weeks."

"What a coincidence, Shwan. So will I."

"It was a long way from our valley to Sulaymania, Najat. We traveled it together and now we will be traveling the road to Baghdad University together."

"It's not far enough for me, Shwan. One day I plan to go to America to upgrade my education and marry a man with yellow hair and blue eyes. My father always used to say I should stop listening to the multicultural radio station and stop watching English and American movies. He said since you were not born English, you are not likely to become English." Shwan began to laugh softly.

"The little girl born in a mud house in the mountains of Kurdistan is off to Baghdad and dreams of life in America?" We had so much to catch up on with our recollections of the lost years; that we were only a couple of streets from my home before we realized the distance we had covered. As we said good bye he asked,

"Will you be at the next meeting, Najat?"

"Yes, Shwan. Will I see you there?"

"Yes, I will look for you."

chapter four

The day Saddam Hussein declared himself the official president of Iraq, northern Iraq became a prison without bars. The Kurdish peoples in the view of the Ba'ath party became criminals without committing any crime. To have been born Kurdish was a crime in itself. We were caught with no defense against the regime and suffered under its whims. Saddam's self directed mandate rid Iraq of Kurds by ethnic cleansing and genocide.

I had reached the point in my life where I could now understand the things taking place in my country. No longer was I a young child able to hide under the arm of my mother, accepting of everything going on around me. To be a Kurd was highly dangerous, to be a young Kurdish woman was even more dangerous. Many suffered rape, torture, permanent disappearance, or out and out murder.

The time had come for me to get to Baghdad in order to begin my university education. My family stood with me in the muddy field of the bus garage, a large field surrounded by a sheet iron fence. Choking fumes from buses hardly able to run, with engines snorting and exuding blue smoke assaulted my nostrils. The noise of taxi drivers yelling out for prospective fares added to the appalling racket while individual drivers yelled out the destination of their buses. Altogether it made for an indescribable noise. My father tried putting on a brave face as he said his farewell but I saw the glint of a tear in the corner of his eye. My mother said,

"I will pray for God to protect you." Then she bent down and picked up the bag of snacks she had prepared with a mother's love for my journey and handed it to me. My sister Shilan hugged me and whispered into my ear,

"No one knows you like I do, Najat. So be very careful and wary, I cannot bear the thought of losing you." Rebwar, now a young man with a highly developed sense of humor and always having the ability to make my parents laugh or calm them down said,

"She is not going away to die! She is going to study with boys and learn about love and flirtation." My father's eyes opened wide when he heard Rebwar's comment.

"We have worked very hard to bring you to this point, Najat. Do not bring shame to our family." I nodded to my father and turned to board the bus. My family waited by the bus window looking up at me until a belch of smoke hid them from view. I was on my way to a new life at the University of Baghdad to study history.

Because of the taboos of our culture, as a single woman I was not able to travel with Shwan unless by accident we were aboard the same bus. I could only be in the company of other women, but both sexes were equally vulnerable to Saddam's vicious freewheeling army personnel. They manned every conceivable route from the North to the South protecting the Ba'ath power from revolutionary and underground groups.

The bus driver explained that every taxi, bus, truck, and private car would be stopped and searched at the numerous checkpoints. Any suspects might be summarily shot at the roadside. We were all aware of the dangers ahead from travelers who had made the journey before us.

Leaving Sulaymania southbound, the surrounding mountains gradually receded bringing us onto a flat plain that seemed to go on forever. It seemed odd to me, never having seen such a view, always having the distant horizon restricted by hills and mountains. Military equipment and sandbag fortifications lined each side of the road where we were stopped for the first time. We could see the sadistic soldiers roughly pulling people from the vehicle ahead of us.

As I looked around the bus it appeared that a number of my fellow passengers were familiar with the routine and held their documentation in their hands ready for inspection so I did the same.

"All off the bus," the driver shouted and we meekly followed him and lined up along the outside of the vehicle. Two soldiers stepped up. One examined our papers without speaking while the second one conducted body searches. My papers were checked and when the inspections were complete we passengers were given the option of walking along one of three white lines on the road. One had the name "Saddam Hussein" in wide letters the second said "Illiterate Kurdish Bastard" and the third "God's line." I of course recognized the deadly game they were playing. We had to walk on the Saddam line meaning we had chosen him in order to survive. I stepped on the Saddam line and was allowed back on the bus. Those who chose to step on one of the other lines were marched off behind a line of military vehicles and machine gun fire rang out. The bus continued without them.

There were many such stops on the road south. With all the delays and questioning, the normal four hour trip to Baghdad took ten hours. On arrival I gratefully exited the bus for the final time.

"Please, Mr. Bus driver, would you find me a Kurdish taxi driver to take me to the university residence as I am alone?" I asked.

The ride through the city fascinated me. It was big, clean, and modern looking. Soldiers or military equipment clogged some of the streets. People were well dressed, the taste of Arab culture abounded, proud buildings adorned the wide streets, and the store windows were filled with goods we in Sulaymania could only dream of. The smells of coffee, fresh fruit, and the earthy aromas of vegetables in plentiful supply wafted out into the streets. It was a huge culture shock for me, having lived my life mostly among relative poverty in a war zone.

Baghdad was a different country. I smelled freedom in my nostrils. I suddenly felt alive as I walked up the steps to the university women's residence. I felt the poverty and brutality was behind me, and I looked to a bright future of peace and learning.

The house mother, Fazila, answered the door after a long interval. I looked through the glass in the door as she approached at her own easy speed. Fazila was big and matron-like. She peered back at me through the glass then opened the door. She fiddled with her worry beads as she looked at me over small, frameless glasses as she waited for me to identify myself.

"I am Najat. I am here to attend the university and have been instructed to come here to the residence," I said respectfully.

"I have been expecting you, Najat, Come in. I am Fazila the house mother. I am in charge of the residence security." She led me into a long hall hung with pictures of Saddam Hussein plastering the walls. All the doors of the room in the hall were open and many young women chatted and glanced at me as I struggled with my belongings and attempted to listen to Fazila's words.

"You will be sharing a room with my two favorite girls, Najat. They are very thoughtful and kind. They are good to me and I return the favor." Fazila knocked, then opened the door of a room with three single beds, a bookcase, and a clothes closet.

"Girls, this is Najat, your new room mate." Fazila left and the two girls introduced themselves.

"Welcome, Najat. I am Salma and this is Sahira. We are in our second year of engineering. As you can see we are dressed to go out for the evening. You may join us if you like."

"Thank you, Salma. But I am exhausted from travel; I would just like to have a cup of hot tea and go to my bed." I noticed the girls looked much like twins; they were dressed in expensive clothing. Their skin was an olive color and had high cheek bones, blue eyes, and silky black hair. Though we had met for just a few minutes, I had a feeling they were the children of wealthy parents.

"We will show you where you may get a hot drink and we will try not to wake you when we come in later."

The following morning I found that my hunch that they were from a wealthy family had been correct. They were in fact the daughters of the rich Abdul Salman and were from the city of Arbil. The sisters, like many others I was to find at the university, treated their sojourn here as a retreat from their stricter home life. Here they enjoyed a lifestyle like those we saw on Arabic soap operas and fashion shows. We students were considered to be educated and responsible adults, able to make the right choices and decisions in life, and we enjoyed freedoms not available before coming to university.

We were expected to discover ourselves, to understand and interact with male students. Friendship without affection was accepted to a degree, but it was not my aim in life to live the lifestyle of my room mates. My goal in life was to try to make a difference for my people and I intended my education to be my tool to do that. Even with the freedom I enjoyed here at Baghdad University, I had to be vigilant. I learned that spies within the university kept a wary eye on all Kurdish students for any activity they deemed suspicious. Even socially one had to be very careful not to say anything derogative about Saddam Hussein, any member of his family, or the Ba'ath regime, for retribution would quickly follow.

In my first year at university I kept a low profile, keeping my beliefs and opinions strictly to myself, trusting no one with them. Genuine generosity created a sense of wariness in me wondering if there was an ulterior motive in the generosity. I felt if I played the part of a naïve student the ones sharing my views would eventually reveal themselves to me. Within the university I created a peaceful environment for myself going along with the Ba'ath party's edicts without comment, speaking neither for the North or South. My primary aim was my education.

Despite the dangers, these subjects were clandestinely discussed between those knowing they could trust the other. I wanted to understand why Saddam held such mighty power over our people and through a professor, whom I came to know and trust, it was explained how it came to be. Sitting under a shade tree far from prying ears the learned one spoke softly to me. I asked,

"Please, tell me the information not generally available to the Iraqi citizen?"

"Let me begin with Saddam's birth, Najat. He was born on April 28 in the year 1937 in the small village of al-Ouja. It is about 120 kilometers north of Baghdad near Tikrit. His mother bore him out of wedlock and apparently made numerous attempts to abort him due to the stigma. The attempts failed and he was given the name Saddam, which means the steadfast one. The father died before the child was born. His mother, Subha Talfah, married Ibrahim al-Hassam who wanted absolutely nothing to do with the child of another man. Saddam was sent to live with an Uncle, Khairallah Talfa, an army officer who had spent several years in prison for his part in a rebellion. Between the years 1936 and 1941 there were six attempted insurrections and so Saddam's childhood was set amid turbulent times. After his release from prison, the uncle turned to crime along with other members of his family. They prospered through robbery, fraud, and illegal trade.

Everyone in the village knew Saddam's history so he was shunned. He rebelled against the society shunning him and he refused to attend school regularly. By the time Saddam reached the age of ten the path of his life of violence had been paved. The path that would lead him to become the sadistic leader of a totalitarian state.

Saddam's toy was a polished iron bar. At times he would heat the bar in a fire until it glowed red. Then he would burn out the eyes of a sheep while other children watched. The iron bar was Saddam's friend and protector. A weapon against a society that excluded him, simply because of his family history. Unable to strike out at them, he used his hot iron upon the defenseless creatures of the village establishing a pattern of violence which grew along with his years.

The uncle moved to Baghdad in 1955 expanding the crime his family had engaged in. The Tikrit mob obtained wealth through robbery often involving bloodshed and quickly made their presence felt in the city. The family had become an Iraqi mafia. Saddam's initiation into the mob was to kill a distant uncle, a robber in opposition to the Tikrit family. Saddam shot him dead and secured his position. He still attended the al-Karckh school and had a genuine thirst for knowledge. Saddam developed an interest in politics. He joined the Ba'ath party (the party of Arab renewal) in 1957 and became a member in staunch opposition to the Iraqi dictator, General Abdul Karim Kassem. The Ba'ath party selected Saddam to help in the assassination attempt of the General on October17, 1959. The general did not subscribe to any of the Ba'ath party's ideals and was reviled by the people he oppressed. The assassination failed and slightly wounded, Saddam fled to Syria.

The founder of the Ba'ath party, lawyer Michael Aflaq, became Saddam's mentor. After several months Saddam went to Egypt and studied law in Cairo. While there General Kassem was deposed by Marshal Abdul al-Rahman and was publicly executed under orders from the Ba'ath party leader, Hasan al-Bakr. Saddam promptly returned home and the knowledge of his part in the assassination stood him in good stead and he was hailed as a hero.

Saddam returned to Baghdad and asked his uncle for the hand of his cousin Sajida. The arranged marriage had been decided when they were both small children and conformed to the Tikrit family rules. Several months after the marriage, Hasan al-Bakr was deposed by Marshal Abdul al-Rahman and his supporters who were bitter opponents of the Ba'ath party. Saddam was quickly arrested and imprisoned. While there he was chosen to be the deputy leader of the Ba'ath party and soon after, Saddam escaped custody. Following several years of civil unrest in 1968, the Ba'ath party succeeded in deposing Marshal Arif.

Hasan al-Bakr became the president of Iraq and Saddam Hussein its strongman. He took control of the infamous Qasr al-Nihaya prison (The Palace Where It Ends). Within weeks hundreds of prisoners were tortured and murdered and a group of one hundred men were publicly hanged in Republic Square. They were accused of being Israeli and American spies. In 1972 he turned the western operated oil industry into a state run concern and signed a friendship treaty with the Soviet Union. In a dispute with president al-Bakr, Saddam shot him in the arm to make his point. Over time Saddam reduced president al-Bakr to no more than a figurehead and eventually it is believed Saddam poisoned him and took over absolute power.

Saddam Hussein made any criticism of him a crime punishable by death. By handing out top jobs to family members his whole Tikrit clan took power along with Saddam. In effect his extended family of criminals ran the country and run it to this day. So you see, Najat, what we the people of Iraq are up against." At that moment I was unsure if the professor was a genuine professor or a western spy.

I now had a much better understanding of the crime and violence rampant in my country, although at this point there was nothing much I could do about any of it. I realized that the greater part of the Kurdish students at the university wore the same mask as I, a survival tactic for all of us. I picked my friends very carefully. Politics were discussed only when outdoors and away from other ears. Due to the spies in the university, over a thousand innocent students were tortured to death or permanently disappeared during my time there.

chapter five

In my stupor I attempted to turn over onto my back. Unbelievable pain instantly brought me back to the present moment as I returned to lying on my stomach. Silence prevailed, save for the moans of an unseen prisoner in a cell down the passage. Hearing them, my own body began to react to my own situation, so I banished the sounds from my mind, returning to my deep memories.

Shwan and I became messengers. Our responsibilities were limited to the organization and distribution of non-volatile information. With our committee we produced and hand delivered informational pamphlets and documents for the purpose of raising awareness.

We knew the primary focus of our group and our job required us to deliver written material in the Arabic language to send a message to every Iraqi to unite and become one in the war against the Ba'ath regime.

Our messages advised them that the Ba'ath military were acquiring weapons of mass destruction to use on our own people which we discovered through delivering documents from inside the Ba'ath Regime itself.

The chemical cloud that had killed my family in Zalan was but one of many experiments with chemical weapons. Numerous communities were taken from the face of Kurdistan in previous years for experiment. The stories of these isolated villages and towns never reached the south of Iraq or the western world's press and so it was our part to courier information between Baghdad and Sulaymania during the breaks from university training. The materials were delivered hand to hand. I never fully trusted the next hand; I always wondered what happened to all the people who just disappeared at that time.

Shwan and I spent a lot of time studying and working together. We had a history, a solid trust, and a strong belief in our cause. He introduced me to the world of men's thoughts and beliefs.

Shwan brought out the best in me and in an odd sort of way took the place of Shanna and filled the void of missing my family. I went back to Sulaymania as often as I could to visit them, but each time I had a terrible fear I might be caught with the pamphlets, that it would be the last time I would see them, and also possibly bring Saddam's wrath down on them. Each trip was a nightmare in itself due to the rough treatment by the soldiers, the searches, and never knowing what went on in the roadside bunkers.

On a trip back home to visit my family, I stood in a line outside the bus at one of the checkpoints as the soldiers went about their routine. I saw the commander, a fat man in a wrinkled uniform looking directly at me. He shouted at the soldier doing the searches,

"Bring that one here!" I felt instant terror. My heart pounded inside my chest. Sweat began to run from my brow and underarms. The soldier brushed his gun between my legs then put it to my head and marched me into the bunker. I had to remind myself the art of a survivor was to put a mask on my feelings. I noticed Saddam's pictures on the bunker walls and the blood spatters on the commander's boots. He blew cigar smoke directly into my face in an act of contempt and stared at me intently with a sarcastic expression on his face. I heard a noise from the next bunker. It was the sound of a man shouting profanities as he took his sexual pleasure with a woman begging him to cease. I though my heart would stop. Would this be my fate too? I felt weak at my knees and struggled to stand.

I knew if that was his plan I was powerless to stop it. I was fully cognizant of the fact that if indeed I was raped, the stigma would remain with me forever. In Iraqi society a raped woman is considered on the same level as a prostitute. As I diverted my gaze from the commander's face and looked around the bunker, evidence of bloody violence marked the concrete walls. Fear for my fate increased as I noted the bullet-pocked walls. This was a place where my life might end.

The commander looked at me intently, searching my face for signs of fear at the sounds I could not help but hear.

"You like that, don't you? Perhaps it's your turn next," the commander said in a suggestive manner. I tried to calm my shaking knees still unsure how to control my terrible fear. I jerked in fear from the sound of a single gunshot from the next bunker. The cries of the protesting woman were silenced.

I had a distinct feeling that someone had just paid the ultimate price and wondered if I would be next. As he pointed to a rickety chair, the commander calmly said.

"Sit down." As I moved to sit, I noticed a soldier walk by from the next bunker zipping up his pants with blood spattered fingers. The commander went through all my university text books looking for anything to incriminate me as I waited, trying my utmost not to tremble or display emotion. He came across a picture of Saddam Hussein with the words Welcome to the Ba'ath party written on it. I had placed it there in anticipation of such a moment.

"You had better be for real.," he said and then he grabbed me by the neck and took me into the next bunker. I fully expected to die, so I drew a deep breath of resignation and momentarily my heart ceased beating as my knees turned to jelly. I drew from my inner strength and did not buckle or whine for mercy. The commander pulled me by the scruff of my neck as though I were a kitten and forced me to look.

A young girl of barely eighteen years lay with her head against the wall, blood still oozing from a bullet hole in her forehead. Her upper garments had been torn asunder exposing her breasts, now stained with her own life's blood. Her lower clothing lay in shredded disarray beside her and she lay naked from the waist down. Even in death the military offered the young woman no dignity.

It was painfully obvious to me that she had been brutally raped then murdered. Even though I was not unfamiliar with death, the sight of this young life snuffed out so violently made me want to vomit.

"You know why she is dead, don't you? Perhaps you already know her." He grabbed some papers that had been taken from her and shook them in my face.

"No." I said confidently.

"Those fighting against the Ba'ath regime will learn a bitter lesson from us. As I said, you had better be for real." He grabbed my arm and threw me out of the bunker along with my bag, then ordered me to board the bus.

Once again I desperately wanted to retch in reaction to what I had just seen, but I managed to control the urge. A soldier pushed me with his rifle barrel as I staggered to the bus. All eyes were upon me. I suppose the other passengers could hardly believe I had gotten out of the bunker alive.

"Move! Move!" The soldier yelled at me. It seemed like a lifetime when I finally sat down in my seat. When the bus began to move away from the roadblock my held back emotions broke forth. I was inconsolable. A man sitting behind me tapped my shoulder.

"I think I know what you have just witnessed. I saw a soldier slip some papers into the bag of a pretty young woman from the bus ahead of us. Then he forced her into the bunker and she never came back out. We heard a shot while you were in there. The girl was set up. At times I think I may one day get used to all this but then I realize I will never get used to it. One learns to face ones fears and build courage.

We were stopped at five more checkpoints before we reached Sulaymania. I felt sick; my mind would not release the vision of the young woman lying raped and murdered in the bunker just because she was pretty.

The first glimpse of Sulaymania through the bus window made me partially forget the horrors I had witnessed on the road. It felt euphoric to be back in the bosom of my family. The house was filled with the smell of mother's baking welcoming me, and lamb soup bubbled on the gas burner. Shilan gave me a warm hug and a kiss on my cheek. After Mother's welcoming hug, she knelt down on her mat to say her evening prayer. Rebwar burst through the door to offer his own welcome to me. Mother admonished him for walking in front of her as she prayed.

"Don't you dare walk in front of me when I am praying, Rebwar. I have told you many times God will punish you."

Suddenly it was as though I had never left. I had formed my own views on religion that I knew conflicted with hers. I had never believed in religion or constant prayer. My also non- religious father broke the acidic atmosphere by saying,

"Yes, Rebwar, listen to your mother. She wants you to go to heaven." Then he grinned at me, "Tell the family about your life in university, Najat. I hope you have been studying hard, for it is my plan to retire when you graduate and open a little shop next to the house."

I told my family about my life at university and about the wonders of the city of Baghdad. But I refrained from describing the events on the road. I felt for them to know would place a burden of fear for my safety upon them.

"Let us all eat. You must be famished, Najat," Father exclaimed. I did not have the heart to tell them I still felt sick from what I had seen on the journey home, so I sat with the family and forced myself to eat. When the dishes were washed and put away, we sat and talked about all manner of things. Then Shanna came over and joined us. We had so much to talk about; we talked until late into the night.

My friend Shanna had become a very attractive young woman and attended the University of Mosul. If our vacation time corresponded we would meet and speak together of the things we witnessed. Apparently she saw much less military violence than I did and I said to her,

"I'm glad you were not accepted at the University of Baghdad, Shanna. I do not think you would make it through the checkpoints. With your great beauty I'm sure you would be taken by the soldiers to be used and discarded."

Often when we walked on the streets of Sulaymania together, young men would whistle at her, or walk behind us singing a song to her but they could never speak face to face. Our old- fashioned customs leave our young people out of modern day thinking.

Shanna's family had promised her hand to a wealthy older man. She thought it quite comical how she would handle being married to a man thirty years older than she since she was having so much fun with the men at Mosul University and had already kissed a young man.

All too soon it was time to return to the university and leave my family to once again run the gauntlet of the southward journey. The routine at the checkpoints was just the same, but all they could find in my bag were Mother's home made pastries and a large bag of nuts, a gift for Fazila. She always expressed joy at my return knowing full well that my mother had sent her some treats. She grabbed my bags and struggled to my room with them and eagerly waited for me to open them. She would often stay and enjoy a cup of strong Arabic coffee and my room mates and I would ask her for a cup reading.

Fazila would solemnly give her readings, which never varied. My fortune was of standing in a castle courtyard looking for someone. Also that one day I would travel far away. She always told the two sisters, Salma and Sahira, that one of them would cause big trouble, but failed to say what it might be other than one of them might put whiskey in her juice. Upon this not so subtle hint, Salma would bring out a bottle from her closet and pour some into Fazila's cup. Within minutes the solemn Fazila began to dance the belly dance. We joined in and went from room to room adding to our numbers, until the girl's dormitory was a mass of laughing humanity enjoying the moment. When Fazila tired she would lie on the nearest bed and fall promptly asleep. All of the girls learned how to speak Fazila's Arabic language.

My room mates, Salma and Sahira, played what I thought was a rather dangerous game. Often they stayed out all night partying at a bar behind the Sheraton hotel frequented by wealthy and beautiful women from places like the Soviet Union and some Arab nations. Europeans and Asians also frequented the place. The bar was the centre for illegal trade, illicit sex, alcohol, and drugs. Saddam Hussein's son Udai often visited with his own circle of friends who pimped the young and beautiful women for him. The bar was owned by a member of Saddam's family who was well known for his acts of torture and murder.

Salma and Sahira knew these most dangerous of men by sight and name. I would often study my homework sitting on my bed in the hope of gleaning some snippets of information about the Ba'ath party that might be useful to the cause. I never did, but I did learn about some of the most debauched parties in Baghdad. I felt fear for my two room mates, for Uday Hussein had a fearful reputation of savage treatment of women. Girls seen with him once were often never seen again. I could never be sure if the stories were campus gossip or based on facts. Nevertheless I had a deep curiosity. Was the son like the father?

chapter six

I sat at the front of the classroom feigning rapt attention to the lecture. I had heard most of the same things about the human race with strong emphasis on Iraqi history a number of times. I refused to be indoctrinated with the daily onslaught of misinformation; instead I watched the face of the professor through the dust particles floating in the beam of sunlight streaming in through the window.

Professor Anthony Christopher appealed to me. He was outspoken and he refused to bow to the constant pressure to change his controversial opinions. He had the courage to challenge convention but never to the point where he exposed himself to any real danger. In my opinion he had the air of an intellectual eccentric. Anthony sported a mass of white hair and always wore a very wide necktie along with a wildly checked

European style sport coat. I think he considered himself a flamboyant genius and with his pointer would wave it around as if we the students were his orchestra.

A sudden change in the tone of his voice and lecture diverted my attention.

"I want to talk about greed and its effect on and corresponding link to the development of capitalism in many areas of the world."

Professor Christopher had my immediate attention, for this was a subject of great interest to me.

"Take your own country for instance. In northern Iraq as you all know Kurdistan was divided into four segments during the First World War, each piece becoming a part of Turkey, Iran, Syria, and Iraq. Why do you suppose each of these countries wanted a piece of Kurdistan?" He paused, eagerly waiting for a response from the assembled students. Receiving none he continued.

"You should know this!" he said with a tone of annoyance, "It is because it was an area rich in agricultural products, minerals, and all manner of natural resources, to wit oil."

"Professor! You are moving precariously closer to topics that a man in your position is not permitted to introduce." The voice came from a student, Shaza sitting in the middle of the class. I turned to look at her with a feeling of dread. I wondered did Shaza have something of intellectual value to share. She continued, "I don't think it is necessary for us to discuss the history of the Kurdish people when we are speaking of the history of mankind. They certainly haven't played any significant role in the development of our country. They are a hopeless bunch and useless! The history of the Kurdish people has documented evidence that supports my point of view. Historically they have put more effort into destruction than construction, in my opinion ever will."

I bristled at the words from a few fellow students assaulting my ears. My heart began racing and my body became tense like a coiled spring. Shaza had my undivided attention. I became completely aware of the hard wooden chair under me. I struggled to swallow my utter rage. My need to vehemently respond was on the cusp of being uncontrollable. But my multiple fears held me back. There was the fear of retribution, expulsion from the university, the fear of imprisonment for the crime of being born a Kurd and as such considered anti Ba'ath Regime. Frantically I looked around the room. I wondered if anyone was going to respond and incriminate themselves. I knew there were other Kurds in the room all of whom stared at the professor as though they had heard nothing, but more than likely sharing the same helpless anger as I.

Professor Christopher defused the situation by repeating,

"We are talking about the history of land and greed, not nationality or Kurds or Arabs. Forgive me for forgetting that I am not in England where individuals have freedom of opinions. You referred to the history of the Kurds, Shaza, and yet we know nothing about them. You know nothing about them."

"The Kurdish people do not have the right to speak up for their own rights. What gives you the right to speak for them professor?"

I knew the professor realized he had allowed the debate to progress further than was wise and so diplomatically ended the discussion. I felt that he was fully aware that the warning Shaza had given him could go much further than the classroom. I also felt that he was wise enough to not jeopardize his position at the university and for that matter his life to make his point understood to a single opinionated student. Sitting quietly, but seething inwardly and fighting the urge to get up and run from the room, I waited with the other students for the bell to signal the end of class.

After a long charged silence, the bell rang and the students shuffled out. I sat still in my chair without expecting a conciliatory word from Professor Anthony Christopher and none was forthcoming. He picked up his books and strode in a determined manner from the classroom. I felt much too shocked and emotional to follow him and sat feeling dejected with my head in my hands. In retrospect I think the amalgam of all the brutality I had witnessed in my short life and the vision of the young girl in the bunker, caused me to seize up with too much anger at a person who had the view that I as a Kurd had no value, or right to an opinion and it left me in a momentary mental void.

I have no idea how long I stayed in the room but I came back to a sense of reality when Shwan's face appeared in front of me.

"How can I possibly make a difference, Shwan?" I said dejectedly.

"Make a difference to what, Najat?"

I explained to him what had occurred in class and how it had a temporary affect upon my thinking.

"I study hard trying to expand my knowledge and I am surrounded by many small minds caught up in their own ignorance. They see nothing beyond the city of Baghdad! In their minds we as a people are insignificant. To them we do not exist, so how can they need to know about us if we are considered as something that does not exist? Why do you look at me this way, Shwan?" I said trying to control my pain and anger, "We have grown older together, but inside we are still the two small children who gasped for a breath of clean air while submerged in a pond above Zalan. The two children who smelled the odor of chemically burned human flesh and the two children who abandoned the bodies of our families to rot in the summer sun. We are the children who wanted to make changes to help our suffering people, and we are the two children who have come to this point to realize that there is very little we can do against a human tide of hatred and brutality."

Shwan, wise as always, looked into my eyes, "Patience my dear, Najat. Only patience and a clear understanding will lead you to know what we must do to bring about the changes we seek. You must listen hard. You must read and question what you see going on around you, so that you have a clear understanding of their prejudices. You must remember the art of survival, mask your feelings, and learn to completely control your anger. If you develop the patience to really listen to what people are saying, no matter how ignorant, it may be you who will learn to see it as an opportunity to teach them about our circumstances even if they don't want to hear it from you. It is up to you as an educated woman to find an answer to a person who doesn't realize they have asked you a question. These trials and frustrations are just the beginning of your life's journey." As Shwan's words sank into my brain I asked,

"What do you mean by saying this is the beginning of my life's journey, Shwan. Surely my life's journey began when my mother gave birth to me?"

"I mean my dear, Najat, that this is the beginning of a life with a real purpose for you. Consider this then as the beginning of chapter two in that life. You have just endured a strong frustration in the world we have inherited. I have a vision of you learning to live with that frustration of which there will be undoubtedly more. My vision includes a strong little girl who has become a strong woman who will one day make sense of all this. A strong woman who will one day find her way to America and tell the unknowing world about our people. This strong woman will tell the world about the slaughter, the disappearances, and the executions of innocent Kurdish people. She will tell of crimes perpetrated by the Ba'ath regime and of how our people have been used in savage experimental gas attacks and bacterial warfare. Without you Najat, it may be too late for the outside world to know there ever was a race of people known as the Kurds. Najat! We have to find some way of getting the information out to the countries in the Western world."

Shwan's words brought me rapidly out of my melancholy frame of mind. As always through his wisdom he had begun to steer me in the right direction. He stood looking down at me, his eyes conveying a positive message of strength. The silence between us suddenly shattered like a broken glass as the hallway bell signaled the resumption of classes. He turned to leave, then he turned again and whispered into my ear,

"Don't forget, Najat. Education is the strongest weapon we have." As he left the room I called after him,

"Don't forget, Shwan, I am going home to Sulaymania for the holidays." With an arm wave of understanding he disappeared amid the group of students entering the classroom.

The three day holiday weekend in celebration of Saddam's 28th of April birthday was a welcome break from constant study, and I found myself amid throngs of people at the Naheza bus station in Baghdad. We were waiting in long lines to purchase bus tickets for a myriad of different destinations. It appeared almost as if everyone in the university had families to go back to on this holiday. Even though it was still only early summer the warm weather added to their discomfort. I too felt a mild distress from the warmth and to relieve my boredom of waiting in a line of almost imperceptibly moving people to buy my ticket, I began a silent study of the people around me.

One in particular caught my attention. He was blonde and blue eyed, and stood taller than anyone around him. My eyes immediately picked up on his clothing. He wore blue jeans worn at the knee, stout military type boots, a white shirt, and he carried a backpack with wide straps. His blonde hair needed a trim and the tangled mass of hair suggested a man with a confident attitude. It seemed obvious to me that he was from some western country.

He saw me looking at him and for a second our eyes met. I immediately averted my gaze but I felt his eyed riveted upon me. I felt slightly uncomfortable at my own attentions on him and yet the man intrigued me. I would like to have spoken with him about where he had come from and what he was doing in my part of the world.

The line moved up and it was my turn to buy my ticket. The ticket seller was a grossly obese man with a face suggesting a general unhappiness with his life. He sat behind a wicket of iron bars. I asked in Arabic with my slight Kurdish accent for a ticket to Sulaymania. He spoke in a vitriolic tone of voice,

"You are one of those wild Kurdish animals from the mountains calling yourselves humans, aren't you? So you are one of the animals who killed my brother. You all live like stinking farm animals, in fact, you remind me of a cow."

Pleased at himself for his cruel outburst he began to laugh out loud and his disgusting breath fanned out into the crowd behind me. His laughter turned to coughing and wheezing and his fat-laden body shook in ripples.

As the seller fumbled with my money and the ticket, I wondered how many times he would repeat this show with each Kurdish student just to empower himself to get over his personal anger. I am sure he didn't understand how the Ba'ath Regime was turning all of us against each other.

I happened to notice that the tall foreigner had got his ticket and stood behind me in the bus line. I heard him mildly cursing to himself softly in the English language.

"Four hours in this damn bus station just in order to buy a bus ticket and now I have to line up and wait to get on the damn thing."

I, of course, had been studying the English language since I was fifteen so I turned to him and said,

"You must miss home." His look instantly became sheepish and he answered in a subdued voice.

"Well, yes. Right at this moment I do. I find the poor system of dealing with simple issues like buying a bus ticket utterly frustrating. You are the first woman since arriving in this country that has spoken to me at all away from my work area."

"Yes." I answered, "We are not so free here as in the West. I'm not speaking culturally. Anyway you wouldn't understand. Where are you traveling to?"

"I'm going to Sulaymania. I have been offered the chance to do a story on the military activities there and I am going to check it out."

Upon hearing the word military it was as though I had set off a land mine; my sense of self-preservation kicked in. No longer could I be the friendly to a tourist Iraqi woman. I knew instantly I had to keep this man at a distance. I chose a seat next to a middle aged woman. The blonde man took the seat behind us and sat with a male student from the university. I overheard him saying,

"A man can actually sit beside a woman in Iraq, not like Saudi Arabia or Afghanistan." The student answered,

"As long as there is a seat available for two women to sit together, they automatically make that choice, but if no seat beside a woman is available then they will sit beside a man. Our country is torn between the old and new generation."

My seat companion seemed to be utterly exhausted from the long wait in the heat and she used her scarf as a fan to cool her face. We exchanged small talk. Then surprisingly leaning close to me she began to confide in me in a whisper.

"My dear, we are a walking dead people. This is not life we are living and I wonder when God will punish this oppressive regime. I have come to Baghdad to visit my son. He has been sentenced to twenty years in Saddam's prison. When I asked what the accusations against him were, they told me he had been accused of spray painting on Saddam's picture. I think we both know, young woman, that had it been true, he would have been killed. I thank God that after several months of searching I discovered he was spared and that he was in the Abbu Kreab prison, but I curse Saddam Hussein for my son's twenty lost years."

From behind my seat I heard snippets of conversation in English between the blonde man and the student. I touched the hand of my seat partner and indicated I was listening to the conversation behind me. She immediately understood and remained silent. Now being able to give my full attention I heard the student say,

"When I finished high school I took a summer break. One evening I and several friends went to the cinema. Shortly after the show started, a group of military personnel stormed into the theatre. They ordered everyone out at gunpoint but my friends and I. We were put in a military truck and driven away. Since I had never been in Baghdad before I had no idea where we were taken to and assumed they were taking us to a place where they would kill us." The blonde man asked,

"Why would you think they might kill you? Especially since you had done nothing wrong or committed a crime."

The student replied,

"We do not need to commit a crime in order to be arrested or for that matter convicted. The soldiers took us to a big building. Perhaps it was a prison or interrogation station. We all were thrown separately into dark rooms. Shortly after a soldier came to my room and started beating me with a club. After a blow to my head I became unconscious, he must have left because he came to my room again later and beat me again. He screamed at me in Arabic and I could only understand a few words which netted me even more torture. This continued for about a month with him demanding me to tell him the names of other revolutionaries. In all truth, I did not know of any. Under torture I gave false names but it didn't stop the beatings.

After a month they dragged me from my cell and took me to a large, brightly lit room and placed me against a wall with about ten other men, all of us battered and bruised. Five armed soldiers and an officer walked in. The soldiers would point at one of us prisoners and the officer would pronounce sentence.

"Thirty years‧ Death by gunshot ‧ Twenty years‧ Death‧ and so on until it came to be my turn. I was terrified. My parent's had no idea where I was and if my sentence was death they would never know what had happened to me. And the thought of many years in this awful prison made death seem preferable. The condemned men were shot where they stood as the others watched in horror. God must have been with me on that terrible day for the officer said I could go free."

The blonde man said,

"So they knew you were innocent of any crime?"

"No. Someone had given my parents the news of where I had been taken and came and paid money to the officer to let me go."

"And your friends?

"I haven't seen or heard from them since. Their families had no money and so two were killed and two were sentenced to twenty years each."

"Your insight and knowledge is most useful to me for I am a journalist. How can I get in touch with you?"

The bus braked for the first roadside inspection and we all filed out of the bus. The soldiers took an immediate interest in the foreigner and more or less ignored the rest of us and allowed us to re-take our seats. I turned to the young student and said,

"You are very foolish to speak so freely to a person you know nothing about. If you expect to survive in this land you should be smarter than that. Can you be sure the foreigner is not working for the military? Perhaps he wouldn't care if they dragged you off the bus and shot you right now."

Having been warned of his foolishness, the student went to sit with someone else so he didn't have to keep in conversation with the blonde man. Finally having satisfied the commander, the blonde man boarded the bus and we continued on to the next checkpoint.

A soldier with his rifle clutched against his side boarded the bus. He made his way down the aisle snatching the documentation from the passenger's hands glancing at them and flinging them back. When he reached my seat he toyed with the two pastry boxes on my lap with the barrel of his gun. I immediately thought that perhaps he recognized me from my last trip and he would order me to go inside the bunker. The memory of the young girl and her brutal rape and murder flashed through my mind and I thought perhaps this time it was my turn. I remembered I must stay calm and unflustered so I smiled at the soldier.

"What do you have in there?" He said pointing at the boxes with the gun.

"Just sweet pastries for my family," I responded

calmly. I handed him my papers and he held them close to his face and studied them. Then he handed back the papers and as my hand closed on them he snatched them back. It was abundantly clear to me that he was enjoying the power he held over us, and as I understood it, a prerequisite for the Iraqi military command. He ran his grubby fingers across my cheek as he returned my papers for the second time. Then he turned to the occupants of the next seat. Suddenly he whipped round again, grabbed the pastry boxes and hurled one of them out of the window and the passengers watched as a box broke and scattered the contents on the dusty grou

He gave me a sadistic grin. The blonde man stood up: I assume to help defend me against any further action by the soldier. The student who had been speaking with him earlier said in English,

"Sit down! The papers from your own government do not mean a thing to these soldiers; you are putting yourself in great danger."

"What are they looking for?"

"This is a routine checkpoint. We will endure several of them before we reach Sulaymania. So get used to it!"

My seat partner, Atte, took my hand to offer comfort. She told me,

"When I found out where they were holding my son I made a home cooked meal and some pastries to take to him in the prison. But on the way the soldier took it from me, threw it away, then took the pastries and ate them in front of me."

"Do you have any other children, Atte?"

"Yes, Najat. I have four other sons. They were conscripted into Saddam's army and all four are on the front line in the war with Iran. I have not heard from any of them and don't know if they are alive or have been killed. I have three daughters also. They are young and all of them beautiful girls. I would never allow them to take this route to Baghdad for fear they would be taken."

Atte leaned closer to me and whispered in my ear,

"If you are carrying anything that could cost you your life, Najat, let me take it to Sulaymania for you."

"I couldn't do that, Atte. Your life is just as precious as mine."

"Not quite, Najat. I have had my time on this earth and I can tell by seeing you look so scared that you indeed have something." She pointed at the second box placed on my lap. Quickly she grabbed it and placed under her abaya.

"I will hand it back to you when we arrive. Do not argue with me!"

The other checkpoints were just as nerve-wracking for me as the first. I felt terribly threatened as I am sure the other passengers did. I felt sick with fear deep down in my stomach. My train of thought became confused and remained that way until I was feeling safe at home with my family.

The bus arrived in the city of Sulaymania which contrasted so vividly with Baghdad. I could see in the faces of the people the exhaustion of being beaten from every direction and I sensed the fear in them. The pressure of their struggle for survival gave them a look of tiredness and a distinct air of unhappiness. Despite all of that, I still called it home.

After the welcome and the special meal Mother had prepared, I felt exhausted and emotionally drained after the harrowing journey. I went to sleep early. After my family were also asleep, I rose and being as quiet as I could, by candlelight I brought my daily journal up to date. When it was done I returned to my bed, but sleep would not come a second time. I could not get the cruel soldier out of my mind. I could see his unfeeling eyes staring at me and how fortunate I had been that he finally left me alone before discovering that I was indeed carrying some information papers for the Musakafin.

The next morning I opened the box of papers entrusted to me by a government official who clandestinely worked with the student underground movement. The same box for which Atte had endangered her life on my account. Without me hearing her enter, my sister Shilan burst into the room. I quickly stuffed the papers under my mattress.

"Hey, what are those?" She demanded.

"Nothing. Just school papers."

"Come on, Najat. I'm not stupid. Something is going on. Your face tells the story." I, of course, knew that Shilan was highly intelligent and could read between the lines. I felt that I could not lie to my sister, but neither did I want to endanger her by taking her into my confidence. I had to make an instant critical decision.

"Shilan! I beg of you not to say a word to Mother or Father. They would be devastated to lose their trust in me and I would be devastated if they forced me to quit university." I remember raising my hands in a gesture of defeat and submission.

I was fairly certain I could trust Shilan with my secret; nevertheless, my stomach began to knot up. I realized that quitting university would be tantamount to failing in my life's quest. I hungered for experience and knowledge I could never achieve here at home. Astutely recognizing my dilemma, Shilan said,

"Don't worry, Najat. I would never do that to you. Tell me nothing. But I want you to be very careful. Remember more people know what is going on than perhaps you think." Shilan left the room and I felt confident my secret would be safe with her.

chapter seven

I began to study the documents from the box. No longer was the information about educating against war or questioning about weapons of mass destruction. Finally this was real evidence. The papers described the chemical weapon's type, the effects of their use, and the way they were to be handled in transportation and deployment. The documents even included the routes the weapons were to be transported on and the detailed maps leading into Kurdistan. The maps indicated where the weapons were to be stored, hidden, and protected against insurgents deep in the mountain valleys. Included were battle and strategy plans to get the weapons to their destination through revolutionary controlled territory. I realized that the information in my hand could be of tremendous importance to the freedom fighters in blocking Saddam's forces from hiding the weapons in remote mountain areas. I realized now why the Ba'ath regime had placed landmines in so many places in northern Iraq. It was well known among our people that walking anywhere but on the beaten paths was highly dangerous.

I scoured through the documents looking for the names of the military officers involved in the program. However, they were encoded and I could make no sense of the codes. Standing with the incriminating papers in my hands I realized I was involved much deeper in the revolution against the Ba'ath regime than I had ever intended to be.

Shilan re-entered the room,

"Will you tell me now what it is you are involved in, Najat?"

Loving my sister the way I did, my heart wanted me to confide in her, but I was fully aware that if I did and she were questioned under torture and broke, my entire family, to say nothing of the rest of our neighborhood, would die an agonizing death for something they had nothing to do with. I knew I could not tell her. I think the look of fear and desperation in my eyes conveyed it to her clearly, so she simply said,

"Mother says the meal is ready, Najat."

We gathered together for the meal and to catch up on the last four months of my university life and progress. The conversation was subdued over the statement Rebwar made,

"Now I have finished high school I feel I am old enough to make my own decisions about my future." Mother sat quietly in a pensive mood but father was angry while Shilan and I sat and listened to Rebwar's announcement,

"I am like most of the young men in the city. I would like to escape to Iran so that I can make my way to Europe. I refuse to fight and possibly be killed for the Ba'ath party."

"I have warned you before about your thinking, Rebwar." Father stated.

"Fine! Then I will join the revolutionary army even though I don't want anything to do with them.

"If you are dead set on your plan to get to Iran, Rebwar, I will pay whatever it costs to get black-market travel papers."

"Well, I'm telling you father. I have already bought a black-market passport and paid for a smuggler to get us over the border."

"Us! What do you mean us? Who is us, Rebwar? What do you mean you have already bought a passport?"

"We are eighteen of my fellow students from high school. We plan to leave in six days from now."

"Rebwar, my only son. I am gone from our home a great deal of the time with my work. Shilan and your mother need a man in the house. Besides this war is not going to go on for ever. It may only last a little longer; the government can't afford it; soon there will be no men left to fight and the people are becoming very poor."

"You have your head in the sand, Father. I should be going and getting a head start for the rest of you. This war is not going to end. Saddam Hussein is a warmonger, not a peacemaker just like Mohammed, the leader of our religion."

"Enough is enough, Rebwar! At least wait until the end of summer and see if I am right."

Mother did not touch her meal and father glared with silent fury. Shilan broke in to the conversation with an angry and agitated tone,

"I support Rebwar's decision one hundred percent! I wish that I too could travel to Iran with him. We are living in a crisis situation, Father! Escaping from our country is not only escaping almost certain death, but it is becoming fashionable for young Kurdish Iraqis to run to seek out life and liberty in the outside world. Our generation is rejecting all the old teachings."

The only sound in the room was Mother's gentle sobbing. Father sat stone faced looking at her. Rebwar sat tall and erect. This day he had become a man with an aim in life and a plan to carry it out. Shilan, too had bravely spoken her mind. I felt proud of them both. As for myself, I did not enter into the conversation, but I sincerely hoped that my brother Rebwar had a safe journey to the outside world. However, I felt a great sadness for my father in losing his son, for I knew once Rebwar had left, there would be no coming back. In an attempt to cheer my father and end the painful silence I said,

"Try not to worry Father. Like you said earlier, things could change tomorrow." I knew I spoke false words, for I knew only too well from the information I had under my mattress, if things changed it would not be for the better.

"How are things at the university, Najat, my child?" I had anticipated father's question and I was well prepared for it.

"Very well, Father. However it is much more difficult than high school. I need to sleep less and study more. Even here at home I have work I must do."

I phrased my answer this way in order that I could have time alone in my room without any suspicion of my real agenda, genuine homework, and my political activities.

"In a few weeks at the end of term we will be holding an open house at the university. The top students in each department have the opportunity to work on a display featuring their best work from the past year. Lots of guests including important Ba'ath officials will be there and will take part in selecting the winners. Father? I am hoping to win an award at the prize giving ceremony and I hope I can make you very proud of me!"

I think father was proud of me already.

"My dear, Najat, I am confident you will win. Then you will be someone if you are in the favor of the Ba'ath."

"That is why I work so hard, Father, so I can earn it on my own."

"Enough work! There's never too much. I know you will make me proud, little one," Father said with a lump in his throat.

The night was long for me. I had arranged to go shopping with my sister Shilan in the morning, although that was not the purpose in going out. I felt very threatened by the documents I was to deliver. Never before had I carried such damning evidence of the Ba'ath party's criminal activities. I hoped fervently it would be delivered into the right hands. I had a very deep feeling that in the right hands the documents may change the very future of Iraq and its people. I searched my mind wondering if the usual recipient of my dispatches was the right one to trust with such important information.

Dawn broke, sending light into the bedroom of Shilan and I.

After our breakfast, Shilan and I prepared for our shopping trip.

"Is there anything we can bring back for you, Mother?" I asked,

"Perhaps you could bring some freshly squeezed grape juice and perhaps some fresh bread."

I went to my room and put the documents in my purse concealing them under a scarf. It was a beautiful late spring morning. Even in our broken city I could still see beauty all around me. Every day the sun grew in strength, the streets were alive with people and the market place a shimmering palette of color. It was a wonderful break from the constant study at the university. We bought the supplies for mother along with a selection of fresh fruits.

"Shilan, I have to go to the main library to get some information for my project. Perhaps you could find something to read while I study. It won't take me long." My instructions were to sit at a table between eleven and eleven thirty with an open book and a pencil lying horizontally at the top with the point aimed to the left.

The main library offered peace and quiet, a temporary refuge from the world outside. It had an excellent selection of reference books and magazines, and in addition the library provided a confidential meeting place for friends of the opposite sex with the table the only barrier between them. More liberal young men and women could enjoy a brief conversation without it being judged as morally wrong. The library was a place where information could be passed along hand to hand with relative ease. I had used the facility for this purpose several times before and this was my purpose for being here this morning. Soldier spies were always in the library keeping watchful eye on the patrons and there was the chance of being caught in the act by the undercover AMN. The library posed an even more insidious danger from fellow Kurds on the military payroll.

In reality no place was safe. The government found it easy to infiltrate Kurdish society. They had a system more effective than executions, by paying for information. They turned friend against friend ensuring that simple trust was no longer possible. The more desperate members of our society sold their souls to the devil, Saddam Hussein, and turned in their neighbors in an attempt to survive.

Shilan searched the shelves for some easy reading while I sat at a table with two books. A text book with a pencil above it lay in a position above the one I pretended to study. A young man came and sat opposite me; he took several books from a satchel and laid them out close to mine. He pushed one of the books towards me a slip of paper protruded from the pages. It contained the typed words (history project) the code for me to pass my documents into his hands. Still pretending to study, I inserted the documents in-between the pages of the book he passed silently across the table. A soldier guard walked by us but saw only two students busy at their work. Shortly afterwards the young man stuffed his books and papers into his satchel and walked out of the building. I felt intense relief that it had gone well and fervently hoped the material would get into the right hands. I gathered my own books and papers and went in search of Shilan.

"I'm all done now, Shilan. We can go." Once outside she said,

"Please be careful whatever it is you are doing, Najat."

My three day holiday at home in Sulaymania came to an end all too soon. My father joined me as I went to the station to get the bus to Baghdad. I purchased my ticket and we stood together as I waited to board the bus. My father kissed my head and said,

"Don't let me down. You promised to make me proud."

"I will Father."

"God be with you! Remember, Najat, that you have already made us proud of you."

I waved a final goodbye and clambered aboard the rickety old bus. The loud music pouring out of the bus stereo system assaulted my ears as soon as I stepped inside. I knew I would have to endure the noise all the way to Baghdad. It was so often the case on these ancient and decrepit buses, with many of them exuding clouds of black smoke which often engulfed the vehicle both inside and out. The buses frequently were unlicensed and carried no destination signs, yet they were always filled to capacity and the driver would yell out the names of the towns and villages it passed through and collect cash fares from those boarding at the unscheduled stops.

This bus was no different. It was jammed with humanity, students of both sexes en-route to the university all manner of adults returning to their work in the city, and mothers taking their children for medical treatments. Others were going to visit family members in the Abbu Khareb Prison in Baghdad along with soldiers returning to their bases after furlough.

The bus was filled with a cacophony of sound, dust from the road, exhaust fumes and the odor of sweat from overheated bodies. By the time we had negotiated the checkpoints and inspections, I was bone weary and my head ached. When I arrived at the women's residence I discovered my two room mates had not yet returned and feeling so grateful to not have to talk about my holiday I flopped immediately into my bed.

The next day was the day of the university open house. I agonized upon what I should wear but settled on a simple green dress. I draped it over a chair by my desk and rummaged through my bag for a matching lipstick and the appropriate cosmetics. I found the shade I felt best would complement my dress and placed it on the chair ready for morning.

I climbed into bed with my mind in a state of turmoil worrying about the possible outcomes of the following day. The way I saw it in my mind was either one of two outcomes. I could be acclaimed as a top student and receive the accolades due me, or I could be expelled from the university for my outspoken views. I was well aware that my outspokenness had created conflict in the past much more than it had saved me. Despite the fear and concern over the latter, I could not help but smile to myself in the darkness as I imagined myself at the podium to receive the top student award.

I knew if I were able to attain the top student award for each of my four years of university training, I would be eligible to travel to Europe to continue my studies in England or Germany. Winning the award was the only legal way to accept a foreign scholarship. Any other was punishable by imprisonment. I knew that even though I was Kurdish. If I won, they would allow me the right to attend a foreign university but I also knew that if I did win, I would have to sign an agreement that I accepted and believed in the principals of the Ba'ath regime.

In order to achieve my objectives I was prepared to make some sacrifices; however, acknowledging the ideals of the existing political system was not one of them. Unable to fall asleep, I began to consider the repercussions such a decision would have on my family producing pangs of anxiety. My work at the university had been compelling and now my feelings turned to self doubt. I wondered if I had been foolish embarking on such a path, perhaps even arrogant by assuming the freedom to display controversial ideas in public. My loss of self-confidence, however, was a temporary one and I told myself, 'I know what I believe and the government of Iraq will not control my mind; I knew that if I projected my views in too loud a voice, it would surely be silenced. I felt there were ways I could communicate controversial ideas without putting my life in harm's way.

I sat upright in my bed. I realized that if I was not free to express my opinions, I would disguise, or mask them. I felt confident that the Iraqi government could not dictate my thoughts. I settled down in my bed again and using techniques I had become accustomed to over the last year, I forced myself to become calm. Breathing slow and deep and banishing troubling thoughts from my mind, I fell to sleep.

chapter eight

I left the women's residence and walked to the main university building. All the halls and doorways were decorated with bunting in readiness for the open house. The students dressed in their finest attire gathered in groups around the main entrance. Off to the side, students from the music department, resplendent in bright uniforms, tuned their instruments. Atop the steps of the main portal the entrance was blocked by a wide satin ribbon. This was attended by a female student in traditional Arab dress. Her ankle length gown was composed of layer after layer of fine cloth with the loosely draped fabric fluttering in the cool morning breeze. She wore a short cropped vest festooned by rows of polished coins which glittered in the sun as she moved ever so slightly. The girl had her hands and arms outstretched holding a wide pillow with a folded Iraqi flag lying atop. In the center lay a pair of gleaming scissors awaiting President Saddam Hussein's hand to cut the opening ribbon and begin the festivities.

Numerous professors strategically positioned themselves around the entrance in order to supervise the goings on. Several others were visible inside the hall checking the last minute details. Like the other students around me I waited for Saddam's arrival. The president liked to put on a military show for any occasions like this to protect his self proclaimed image. The route to a particular event often choked with up to five thousand troops marching in full military dress with boots and buttons polished. Saddam often arrived standing in the turret of the leading tank followed by many others. It was no error on his part that there were more secret service intelligence officers and soldiers to listen to his speech than students and dignitaries.

I was to find out later that long before dawn, the presidential guards were at the university to check anything and everything they considered a possible threat. The guards were positioned all over the university grounds. Anything that Saddam might touch including the scissors was washed down and disinfected. Even the flag the girl held on a cushion had been put there by a guard as a security measure. Special instructions on protocol had been given weeks in advance to the university president, Mehdi Sumaid, and these had been practiced for many days.

Away in the distance, the roar of motorcycle engines broke the quiet of the morning. The student band took its cue and began playing the National Anthem of Iraq. Seconds later a motorcade of gleaming black Mercedes Benz sedans led by motorcycle police entered the university gates. This day Saddam was making his entrance in style. I think we all knew the cars contained the most important and influential men in the government including Saddam himself.

The first car emptied its cargo of heavily armed bodyguards. Saddam alit from the second car and immediately the bodyguards surrounded him. In finely rehearsed motions, the doors of the other cars opened and Saddam's entourage stepped out.

I was able to recognize the Minister of Education, Hamed Yousef Hamady. It was widely rumored that Saddam was servicing his wife. I also recognized Zyad Hassan Hashim, Roukham Tekritey was Saddam's special palace soldier. There were about a dozen in all that I recognized mostly by reputation. As Saddam came closer to the door surrounded by his men, I stood on tiptoe to get a better look at the man so bitterly reviled in our country. I watched his body language and despite the fact that we all knew Saddam had a number of doubles masquerading as him, I could not help but wonder was this the real Saddam. I, of course, knew his history, but still wondered how such a thug could have risen to be the president of Iraq.

The music stopped abruptly as Saddam stepped onto the red carpet leading to the main door. He snatched the scissors without a word from the trembling girl and sliced through the red ribbon. Saddam raised the scissors to the sky the way he often did with a rifle. The crowd cheered as Saddam and his entourage entered the building. Then we students dispersed and made our way to the presentation area while the dignitaries examined our displays. We all knew that they would examine some of the works more closely than others perhaps to look at an essay or study photographs. We knew also that if they found something offensive or considered it to be subversive there would be no second chance. This was Saddam's way.

We stood behind the table containing the display of the work by the students taking history. I felt my palms begin to sweat as the President and his entourage approached. I could not turn back now. The die was cast and I would know very soon what the future held for me. As Saddam looked at the work next to mine, my blood ran cold. I felt chilled by the realization that I could reach out and touch the man responsible for so much suffering and death in my country.

As I looked at him, making sure I made eye contact, joyfully I saw his gaze concentrating on the display. However, one of his entourage focused his gaze upon me. It was impossible to ignore and I felt the invasion of his eyes. Knowing I had gotten myself into a do or die situation, I elected to respond with similar intensity. I was fully aware of the impression I was making, for I had intended that this would be the day I would be noticed. For this very reason I had chosen the crisply tailored green dress, the official color of the Ba'ath Party, picked out a complementary lipstick and had carefully groomed my hair and eyelashes and brows. I looked directly into his eyes and gave a quick smile even though I knew a smile would be interpreted as provocative.

He smiled back. I stood stock still with my hands held together at my waist in a manner befitting a subservient young Iraqi woman. His gaze was fixed firmly upon me as he followed the President. Saddam smiled at each student as he examined their displays, occasionally asking the students of their future plans. For an instant my heart stopped beating as Saddam Hussein stood in front of me. Still I showed my excitement at the possibility of him shaking my hand, as did the other students.

The man who had been watching me directly stepped up to the table; I examined him closely. The man was tall, well built, with an unmistakable air of authority. Thick black hair, freshly trimmed, framed, strong features. A neatly styled mustache covered his upper lip. Dark piercing eyes with a look of high intelligence were fixed upon me. He surprised me by extending his hand to me. Out of respect for his gesture I accepted it and he held my hand far longer than seemed proper as he formally asked me for my name.

"Najat, sir." I responded. One of the other guests spoke to the man. I heard him say,

"Sa'adoun, have you noticed this student's work?"

Instantly I recognized the name. I had seen his name on one of the documents that had passed through my hands. He was one of the members of the secret service intelligence for the Ba'ath Regime. Ali Hassan al-Majid had a reputation of using chemical weapons on the Kurdish people. I wondered what kind of position Sa'adoun occupied since he had worked for the devilish al-Majid, known widely as chemical Ali.

There was much speculation about Sa'adoun Alwan, for most of us knew that the Ba'ath Regime had three separate layers of command. The first layer consisted of the Tikrit family, members of Saddam Hussein. The second contained the higher level government men and the third layer consisted of secret service agents. It was also well known that the two lower levels spied upon each other in order to gain favor with the top level.

I suddenly realized I was engaged in staring blatantly at him, my nervousness rising by the second. I saw him speak softly to the man who had mentioned his name. His gaze never left me, and I felt as if he could see right through me. I had to break the impasse.

"Please, Sir." I addressed Sa'adoun with my practiced Arabic accent, "Feel free to browse through the work. The display represents our best efforts during the last few months of school. I would be honored to answer any questions you may have." Sa'adoun's attention was diverted from my work by a professor who stepped forward with the obvious intention of steering him away from my display. Sa'adoun ignored him and picked up several articles from my display and began to read aloud.

"The capitalist system;" "The impact of war on the economy;" " The Function of Religion in Modern Times;" "The Cycle Famine and Starvation;" "The Western Impact on the Middle East!"

His voice trailed off and he paused, staring wide eyed directly at me. I felt at a loss that I could not judge his reaction. I glanced at Sa'adoun who glanced at the professor who had tried to divert him from my display. He kept on reading while my ears keenly listened. His voice had remained constant through his reading of my titles, and I had detected no anger or dismay in him. The air in the room was charged with high voltage electricity and the clean, sharp, acidic fragrance one notices after a thunderstorm, as I, the professors, and students waited for a response, expecting an explosion of anger. We all were frozen in silent anticipation. Continuing his rigid stare he said,

"You have been studying extremely complex topics, Najat. Is this work supposed to be your agreement or disagreement with the Ba'ath party?" Every nerve in my body tingled and my saliva had a bitter taste. The wrong word here could mean my death.

"It is important for all people to learn that Marxism promotes enlightened thought and that the integral message is not to promote war and violence."

Sa'adoun spoke, "You have a very soft accent; are you from Arbil?"

"No. Unfortunately I am from Sulaymania." I answered with all the diplomacy I could muster. I knew most people of Arbil strongly supported the government while the population of my home city hated Saddam and his political party. I wondered if I had thrown the fat into the fire, and I knew the next few seconds would give me the answer. Sa'adoun's face carried a stern expression, but his words gave no indication of how he really felt.

"You are very young, Najat, to have such passionate ideas and opinions on such a diverse array of complicated issues. However, we must move on and view the works of other students. You certainly have captured my interest, and I would like to speak with you again sometime. A mild shiver ran through my body at hearing the words, but I smiled as warmly as I could to suggest agreement.

The two men walked away from my table to join the rest of the bodyguards. Sa'adoun paused and whispered something into the ear of the other man. I wondered. Was this the beginning of the end? I became increasingly uneasy witnessing the exchange. In order to control my feelings I decided to tidy up the display table. From the corner of my eye I could see the soldier watching me. Upon realizing that I was aware of his gaze, he turned and left the room.

When all the dignitaries had gone, I picked up some books intending to return them to my supervisor's office. I walked slowly with as much dignity as I could. I was engaged in placing the books in the proper location on the shelves when I heard loud voices from the next room. I peeped furtively round the corner and saw my supervisor in heated conversation with the man that Sa'adoun had been whispering to. He held a buff file folder in his right hand, but I was too far away to be able to read the name on it. Unwilling to be discovered snooping at them, I walked softly down the hall and back to my station with all manner of questions rushing madly around in my mind.

I spent the day with my stomach in knots wondering what my fate would be. Would it be accolades or a bullet through my brain? The blaring public address system pierced my melancholy with the announcement to assemble in the main auditorium in thirty minutes. My heart rate increased rapidly in fear of what would happen to me.

We students rushed around folding the tables and stowing them away. We took our displays back to our rooms before hurrying to the auditorium. A display of music and dancing (to be performed by the music department) was to precede the actual awards ceremony. I saw groups of excited students proceeding down the halls speaking in high anticipation of being the chosen ones. I heard that Saddam had left the university after only a couple of hours.

After the music stopped I sat with my head bowed, expecting the worst possible outcome. I was Kurdish. I had dared to display my thoughts, and now it was just a question of time before I paid the ultimate price. The chancellor droned on, reading the names of the winners of the different categories with cheers and clapping from the students as each name was announced.

"In the history section the winner of the top student award goes to Najat Sabir!"

The words reverberated around my mind like a series of rifle shots. I felt this could not be real. I rose unsteadily to my feet. As if in a dream I staggered toward the stage. My feet felt like lead diver's boots. As I climbed the steps to receive my award I found myself to be utterly astounded that I, a Kurd, was making this journey. I stood in front of the assembly as the chancellor handed me the award, a gift tied with a brilliant red ribbon.

I shook his hand in respect at the honor, but in a flash my mind suggested that perhaps the honor had been chosen as a ruse to have me disappear. I wondered too if they had discovered that I had handled documents pertaining to chemical warfare. As I straightened up I could see Sa'adoun watching me with a piercing stare as he clapped with the assembly. I gave him a fleeting smile for I thought perhaps he had helped select me for the award. He sat looking smug and powerful with a curious smile on his lips. An odd feeling came over me, and I sensed that I had not heard the last of Sa'adoun Alwan.

When all the dignitaries had left, we students gathered in the great hall in a party atmosphere. There was music, dancing, and much excited conversation. After darkness had fallen I left the gathering and walked alone back to the women's residence. A shiny black car drove past slowly. It went around the block, returned, and then it traveled at walking speed alongside me. It moved ahead, then stopped. There was no doubt in my mind now that I was being watched. Through a partially open window I saw the figure of a man holding a cigarette in his hand. The tip glowed in the darkness. Would this be the moment that a bullet came to silence me forever? The car followed my progress to the residence. With my heart in my mouth I climbed the steps and went inside.

I remember well the roller-coaster ride of emotions; the day had equal parts of pride in myself for my achievement coupled with fear for my future. I climbed into my bed only to discover that the fear for my future prevented me from sleeping. Hearing each small sound from outside in the hallway, I imagined the security forces were coming to take me away. After hours of tossing and turning in my bed I heard the door open. They had come for me! I sat up and drew the sheets around my shoulders. Sahira, one of my room mate sisters, walked in.

"Sorry, Najat, did I wake you?"

"No, I was awake. What time is it?"

"It's three a.m." Having Sahira in the room with me had a calming effect. My fears dissipated and I fell into exhausted slumber.

For the next few days I kept looking over my shoulder expecting someone was following and observing me.

However, my fears were unfounded, and I put it down to an overcautious imagination. We had a short break just before the long summer break. I was eager to get back to Sulaymania and see the pride in my parent's eyes as I told them I had won the top award.

Once again I acted as courier, carrying documents which I hid inside the insole of my shoe. After the usual nightmare ride to Sulaymania by bus along with the degrading inspections, I arrived at home and shared the triumphant news of my award with my family. Much to my surprise I found Rebwar still at home after our tearful farewell when I left earlier to return to university. I had thought that by now he would be safely across the border in Iran,

"Did you change your mind about leaving the family, Rebwar?" I asked.

"No, Najat. I did leave with the group of students I told you about, but it all went wrong. The smuggler got us close to the border but we could not get across. There were too many Iranian Pasdar (soldier guards) watching. We hid during the day and tried two nights in a row to cross over. On the third night another group of would-be-escapees were discovered not far away from us. We saw them rounded up and gunned down. Our smuggler gave up and said it was much too risky, so we followed his lead and gave up the attempt and returned to our homes." I spent the first day at home helping and chatting with Mother. On the second I elected to make my delivery. As usual I went to the main library and followed the same course as before and completed the transfer of documents under the noses of the guards.

It came as a great relief to be cleared of the incriminating papers. Crowds of people filled the streets. Taxis honked their horns in frustration. Drivers cursed at the congestion as pedestrians hurried and jostled from one side of the road to the other. As I weaved my way through the throngs of shoppers, I became aware of a well dressed older man close to my side keeping pace with me. As a shopper approached the man stepped to my rear, far to close for my comfort. Before I managed to evade the man, I felt him firmly grab my buttock. In an instant reaction I elbowed him in the stomach. I felt as long as tradition, religion, and customs forbade us from love, affection, and sex before marriage, the behavior of these hungry men would not change.

On the next corner the delightful aroma of fresh crusty bread surrounded a bakery. Unable to resist the tantalizing smell I purchased some hot loaves and put them in my bag. As I did so, I saw a group of soldiers standing on the sidewalk up ahead with a crowd of people surrounding them. I paused briefly to look as I passed by. The center of attention was a young man lying on the ground. His blood was spattered all over his clothing and running onto the sidewalk. The unmistakable smell of spent gunpowder from the soldier's gun drifted in the air. The young man's hand gripped an aerosol paint can in a grotesque fashion. His intended message to Saddam dripped paint from a half finished word down the wall.

I felt highly nervous now. The presence of the trigger happy soldiers reminded me of my own precarious position. I suppose in hindsight, the presence of the soldiers upset me much more than the sight of the brave young man who had met his end making a simple statement. My initial joy of shopping had vanished, so I hurried toward my home clutching the bread close to my body. Turning the corner onto my street my heart stopped for much longer than a moment. Several army vehicles were parked in front of my parents' house. Some of the soldiers stood in groups around the trucks smoking cigarettes while others leaned against the house wall squinting in the sunlight.

With fear rising in me like a volcano, I stepped into a

shaded doorway. Sweat began to trickle down my brow to my cheeks then down my neck. I wondered what they were doing here. Had my family been arrested and they were waiting for me? As I looked, it didn't seem like the usual military raid where highly agitated soldiers rushed around like dogs after a rat. These soldiers were relaxed and chatting together. Perhaps they were watching a family across the street.

I considered the options before me. Perhaps I could run and get away. But I knew that if my activities had been discovered, I could not let my family pay for my involvement in them. I drew courage from deep within, preparing to accept the consequences of my deeds to save my family. I would admit my guilt but resolved that I would not give out any information on others in the cause.

I stepped out from the shadows and forcing my legs to move. I walked deliberately to the door of my home. A soldier went to open the house door for me. Not only was this highly unusual, for me it was a foreboding of terrible things to happen once inside. So far no one had spoken to me. This too I found unnerving. I stepped over the sill and heard raised voices from the next room. As I approached I heard my mother saying,

"But she is still my little girl. My little baby." Entering the room I saw Sa'adoun Alwan standing tall over her. He saw me enter and turned to face me.

"Najat, I have been expecting you." I was paralyzed with fear. I had no idea what to expect and my face remained expressionless. I looked into his face for a sign of anger or hidden agenda but I saw none.

Sa'adoun smiled at me. His eyes were warm and showed no sign of malice.

"So nice to see you again, Najat. I'm sorry it took so long." His words puzzled me and I looked to my parents for an explanation. They both stared at me wide eyed with blank expressions. I had the distinct feeling that Sa'adoun was the only person in the room that knew and understood what was occurring. My gaze left their faces and I spotted a hard-sided, polished tan coloured briefcase open at their feet, filled to overflowing with American banknotes. Instinctively I knew this scenario had to have something to do with me, but what?

Gesturing down to the case Sa'adoun announced,

"Don't worry, Najat. Your parents have been adequately compensated. You will have a much better life with me. You will have everything and anything you could possibly need." He turned to my parents who appeared to be dumbfounded and continued staring vacantly. "I expect Najat to be ready in three days," he said in a commanding and stern tone. "I give you three days only because I am a busy man." I could not help but notice how his first soft words to me had changed so quickly to the barked commands of a military leader.

Without another word he turned and abruptly left the room. As the culture of our country demanded, we showed our guest to the door despite our feelings of being violated by him. As the military vehicles started their engines and Sa'adoun Alwan stepped into his military jeep, all our neighbors crowded round to see if someone had been killed or arrested. Others drew their children into their houses in fear. The motorcade moved off down the street covering everyone in fine dust that billowed up from the wheels. We did not want to tell our neighbors at this moment about what had transpired. Instead we told them that the soldiers had come to inquire why Rebwar was not in the military, and we said it was because he was still going to school.

We came back into the house, and I saw that my mother's eyes were tear filled. My father's arms were wrapped around his head as if he were fending off blows. He sank to his knees with an air of helplessness washing over him. Mother lowered herself down beside him. She extended her arm to offer comfort to him but as she did, he exploded in violent anger He reached out for the briefcase and hurled it against the wall spilling its contents all over the room.

I recoiled in utter shock. I must have loosened my grip on my bag, for the loaves of still warm bread spilled to the floor. Knowing only too well that I had brought such pain to my parents, I slowly backed out of the room and stood in the semi darkness of the entrance hall. My legs and knees turned to jelly and would not support me. I slowly sank to the floor with my head in my hands. In the fog and confusion that raced through my mind I tried to think logically. Was this an absurd daydream or the answer to my grand master plan for my people?

Sa'adoun obviously intended to take me as his wife. While the words had not been uttered to my ears, it was obvious it was his intention to have me. How could I, fighting in my own way to overthrow the Ba'ath regime, reconcile myself being the wife of one of its leaders? Sa'adoun was one of the men who stood for everything I despised. A man whose complicity with the crimes of the regime was legend. Or was this an elaborate ruse to spirit me away to some torture cell with no public fuss?

As I sat on the floor behind the entrance door I could hear the chatter of our neighbors as they remained gathered outside our door.

"Who would have thought the Sabirs would have attracted the attention of the army?   I wonder what they wanted in there."

I knew the people outside were used to surprise visits to houses in the area by the army. They had witnessed shootings and beatings with rifle butts. They had seen entire families spirited away, never to be seen again.

chapter nine

The sound of my cell door opening broke the memories. I wondered; was I to undergo a further torture session so soon after the last? If I were, I had a strong feeling I would not survive it. A guard stepped inside. He grabbed my arm and turned me onto my back. The pain was excruciating. In the dim light from the open cell door I saw him unzip his pants. He lay atop me in his violent act of rape. I had no strength to fight him. "Kurdish bitch" were the only words he spoke before leaving me. I had long since ceased to be able to cry so I turned onto my stomach and recalled the words of my father spoken in anger. "I don't know what to do! I just don't know!" Father slammed his fist down on the bench they were occupying. "I'd rather bury my daughter with my own two hands than give her to that murderous Sa'adoun as his bride."

"But surely he must love our daughter. I cannot think he would want to destroy her. You heard him say as I did that he has plans for her future." I knew my mother was trying to calm him down. "Try not to think the worst, my husband. Perhaps Najat will learn to love him."

"Learn to love him! They have obviously met before! Our adopted daughter brings shame to our family!" I saw father turn to look into Mother's reddened eyes.

"How can this be happening? Please can someone. Tell me why? I tell you Najat could never love such a man. Our daughter is no fool. I think she knows much more than we give her credit for. She must know of this serf of Saddam Hussein. She must know of his background and his history." Silence ensued between them only to be broken by the squawk of the dry hinges on the back garden gate as Rebwar sauntered in.

"What's going on? I thought I heard a shout. What's for dinner Mother?"

"Pal-pina." (A traditional Kurdish soup.)

"Oh, no. Not Pal-pina again!"

"I did laundry today. I can't do that and cook your favorite meal as well, Rebwar! Besides, after what has just occurred probably no one wants to eat anyway." she replied in annoyance.

"So what has happened to reduce everyone's appetite?"

"One of the Ba'ath men, Sa'adoun Alwan, has demanded Najat's hand in marriage. He has given us three days to have her ready for him. He seems to think that by throwing money at us everything will be all right."

"Money? So let her marry him. Maybe we won't have to eat Pal-pina all the time." As he often did, Rebwar had not chosen his words wisely when speaking in front of my father.

My father jumped to his feet and towering over

Rebwar, he shouted,

"Shut your mouth, Rebwar! Your trouble is that you never think before you open it." Father stormed off yelling "Are you completely crazy?" Rebwar stepped up to Mother and put his arm around her.

"I'm sorry Mother. I was joking. Father was right. I didn't think before speaking. Just the same I am sick of eating Pal·pina." I heard Rebwar say softly to Mother,

"Think of it this way, Mother. This is an opportunity for us all to get out of Iraq. I can talk to the smuggler again. You say we have money now? Perhaps we can pay him to take us over the border to Iran and from there to Europe. But don't repeat this in front of Father right now. He is probably too upset to consider it at the moment." Rebwar went into the house, and I went out to the garden to speak with mother. I did not cry on her shoulder, for that would have added to her pain and extend my own. My mother held me and said,

"My beautiful daughter, listen well to what your mother has to say. Your generation is much different than mine, but when it comes to love and marriage there is very little difference between us. I used to think that love is a magical thing that would rescue us and be the beginning of something significant. The first sight of love is attraction, but it is only the beginning of a series of complications. Learning love is also responsibility. Discovering that marriage is like a tangled fishnet takes a lifetime to unravel. I am referring, of course, to your future husband. Whether you are in love or not would not make much difference in future years. Why would you want that tangled net to unravel?"

I truly didn't understand what Mother was trying to impart to me. Did she mean that loving or not loving the man I would marry made no difference?

"Were you and Father in love when you were married, Mother?"

"Let us think only of you right now, my child. Some day I will tell you my story." Then she left to join Father in the house.

The atmosphere in our living room that evening was one of somber thought as each of us contemplated my future. Darkness closed in on our suburb of Goyzha. From the window of my room I saw a myriad of stars lighting the streets with a pale glow. There was no way I could get to sleep. Thoughts of my impending future rushed unresolved through my brain. The rest of my family were in bed when I heard a sound, and I glanced toward the entrance to my room. I saw the shadowy figure of a man holding a large knife with a raised arm. The blade glinted in the pale light. I knew the blade was intended for me, but at whose hand I did not know.

In an act of self-preservation I rolled from my bed to the floor and curled up into a ball. The sound of running feet preceded a terrified scream. Then the sound of more running feet and yelling filled the room. A mass of bodies fought under the window as I cowered in the corner protected by the darkness. I heard my Mother's voice shrieking,

"No, I will not let you!" Then the voices of Shilan and Rebwar joined in the vocal fray.

"You cannot do this, Father! Najat has to have a say in her future! You do not have the right or moral authority to take it from her! Only she has that right!"

Someone turned on the light. Mother and Rebwar sat on my Father holding him down. His hand still clutched the knife. From the corner of the room I saw it all as Mother continued to scream

"No one can take my children. No one. And least of all, you, her father!" Shilan stepped forward and stamped on father's wrist forcing him to let the knife slip from his grasp. She then kicked it out of his reach.

There were two ways that I could interpret the scene

before me. First that my father felt I had brought a terrible shame to his family. A shame that he felt he could only erase by ending my life. Or secondly that he loved me so much that he felt my death was preferable to being married to a despot. Either way I never imagined that he would consider taking such extreme measures let alone acting upon it. Then I remembered his words in the garden when he said,

"I'd rather bury my daughter by my own hand than see that murderer take her from me." Instantly I knew what I had to say,

"Father! How could you think that I had a relationship with this man? He may have seen me at the university. Yes, he seems to know a great deal about me. You know that the Ba'ath knows everything about everybody. I have not shamed you, Father. Sa'adoun Alwan is a clever man, a military strategist, and he has succeeded in making you believe something that is not true." Summoning up all my courage I made a request,

"Let me marry this man, Father. Please do not allow this situation to destroy our family. I would be living in Baghdad and no one need know about the marriage if this family vows to keep silent about it. The whole thing can be handled very discreetly. Besides, I see no other way and for you, Father, there is a bonus. The money will allow you to retire and open the little shop you have often spoken about." Having calmed somewhat, father got up from the floor. With anger still seething in his breast he said,

"The money is blood money, Najat. Are you for sale like a goat or sheep? How can I spend the ill gotten dowry knowing I too have sullied my hands?"

"I beg you not to think of it in those terms, Father. Like Shilan and Rebwar said, I have a right to my own destiny. The world is changing. Our Kurdish world is changing, like it or not. I have made the decision, Father.

I will marry Sa'adoun Alwan."

I knew full well I had gone against the teachings my parents had grown up with. I had made decisions based on my own wants and needs. I had made those decisions as a free woman and not as one enslaved like a tradition Iraqi woman. But I felt that perhaps I had severed forever the feeling of family between the Sabirs and me. The security I had always felt in this home had been impaired by both the actions of my father and me. Shilan helped me push the drawer chest in front of the door saying,

"I will stay close to you tonight. I really hope you had nothing to do with this mess, Najat. Now try to sleep."

Far too shook up, I could not sleep. I lay wondering why Sa'adoun had chosen me? I knew he had spent a great deal of time observing me at my display table at the university. He had not indicated that he particularly admired my work, and he must have known my ideas and politics were not those of the Ba'ath regime. So why had I been chosen to be his wife? Until the dawn light entered my bedroom I lay thinking of the possible nightmare ahead of me. How would I feel when he wanted me sexually? Would I grit my teeth and close my eyes as though I were at the dentist. Would I have to live a life of pretense as his wife in social functions?

The dawn arrived. I had spent a sleepless night contemplating the immediate future. No matter how my mind re-arranged the facts I could not get any comfort from them. With my stomach in turmoil I left the house without eating or seeing my parents. In a way I was glad I did not see them, for a re-hashing of last night's debacle was the last thing I needed right now.

I made my way through the early morning streets to Shwan's house. He lived near the market in one upstairs room of his adoptive parents' house on Sarshakam Street. The sparsely furnished room contained a bed, a bulging book case, and one chair set by a small desk holding up an ancient typewriter. The ownership and use of these writing machines was illegal by private citizens in Northern Iraq, so the machine had to be stowed away when Shwan was not using it. To request a permit to own one would be an admission of guilt, and the applicant an enemy of the state. This early in the morning Shwan answered the door in his night attire. Wearing light blue pajamas he sat down on the bed while offering me the chair. Feeling tired still and highly nervous, I found it difficult to settle. I blurted out,

"I really don't know what to do for the best. I need your solemn judgment." I explained the situation. Then having told Shwan of my dilemma, I began to pace the floor while he sat silent contemplating,

"You know my friend, Hoshman? He is working for Rangdaren who can arrange to get you and your whole family into Iran without too much difficulty. From there you can travel to Europe and perhaps eventually to America as I can remember you once saying was your ambition."

"Shwan, there must be a million Kurdish people trying to leave Iraq and get to Iran. The danger is much too great. My brother Rebwar tried it and gave up after seeing other escapee's machine gunned down by the soldier guards. Besides I don't think my parents would attempt the trip. They are of the old school and trust that God will eventually fix everything in Iraq. If I were to leave alone, it is almost a certainty that Sa'adoun would have my family liquidated, especially after handing my father a briefcase of American banknotes for me. So you see my situation is impossible. I cannot win under any circumstance, the way I see it, the only thing I can do is to sacrifice myself to Sa'adoun Alwan."

"Consider the possibility you are wrong, Najat. A great many people cross to Iran. Yes, some get caught and receive Saddam's justice. But there is political motive involved here too. Each side, both Iran and Iraq, offers help to those crossing in either direction in order to weaken support for the other side. Let me explain. If Iran helps our people who make it to their side, it is assumed we will look upon the Iranians with favor and fight for them against Iraq. We, the people, are but pawns in a political war, Najat. But having said that, there is still a possibility for us to achieve personal freedom."

You don't want your family to leave and you don't want to stay. Only you can make the final decision. If you don't marry Sa'adoun Alwan I have no doubt that he will make your life and the life of your family unbearable or even terminate them. On the other hand if you go ahead with his plan to marry you, your family will be the talk of the entire city of Sulaymania. The way I see it, Najat, is that no matter what route you choose to travel, your family will suffer for your actions anyway."

I realized that Shwan had spoken wisely and with conviction.

"It just gets worse, Shwan. It just gets worse by the minute." He did not answer and a long silence between us ensued, and the noise of the morning traffic penetrated into the room.

"I have been thinking, Najat. Please don't take offense at what I am about to say. Perhaps you should marry the man. Not to, would mean almost certain death, not only to you but perhaps to your entire family. But I suggest you do it very quietly with no fanfare or publicity." He returned to my side and placed his hand on my shoulder again. "Marrying him could certainly be helpful in terms of your political work. It would be dangerous but a valuable place to be. You could never trust anyone. You could never let anyone know who you really are, or any of your history. You would always have to be vigilant, as smart as a whip, and never let your guard down."

I felt shocked and astonished hearing his words. My lifetime friend, the one I looked to for sound advice had scraped a raw nerve.

"You are suggesting I marry this depot! That I sacrifice any chance for personal happiness, if not perhaps even my life, to further a political cause? A political cause that has gone unresolved for a multitude of years? You are also suggesting that I carry out this mad scheme clandestinely and without any chance of any recognition if I were to succeed?"

"Najat, think back to some of the conversations we have had in the past. I believe this is something that you have thought of yourself. However infiltrating the seat of power, perhaps you were not aiming this high. But I know you have considered this as an option several times. Think of this as your revenge, Najat. Remember how on that fateful day back in Zalan your real parents were gassed to death simply because they were born Kurdish. Think of them and the rest of our villagers the day after the attack when we returned to find them all bloated and burned in the Zalan sun. You found the courage on that day to travel with me and begin a new life. Summon up the anger you felt on that day. Do not waste the energy in it. Control it, use it, fight with it. Consider this wedding to be an opportunity unique for the Kurdish people, Najat. I will do everything in my power to protect both you and your family name from Kurdish society."

I stared at Shwan incredulously. I had come for advice and heard things I didn't want to hear. I had come for an answer to my dilemma. What I received from him was what I had really known all along. I would marry Sa'adoun Alwan.

For the next three days our home became a prison without bars, a prison of our own making. We totally avoided the world outside our door, unwilling to offer explanations of any sort to our neighbors. In effect we left the entire neighborhood in the dark as to why the military had come to our house.

Being more attuned to matters of security than my family, I sensed that unseen eyes were watching the house. During those three days Father never spoke to me. Shilan offered comfort while Rebwar tried to humor everyone. Mother tried her best to create peace among all of us as she worried about what our neighbors were thinking about our family.

chapter ten

Sa'adoun Alwan strode imperiously through the front door of my family home at the end of the third day. He greeted my parents in an offhand manner, and my parents resignedly returned his greeting. The great one had come to claim his prize and he did so with flourish. His soldiers waited outside as the dust from the jeeps slowly settled. Sa'adoun once again attracted the attentions and suspicions of our neighbors with his presence. With an air of absolute authority he spoke to my family.

"As you can see I have returned. Due to the pressing demands of my schedule some tradition must be sacrificed. I'm sure you understand that because I am indispensable to the government; I am a busy man. Najat, of course, will be returning to Baghdad where she will continue her university training. You will have no cause to worry about her. My mother and sister will accompany her while shopping for clothing and jewelry." Glancing at Mother he said,

"Perhaps you could join them. You must understand that my family will take care of all the wedding preparations. You have no need to concern yourself with any of them. However, you will participate as honored guests. You may trust that I will arrange an outstanding wedding for my bride and me."

I watched his face as Sa'adoun looked at my parents. I knew he was judging their reaction to his words. He was fully aware that his plans for the wedding were completely contrary to the customs of the Kurdish people, and he wanted to know if my parents would create opposition to it. I knew that Sa'adoun was a powerful, intimidating force and my parents were both cowed by it. They feared this commanding man and so they offered no resistance. They abandoned the tradition of the groom's family traveling to the bride's city to marry. I'm sure Sa'adoun suspected that the family was silently cursing him, but to him it was of no consequence. His will would be done. Despite that, he baited them by saying,

"Whatever you prefer, of course." After studying my father's face for a moment he said, "I must go now; I have business to attend to."

I had, of course, expected that he had come to whisk me away in his military jeep, but apparently I was to return to Baghdad on the bus as usual to finish off the rest of the term. At ten p.m. after an interminably long day, the residential electrical power was shut off. Fans and air conditioners stopped working and the lights went out. Rebwar lit a couple of lanterns, and we all went up to the flat roof of the house to enjoy the coolness of the night. The outer edge of the roof had a wall of cement blocks. Our rooftop bed had been made up with colorful embroidered sheets. The sky, lit by a million bright stars, cast a low light over the city. Lying back looking at them, they were like brilliant diamonds cast upon a tray of black velvet. Soon the cool breeze drifted down from the mountains to caress the city night. Father and Rebwar leaned over the wall carefully checking out the street below and whispering in quiet conversation. Mother sat on her bed fingering her worry beads, deep in prayer. Shilan and I lay in our bed taking in the myriad smells of the city drifting through the air and looking up at the night sky. We remembered our childhood as we tried to count the stars or watched the tracer bullets crossing the city and wondered and guessed how big the galaxy was.

Suddenly Father and Rebwar ran for the stairs and down into the house ordering us to stay put. I had an intuition of what was occurring as I heard a knock on our front door. Ignoring father's warning, I went downstairs followed by Shilan and Mother. I heard my father in intense and loud conversation with a few peshmarga (Freedom fighters) standing in our doorway. I heard Father say,

"You had better do some research before you take my daughter away."

My concern was for my mother. I could see even in the dim light she could barely hold herself up. Without any hesitation I forced myself in front of my father and exclaimed,

"I'm not frightened by you! If you wish to take me away to kill me perhaps the ones who sent you would like to hear the truth." One of the peshmarga grabbed my arm.

"You are coming with us!" Father pulled me back. From out of the gloom my friend Shanna's father stepped into the scene.

"You people should be ashamed of yourselves to be in

this house and confronting Najat with horrible accusations! I have been working with you for twenty years. This is how you return the favor? I have fed you! I have sheltered you from our enemy. I have delivered all your needs and you come here and shame me?"

"Be calm, sir. We have orders that she must go with us. It has been reported that she works for the higher end of the Ba'ath regime. She is dirty!" Shanna's father replied,

"You fools! You will not take her without me and her father coming along!"

Though my mother gripped me tightly as though she would never see me again, the three of us were hustled into a vehicle leaving her and Shilan crying outside the house. With no lights on, we drove until we got away from the immediate area. About fifteen minutes later we arrived at a residential area known as HawaryBarza which had a fast, easy exit to the mountains.

The peshmarga men pushed us into a house, and I noticed a pile of shoes at the entrance. Inside the large room a large number of Peshmarga were sitting on cushions around the walls drinking tea. The room seemed to be too small for so many, and they sat shoulder to shoulder with their weapons close by. My father was refused admission to the room. They placed me in a corner and forced me to listen to the accusations against me. They had all heard the rumors. Some believed them while others didn't, and a disagreement rose among them while Shanna's father fought for my life.

The outcome was that I was to be killed. I changed from my sitting to a kneeling position with my hands on the floor. My tears began to cloud my vision as I looked around without making eye contact with the men around me. I began to speak in my own defense,

"A few months ago I was on my knees at a military station on the road to Baghdad. I begged not to be raped and shot like the girl a few feet away from me. Now I'm on my knees begging you. Tell me what is the difference?" My stomach was in knots as I continued. "If you kill me and leave my body to rot in a field, or if you hurl it in front of my parent's house for everyone to spit upon, it makes no difference. For either way I shall die proudly knowing that I have saved many lives without firing a single shot unlike you with your weapons at your sides. Silence descended into the room as my words were digested.

"We follow orders, Najat!"

"Like other orders, you throw away the lives of innocent women. By not doing a thorough investigation you bring shame to their families. In this case you do not know who is secretly working for you and our country, and our identity as a people or the Ba'ath party. You men embarrass me!"

"We do not need another lecture. Take her away." My father heard his edict and struggled to get into the room. Two men grabbed me and forced me between them and Shanna's father. I struggled. But I had not sufficient strength to break free. At this point I felt great sorrow for my father and wished that he had killed me. Now these foolish men would kill me instead. I tried to reach for him and beg his forgiveness. Suddenly the door burst open and Shwan and Rebwar leapt into the room pushing my captors aside. Rebwar yelled at the top of his voice,

"Take my life. Not hers." Always diplomatic, Shwan said in a firm voice,

"Everyone stop. No one is going anywhere!"

Shwan was well known in the underground as a messenger for them. As such he commanded their respect.

"Listen carefully. Najat is a member of our group, the most valuable contact we have with the other side. She is pure gold to our cause. It is I who guided her in many

things in order to favor us with unique inside
information on the activities of the Ba'ath party. Her
information has saved lives. Kill her and you will have
severed the best link we have."

My captors released their grip on my arms and my
father and Shanna's father came to my side. For the first
time ever, I heard anger in Shwan's voice,

"Whoever gave you these rumors and reports know
nothing of our struggle. Take my advice and stop killing
innocent people just because someone says so. We know
our duty, and we in the know are well aware of who is
dirty or clean. You owe Najat an apology."

I did not hear muffled apologies offered. I felt sick.
It was as though I had died and suddenly returned to
life. Then as if it were compensation for my trouble, the
owner of the house offered to take us all home in his
minibus. It was six a.m. when we arrived at home. As I
opened the door, Shilan ran to me crying.

"I have been expecting to find your dead body thrown
in front of our house. I told you to please be careful!"

"Mother broke into a sweat, then she got very cold. I
think she is suffering from shock and pain. I forced her
to swallow a couple of sleeping pills, and now she is in a
deep sleep. I will make some breakfast. It's too late to
go to bed now."

After my ordeal I needed something physical to do,
so I went to help Shilan make the breakfast. For the
first time since I had come to live in this house, Shilan
was angry with me.

"Najat, I told you to be careful. Who are you working
for? Why is there is there no longer trust between us?
It seems we are all accused no matter which side you
are working for. This regime has made a mess in our
country. The damage is so bad it could take a century for
it to be cleaned up! Look what you have put our mother
through. It seems you forget about us by giving your life

to be a revolutionary, and that they are more than willing
to take your life anyway! I wish you would leave politics
and the university behind you! Rebwar is right; we
should all try to leave this country!"

"You are very upset, Shilan. I'm not involved with
anything. You know what is going on."

Shilan refused to give up and recited the names of
girls we both knew who had been killed.

"Runak, Neagar, Rezan, Awaz. Are they all mistakes
too? Everything is a mistake! Living here is a mistake.
This bloody country is a mistake!" What if you hadn't
told me about Shwan, Najat? You would be dead by now
if I hadn't sent Rebwar to go for him so he could come to
our aid and save us all."

Shwan, who had returned to the house with us, and
had been in the living room talking with Father and
Rebwar, declined to eat breakfast. My father shook his
hand with great respect and then bent to kiss his hand.
Shwan quickly pulled his hand away.

"As I said, Rebwar is my dearest friend. He is like my
brother. I was just glad I could come to your family's aid
and tell them the lies the Peshmarga needed to hear. I
am especially happy that your daughter is now safe."
Shwan left and we sat down to eat; then Shanna's father
walked in.

"I want you all to promise never to discuss the night's
happenings with anyone and that, in fact, it never
happened. Especially do not involve Shanna with this."

Conditions in our home were quite strained for next
two days, and frankly I was glad when it was time to
return to the university. My father took me to the bus
depot and just before I boarded he whispered,

"Najat, my child, I am both angry and disappointed
in you. I know I project the image of a man who knows
little. For my family's sake it is safer that way. But I do
know more than you may think. So as you go into the

future be very careful." I climbed aboard the bus for the usual nightmare ride to Baghdad. I had plenty of time to think of the recent past and of my future.

I, of course, rejoiced that Sa'adoun was a very busy man because I wished for continued freedom. According to Iraqi tradition there could be no consummation of the marriage until the wedding day. Classes resumed and I was unable to occupy my mind by reading and studying. I was aware that one day soon I was to be married, but Sa'adoun's absence made keeping my secret easy.

Several week's had passed when Sa'adoun stood in front of the women's residence door late one afternoon. Fazilla told me later that she had been sitting on her low stool behind the door as usual, guarding the residence from male intruders. She saw the male figure through the frosted glass in the door but waited for him to speak.

"I am here to see Najat." Fazilla, the protector of the women in her charge, exclaimed through a crack in the door,

"No one can take my girls out. It's against the university rules."

"Then you are doing a good job madam. You serve your people well as I do. Now! Call her down; she is my wife." I remember Fazilla telling me she was flabbergasted. This excuse was a brand new one she had never heard before.

"Najat is unmarried, sir. You look more like her father than her husband."

"Call her! I said!" Now thoroughly intimidated by the impeccably dressed military officer, Fazilla ran to my room and breathlessly announced,

"Your Sheik is here. He almost put a bullet through my head so you had best hurry down." I took a few moments to check my appearance and my clothing. Then I went downstairs in utter dread of this meeting. This I felt, was the day when my role of deception would begin in earnest. I forced a smile to my lips as I approached him,

"How nice to see you, Sa'adoun. Should I have expected you?"

"I am taking you to a special dinner tonight." He handed me a box tied with a royal blue ribbon. It is something for you to wear, Najat; I want you to look especially beautiful. It is a very important evening."

"But I have an exam tomorrow. I need to study."

"Understand, Najat. I am not accustomed to have my motives, plans, and wishes questioned. Don't worry, I will take care of your exam for you." I quickly realized that living with Sa'adoun would not be easy. I had just tasted a morsel of the life I would be living. "By the way, Najat how is your English?"

"My English? Reasonably good, I believe. Why do you ask?"

"Most of the dinner guests will be European. German, French and British. There will also be some Americans and Russians, mostly journalists and business people. The majority will be speaking English, and I want you to be able to communicate with them."

A loud crashing noise made us both jump in alarm. My first thought was that this might be an assassination attempt. Our attention was diverted to Fazilla who while trying to eavesdrop had spilled the trash container into the foyer. Sa'adoun's demeanor changed instantly,

"What are you listening for, woman? Have you nothing better to do? Leave the area now!" I felt badly for Fazilla, but I kept a closed mouth. I had a distinct feeling that as Sa'adoun's wife there would be many times to come when I had to maintain an uncomfortable silence. I watched a frightened Fazilla hurry away, then I turned to look at Sa'adoun.

"I will pick you up at eight o' clock, Najat. Be ready

and remember, I want you to make a big impression."

Back in my room I opened the box. Inside I found a stunning ankle length gown with a deep vee neckline, bronze in color and trimmed with gold braid. There were matching shoes and a ruby pendant necklace with ruby ear rings. I bathed, put on my makeup, and dressed. For the first time in years I removed the coin necklace that I had taken from the side of my real mother's body in Zalan. It was the only tangible link I had with her and my childhood. Tonight I would forgo wearing it for this special occasion.

I looked at myself in the mirror. Seeing myself dressed this way gave a huge boost to my ego. I could not help thinking, am I the same little girl who walked from Zalan dressed in homemade clothes with the skin peeling from her face? Continuing to study my image, I drew up the courage to meet the challenge of this first outing with Sa'adoun, despite the fact that I had the feeling he expected me to be his spy, his Mata Hari.

I could not wait to get to the event with Sa'adoun to have my mission begin. Just then Salma and Sahira returned to the room. Upon opening the door they gasped when I stood before them. Previously they had never paid much attention to me, for they considered me just another student and roommate.

"Oh, Najat, let's have a look at you," they said in unison. "Where did you get that beautiful gown?"

"It's a present from the man who is to be my husband. He is taking me out tonight." It seemed rather humorous; I was finally on a par with Salma and Sahira. Salma looked at the label in the back of my gown.

"It's from Geneva in Switzerland! Are you going to marry someone important?"

"Yes. I'm to marry Sa'adoun Alwan."

"You don't mean Sa'adoun Alwan, secret service working under Ali-Majid for the Ba'ath government, do you?" They stared, waiting for me to confirm their question.

"Tell me, Najat, how do you know him? It's not like he was a public figure?"

"Sahira and I have spent the last two years of our evening leisure times with Saddam's government circle of friends. We have partied with them, and they have treated us with everything we could wish for. Surely, Najat, you didn't think our father could have provided us with all the fine clothes and jewelry we have, did you? We have been to almost every party that the Ba'ath's most important men threw for friends. Whenever they go to Europe they bring back perfumes and clothing for us." As I glanced at their bedside tables I noted they could hardly have held one more perfume bottle or makeup. "If Sa'adoun has chosen you for his wife, Najat, you are the lucky one." Sahira, the more cautious of the two, changed the subject quickly. I think she felt her sister was saying a little too much.

"So are you still to live here at the university after the wedding?"

"I'm not sure but I doubt it."

I felt I had secured my position as an equal with the sisters. Modeling the dress for Salma and Sahira's eyes had been fun, but never before had I been out in public with such a revealing garment. I had, of course, seen such revealing gowns being worn on television and movies and on the upper class of our society. I had doubts about going out in public dressed like this, but Sa'adoun had specifically wanted me to wear it. At exactly eight o clock I went to the foyer where he was waiting for me.

I could tell by his eyes he was more than pleased with my appearance. He held my hand and looked at me as though he were admiring a fine jewel. He took my arm and led me to a waiting silver Mercedes. Shortly afterwards the car pulled into the driveway of a magnificent house. I was astounded at the incredible façade. To my eyes, Sa'adoun had brought me to a palace. In my mind I had become an important person; while mere months ago it would have been a crime for me to even have an identity.

The house, perfectly placed amid manicured lawns, well tended flower beds, and surrounded by walls and arbors with flowering vines creeping over it created a scene of opulence. The car stopped at the foot of a flight of steps to the main entrance. Tall Grecian pillars stood in front of walls built with cream coloured marble, and a huge sculpture of an Arab warrior guarded the massive entrance doors flanked by soldier guards. Beyond, soft lights beckoned us from the interior. Once inside, my senses were overwhelmed. The interior walls were crafted of marble. Priceless, traditional Arabic art abounded along them. Light sconces carved from ivory were spaced along the hallways, and massive chandeliers hung from the high ceilings, each with up to a thousand tiny light bulbs. Uniformed black servants in pairs led the guests toward the ballroom and as I walked daintily on Sa'adoun's arm, shimmering light reflected from a multitude of surfaces. Somewhere up ahead I could hear sweet music. As we moved toward the sound, Sa'adoun shook hands with the guests acknowledging him.

Everything seemed to be in slow motion. My mind tried to absorb a multitude of sensations completely foreign to me. At that moment I realized that the Ba'ath regime proclaimed hatred of the Western world, yet lived the much maligned lifestyle of the West. Immediately I made the decision not to be swayed by the opulence surrounding me. I had a job to do and I would give it my utmost.

The music came from an exquisite inner garden. As we entered, a light breeze sent my dress fluttering against my legs, and my lungs were filled with the fragrance of night scented tropical flowers. A shimmering reflecting pond adorned the garden's centre. Around it the guests were enjoying pre-dinner cocktails. My ears picked up words from many languages. I clung to Sa'adoun's arm as he chatted with other guests. When he introduced me I responded shyly.

I found the manners and sophistication of many guests intimidating. I had always been confident and even outspoken in my own environment, but I could not own my own thoughts and opinions here. Sa'adoun whispered in my ear,

"I can tell from the glances of the envious eyes of other women looking at you, that you are possibly the most beautiful woman here." I felt a little inadequate in such foreign surroundings. I had always been accustomed to being considered quick witted and highly intelligent, but here I felt myself much too overwhelmed to absorb the culture of the rich and powerful. I did speak softly and genuinely when spoken to, but I kept my utterances as minimal as possible.

In retrospect it is hardly surprising that I felt the elite were superior to me in many ways. Large numbers of them had a distinct advantage in that they had traveled and learned from other cultures. Now as Sa'adoun's wife I too would learn these things. Aristocratic guests and multi lingual conversations would likely be my future, and the luxury of second impressions would not be mine.

Beyond the shimmering pool, sturdy tables groaned under the weight of covered dishes. There were huge platters of fruits (many not native to Iraq) roasted whole chickens, and platters of fish. Off to the side, three whole lambs roasted on spits tended by a chef. Servers wearing long white traditional Arab dress with red turbans mingled with the guests serving potent Arak liquor or a choice of other beverages to everyone. Several women, dressed in bright red and blue dresses, acting as hostesses circulated among the guests.

Sa'adoun was remarkably sensitive and attentive towards me. In one sense I felt he was showing me off like a trophy. In another, I wondered if the actions of Sa'adoun and the local dignitaries were for the benefit of the foreign guests. In any event I was very grateful to him for steering me through the evening without allowing me to feel embarrassed. Sa'adoun had allowed me to enter the upper echelon of Iraqi society not with care or consideration for me but to secure making his moves in his own best interests. I knew that Arab men in general were attracted to the Western lifestyle behaving as if they were liberated and open minded. I perceived that at this gathering, the elite men were attempting to show the foreign guests that they were better and more powerful.

I began to grow increasingly nervous about the first meeting with his family. He had said his mother and sister would take me shopping for the wedding. However, since he had agreed that I should finish university before we married, there appeared to be no hurry to meet them. This feeling came to an abrupt end. Before we sat down to dine, Sa'adoun took my arm and gently steered me to a very well dressed middle aged woman sitting with an impeccably dressed younger version of her. I had the shock of my life when Sa'adoun said,

"Mother, this is Najat." I saw the two women measuring me up. "Najat, this is Hayfa, my sister." The sister, who was slightly older than I, stepped in front of me. She nodded briefly, and then began speaking with a woman beside me. I suppose she was unaware that I had a rudimentary knowledge of several languages and that I could tell what she was saying. Sa'adoun steered me away and gestured to a group of young women having animated conversations in a corner.

"Those are all my cousins, students about your age." I fixed a constant smile to my face and tried to regain my shattered confidence. I was determined to charm each guest I was introduced to. There were journalists, military personnel, and foreign businessmen just as Sa'adoun had said there would be. I was determined not to forget a single name. There was the fact that some of the government and military names would be useful in my underground work and the fact that foreign involvement is everyone's business in Iraq. I felt motivated to initiate certain introductions without being obvious, and I paid very close attention to what was said.

Some of the cousins wandered over and began to ask questions about my life at the university. They appeared to be snobbish, self-centered, complacent, and sheltered, given the fact that their lives had been so different from my own. Hayfa, having joined them, graciously advised me how to camouflage my unacceptable background.

My uncanny sense of perception told me that I was being watched. I turned away from the cousins and scanned for the culprit. A pair of dark brown eyes appeared to be riveted on mine, and it surprised me to see that the owner was speaking with Sa'adoun. It looked like they were well acquainted with each other and were deep in conversation despite the fact that the man was obviously staring right at me. In order to break the impasse I rejoined Sa'adoun.

Clearly, the man was having difficulty concentrating on the conversation. Hearing him, I immediately ascertained he was American even though his appearance could pass for Arabic.

"You were saying, Sa'adoun, something about the president of France? I'm afraid I didn't quite understand. What about Mitterand?"

"I was just saying that he is to be our guest tomorrow

morning at ten. I'm expecting you to be there."

"And who is this lovely woman, Sa'adoun? Another of your cousins?" The American turned to face me in anticipation of an introduction.

"Forgive me! Time never allows for-I haven't had the opportunity to inform you of a new addition to my personal life. Najat, I would like you to meet my dear friend Russell MacMillan. He is a reporter."

"Good evening, Mr. MacMillan," I responded in a dignified manner.

"Please, Najat, call me Russell."

"Russell. This is Najat. The woman I have chosen to be my wife." I saw a look of disappointment cross his face and he tried to hide his surprise at the news.

"Your wife!" When did you get married?"

"I haven't yet, Russell. You'll come. You will be invited, of course, as soon as I can arrange it. I have been so busy this last month it has just flown by. Najat is busy too; she is studying at Baghdad University."

Russell McMillan's eyes were even darker close up. I found myself immediately drawn to him. He was moderately attractive and his face bore a permanent kind of charm. He had dark coloured hair, his complexion was lightly tanned, and his build was not much taller than Sa'adoun's, I knew he was American by the way his face structure was defined; however, he could also pass as an Iraqi.

Hayfa sidled over. Momentarily Russell took his eyes off me and glanced at Hayfa. Moistening his lips he said,

"Hello again Hayfa. I hope---," He was interrupted by Sa'adoun in mid-sentence,

"Excuse me. There is someone I must speak with." Glancing at Hayfa and I, he said,

"Will you two ladies keep my friend company until I return? I know how Russell likes the companionship of young women." A waiter passed by with a tray of Arak. I asked him if he would bring me a glass of juice. As I did, I heard Hayfa say to Russell in an exaggerated whisper,

"It seems that my brother suffers from blindness. In all of Iraq he could not find an Arabic wife, only this Kurdish woman." I felt humiliated. My gut told me to respond with equal rudeness, but my brain told me to let her ignorance pass and to act in a dignified manner. Hayfa went back to join her cousins. I looked at Russell and saw he was clearly embarrassed and attempted to make a blustery apology for Hayfa's behavior.

"Really, Russell, it is fine. She is entitled to think whatever she pleases."

I could tell that Russell had clearly been impressed by my show of dignity and calm cordiality and in him it produced shyness. Stumbling over his words he said,

"I was just telling Sa'adoun how beautiful I thought you were. He is indeed a fortunate man." I began to blush.

"You are very kind, Mr. Macmillan. I mean, Russell. Now tell me what kind of reporter are you?" I could see my question had confused him, "I mean, do you report just what the Ba'ath regime expects you to, or do you follow up on their stories and create your own?"

"Well, Najat isn't that what reporters are all about? I was hired by the Iraqi government to tell their story. As a journalist one can be employed to represent a specific group."

"Not exactly, Russell. To my mind that is not journalism, it is more like propaganda. In that case it is not the whole picture. For example, I doubt that they let you know everything about the domestic action or what the regime is really all about. Doesn't journalism by definition require complete factual information that is reported with objectivity?"

"I can best answer you, by saying that these days it's getting harder to follow the politics of this region- actually no, the political history of the Middle-East has always been complicated by itself and the influence of others. You make a good point, of course, but I do this as I would any other job. I meet the expectations of my employer and I get paid for it." Russell shrugged and grew thoughtful. "I do understand there are problems in the north, but I would-well, never mind. Let's not get into that discussion here." I stared at him with an inquiring look. "I mean, I would rather not talk about it. Not now anyway. You speak English very well, Najat. Where did you learn the language?"

"For the past three summers I have taken private English lessons. They are expensive, but my teacher and I think it is a wonderful investment. Actually I have found the language difficult to master. Unfortunately I don't get to practice it too often, except with an English professor at the University and when I watch English movies I repeat word by word in order to practice. "

I had spotted a woman standing behind Russell. She touched him on the sleeve. She gave me an odd look and after I had finished speaking with him, she broke in with perfect English.

"Russell, why don't you come and watch the dancers with us? They're having fun out there. Come, you will enjoy it."

"Roza, I'd like you to meet Najat, Sa'adoun's fiancé. Najat, this is Roza Bykofski, a Russian reporter from Moscow. She is my date for this evening." We clasped hands and Roza gave me a genuine smile. I think she was relieved that Russell was not about to ditch her.

"Won't you join us, Najat?" I nodded agreement. We went to mingle with the boisterous crowd gathered around the dancers. Ornately costumed and exuberant belly dancers whirled and undulated to the music, creating a festive Middle-Eastern atmosphere. I couldn't keep myself from smiling. A number of times Russell and I caught ourselves focusing on each other for an instant. This was forbidden for me as I was already claimed as Sa'adoun's wife. Even if I wasn't it would still be prohibited to be attracted to or to marry a Western man. However, in our male society men were allowed both marriage and intimacy with Western women. Because of my belief as a free woman, I always had the courage to break the rules. So I enjoyed each momentary smile and temptation, but still the fear of the society attacked my courage.

Sa'adoun and Hayfa strolled out to join us. Sa'adoun behaved in a charming manner toward me, and I had difficulty understanding how he could be the same person who brought such suffering on his people. He placed a protective hand on my back, then turned to Russell. "Where is your drink, my friend?"

Hayfa said to me, "Oh, look! Here comes my other brother, Hassan, with the invitations to your wedding celebration. You must be terribly excited!"

Hassan Alwan, circled the ballroom, offering each guest a bone white invitation card trimmed with red satin ribbon from a large silver tray carried by a servant dressed in bright regalia. My stomach churned. My nightmare was about to begin.

"Isn't this exciting, Russell?" Hayfa asked leaning over me. I wondered if she had momentarily forgotten that she disapproved of me for her brother's bride. Somewhat distracted, Russell nodded agreement.

"You know, Najat, I spend a lot of time with Sa'adoun, and yet he never told me about you."

I knew by now that cultivating a relationship with Russell could serve my purpose well. I felt comfortable with him and even in the short time since we first met I had come to like him. I gave an answer to his question,

"Because it took him just three days. He saw me. He got me. He bought me."

I startled myself with my flippant and irreverent

reply, and I knew I had confused Russell. I knew also I had gone too far and said more than I should. I reminded myself that I had been incredibly stupid. I knew I should not let our attraction to each other lead me to foolishness, making me forget why I was here. Besides Russell worked for the government. My position in this living nightmare was far too precarious to be trusting of anyone. Now I had to play the part of the dutiful and loving wife.

"Well, all I can say is, he is lucky to have you, Najat."

Sa'adoun had ended his conversation. He came and stood at my side and took me away to join the other guests as they slowly left the party. Sa'adoun's demeanor suddenly changed,

"You have been much too forward with my friend Russell! You have shamed me, Najat!

I have been watching the both of you. I could see how you were looking at him!" He began to pace waving his arms and berating me.

"I was not certain of your family, how they brought you up, what kind of respect they taught you until tonight. I know your confidence and your outspokenness from now on is not acceptable to me! You are to be my wife! That means that you represent me! Not yourself. You must impress others so they believe I made an excellent choice in a wife." Just as quickly his demeanor changed again. He quieted down, came and stroked my face, and in a patronizing voice he told me,

"You don't know much. You haven't seen much. In fact you have seen nothing. But you will learn, my dear." His demeanor changed again. Now he was the military commander addressing the troops,

"You will also learn to follow orders." I felt the need to respond.

"I did follow your orders when you desired to bring me here, Sa'adoun, and left me to accompany Mr.

Macmillan. Now I really must get back to the university. I have much studying to do." A rustling sound startled the both of us. Sa'adoun's mother entered and announced, "Najat, your bed is ready upstairs." At that moment I came to realize that the palace belonged to Sa'adoun's family.

"Thank you. Oum Sa'adoun. (Mother of Sa'adoun) But I have to get back to the university. I have an exam to write in the morning." Sa'adoun looked at me icily.

"Then I will drive you there." I detected suppressed anger in his voice but I had things to say. He and his mother stared at each other until I broke the silence.

"I would like to speak with you about something, Oum Sa'adoun. I hope I am not being presumptuous or difficult with this request, but I would prefer the wedding to be a quiet one, private, intimate, and small. I hope you understand?"

While I spoke I watched Sa'adoun's face for his reaction. His lecture had humbled me, and I had been unsure about how to ask without bringing more trouble upon myself. He had said I didn't know very much and, of course, he was correct. I knew now, in order to get what I wanted I would have to be an obedient and perfect wife to him.

"Why? Are you not proud to be my son's wife?

I began a desperate attempt to make Oum Sa'adoun understand the importance of my request without making her angry or feel I was belittling her son's achievements.

"Of course I am proud. I am very proud Sa'adoun is giving me the best that life has to offer. But can you imagine how it is in the North. The talk in my home city will endanger my parent's lives if someone finds out just how important Sa'adoun's position is. I would have to look over my shoulder all the time. Some political group might kidnap me to exchange me for my husband's life. I have no wish to be involved in politics, or cause talk in political circles on either side. I have no wish to destroy my future, nor that of our children."

Oum Sa'adoun's eyes lit up at the mention of grandchildren.

"Enough, Najat. I will support your family. Bring them to Baghdad." I must admit to being surprised at Oum Sa'adoun's ready compromise, but I knew my family would never move to Baghdad and certainly not for Sa'adoun's sake. Oum Sa'adoun turned to leave and I heard her faintly saying to herself,

"When he could have had any woman in Baghdad, why did my son choose this one?" I walked over to Sa'adoun and looked pleadingly up into his face and gave him the smile of a doting wife.

"Come, Najat, let me take you back to the residence. This has been a long night."

chapter eleven

Back at the university, Sa'adoun insisted on escorting me to my door within the women's residence. Fazilla had to be roused from her bed, but upon seeing Sa'adoun accompanying me, she made no comment despite the fact that she had been disturbed, and she moved even more sluggishly than usual.

First checking to see if Salma and Sahira had returned yet and seeing that they were absent, I signaled Sa'adoun to enter my room with me. I took a key I had hidden in the pages of an old book. I proceeded to unlock the heavy chest at the foot of my bed. I noticed that he looked on with some amusement; I suppose wondering what I was up to. I lifted the lid and withdrew the cash filled leather briefcase he had left at my parent's house.

Please, Sa'adoun, take this. My family is more than happy to return the money. They prefer me to marry you out of respect, rather than for you to buy me. I am not for sale and my family will not sell me. The money you left in my home is all there, they did not touch it, and my family, just as you pointed out to me earlier, taught me also to represent them and not myself." I saw a smile come to his face as he grabbed the case. It turned to soft laughter as he reached for the door handle, and it occurred to me that he probably thought my family to be fools.

"Good night, Najat." he said as he closed it.

June and July were the months of my engagement to Sa'adoun Alwan. In one sense I had a feeling of fascination about where my life's path was leading me; however, it was tempered by a feeling of anger that my dreams of the magic of love would likely never become true. My choice of a man to love with mind body and soul had been taken from me by fear and force. In the moments when I thought logically and without emotion stirred into the mix, I knew that my marriage to Sa'adoun had a more powerful and meaningful purpose than my own selfish emotional feelings and needs. I understood completely that my purpose in this marriage was to serve my people and save the lives of as many as possible. I must also somehow assist in the bringing of peace to Iraq without war or weapons. Without a concrete plan, I had no idea at this juncture how I could or would accomplish my aims.

Since that first outing with Sa'adoun at the party, I had a fairly regular visitor. Shabeah al-Azime was Sa'adoun's military servant. Shabeab was quite young, probably about twenty years old. He was quite small in stature and dressed in his army uniform looked much too immature to be a soldier. He had a very dark complexion which had the appearance of having been out in the blazing sun too long. Shabeab's purpose for often standing on the front steps of the women's residence waiting for me to return from classes was to deliver gifts on behalf of Sa'adoun. Sometimes it would be expensive Parisian perfumes or exquisite jewelry from London, Paris or Geneva. At other times he had beautiful clothes hand picked for me at expensive European salons or handmade shoes from Italy.

With all this attention, I soon needed another place to store all my new things as Salma and Sahira also had many expensive belongings.

Sa'adoun himself from time to time would come to the residence's front door, surprising me with instructions to escort him in his big black Mercedes. My future husband took me to high end restaurants in the big hotels in Baghdad. At other times he would spend lavishly when he took me shopping in Karakh or Mansure. Sometimes we went to Multasam or the Karada-Maryan district near Al-karkh on the bank of the Tigris River and the Palace of the Republic where a natural boundary created a sense of security for the richer society.

"Everything in this area, Najat, is untouchable. In the part of Baghdad around the Palace of the Republic, where you see the palace and all these elaborate and opulent houses, is where we, the powerful of Iraq live. Security here is tight."

I had already found out that most of Sa'adoun's conversations were about power and control. Pointing he continued,

"This building is Saddam's secret nerve centre under the control of General Capp Curnel. This next one is the head offices of the Ba'ath Secret Service under Amn al Khassa." I could smell blood on each name Sa'adoun uttered and shivers ran rampant through my body. We were approaching the Palace of the Republic, and he began to describe the four entrances to it. Pointing to the first entrance he remarked,

"This is the number one or western door. Only the president and his immediate family can use this entrance. His ministers, who are all Tikriti, may also use the western door," he said with a tone of envy in his voice. "This north facing or number two door is to be used by members of the National Committee and by the Revolutionary Command Council. The third door is to be used only by the palace personnel." As we approached, a guard recognized Sa'adoun's face as he continued.

"Number four is known as the Lion's Gate. This door is the door I use. This is for the director and members of the intelligence service. Only Amn-Al Khass and Jehaaz al-Mukhabarat al-Amn are allowed to use this door. It is unbreachable. This door controls the security of Iraq. Its members have been given the authorization to control the peace of the Ba'ath regime, whatever measures it takes."

Sa'adoun's information stunned me. He had revealed to me details that only a few people in our country knew. I hid my feelings of revulsion and fear at the knowledge I possessed and instead fed Sa'adoun's ego. I falsely suggested how impressed I was with his power. He began speaking louder with a more controlling tone,

"So you see, Najat, this is our city, our country. Next it will be our world and you, Najat, will be with me at my side."

I could not help but think which world did he mean? I shivered as I wondered where in this world of his I would fit. When Sa'adoun had finished bragging about his position and power, he remarked that he would take me to a place I had heard a lot about. He wanted to take me to the al-Alvia Bar to meet a group of foreign and local friends for a drink. On the way over I began to think about the things he had told me and how they fit in well with what I already knew.

My country had no constitution or constitution based

law. We had what was known as Saddam's Law which changed as often the wind changes direction. We had a military government and a good many of the positions within it were enlisted from the secret service organization. Others came from Jehaz al-Amnal Khass, the secret nerve center. All of the occupied positions had been given according to Saddam's whims or to members of his extended family. No positions were available to ordinary Iraqi citizens. For this reason positions within the government were often changed by disappearances and murder. Knowing this, the occupants of government positions were all spies reporting on each other in order to gain favor and stay on top. Over and above this level of self preservation, the Ba'ath party had its own secret service reporting on all of them.

Sa'adoun pulled to a stop in front of the al-Alvia Club. He led me in and we sat down with a group of people. Sa'adoun had already told me about the opulence of this place, but even forewarned, I was stunned at its magnificence. It was obvious that millions of dollars had been spent in its construction exclusively of rich marble. The club catered to each whim of the wealthy. Scanning the group, I saw some faces that I recognized from television and the press and some that I didn't know. At the introductions for the first time I met Ali Hassan al-Majid. He was a man with a reputation as a butcher of indescribable brutality. Al-Majid had no scruples, particularly against the Kurds. They were fighting the regime and his answer was genocide for Kurds and Shia Moslems.

He extended his hand in greeting as Sa'adoun introduced me. Mustering all the self- control I could, I smiled and politely shook his hand. Sa'adoun mentioned that I was a Kurdish woman.

"For a change a smart one."

Al-Majid could not disguise his disdain at touching

my hand, but like me he exercised his self control since he was in the company of other powerful men. I could not help wondering what he thought about a Kurd sitting at the same table and if his secret service would launch an investigation into my background. The next hand to greet me was Hussein Kamel Takrite, a relative of Saddam. This man was in charge of control and manufacture of weapons. He had been the driver for Ahmad Hassan Al-Bakr, the former President of Iraq who reputedly had been poisoned by Saddam and had been involved in Al-Bakr's assassination. Al-Majid and Takrite were drinking buddies and dined and drank together. Never in my presence did they discuss their government roles. After a few drinks, the two men became sexual predators and hunted down the most beautiful women in the room using their power to gain submission. They seemed to prefer European or Oriental women. Like children in a candy store unable to choose and occasionally they took home more than one.

I spotted Russell within the group. He caught my attention. I saw him behave differently than the others. He was soft spoken and polite and his words were respectful and humble unlike a number of others in the group. Perhaps the culture of his country dictated that men did not go about hunting conquests. Nor did they talk loudly in mixed company about women as though they were in the world strictly for the pleasure of men.

A woman identified as a Canadian doctor came over to the table and sat next to Russell. For the benefit of the group she flirted a little then left shortly after speaking with him. The other men in the group began taunting Russell about his sex life suggesting that he had no appetite for women. As the jokes flew around the table Russell did not take the bait but laughed along with them. I sat next to Sa'adoun while all this was going on. I said nothing unless I was asked a direct question. Then I answered respectfully. Russell was engaged in conversation with the others at the table until they left one by one to seek out a woman for the night, leaving him, Sa'adoun, and me alone.

Remembering the lecture Sa'adoun had given me on the night of the big party, the first time I had met Russell, I tried to avoid eye contact with him unless he spoke to me directly. Each time I did, I blushed. I knew he was looking at me differently and it pleased me.

"Excuse me for a few minutes." Sa'adoun said as he got up to leave. Free to speak, Russell asked,

"How are you doing Najat? How is university? Are you going home for the summer break to your family?" I answered his questions correctly and politely. Then he said,

"Your eyes, Najat?"

"What about my eyes?"

"Your eyes are telling me a lot, Najat."

"How so?" I asked.

"They are far and way too distant from the present moment, Najat. I see them crying without tears." I could not respond as Sa'adoun had returned. But I admit I did want to tell Russell that while my eyes might be crying, his were full of secrets. Just before he sat down again Sa'adoun announced,

"The cowboy is here."

He spoke the words sarcastically as though he couldn't stand the sight of Uday, Saddam Hussein's son, as he strutted into the room with his five bodyguards. Suddenly it seemed as though the excitement of the bar had been handed over to Uday Hussein. The awesome power of the president's son took everyone's attention. Accompanying him was Barzan Al-Tikriti. He was the head of Mukhabarat Intelligence Agency later serving as Iraq's representative to the U.N. in Geneva. He

administered Saddam and Uday's fortunes abroad and
was in charge of procuring armaments.

"Don't even look at him or his men, Najat." I thought
I had better get used to Sa'adoun's control and jealousy.
Then Russell spoke in a quiet voice,

"I haven't seen him in this bar before."

"He does come here from time to time but mostly he
goes to the Al-Said Bar. It belongs to the most trusted
men in his father's family." Sa'adoun pointed out each of
the five bodyguards and identified them.

"That one there is his pimp, Ahmude Salman. He is
educated and charming. Women are attracted to his style
so Udai employs him as his pimp. It is his job to find
women suitable for Udai's desire for the night. If he fails
in finding a suitable victim, Udai kicks him. That man is
next to him is Namir Tiktriti. He arranges Udai's wild
parties."

"What do you mean by wild?" Russell asked,

"Don't even go there, Russell! Salam Aoussi on the
right is Udai's personal spy. I can't stand him. Actually,
Russell, I believe that Udai is mentally ill. Perhaps as a
result of his father beating him with an iron bar and
forcing him to witness the most awful and graphic
torture in order to give his son strength and to control
him. Udai has learned that without pain there will be
no peace or pleasure. Stories emerge of terrible things
happening at his wild parties."

It was painfully obvious that Sa'adoun was not
impressed with the President's son. On the other hand,
perhaps it was personal since he didn't have Udai's
power. I think Sa'adoun realized that possibly he had
said too much to both of us. He excused us and we left
the club and he drove me back to the university women's
residence.

It was two a.m. and rather than sleep, I began to study
to be ready for the next day. I never shared my real

experiences with Salma and Sahira. They always wanted to know how my evening had gone, but I lied and told them about romance with my fiancé which seemed to satisfy them. I could barely stay awake the next day and made my way through it by drinking strong Baghdad coffee. It was a trick that Fazilla Hunnen taught me.

The month of August arrived. I had been trying not to think about it too much. I had grown accustomed to the fact that I would be Sa'adoun Alwan's wife whether I wished it or not. At this stage there could be no turning back. It was far too late for regrets. There were times when I got a headache thinking about being married, even if it were not to Sa'adoun Alwan. I had no experience on what it meant being a wife, and the man I was to marry was a mass murderer.

When my mind was not occupied with my studies, it would spin with thoughts of what the future would bring. I can barely imagine the opulence I would be living in. It was such a far cry from my beginnings in Zalan with dirt floors and the canvas door covers in the houses. How could I live in such a house as he had shown me the night of the party? Would I be expected to live there along with Sa'adoun's mother and his snobbish sister? What would be my role in such a household and, indeed, what would my role be in my husband's life. He had such incredible power over people's lives, terrifying power.

In some of my sleepless nights, to blot out these thoughts, I would remember my thoughts as a young girl. Then I had dreamed I would marry a strong man one who was both intellectual and dedicated to bringing peace to Iraq. But the memories and dreams soon died upon the realization that I would marry a man whom I did not now nor ever could love. The man whom I would marry was arrogant. He was cruel without compassion and had no empathy for the things I believed in. I felt he had no interest in my thoughts. I would become a possession, a woman who must obey her military husband without question. He would never ask or value my opinions. I was to become his prisoner, snared and trapped. I was to marry the enemy.

It was Friday at noon. I stood in the foyer of Hayfa's bedroom. The four Arab serving women who had just finished preparing my wedding gown waited anxiously for a reaction from me. They glanced at each other. I assume they were wondering why I wasn't ecstatic, possibly thinking I was highly nervous. I am sure they were aware that I was Kurdish and that Sa'adoun Alwan would be a far cry from the reputed rough Kurdish people I had grown up with. He was highly civilized and charming, and a powerful man in the Ba'ath regime circle. Despite their subservient role in the house, their envious attitude toward my impending marriage was very evident as they waited for the signal to escort me into the next room.

Anxiety squeezed at my throat, choking me. I craved sweet, fresh air that did not have the smells of other human breaths. Cool air, mountain air, but it would not be so. I examined my image in the mirror. Oddly the image did not appear to be me. A young woman in a wedding gown looked back at me with eyes that had a far away look. They were the eyes of a stranger: dull, dark, resigned. My mind asked me silently the same question I had asked myself numerous times. What was I doing here? What was she doing here? Still staring at the image I began feeling as if I were dirty. Very soon I would have to submit to the sexual advances of a husband I hated even before the act. Sa'adoun had taken many dalliances with other women while I had no such experiences. Would he treat me with dignity and respect, or would I be just another prostitute in his mind? Would he be gentle and considerate or would it be like the men in the bar had joked about, rough and without regard for my feelings?

These moments before the mirror were my last minutes of freedom as I had known it. Bile burned at the back of my throat. I swallowed hard and commanded my mind to stop anticipating my walk into the Devil's cave. my body finally ceased its trembling. Words spewed from the mouths of the Arab women surrounding me, trying to address me all at once. I could not think straight. Their words were a blur of incoherent sound. I could not concentrate or discern a single word of what I thought were complements. I could not respond or thank them. My head was spinning. I had to get away. My legs began to propel me behind a carved dressing screen and I found refuge in an alcove overlooking the ornate gardens. Now I found myself alone with my thoughts.

I wondered, was I quite mad when I agreed to this marriage? I told myself. You are about to marry a man with whom you share nothing. Our values and convictions could not be further apart had we been born on different planets. I, Najat, am about to forfeit my very future and perhaps my young life on the sacrificial altar of patriotism to aid the ones who are trying to bring peace to the Iraqi people.

I stared down at the white dress draped around me like a burial shroud. For a second I saw myself as a corpse ready for the grave. I struggled to bring air to my lungs and pressed my hands tightly to my chest. My birth mother's coin necklace dug into my flesh flooding my mind with the faint memories of the ones who had brought me into this world. I wished they were with me now at this moment to give me the love and support they had when I was small and dependant upon them. I recalled a wishful childhood dream where Mother floated to earth to assure me that all answers would come to me in time.

For only the second time I could remember, I removed

the necklace. I did not want it tainted by being on my body on this day of all days. Nor did I want to have to explain to Sa'adoun why I wore such a simple piece of peasant jewelry on my wedding day. The necklace was my connection to my family who had been annihilated by the Ba'ath regime and only Shilan, Shwan, and I knew of its origin and significance. I slipped the necklace into my white glove. It would share my day with me, but not my marriage bed.

My family had traveled to Baghdad to attend the wedding. Sa'adoun had established them in a suite at the Sheraton Hotel where the reception was to be held and had his sister, Hayfa; take Mother and Shilan shopping for fine clothes for the occasion. Shabeab Sa'adoun's driver had instructions to take Rebwar to a high class tailor shop for suitable clothing for the wedding. To say the least, Shilan was completely impressed at this new exciting and opulent world she suddenly found herself in.

"There you are!" Shilan said, ducking into the alcove with me. Seeing her at this moment distracted me from my morose thoughts.

"You are the most beautiful bride, Najat," she said touching my cheek. Her eyes told me that she understood and felt my inner conflict despite her words of encouragement. I smiled but dared not utter a word lest my real emotions burst uncontrolled into tears.

"Its time to go, Najat. Everyone is ready." Shilan took my arm and led me blindly, feeling weak and ill, out to the waiting black Mercedes. There were other elegantly dressed ladies waiting but I saw them only in a blur. I had none of the feelings a bride ought to have at this moment. I felt only numbness as I sat between Shilan and Hayfa on the rear seat. The two girls seemed to get along together admirably and began to sing little songs as the motorcade got under way. I sat staring blankly at the back of the driver's head.

Shilan sensed my dejection and reached for my hand. She felt the necklace inside the palm of my glove. She glanced at me and I knew she understood. She leaned into me and whispered,

"We shall miss you terribly." she said high spiritedly, in an attempt to cheer me on this the darkest day of my life.

"I shall have to get married and move to Baghdad to be near you." It was quite obvious that she was besotted by all she saw in the city.

"You can't leave Daya (Mother) too," I snapped. "She does not deserve to lose everyone." Sensing my serious tone Shilan laughed softly.

"Relax, Najat," she said gripping my hand, "I was only humoring you. I will never get married. I will grow old and gray and stay with Daya always." Outside the car I vaguely heard horns honking at the crowds on the sides. Suddenly we were there. The car turned into the grounds of the Sheraton Hotel. The exterior was calm and refined looking. The architecture elegant and imposing, the grounds exquisitely manicured. To date I had not had the privilege of being here.

My throat tightened as I held back a tremendous urge to sob. The sheer splendour of the hotel, contrasted sharply with my feelings of despair and sense of loss of self. I had a strong feeling that the beauty surrounding me was a waste of time, money and effort. It was all a sham. Despite my quiet desperation, I knew I had to control my emotions. Once again I reminded myself that I had a job to do in serving my people no matter what the personal cost. I gripped my mother's necklace inside my gloved hand and stepped toward my fate.

chapter twelve

My cell door opened. The sound tore me from the memory of my unhappy wedding day. A guard stepped in and placed a piece of bread and a container of brownish water on the floor. Then he left without a word. It became immediately apparent that they intended to keep me alive, hoping to break me by more torture. I knew it would make no difference whether I told them what they wanted to hear or not. The end result would be the same. I knew enough about the regime and this prison to understand that virtually no one ever left this place alive. But I was not ready to die yet, so I gulped down the water and ate the bread. I lay down again and forced the bad thoughts from my mind, returning them to memory.

Inside the private ballroom large numbers of guests were noisily engaged in celebration. A costumed belly dancer, draped in jewelry, greeted my wedding party. Two drummers leapt to each side of me, drumming and moving to the rhythm of the music as they directed me to my place, a throne on a stage two feet higher than the floor.

Despite the internal churning in my stomach, I managed to portray an impression of cool composure. I told myself, I will not shame my family or embarrass myself. I made this decision without the counsel of my parents. There can be no second thoughts. I forced my lips to smile but felt grateful for the fine veil covering my face which hid the sadness in my eyes. I willed the perspiration to stop beading upon my forehead.

Sa'adoun had arranged for our marriage certificate without my being present. It was a veiled insult to the culture of my family. It should have taken place at the time of the engagement as our culture demanded. I felt lost and disoriented. When the actual ritual had concluded, Sa'adoun simply disappeared. Being on new ground and not knowing what was expected of me next, I scanned the crowd. My eyes searched not for my husband but for Russell. I was desperate to catch sight of him. I needed a sane voice amid the insanity I found myself in.

All I could actually remember of my wedding was Sa'adoun lifting the veil from my face, taking my hands, and directing me to my throne. It was a gilded, high backed chair festooned with fresh, scented flowers. Behind me a blanket of pale pink roses shrouded the entire wall. Before me on a small table, with a crisp linen cloth cover, two silk brocade covered boxes were placed slightly to my left. I sat on my throne gazing out over all the assembled guests. My eyes found Russell sitting with a group of foreign guests. He was behaving warm and gregariously, conversing comfortably. I felt envious; he was clearly enjoying the festivities. Just as suddenly as he had vanished, Sa'adoun reappeared and came to my side.

His relatives began dancing toward us, all of them singing and shouting,

"Cheers to the bride and groom, Haz Halla·· Haz Halla." Off to one side Hayfa was attempting to teach Shilan the undulations of a belly dancer. They laughed together and I envied them their freedom. Rebwar stationed himself at the entrance aided by Harif, Sa'adoun's youngest brother, to greet the late arrivals. I located my mother sitting at the same table as Oum Sa'adoun. She was speaking with my aunt, Dlshad, her favorite sister with whom she shared her secrets. My gaze darted around like a woman possessed, looking for my father. My heart sank even lower and tears came to my eyes. Mother, aunt Dlshad, and Oum Sa'adoun were looking at me. I tried to smile for them.

Sa'adoun glanced at me and saw the glisten of a tear. With a voice suggesting genuine concern he asked,

"What is wrong, Najat? You seem upset."

"Do not worry Sa'adoun. I have not seen my father yet." His response was cold, without feeling,

"Perhaps he is not grateful to have me as his son-in-law?" His words made me realize that my father simply could not bear to be here to see his child enter the jaws of the lion. He had disowned me. I wanted to scream. On top of all the other emotional pain I had been dealing with, this was the worst.

A signal announced it was time for the exchanging of wedding bands. Sa'adoun took my hands and raised me from the bridal throne. We exchanged wedding bands. Then with a sly smile he picked the largest brocade box from the table and lifted the lid. He extracted a delicately crafted golden necklace laced with diamonds and placed it around my neck. Then diamond studded gold bracelets were placed on my wrists, followed by earrings.

The orchestra played traditional music to honor the bride and groom and then to honor the families. My mother stepped forward to place another necklace upon me. This one I noticed above all the others. It was exquisitely crafted of finely worked gold so long that it fell half way to my waist. My body heaved in a silent sob. I knew it was much more extravagant than she could possibly afford. The pride of my family had most probably put them in debt for the next decade. My mother kissed me on the cheek and I know she tasted my silent tears. She was followed by a parade of Sa'adoun and his immediate family and guests, each draping my body with fine gold jewelry. I began to become so heavily laden with gold I could barely hold my head up straight.

The sentiment behind the array of gifts held little interest for me nor did the beauty and quality of the craftsmanship.

My attention was diverted to a figure striding toward me. Russell, who had been conversing with a group of what appeared to be foreign guests across the hall, headed determinedly my way. I looked at his eyes as he approached. They were smiling as though he were a man with a secret to keep. Forgetting for a moment the somber reason the both of us were in the hall, I felt a mild excitement in the presence of this very different American man. Each time I had caught sight of him fading in and out of my vision, I became very aware of my surroundings. Russell seemed to be the only anchor that secured me to the reality of my wedding celebration. He drew near. Russell smiled broadly and approached Sa'adoun with open arms. Russell and my husband clasped each other in an affectionate embrace as he offered his congratulations. Russell took both of Sa'adoun's hands in his and together with a strong handshake they turned to face me. Instantly I realized I was staring. I snapped out of it before Sa'adoun perceived it was not he I gazed at.

Just as quickly we were both distracted by Russell reaching into his pocket and bringing out a small box. Without a word he removed the tissue paper to reveal a spherical pendant suspended from a gold chain on which words were engraved in the shape of a crescent. He looked at Sa'adoun and asked permission,

"May I?" Sa'adoun nodded. I could feel the warmth of Russell's hands, although they never touched me as he fastened the chain behind my neck. He recited the words of the ancient parable, the inspiration for the inscription, as his fingers deftly fastened the clasp. When he had finished he shook my hand.

"Now you are Sa'adoun's wife. You are very special to me, Najat." Turning to Sa'adoun he said,

"You and Najat are much more than friends to me, you are more like family." It is hard to explain but after the sensation of the touch of Russell's hand, I began to relax and even enjoy some of the festivities.

A band played throughout the wedding dinner with local singing stars performing some of my favorite tunes. I was delighted to meet several of the stars and admitted to myself that I was impressed by them. Suddenly there came a realization that from this point on it would be possible to meet almost any celebrity. Just as quickly, reason spoke to me, 'Why would you be interested in such meetings when you have an important destiny of helping to free your people?'

As the guests danced, relaxed by alcohol, free expressions of sensuality emerged. The belly dancers were professionally trained and did traditional dances expressing their folklore while I as a bride sat watching with my husband. Few words passed between us. As the final courses of the sumptuous banquet were served, it became apparent that this was not completely a traditional Iraqi wedding. It had been influenced by

Western culture and it fascinated rather than disappointed me.

As the evening progressed the atmosphere threatened to engulf me. Over and above the heavy emotional environment, the air in the hall was humid, thick with spiced and alcohol laden breath. The doors and windows were thrown open to the night which did not alleviate the feeling but added to it with the warm night perfume of flowering plants and trees outside. I sat alone on my bridal throne and dared not leave it without my husband at my side. For if I should eyebrows would certainly have been raised.

I yearned for the feel of fresh, cool air upon my skin and in my lungs, a brief respite into the garden, a breath of cool mountain air, a breeze. My eyes scanned the ballroom until Shilan came and rescued me from the oppressive air. She took me outside for a few moments. My discomfort was to continue as I returned. I saw Sa'adoun seated at a table with a group of men, undoubtedly government representatives, in heavy conversation.

At the table, seated among Sa'adoun's family, Mother looked terribly out of place. I knew she struggled, felt lost, entirely out of her own environment and customs. Knowing hardly any Arabic, she could converse only through Shilan as interpreter. I knew my mother very well. Her very upbringing, like most Kurds, had prevented her from wishing to learn the language of those who had oppressed our people. Sa'adoun's family chatted gaily among themselves as though mother were invisible though she was amid them.

At a later date, Shilan told me that the family had made unkind remarks about Mother and her background, knowing she did not understand. It became painfully apparent through the conversations at the table, that the Kurdish peoples and their concerns were treated with complete indifference. Shilan also divulged that she had left Mother alone to try to meet Russell. I remember seeing Shilan walk up to Russell and introduce herself.

"Hello, you must be Mr. Russell." At the sound of his name he turned to face a small dark haired girl.

"And you are?" Russell asked in English.

"Shilan. Najat's younger sister."

"Oh, really! Come and talk." Russell led Shilan away to two seats at an empty table. Shilan remembered the conversation and repeated it to me. She told me she struggled with the English language.

"You and your sister do not look very much alike. Other than that you are both beautiful women, you do not share the same facial features."

"Yes, I know. But Najat is the more beautiful one. I hope that she retains her beauty and that marriage will not destroy her."

"By the way how did you know my name?" He glanced at me then back to Shilan. Blushing, Shilan realized she had possibly said too much.

"Oh, no, of course not. Najat does not talk as much as I do. Hayfa told me your name. Najat is?"

"More private?"

"Yes, that's it. More private."

"Yes, I think I understand, Shilan."

Sa'adoun returned and the conversation ended. From my throne sitting above the guests I had seen Shilan and Russell talking together and I envied her.

I did not wish to see the night end. Its conclusion meant possible new discomforts. Gradually the guests filtered out one by one. My innocence as a woman was leaving at the same time. It came much too quickly. I had no idea if Sa'adoun intended to whisk me off for a honeymoon in some neighboring Arab country, Europe, or stay in Baghdad. Or possibly here in this building.

He had made all the arrangements and had told me nothing. His arrangements were all according to his lifestyle, not Iraqi tradition. When the last guest had left he took me to an upper floor room.

We were alone. For a few moments Sa'adoun's fingers toyed with my hair and stroked my neck. His hands, rough and powerful, began to remove my bridal gown pulling it away from my body. His actions were clumsy, lacking in gentleness. I closed my eyes while my fingers grasped at my palms.

Then my eyes opened wide. I knew what was to happen was not to be an act of love, but more like a rape. He kissed me on the lips and revulsion overwhelmed me. I sensed I had angered him and to diffuse his possible wrath, I attempted to explain that I was simply nervous and I needed time and gentleness.

Completely absorbed in his quest to take me, his feeble attempts at tenderness were quickly forgotten. Apparently he did not consider my participation to be of any consequence. His naked body forced mine onto the bed. Without success I tried to choke back the sound that escaped my throat the moment he penetrated me. My eyes were wide open focused on the shadows on the ceiling. My body was in excruciating pain but my mind had numbed. I had always assumed that rape was a quick act of violence, but this was a slow agonizing torture.

Soon silence descended upon the hotel. I pulled the sheet up over my body to cover the shame of my brutal rape which had overwhelmed me. Turning slowly so as not to waken Sa'adoun, I curled up in the furthest corner of the mattress. Eventually the numbness subsided.

My head throbbed and I could not remember a moment in my life when I felt so alone. Even on that awful day when I had to walk away from Zalan, I had Shwan to offer me support and comfort. I felt fear and anxiety for my future. I wondered how many nights like this I could endure. I lay awake questioning my decision to enter into this sham of a marriage as well as my ability to carry out the grand scheme of espionage Shwan and I had so naively plotted. I wondered too, how I could look into my husband's eyes in the morning feeling the embarrassment and shame within me. I had not been ready to lose my virginity to a man for whom I felt nothing but hatred.

Some time just before the dawn I fell into a deeply troubled and exhausted sleep. By now I was utterly exhausted with the terrible long wedding day and the equally long night filled with all manner of bad dreams and ghastly realities. I fell asleep again and as far as I can remember I did not dream. I awoke with the sunlight streaming in through the open window. I carefully opened up one eye and looked to see if my husband was also awake.

Mercifully Sa'adoun had left our bed. I had no idea what was expected of me. Sa'adoun had been absolutely right about situations like these when he had said that I knew nothing. Nonetheless I felt grateful that I did not have to speak with anyone, at least not yet. I decided I should remain in bed. My body felt bruised and I longed for a cup of hot, sweet tea. Thinking of the tea, memories came to me of my mother bringing it to me. How I would welcome her if she were to come to me now!

Slowly clarity came to my mind and I began to relax a little, although frankly I was still in a state of shock With the cool morning breeze drifting through the window cooling my skin and the sun now high in the sky, life had begun to look a little better. Though extremely dangerous my situation no longer seemed to be impossible. Lying back into my pillow I thought about the challenge I had undertaken. To ensure that no child would experience pain and loss the same way I and many other children had, I visualized the great benefit that could come from my actions. I reflected on the lives of men, women, and children for whom any action was far too late. My resolve had returned. I could uphold my vow. I would use my resourcefulness and intelligence to be both a dutiful wife and a cunning spy.

I had much to learn. I knew that. In particular it was necessary that I learn and practice silence and obedience.

chapter thirteen

In the early days of our marriage I confess I experienced considerable difficulty. When certain subjects were discussed in our home it was too great a struggle to maintain my composure. I was not accustomed to be unable to offer an opinion. Any attempt to participate in conversation with Sa'adoun and his associates would not only be unacceptable, but downright dangerous. Many times I sat and seethed in silence with an almost unbearable need to include my own personal point of view. As a survival tactic I learned to disconnect. I managed eventually to live within myself while outwardly appearing detached, calm, and unemotional. Nothing could touch and stir my thoughts to respond and I was thankful. I remained silent but within my silence, spoke the voice of others. There was a reward for my continued self-control. The more silent

I remained the more I could hear and digest.

Both strange and at times familiar faces came to visit, and Russell became a frequent visitor for both business and pleasure. Once in a while Sa'adoun's mother and his sister would give us a surprise visit. I always suspected that the visits were an inspection tour in disguise. I felt sure that they never totally accepted me as a member of the family. I had been tested but never really considered good enough for Sa'adoun. They had no generosity in their voices as they spoke to me. I retaliated by being far too generous in return, and so I never accepted them as an important part of my life.

I kept the difficulties of my sheltered existence to myself. I lived with a man who always afforded me the highest respect when in front of guests and family. But in the privacy of our home and more so in our sleeping quarters, Sa'adoun alternated between scorn and indifference, and he never did master the art of gentleness.

Each day of my new reality had its own challenges, but with perseverance I adapted to them. Russell had become a frequent visitor to our home and as I have stated before, he was a kind considerate guest who became my only friend within Sa'adoun's large circle of friends. Sa'adoun eventually relaxed and appeared to have forgotten his little spat of jealousy concerning Russell. As time passed, Sa'adoun indulged me with permission to engage in conversation when Russell was present. It would appear that I had become quite proficient at concealing my emotions, for my husband failed to notice the anger that his condescension fueled in me. He seemed oblivious and undisturbed by the camaraderie developing between our American friend and me.

I eagerly looked forward to the start of the next semester. Returning to the university would renew my intellectual stimulation. I felt a great need to be with people like myself, ordinary with both feet on the ground. I needed conversation and debate. I needed more companionship than Russell and his visits could provide. Also I missed Shwan terribly.

The first months of my marriage were relatively uneventful. No major disagreements erupted. Having some experience in clandestine activities I knew that Sa'adoun had me watched, both at the university and at home. He was informed daily about what I wore and whom I spoke with. Even the food I ate for my lunch was reported to him. Wisely I discontinued trying to pass along information. I knew I must wait until I had earned Sa'adoun's complete trust. Instead I pushed myself to excel in my studies and at home I played the part of a devoted wife.

We lived the life of the privileged and enjoyed the benefits that accompanied a high level government job. Not long after our marriage Sa'adoun purchased a well appointed palace in the elite Baghdad suburb of al-Azaminya with exquisite Arabian and French architectural taste. The area turned out to be one in which I had nothing in common. I was unable to find a friend or another person I could trust. Oddly this turned out to be a benefit. I thought that if I kept everything to myself I would have no questions to answer. In effect this gave me a certain amount of freedom and a life of relative ease, albeit in a completely sheltered environment.

Sadly I did not get back to Sulaymania very often to see my family but when I did my high profile identity papers eliminated the travel hassles. Rebwar took the documents and had identical copies made on the black market so others could travel more safely. I did invite my family and dearest friend to visit me in Baghdad, but no one ever came so I kept my shallow life to myself.

At the beginning of the semester I had already become pregnant and although Sa'adoun was away for up to a week at a time, he received daily reports about my health and progress. Of course with him being away in the war zones, I never knew if he was in or out of the country. It gave me more freedom within the scope of my usual restrictions to gain access to and start gathering information. I used every resource I could think of to gain information and news about what was occurring in the north and the rest of the country

The apparently endless war with Iran magnified the difficulties of the northern peoples including the members of my family. Unrelenting bombing and armed conflict continued to destroy the lives of my countrymen. Massive sections of the dry grasslands having been ravaged by fires, became blackened useless earth. Any evidence that these areas had ever supported life had been obliterated. Towns too, had been razed. Virtually no building stood undamaged and the people found no safe secure place. Saddam's army attacked from the south and the Iranians from the north. The Kurds were trapped, helpless and unarmed between the vice-like actions. My country had become a wasteland of rubble, downed trees, and stank of bloated human and animal bodies.

Now the south of Iraq became as restless as the north, with Baghdad no longer a paradise for its residents. A defeated section of the army had retreated from the fighting in the north back down to Baghdad. In Saddam Hussein's eyes these were cowards and traitors who had brought shame upon Iraq by not fighting to the death. As a result the city centre echoed with the screams of dying men as soldiers loyal to Saddam beat the vanquished troops to death with iron bars. Blood spattered residents watched in horror as the slaughter continued with the vanquished on their knees, pleading to no avail. The streets and the bodies were so blood soaked the only skin color was red. When the carnage was done, the Ba'ath party supporters and residents walked among the bodies cursing and spitting upon them. Saddam decreed that the corpses be left to rot in the streets to remind those who had any inclination to refuse to fight for Iraq that this would be their reward for bringing shame to the country.

One of Saddam's best friends, Salah al Khady, a general in the Iraqi army, withdrew his troops from the battlefield. Saddam hung him and shot the troops one by one. Saddam stated, "If these men do not have the will to fight for their country, they do not have the right to live in it or breathe the air of our land."

At the same time thousands of Iraqi citizens who committed the most miniscule of crimes against Saddam were installed in abandoned bunkers deep underground then sealed shut. Every single one starved to death or asphyxiated.

Saddam gave al Khady's family some money as though nothing had happened. Iraq became a gigantic burial ground with Saddam as its chief supplier of corpses. My husband Sa'adoun, like many others, was partly responsible for murder, torture, and untold killings, delivering what the Ba'ath Regime expected of them.

The Sa'adoun Alwan household became wealthier. He received more and more money as well as leisure time to enjoy himself. Often he took me to the al-Alvia Bar. I discovered that the bar was a place not only for drinking, womanizing and gambling, but for the laundering offshore money brought in by foreign men, it was then in exchange for illegal oil. The money was then used for the purchase of weapons of mass destruction, chemicals, equipment and supplies for Saddam to build nuclear proof bunkers. The Regime brought in mercenary military instructors from Western countries and specialists in torture techniques. I learned from careful listening that most of Saddam's torture methods had been adopted from the Soviet Union's intelligence services the K.G.B. and the G.R.U., while other techniques came from Eastern Germany. More than a thousand Soviet military experts were serving in Iraq. Weapon manufacturing facilities were brought in. All of these things were discussed openly in the Al Avia Bar and it reminded me of my mother buying vegetables from a donkey cart where bargaining for prices was carried on in loud and heated voices. The monetary costs for ending human life was just that simple and I realized that human life to the Ba'ath regime had absolutely no value.

It occurred to me what fools we Iraqis are. With this atmosphere in our country, who of the Western countries will believe what was happening here and who would come to help save us? When the Alcohol flowed freely and the discussions on war and its costs and benefits were often forgotten by the prostitutes frequenting the bar. They would entice the men away from the heavy talk or bargaining, taking them home, while I would sit listening intently. At times Sa'adoun ordered his driver to take his pregnant wife home while he stayed behind. I was sure he chose a prostitute just like the others. This did not cause me any real concern since I did not love my husband, but I did have reservations about his behavior because of the baby within my womb. I did not want my innocent child to become a carbon copy of his father.

There were times when I placed my hand upon my belly and felt the movements of the child. The concerns I had for the new life growing there overshadowed my purpose in being here in Baghdad, trying to aid my country and people. At other moments I felt a great loneliness for my family and my old friends with whom

I wished to share my joy in motherhood. I wondered if I might lose my passion for politics. But I knew if I did the project of marrying Sa'adoun would have been an exercise in futility. I realized that I was losing my strength and resolve. I knew I must get a grip on myself. I needed to concentrate on my real purpose.

The clandestine news I received from the north helped to strengthen my determination again. Stories related a scorched earth, putrid smells of decaying corpses in the streets, no electricity, and no water supply. Operating telephones were as rare as summer rain and for my people, the Kurds and the Arab Shias, it was impossible for them to know which of the invaders were trying the hardest to eliminate them.

I knew desperate children orphaned or separated from parents gathered in packs like wild dogs, some as young as three years of age. Others carried sibling babies with them, in search of food and safety careful to step over rotting bodies in the streets. Still others mainly maimed and injured children dressed in rags, spent every waking moment in the search for comfort and sustenance.

Russell MacMillan and my husband appeared to have become great friends, spending many evenings together. Occasionally Sa'adoun's brother, Harif, joined them. According to Arabic custom the men often sat until the early hours of the morning swapping stories as they imbibed Arak. Periodically they would frequent bars and nightspots. On other nights they would stay at home where I was able to quietly listen to my husband reveal things that were not meant for my ears.

When it became too late for Russell to go back to his apartment he stayed the night in a guest room. I gathered from these random conversations with our guest that Sa'adoun expressed an attraction for Western culture and an interest in the liberty of women there. I also learned that women living in Iraq had infinitely more liberty than women in Saudi Arabia and Afghanistan. Despite our lack of personal freedoms, we shared while in same sex company gatherings, views on education, dress code, and respect. The first night I met Russell, Sa'adoun had made it abundantly clear that a woman could accept only one man in her lifetime regardless of how the choice is made. Nothing was to break the societal rule and should I break it, society would destroy me even before he did.

While Russell was a constant visitor we had very few moments when we found ourselves alone, although Sa'adoun allowed me to participate in conversation when the three of us were together. Were it not for our guest's visits I would know far less about my husband and his activities, for Russell was a window into Sa'adoun's world. At times their conversations were lively and animated, aided by generous amounts of Arak. It was only at these times that Russell dared to express a conflicting opinion, having learned I assume, that disagreement with my husband could be fatal. These discussions furnished me with information that Sa'adoun would never have revealed to me and afforded me the opportunity to get to know Russell and to gauge how far I could trust him.

However, no matter how much I valued Russell's friendship, I could never disregard the fact that both he and my husband worked directly for the Ba'ath regime. Most nights when it became apparent that the drinking and talking would go on until dawn I would slip away to bed leaving them to entertain each other. I never once attempted to discourage the drinking. In fact I made quite sure that the Arak or Scotch Whiskey would not run out. By observation I had learned each man's capacity for drink and could gauge when tongues were loose and arrogance on Sa'adoun's part reached the flashing point.

The first time I saw my husband utterly drunk, he was filled with such rage that all rules of discretion were abandoned. He became utterly carried away with his own importance and then combined it excess pride in his ability to drink all others under the table. In spite of his inebriation he spoke in an unwavering voice, clear and concise with complete authority, forgetting that I sat close by quietly listening

"Another conspiracy and then another! These traitors will wish their mothers' had never given them life! I would like to pull the trigger myself."

In his drunken rhetoric Sa'adoun revealed there was to be another purge, one more in the endless stream of purges, expulsions, eliminations and executions of anyone thought to be a threat to the Regime.

"Purges are power! Throughout the history of this country, purges have controlled the dissidents. This is the only way to maintain the power structure within our land."

He spoke of Saddam Hussein with admiration. All the members of the Ba'ath party thought exactly like Saddam, just as if they had been brainwashed.

"From the very first day of his rule our glorious leader Saddam has been up front and center with the people of Iraq. On every television channel he has openly made his promises to them. He said, 'Give me your loyalty, and I in return will make all your dreams come true. I will bring wealth to every home, educate every child. I will bring you state of the art medical care, free medicine, and political security. Our country must be purely Arab. And in order to bring you lasting peace, I need your unwavering dedication to the Ba'ath Government of Iraq."

I looked at Russell's face. I discerned that he felt Sa'adoun's drunken outburst meant the end of his diatribe. But alcohol had its grip upon Sa'adoun and he continued with his voice slurring.

"In the 1979 purge, President Ahmed Hasan al-Bakr was placed under house arrest and Saddam installed himself as the supreme head of state and government of Iraq. At the same time he became Secretary General of the Ba'ath party. By 1980 he assumed the position of Supreme Commander of the Armed Forces. But we in the government positions knew he had been in supreme control in Iraq for a decade. In a brilliant move he announced that a plot to overcome the government had been foiled.

He called an emergency meeting of the Ba'ath leadership. Almost a thousand members gathered in the Mustan Sarya Hall. Saddam addressed the assembly, clarifying the new limits of its authority and reinforcing his own. Any doubts as to his supreme power were dispelled by the events of the day. Our glorious leader began to rant about spies and traitors in our midst. He spoke of a major plot to overthrow the government.

A man known to all the assembly as a loyal party member was marched in shackles to the front of the hall. Utterly terrified he turned to face them and made a confession of treason, then proceeded to read from a list of co-conspirators. Sweat poured from the brows of the assembly as one by one names were read out until one third of the members had been labeled as traitorous. Some were taken from the hall to be shot immediately as the others listened in horror.

Hundreds of men were forcibly removed from the hall and taken to the Abu khreb prison and the Qasr al-nihayah Prison known as the Palace Where it Ends. Some were shot while others were hanged.

Then Saddam addressed the remainder of the party. He demanded that they swear allegiance to God and Saddam Hussein. He outlined what was expected of them with the promise that if they made a mistake they would pay the ultimate penalty.

Saddam performed exactly as he had before in 1968. When the Ba'ath returned to power Saddam was the strong man in the regime. He tortured and murdered a great many politicians, hanging others in the Baghdad public square. "All were accused of being American or Israeli spies."

Sa'adoun poured himself and Russell another drink and continued. "The following morning the three hundred traitors were executed by senior squads of party officials using their personal handguns. When they had run out of ammunition, soldiers opened fire on the remaining prisoners with automatic weapons. During the night the military had rounded up the families of the traitors and most of them were also questioned and executed. So you see, Russell, when there is conspiracy against the seat of power, it must be cut out at the root. The cleansing must be absolute."

I watched Russell's face. I had the feeling that my husband's drunken revelations had shocked him. Possibly for the first time he saw behind the mask of gentility and friendship instead he saw a man with no regard for human life. I saw him shake his head. Then he arose from his seat and poured another drink into Sa'adoun's glass.

"Were all those men and their families against the Ba'ath regime, Sa'adoun?"

"No, not necessarily. You see, Russell, we held power once and we lost it and so we learned well from our own experience and their error. We fought our way back into power. Then we cleaned house completely, leaving them no chance to stage a coupe and seize power again and guaranteeing the power is ours in the future."

"Power is a terrible thing in the wrong hands, isn't it?"

"Yes, Russell. Authority is also, but everybody wants

it. Power is a perfect ingredient of threat, wealth, and greed. It ensures respect."

"Now that power has fallen back into your hands, what does the Ba'ath party want to prove to the world?"

"When the world wakes up and studies one man and one man only. The way Saddam appears in pictures, books and statues, they will come to understand he has a theory. Once the power has returned to his hand, nothing will stop him from having Holy Babylon fall into his hands again from the Ottoman rule to Persia to Basra and Kuwait."

"Back up my friend! You are losing me." Watching and listening, I felt that Russell was on dangerous ground. Sa'adoun was unaccustomed to being interrupted and could become aggressive quickly.

"Where do you want me to begin, Russell? When the Persians occupied Basra for a five year period in the mid 1770s the trade route between India and the West was diverted to Kuwait creating an enormous economic boom matched only by the discovery of oil some 160 years later. Our problems began with the Dutch. Then at the end of the eighteenth century the entire responsibility for policing the Gulf was taken over by the British, then France, then everyone else. Suddenly everybody is running the show except us. Wealth and greed were rife until 1908." Sa'adoun took another sip of his drink, his speech now becoming even more slurred. Clearly he was having difficulty concentrating on uttering a perfect sentence and apparently he had lost control of his secretive nature.

"Maybe I should talk about nine eleven. Suddenly he stopped himself. I mean 1911."

"But what happened in 1908, my friend?" Russell asked.

We Arabs guessed that the oil discovered in Iran in 1908 would become the black gold of the future. Because of 1911, I mean Nine Eleven." Russell corrected Sa'adoun on the year,

"I mean 1911. On the advice of Winston Churchill, the Royal navy converted its ships from coal burning to oil. Do you get it now, Russell? The greed and power of the West took us over. They took our oil, however, they wanted to take it and at whatever price they could get away with. They took over our land for drilling and basically ruled our country."

"Yes, but what has that got to do with today?"

"It's not much different today, Russell. The oil and its production are still controlled by America and the Western powers. The oil at the Iraqi - Kuwait border is supposed to be shared equally. But it is being stolen from us and that's where nine eleven will come back." Russell ceased trying to correct Sa'adoun on the dates and allowed him to continue uninterrupted. "If we don't get the Arab nation back with oil power then we will convert the oil back to coal."

I could tell that Russell was speechless at Sa'adoun's drunken diatribe. I had heard stories about the massacres, but now my husband had stated that he was very much a part of it.

"What's the matter, Russell? That's what it takes to clean things up. There has to be a purge. Saddam knows what he is doing, you know. The entire thing was mostly filmed. It had to be done, Russell. It had to be done." It suddenly occurred to me that my husband was responsible for fingering the men in the hall who were picked to be executed.

"Besides, you haven't heard anything yet." Sa'adoun's bleary eyes fixed on Russell. "This was just cleaning up the government, not the country. Saddam will make sure that this country is not contaminated by Kurds, Shias, or Jews. I am sitting in the corner of this coming show. I have the best position on the third level and I will move up to the first to make it happen."

He made this awful statement without any embarrassment and yelled at me to refill his glass. With my back to him I partially filled it then spat into it and dropped in two ice cubes. I think my act caught Russell's eye for he looked at me with a wry smile. As I handed back his glass, Sa'adoun grabbed my arm. Drunken voiced he shouted,

"Sit down! Listen and learn what it takes to run this country and gain strength and power. Never mind, go to bed. You are too stupid to learn anything anyway."

Alone in my room I choked back tears, not on account of my husband's stinging remarks, but rather because I finally knew the depths of my husband's depravity. This night was a turning point for me, hearing my husband telling what more the Ba'ath regime intended to do in the future, not only to Iraqi citizens but other nations too. His drunken disclosures motivated me to once again try to help alleviate this terrible future situation.

Shortly after my husband's drunken revelations I witnessed first hand the depths of his depravity.

chapter fourteen

Having overheard there was to be an assault in the district of Fazil a short taxi ride from where we lived, I wished to learn more about it. Sa'adoun was not at home and I looked through the papers on his desk. There was no official directive since paper trails were often avoided. There was, however, a list of the names and addresses of the proposed victims, some of which I memorized.

Finally I had information I could act upon. However, the raid was to take place at midnight, less than two hours from now. I was unable to contact Shwan or any other member of my resistance group on such short notice. The only thing I could do was to go to Fazil and try to warn some of the people on the list and hopefully they could alert others.

I wondered how I could travel the streets of Fazil

without attracting attention to myself. Then I
remembered how one evening Sa'adoun had brought
home a smaller sized military uniform and instructed
me to wear it saying,

"If the women of Iraq are required to fight for our
country you will find yourself fighting alongside them."

It had been one of his cruel jokes, but I had gone along
with it and now the uniform could serve a real purpose.
Dressed in the uniform with my hair tucked into the
hat, I took a taxi to the outskirts of Fazil. With my heart
beating wildly, I stepped into the fray. Soldiers were
stealing furtively from corner to corner, gathering in sub
groups, and storming into houses. The sound of boots
resonated through the streets as though the entire Iraqi
army was on the move. The shouts of soldiers
interrogating the occupants spilled out into the streets.
Entire families were herded onto waiting buses to be
shipped out for slaughter or dumped at the Iranian
border.

I walked though the melee determined to warn those
not yet targeted. A soldier passed me and spoke in a
harsh tone,

"Come on! Pick up a weapon from the Zeal (military
truck) before the officer sees you without one." I grabbed
a rifle from the truck. The weight of it surprised me. I
proceeded down the block, then crouched down to watch
with the rifle across my knees. Numbness pounced upon
my body. In the middle of the block under the light of a
street lamp I saw my husband leading a team of soldiers
who were herding a group of terrified prisoners. Many
who had not followed the orders had tried to run.
Sa'adoun did not stand back as the beatings progressed.
Instead he led the brutal assault and used his heavy
boots to kick them viciously. This was not an arrest I
observed but wanton torture. I saw the look on Sa'adoun's
face. It was one of twisted pleasure. On the sidewalk

Russell MacMillan aimed his video camera into the fray, concentrating on Sa'adoun, in order to capture documentation of the raid. I felt utter shock at seeing Russell in this scenario; I had always assumed he filmed only in active war zones.

I felt nauseated. The man, whom I secretly loved and in part naively trusted, had the same blood on his hands as my husband. I remained in my crouching position and a soldier running past not seeing me there, knocked me over. My hair spilled out from my hat which was now lying on the ground. Leaving the rifle on the ground I forced myself to stand. A Mulazim (officer) stared at me. He began to approach me, first walking, then running. In utter panic I too began to run. I ran back the way I had come and the officer kept pace with me but could not catch up to me. I hurled myself into a darkened street and part way down I pressed my body up against a wall hoping he would pass without spotting me. I held my breath so I would make no sound. Sweat poured from my brow and my heart beat so wildly I could hear it.

The sound of moving feet ceased. I heard deep breathing behind my back. A hand grabbed my shoulder. It was now just a question of time before my life came to an end either at the hand that held me or at Sa'adoun Alwan's hand. A second hand closed tightly over my mouth. Hot breath made the hair on the back of my neck stand up.

"Don't make a sound. I'm here to help you." Shielding me with his rugged brown djellabas (coat), he maneuvered me toward a partially open door. Pushing me into a dark, narrow hallway he closed the door behind us without making a sound. A woman carrying a lighted candle, shielding the flame with her hand, emerged from an adjoining room. A number of children of various ages followed her into the hall, some of them whispering,

"What is going on?"

"I was watching from the roof and saw in the moonlight that this girl was in big trouble." The man who had brought me in said. "I saw a soldier following her so I distracted him and brought her inside for safety. Tell me, why is a young pregnant woman wandering the streets dressed in an army uniform?"

"I am wearing it for a disguise. I have come to warn the people here in Fazil that a raid was planned for tonight but I fear I have come too late." I began to tremble. This unknown young man had probably saved my life. As I began to calm down I explained.

"The soldiers are raiding this area to take citizens of Iranian background and remove them in trucks and buses. You may not know that before Ayatollah Kohmeni took over power in Iran, he was forced to leave the country by the Shah of Iran. Kohmeni made his home in the city of Najaf here in Iraq with the support of the Shia Muslims leader, Ayatollah Bakkar-Al-Saddr. In 1978 Iran and Iraq signed a treaty. When Saddam forced Kohmeni to leave Iraq, he went to France. Ali Hassan Majid hanged Al Saddr's family and supporters. Many Iranians, in fear of what might happen, have already left Iraq. Most of them were deported at the border. Saddam Hussein has ordered that any Iranians still in Iraq are to be located and deported as a threat to the Regime."

"Young lady, none of what you have said is a secret to us; we just pretend to be blind and mute. Tonight's actions have been going on for quite sometime."

Both the mother and her adult son tried to convince me to stay until daylight. But I had to get back. Either way my life was in grave danger. The mother offered me a long abaya and sandals in order that she and I could walk together along with a little boy, appearing like two harmless matrons making their way in the night, unlikely to attract any real attention. We passed the occasional soldier completing his area inspection. We walked steadily with lowered heads greeting each soldier that we passed. She led me through unfamiliar areas. It took an hour before I could hail a taxi to take me back to my home. The woman asked no explanations of me, but wished me well and left me. Thankfully my husband had not returned before me, so I took a long, hot, shower trying to scrub my body clean of the filth I had seen earlier. Settled in my clean warm bed I tried to erase the memories of the night. I realized what I had done had been with the best intentions. However, it had been a foolish gesture that could have jeopardized the unique position I commanded. By the same token I had seen the brutality with my own eyes. Never again would I look at the man whose child I carried and doubt his capability to inflict pain upon others. At five a.m. I heard his feet on the stairs. I shook in fear wondering if I had been seen and recognized.

Later that evening I was in my kitchen assisting my maid with the preparations for a big dinner Sa'adoun had organized. He had given me a guest list. Next to Sa'adoun sitting in the living room on his right was Ali Hassan al-Majid. He was the man who was in charge of the chemical weapon experiments. He was Saddam Hussein's cousin and had been responsible for the genocide in Kurdistan. He had been a non-commissioned officer when al-Bakr was in power. He had been captured by the Kurdish revolutionary and sentenced to hang, but an insider had been extremely well paid for his release. Next to him sat Russell MacMillan.

On Sa'adoun's left was Hassan Kamel, the regime's weapon control officer. Next to him sat Adnan Khayrula, Saddam's defense minister. He was Saddam's cousin and brother in law, his closest friend since childhood. He had become a threat to Saddam's power by earning a

good reputation with the Iraqi public. Next to him sat
the chief of police, Physal Brat, and Zead I Brahm, the
minister for health. Several foreign business men and
other Regime officers of lesser importance were seated
randomly around the room.

Usually most foreigners I met had subtle differences.
Normally I couldn't distinguish between Westerners, but
I never mistook Americans. Their physique and
confident overbearing manner always gave them away.
I knew the foreign guests were all Americans.

They were conducting a meeting with Sa'adoun and
Saddam's ministers. I tried to listen to the conversation
with my ear to the door. I could only glean small parts of
what was being said, but I gathered that they were
conferring over the prices for an important deal on some
kind of ingredients. From my listening post I heard one
of the American's say.

"What is the importance of this product to you? Why
do you need it so badly? What would you use it for?"
Sa'adoun sidestepped the question.

"Our country is not only offering oil. We have many
other products and natural resources. We have many
farms and this is the reason we need this particular
chemical. We may have other uses for it. That is no
concern to you or your country." Ali Majid stepped into
the conversation.

"So gentlemen, if you have no problem with that, we
are prepared to meet the agreed price per ton." Over a
few glasses of Arak the deal was done.

Fawzia, my maid, whom I had sent out to buy some
more fruit and deserts, returned and hearing her, I left
my listening position at the door and joined her in the
kitchen. I satisfied my craving for fresh dates and took
a tray of fruits into the room. I had hoped to hear more
but the room went silent until I left. About two hours
later the Americans left without accepting the

The Terrors of Toxins

The science behind Saddam's scary weapons
BY GEOFFREY COWLEY AND ADAM ROGERS

FOR ALL THE UPHEAVAL IT CAUSED, the last gulf war was essentially a regional dispute. The current crisis centers on a far bigger and scarier issue: the growing threat of chemical and biological weapons. Saddam Hussein has used chemical weapons on Iran and Kurdistan, and he has a long-running infatuation with germ-warfare agents as well. U.N. inspectors have established that Iraq produced some 8,000 liters of anthrax spores during the '80s—enough, by some estimates, to kill every person in the world. Saddam's forces also manufactured 20,000 liters of botulinum toxin, a deadly bacterial poison, and packed much of it into warheads. Saddam has the facilities and expertise to produce weapons of mass destruction—and he's pointedly blocking outside monitoring efforts.

International conventions have long prohibited the use of chemical weapons during war, and they bar any country from even making or acquiring biological weapons. But intelligence experts believe that 16 countries, including China, Libya and North Korea, maintain biological-warfare programs. Small-time terrorists are getting into the act as well. Aum Shinrikyo, the Japanese cult whose 1995 nerve-gas attack killed a dozen people on a Tokyo subway, was reportedly stockpiling anthrax and botulin toxin—two of the deadliest known germ-warfare agents—and U.S. extremists seem to be following the group's example. Federal law-enforcement officials say the volume of credible domestic threats has doubled in the past year; the FBI is currently investigating several dozen.

Modern chemical weapons date from World War I, which brought us chlorine gas and mustard gas, and they've grown ever more deadly. Just before World War II, German scientists looking for a better insecticide developed the first nerve gas, tabun, which led to deadlier agents called sarin and VX. All the nerve gases block the body's production of acetylcholinesterase, an enzyme that regulates the nerves controlling the action of certain muscles. When you lack acetylcholinesterase, your diaphragm tightens, you suffer convulsions and you die gasping for air. Sarin is deadly as long as it lingers in the air, but it dissipates quickly. VX is thicker and more persistent and makes a far more dangerous weapon. The substance is readily absorbed through any orifice; even a drop on the skin can kill within minutes. And because the key ingredients can be stored separately, it's easy to hide and transport.

All of Iraq's known chemical-weapons facilities were destroyed under U.N. supervision in 1994, but experts suspect that Saddam still has stockpiles of VX—as well as bombs, rockets and missiles capable of delivering the stuff. Civilian populations are largely defenseless against nerve gas, but there are ways to counter it. A drug called atropine can reverse the effects if administered promptly, and pretreatment with pyridostigmine can help shield the body, by sealing off acetylcholinesterase molecules. Some 400,000 U.S. troops took pyridostigmine as a precaution during the gulf war.

Chemical weapons are frighteningly easy to use. Because they're often toxic on contact, says Col. David Franz, commander of the U.S. Army Medical Research Institute of Infectious Diseases, "you can basically fly over and toss a bucket of this stuff out on troops." Germs and bacterial toxins are harder to preserve and deliver, and they tend to act more slowly. As a result, they're not very useful for stopping a line of infantry on the battlefield. Yet as instruments of terror, biological weapons may pose the greater threat. A few grains of the right toxin can cause more harm than a ton of nerve gas, and a test tube's worth of infectious material can start an epidemic that sustains itself. What's more, any laboratory equipped to make vaccines can easily churn out deadly biological material. "A U.N. inspector may think everything is fine if he visits on the day you're producing vaccine," Franz says. "A week later you can be producing biological-warfare agents." Here are some of the agents that Saddam, or a freelance extremist with access to a lab, could be cooking up:

Anthrax. Spores from the soil-dwelling bacterium Bacillus anthracis are very hardy and very dangerous. They survive for decades, even in harsh environmental conditions, and can enter the body through the stomach, the lungs or even small skin lesions. Warheads designed to disperse dried, ground anthrax spores into the air could wipe out large population centers and leave them uninhabitable. Iraq procured the anthrax organism from U.S. suppliers during the 1980s, and cultured it to produce crude bombs that were never used. Inhalation of just 8,000 anthrax spores can cause woolsorter's disease, a condition that textile workers sometimes contract from the wool or hides of infected sheep. The condition starts with fever and malaise, and progresses to respiratory failure, septic shock and, in many cases, meningitis. Penicillin, injected every two hours, can save an infected person if administered before major symptoms set in. But once the symptoms appear, death usually follows within 96 hours. Researchers have developed an experimental vaccine that involves six shots over 18 months followed by annual boosters. But it hasn't been fully tested in humans.

Botulinum toxin. Though it's technically a biological agent, botulinum toxin, or "botox," behaves more like a chemical weapon. This poison, which is produced by the bacterium Clostridium botulinum, doesn't cause infection, as anthrax does. Once it gets into your system, whether orally or through inhaled particles, it blocks nerve transmission, causing paralysis that can lead quickly to respiratory failure. Gram for gram, botulinum toxin is the deadliest substance known to science—15,000 times as powerful as VX and 100,000

counterparts used one to assassinate defector Georgi Markov in London. In 1969 the Iraqis tried to build weapons that would release ricin into the atmosphere, but their efforts apparently failed.

Smallpox. Vaccines finally eradicated this ancient scourge in the late 1970s. Officially, there are only two samples of the virus left on the planet (one in the United

Saddam could repeat what he did to the Kurds in 1988—deploy deadly chemical weapons

Tailor-Made for Mass Destruction

Just how much mayhem could a few planes carrying a small payload of chemical or biological weapons cause? On a clear, breezy night, they could spray a sleeping city in minutes—and kill thousands, even millions. What 300 pounds of the leading killers can do:

WEAPON	WHAT IT DOES	INGREDIENTS	FALLOUT
Anthrax	Black pustules, vomiting, fever and suffocation in 2 to 4 days	Inhalable spore from bacteria. Can lie dormant for decades.	Sprayed over a city the size of Omaha, it would kill up to 2.5 million
Botox	Attacks nervous system. Causes respiratory failure in 2 to 12 hours.	Toxin produced by botulism bacteria; Iraq first acquired from U.S.	Could kill up to 40,000 in an area the size of the Mall of America
VX	Paralysis; involuntary muscles eventually strangle vital organs	A phosphine oxide nerve gas 100 times deadlier than sarin	Sprayed over a site the size of Disneyland, it would kill up to 12,500

SOURCES: RAYMOND A. ZILINSKAS, PH.D.; ADAPTED FROM OFFICE OF TECHNOLOGY ASSESSMENT, 1993

times worse than sarin. The effects depend on the dose. Ventilators can usually keep a victim alive until the paralysis passes, but recovery can take months. And though an antidote made from horse serum can prevent illness if administered early, some people are violently allergic to it.

Ricin. This toxin comes from castor-bean plants, and concentrated solutions can be very nasty. Inhaled ricin is inevitably fatal in animals, and there's no antidote. The Soviet secret police developed ricin-firing umbrellas in the 1970s, and their Bulgarian

States and one in Russia). But intelligence officials suspect that several governments, including Iraq's, may be cultivating it as a weapon. Smallpox is an airborne agent that one could easily spray into a crowded public space. But unlike measles or chickenpox, it kills a third of its victims. When European settlers unleashed it on the Americas in the 16th century, tens of millions of previously unexposed people died. Now that we've curbed the disease, and stopped vaccinating against it, we're as vulnerable as they were. ∎

If the U.S. does take military action against Iraq, 58% believe a strike would make Saddam less of a threat to the rest of the world; 33% disagree

iso. ZYKLON-6   which germany used on   SEPTEMBER 24, 1997 NEWSWEEK **37**

A document showing types of chemicals sold to Iraq used to make chemical weapons. Their use experimented on the Kurdish population.

hospitality of dinner in our home. The Arab guests and Russell stayed behind talking to Sa'adoun and al-Majid while I occupied my usual place at my listening post outside the door. My husband and al-Majid expressed anger at the departed Americans. They were completely unaccustomed to being questioned. Sa'adoun repeated,

"What has it got to do with them what we do with anything?" The Americans are ignorant and uncultured. They are the whores of Saudi Arabia. They support their terrorists, investments, and wealth like they are not aware of the facts. America wouldn't be the power that it is without Saudi Arabia." For the first time in the meeting I heard Russell's voice.

"So what have the Saudis got that you don't so that they can be your whores just as easily?" Ali Majid spoke up,

"They will one day. You see we make a little investment in America, and. in return; we let them make a bigger investment here, just the way they run the show in Kuwait and Saudi. Wait until one of our Saudi brothers gets upset; then things will not be so pretty." Russell interjected,

"America already has plenty of oil." Sa'adoun answered him,

"Not enough. Never enough. What do you think this meeting is about? You see America has been trying for the longest time to install a pipeline in the Caspian Sea through Kurdish territory which is partly Iran, Turkey, and North Iraq, through us to the Persian Gulf which is Arab Gulf. But war is everywhere. Besides Russia would not allow it; forget Iran. So America has two choices, either lay a pipeline from the Caspian Sea through Turkmenstan, Afghanistan and Pakistan to the Gulf. This requires the consent of many nations asking them to sign contracts or arranging the selling of their chemicals to us. Then there will not be a place on this earth called

Kurdistan and then the pipeline will come through easily. At least America will think so but that is not what is going to happen. We will get the ingredients, and we will put the pipeline through ourselves using French and British engineering assistance just like all the other high tech implements they have already built for us."

My knees felt weak, and bile came to my throat hearing of the appalling plans to eradicate Kurdistan and my people. Sweat came to my brow and I wondered what I could possibly do to stop it. I struggled hard not to vomit, but managing to contain myself. I heard Russell begin to speak.

"No, America would not go along with the eradication of a nation. They are hard-headed businessmen but would not do it on the blood of a people." Ali Majid responded to Russell's outburst.

"It's cheap blood and wouldn't cost America anything unless whoever we are dealing with thinks so." Sa'adoun interjected,

"Besides we are not fools. We are the heart of the Middle East. If we fall into America's hands they will have control of us all. This is not about America. This is about us and our Arab nation brothers." Ali Majid spoke,

"Wait. Time will allow us to prove it all with every plan we have. We control money and investments. Now let's get back to what we are here for."

There arose some disagreement in the room. Adnan Khayrula spoke,

"I am against this plan and the rest of the regime's plan that you have for our country: for the Kuwait war, for the Arab nations supporting terror, and God knows what else." Zead I Brahm gathered courage from hearing Khayrula speak his mind.

"I too am afraid of the dangers of this product, the results we might face by using it and the effect on generations of Iraqis to follow us. It could create deformities in children, brain disease, things we may not even know about. This is madness." Hassan Kummel interrupted him,

"There would be accusations from the international community; they would check us out before we could eliminate them." Physal Brat the police chief reaffirmed his agreement and said,

"Speaking as chief of police I say this is not going to succeed. We cannot win this war or any other war. Nor can we control the world of Arab Nations by doing this." Ali Majid spoke,

"I assure you and the others that you are being naïve in your concerns. Who do you think helped to put this regime in power and put Saddam into his chair? After all, it is America who is controlling this war. They have given us the maps and the targets within Iran to allow us to win this war. We have money, they have the technology. My brother, do your homework! If we don't destroy the one we fear the most, how can we go on to succeed with our plan?" Physal Brat asked.

"Whatever your plan is, you should explain it so we can all make sense of it together, Brother!" Al Majid retorted.

"You are too small a minority on our list to know or even understand the plan of the Ba'ath regime. Besides, the decision has been made long before you were invited to this meeting. There is nothing left to discuss so you might as well all go home."

The men left leaving Sa'adoun and Russell alone while I sat quietly in my corner of the room. Sa'adoun expressed puzzlement at the questions and disagreements among his closest officials.

"Russell, my friend, everything will come given time."

"Sa'adoun, my friend, you have been sharing too much information. Thank you for honoring me with your trust."

"Don't worry, Russell. You will never leave this

country or my side." Russell did not respond.

"One day, Russell, you will understand my sense of humor."

"I think I understand. Anyway I'm not looking to leave this country either." Sa'adoun stood up to stretch and noticed me sitting in my corner with a newspaper.

"Look at her, Russell. Finally she is learning how to cook. How it is a girl can grow up to be a woman without having learned to feed her family."

"But you spoil her, Sa'adoun. She does not need to learn how to cook or do housework."

"When I first met her it was her political savvy that attracted me. With her talk of politics and capitalism I had thought I might be able to use her politically by using her active mind and strength for the regime's benefit and put her thinking in the right direction. However, she has turned out to be quite stupid." In a further attempt to belittle me in front of Russell he said,

"Why don't you tell us, Najat, if you could make any changes in this country what would they be? You are so ignorant of politics." I did not have to search my mind for a topic and responded confidently,

"I would provide a healthy lifestyle for children. I would let them be children so they wouldn't grow up the enemy of adults. Children are bored in this country. We don't provide them with anything to stimulate their talents, creativity, and things to challenge their age. They only have school and that's not enough. Add the horror of war and before you know it these children are indoctrinated and taught to be soldiers without ever understanding the meaning of war."

"Would you like to add anything else before you bore Russell to death?"

"But I'm listening to her Sa'adoun." Having the opportunity to continue, I asked.

"So how do children live in America? Are they the

last resource of your society?"

"No, Najat. Absolutely not! Everything is dedicated to children, even before they are brought into the world. We value life from the points of medical, clothing, nutrition. We provide playgrounds and recognize children's needs from the talented to the untalented. We try to steer them in the right direction and we let them challenge the basic rules of society, for every new generation are the protectors of our past and future." Sa'adoun spoke with scorn,

"It seems so perfect. It's a perfect world you people live in. So tell me. are there no broken homes or children desperate for love and family union? Is there no child abuse or molestation, no rape or killing of children in America?" I was unfamiliar with the term molestation and did not know what it meant.

"You are talking about social crimes, Sa'adoun, Not the lives we give to our children." Sa'adoun responded, "Shortly I will show you the Koran which we live by. It outlines the map for our children's future and new generations showing what they can do. You are right, they do have amazing imaginations, thought, and courage. Forget about the strength and power they would have." Russell asked me, "By the way Najat, are you eating properly to feed the baby?" I nodded. He went on to say, looking at my husband, "I have taken the liberty of ordering some books from back home in America which specialize in pregnancy and the care of babies for Najat. I hope they arrive before she delivers the child," Sa'adoun answered Russell sarcastically,

"In this country women have given birth for centuries as easily as a dog delivers pups. So there is no problem. Besides, Iraq is the birthplace of mankind and civilization. Education began here and there are more books read by more people than ever could be read in America. Schooling here is free for all children, as is university to those who want it."

"Sa'adoun, please understand that I had no wish to insult the people's talents or Najat. The gift of the books is just our way of showing a little generosity in your happiness." Russell's amazing talent for diplomacy in the face of my husband's ignorance and rudeness never ceased to surprise me. Picking up his glass Russell proposed a toast.

"Here is to your continued happiness and to the expected safe arrival of your first healthy child."

"I'm not worried about the safe arrival. I have already made firm plans for his life. He will go to the Azamiya School. You know about it, Russell. It has the most sophisticated system and bunkers built by the Americans that offer protection against a possible nuclear attack. Also it is under the protection of Jehaz al-Amn Khass with all staff members selected by the secret service. No one can enter without high level clearance or proper authorization. Excuse me for a minute." My husband left the room and I took the opportunity to say,

"I must apologize for my husband's rudeness, Russell." He smiled with a sense of high regard for me, suggesting everything was just fine. No other words passed between us, but a strong feeling of mutual admiration caused my surging blood to warm my face.

Sa'adoun returned carrying the Koran and proceeded to unwrap it from its cover of green silk as he sat down next to Russell.

"Excuse my lack of protocol, Sa'adoun. I understood that you are supposed to wash and pray before opening the Koran? Also I understood one was supposed to be alcohol free at the time?"

"Don't you dare turn Shia on me! Besides, religion is what the individual wants to make of it."

Moistening his finger, Sa'adoun turned over a few pages.

"Look at this tree. Each branch gives you different ages of children, their abilities, and we can stimulate those abilities to make of them what we want them to be."

"Would you translate it for me?"

"Not now, Russell. Perhaps sometime when we are in the privacy of my office. Najat is not religious. In fact, I think, she is against it." I studied Russell's face as he looked at the book. He seemed to be uncomfortable and in my opinion Sa'adoun was not showing him religious Arabic writing or his expression would not have been so rapt. I was convinced that my husband was showing him something else. A sudden change came over Russell's face and he excused himself saying,

"My kind and generous host I do believe I have eaten and drunk too much. I need to take a long walk to appease my system." As always I had been happy to see Russell arrive and sad to see him leave. I sat awaiting whatever punishment Sa'adoun might dispense since I may have said too much and offended him. I never really knew what to expect of him, but he brushed his hand across my swollen tummy and went upstairs without a word.

I learned later that four men had been put to death at a later date for voicing opposition to the plans of the Ba'ath regime. One of them, Zead I Brahm was hanged. The chief of police, Physal Brat, was shot and his twenty eight staff members were also hanged. Adnan Khayrula perished in a rigged helicopter accident arranged by Saddam Hussein. I did not receive information on the fourth man's method of death.

A month went by after that evening and I had not seen Russell at all during that time. I felt empty and I suffered great anxiety. Russell had spoken his mind about chemical purges and I felt sure that he had already been put to death. The thought of it brought tears to my eyes. My pregnancy progressed and I found that I tired easily. Rather than subject myself to the noises of the day, I rested and took my daily walk in the early shadows of evening in the cool of our courtyard. Our maid had usually left for her home, and I strolled in silence without fear of interruption. But I never once let my mind swerve from my purpose. After my stroll, I washed my face, brushed my hair, and changed my clothes.

I had almost convinced myself that Russell was dead, but still I kept my eyes on the door and the hope in my heart that Russell would enter. I dared not ask Sa'adoun why he had stopped bringing my friend to the house, for I feared for Russell's life should I show too much concern. The not knowing led me to even more anxiety and sleep loss. There would be some who judge me for having the feelings I did for Russell, but I craved the sound of his voice and his easy smile. I yearned for his presence, I wished I could touch him and to experience his love. There existed a charge of electricity between us when he sat in the same room as I. While I could never be sure he shared the same feelings, I hoped that he did. Having to live with and endure the beast who was my husband, Russell was a dream that helped me cope with the reality of my life. At the times when these thoughts invaded my mind, I could only allow them to stay for a while. Then I had to wrench myself back to reality. Then I would blush and feel embarrassed, for I had made the vows of marriage to Sa'adoun.

As time passed, without further word of him, I wondered if my husband or Al-Majid had ordered his death or if he had been killed covering one of the war zones. The not knowing deeply troubled me and the worry of it began to affect my health. I could not sleep well and I neglected my diet. For most of the time I forgot about the innocent life growing within me and upon thinking of the child I forced myself to eat something. My evenings were spent in lonely silence except when

Sa'adoun was at home, and I sat with him as he glued his eyes to the television set watching the mass slaughter of soldiers on both sides of the conflict. Since the war coverage was piped directly into our home, Sa'adoun watched the carnage hour after hour.

I became sickened of the constant visions of conflict even though I had been raised in the atmosphere of war. Suffering in many forms became the lot of most Iraqis. Lack of money prevented the citizens from obtaining basic food items. Prized possessions were sold to the better advantaged members of society and the poor became poorer or destitute. The long-suffering society read articles in the daily press about the "Hero of Iraq" Saddam Hussein and his accomplishments. State television showed him proudly detailing the scorecard of war, how many thousands of the enemy had been killed and wounded. Often he pinned gold medals on his generals at the Palace of the Conference for the country to see his glory. Hundreds of others were executed by the Revolutionary Court.

It seemed in this juncture of my life that the war had gone on forever. The wholesale disappearances and assassinations appeared to be endless. Whether one was Kurdish, Shia, Iranian, or Iraqi made little difference. Everyone was victimized. There were not enough doctors, nurses, or medical supplies to care for the victims of the war or to aid the sick. When our nation's blood supplies were severely depleted, it was reported that the regime used Kurdish orphans and prisoners to provide blood for transfusions. Prisoners were delivered to the medical school and laboratories for experimentation, and the children were transported to the Midseris Land Hospital. Their blood was drained from their bodies these in turn then dumped into the Euphrates River to rot and be devoured by the fish.

By now even the wealthier members of society were

losing their homes. Salaries were no longer being earned. They were replaced by gifts from the government in the name of God and war. Every day new rules and pronouncements emanated from the palace, further confusing the people with complicated or subliminal warnings. Those daring to speak a single word against Saddam's rule found it would be the last word they ever spoke.

The history of my country has been re-written frequently to meet the specifications of the current ruler and in this present time changed to celebrate Saddam Hussein as Iraq's Hero, Savior, Warrior, God. The face of Saddam Hussein filled the television screens and billboards. It was painted on blank walls and depicted on flags and banners. His image adorned book covers, clothing. No goods were without Saddam's picture plastered upon them.

From my position of viewing the inside and outside situation within our country, I could not get my head around the level of co-operation that Saddam Hussein received from other governments around the world. I was by no means naïve about the economics of war. I was fully aware of the profits available in the war business to outside countries from the sales of arms, ammunition, chemicals, and a multitude of other war related items. Surely these foreign suppliers saw what was happening in our country when they watched the international news, and yet the blood soaked trade continued.

Saddam found it easy to procure all kinds of equipment, military, and otherwise. Weapons and technology including lethal gasses and deadly strains of bacteria were acquired. He placed orders for anthrax, smallpox, plague, and the items were shipped regularly into Iraq and stored and maintained by the foreign suppliers. It is beyond the realm of common sense that the foreign governments and suppliers did not know what Saddam Hussein intended to use them for. I could not help but ask myself why? Did the western powers hope to annihilate the entire Arab world for purposes I was unaware of?

chapter fifteen

Through their television and the press, it appeared that the world watched the happenings in the Middle East dispassionately. From my vantage point it seemed the outside world did not care about the death and destruction. I heard all these points discussed in my home. According to my husband, the end of the conflict was just part of the plan the Ba'ath party had in mind for the country.

Sa'adoun called a meeting of his military cohorts at our home, but at this gathering a new face graced the group. Abu Jamsher stood much taller than the other men in the room. Abu Jamsher in traditional Kuwaiti dress was an emissary from Kuwait. He wore a long pure, white silk Disdasha with a matching silk Agala accentuating his black mustache and eyebrows. His skin was whitish and clean looking unlike the tanned faces surrounding him. When the group were behind closed doors in the library, I took up my listening post at the door. Sa'adoun made it perfectly clear to Abu Jamsher that Iraq intended to use force to bring about changes in Kuwaiti policy.

"Our attack upon Kuwait is no longer an option! Your country is stealing oil out of the Ramela oil wells on our border. There is an agreement that we share equally the oil from that source, and Kuwait is selling the resource at less than our agreed price. You have betrayed the Arab nations and have stolen from us. We should be united!"

"Sir, you have got it all wrong. This is just business, trading, importing and exporting. We are using technology like any other country on the planet." With a sneer Sa'adoun answered,

"You use your expertise to steal from us to buy Western technology, Abu Jamsher. You, like us, buy weapons from the West. We have developed the technology to build our own and now we have become experts. We now have the capability to blow up Kuwait in a breath and we can flatten New York in seconds so that they will never make another business decision in that city." Flustered by Sa'adoun's accusations, Jamsher responded,

"Sir, the Kuwaitis are developers; you are warmongers. You are not only a threat to Kuwait you are a threat to the whole Middle-East." My husband answered him,

"We are fully aware of the American support and technology that is pumping out more oil in one day than we do in a month. You have also signed a contract stating that America will take that oil for the next forty years. Kuwait belongs to us. It is a part of Iraq and it will be returned to us as a part of Iraq again." One of the other military men spoke up,

"Not only are you stealing from us so that we are

bankrupt, but then you lend us back our own money. How very ironic. Therefore, we will just invade you and get even." Abu Jamsher responded,

"I will cooperate with you. I will give you information on all the major powers involved, but I cannot prevent how much oil is coming out of the ground on our side of the border."

"If you want to save Kuwait from a bloodbath I suggest you find a way to stop it before we make you drink the oil instead of selling it," Sa'adoun snarled.

"How can I fight and stop a larger force than our own without telling the other powers of Iraq's intentions. I am begging you, do not bring war and hunger to our people. We cannot afford to fight back."

Sa'adoun laughed. "Of course not." With his voice raised in arrogance he asked,

'What is your population in Kuwait? Two million eight hundred thousand? Many of them are Palestinians. One thousand are the king's family, one and a half million are foreign workers and you have only several thousand soldiers and a few marines." I heard Sa'adoun's fist strike the table top with a loud crash. Then his voice filled the house as he yelled,

"So make your choice here and now! You know Kuwait inside and out and you know all about the oil production. Save your country, it's up to you!" Abu Jamsher must have realized that Sa'adoun had put him solely in charge of his country's future and that his life at this moment was in question.

"Perhaps you wish to kill me?"

"Not yet, Abu Jamsher. I am giving you a month no more, no less. Come back with what we want and you will be welcome."

Given the volatility of the discussions, I felt that Sa'adoun might kill the visitor in our home. I tried my best to hear but I lived with the fear of being discovered listening at the door. Without warning I heard the front door squeak as it opened. I moved away from the library door and saw Russell MacMillan enter the house. His bedraggled appearance startled me and my words of welcome were,

"Russell, you look terrible! What have you been up to?" I felt a great joy and relief to see him after such a long absence. My fears of his demise vanished instantly, my secret feelings surged forward, and I wanted to hug him and to feel his heartbeat against my own. My lips trembled and my eyes moistened. I could tell by the look in his eyes that Russell understood and I felt sure he too would have liked to hug me, but as always, the fear of tradition and my husband's unpredictability created a high wall between us. I stood back and looked at him. Generally Russell exuded the well fed and robust American. Today his face looked gaunt and pale and dark rings underlined his normally bright eyes. He reeked of stale sweat and I had the feeling he had just come through some kind of battlefield nightmare.

Sa'adoun must have heard my voice for he burst out of the library door and saw Russell.

"You look like Hell, Russell. What have you been up to?" He led Russell into the library to introduce him to Abu Jamsher. Then Abu Jamsher walked out of the library heading for the front door with Sa'adoun. As they left Sa'adoun pointed at Russell and said,

"America is supporting us too." He spoke to one of the officers, "Do not leave his side." Looking at Russell he said. "How can you turn a donkey into a lion? My apologies, Russell. Where was I? Yes, you do look like Hell."

"I expect that I look more rested than I feel right now. I have covered a lot of ground recording the battles in regions that have only sand, dust, and smoke. It is not easy to look at, but for now I need to get cleaned up and enjoy some sleep."

"Yes, you look like you need to unwind." Sa'adoun turned to me and ordered,

"Run Russell a bath and supply him with clean towels." Russell nodded in gratitude as he said, "I have become accustomed to your hospitality and know better than to insult my host. Therefore, I shall gratefully accept. Please know I shall never survive in my own culture again. You spoil me, my friends." After a long soak he ventured out of the bathroom wearing clothing belonging to Sa'adoun. I smiled at him noting the pants that were much too short and shirts that barely reached his wrists. My husband had taken over the bathroom so Russell and I were temporarily alone. I had a huge smile on my face from the sheer joy of seeing Russell alive and having returned to my home. At this moment in time nothing mattered but him.

"May I make you a meal, Russell?" He declined saying he had already eaten but offered me his thanks. I placed my hand upon my enlarged stomach.

"Has your health been all right, Najat? Tell me what are you thinking right now?"

"I must find a way to raise my child away from this place. I have been trying to think of the way to accomplish a healthy life for my baby without provoking my husband and more importantly without confusing the child. Also I have other pressing matters to deal with."

"I have faith, Najat, that you will make a wonderful mother. Even in the face of fire you will find a way. You are a smart and astute woman." I heard my husband coming from the bathroom and so I stood to go to my bed.

"I bid you goodnight, Russell."

"Good night, Najat." It was always the same. We both blushed, my heart quickening, my eyes saying things my lips could not. I know Russell felt the same things I did, but we had no language we could use but our eyes, given the circumstances we were in.

I fell asleep listening to his voice downstairs trying to separate the sound of it from Sa'adoun's and awoke about midnight hearing the two of them chatting in much louder voices. Unable to sleep any longer I crept to the stairs to listen. It became obvious that they were drinking and Sa'adoun regaled Russell with all kinds of stories. I heard Sa'adoun say,

"Initially this was a difficult war to take seriously. We all thought it wouldn't even last six months." Russell asked,

"What was the real reason the regime wanted to invade Iran?"

"To make the story short, Russell, we wanted to challenge the treaty of 1958 promising that Iran would give us four wealthy lands; Tumbel Kubra, Tumbel Sukhera, Zaen Kaus, and Zerbateu. We signed that treaty in 1972 and the promise was kept until Khomeini took power. The Shah wanted Kohmeni returned to Iran in order to administer the death penalty. This is where we made a serious mistake.

Khomeini's followers are Hezbollah. They have a passion for their faith but they not only have faith. If the Middle East doesn't wake up they can possibly control all of us. You see we don't have a constitution and law like you do so society and religion rule the people's behavior and dedication. So Hezbollah or other religious groups use it to control others. Some by force and violence, some by peaceful means. So you see we should have just returned him. Under Khomeini Iran was in political turmoil, so we took the opportunity to invade and take our four lands back. The Western powers assisted us with full information and weapons in order that they could continue pumping out the oil they had paid and contracted for. Now it became everybody's war. All the Western powers sat down at the table with us. We drank, ate, and talked together in a civilized manner. Kohmeni is bad for everyone's business. By now you know how we run the business.

I did not hear Russell say much but his few questions were probing and bold. I felt grateful that my husband slurred his speech and spoke freely where he might otherwise not have.

"Are you saying, Sa'adoun, that we Americans helped place the Ba'ath party and Saddam in power?"

"The Americans, along with England, Sweden, Germany, the C.I.A., and others put us on the road to Iran."

"Are you making accusations or do you have proof and facts?"

"My friend, do you think we are stupid? We had it all figured out. First we attack Iran. We destroy them and ourselves. Kuwait will stay safe and install the American puppet. Now the Persian Gulf traffic will be free to come and go. We are the center of the Middle-East and will be blamed. Then we will fall into the hands of America and America's economy will be safe. America will be safe."

"You have totally lost me, Sa'adoun. Why would America do this when they could have friendly relations?"

"If all this falls into the hand of America they would not need to be the whore of Saudi Arabia." Russell began to laugh,

"We have had this discussion before, my friend." My husband joined him in laughter. The two of them couldn't stop. With each fresh drink Sa'adoun's speech grew even more slow. As a man accustomed to being in control, he remained quite articulate in spite of the drink. Finally Russell asked,

"What do you mean?"

"Russell, what do you know about what you guys call Muslim terrorism?" Russell did not respond. "Ha ha, obviously not very much. Saudi Arabia is run by the king's family. They are a very rich country. Most countries are in debt or extend their budgets. The Saudis always have a huge surplus so they have billions of dollars to spend. America wants oil and the Saudi's invest the money gained from its sale in America. There is a powerful Muslim group known as the Wahabe. In exchange for Saudi oil money, they allow the king's family to stay in power. Both Saudis and the Wahabe have what they want. The White House lobby in Washington is packed with Saudis. They occupy positions of power in diplomacy and investment. Some are employed by the C.I.A. Tell me, Russell, has America ever questioned who these people really are? I can tell you that many of them are students of the Wahabe, the mother of all terrorist groups. They give birth to terrorism every minute. They are rich, they are powerful, and every country tolerates them. Believe me they are a huge threat to America and they know it. So we can leave everything just the way it is, or we can turn the tables and make America fall into our hands as I have told you before."

If you have all this information on paper, Sa'adoun and can back it up with facts just as you have described it to me. I will personally take the information to the Western powers."

"Don't be naïve, Russell. You will be killed long before you arrive wherever you think you will go."

"You would do that to me, the one who calls you his friend?"

"No, not personally. But you know too much, Russell. Even if you didn't know these things before, and I assume you did, you are much safer here in this country where I can protect you."

I heard the chairs move and guessed they were

calling it a night. I slipped back into my bed and digested what I had just heard. Sa'adoun was correct; we are all naïve in this game where thousands lose their lives annually. I tried to think of what documents I might lay my hands on in order to alert the West to come to save us. But I realized that since the West and Iraq ate, drank, and negotiated at the same table, there would be little chance that a message from a Kurdish woman would be read and even less that it would be acted upon. I wondered if America knew that the regime had practiced genocide on the people of Kurdistan. Would it make a difference if they did? Were they really selling the chemicals to the Ba'ath regime to clean up the Kurdish nation to make oil investments? No! That can't be happening. This is all the Ba'ath's plan, not the Americans. But one day they would make the world point the finger at America and manipulate us all.

I lay still, unable to sleep. My baby moved his tiny limbs and I could feel him, adding to my discomfort about what I had just heard. I heard the guest room door closing and my husband staggering up the stairs. He flopped into bed beside me and fell immediately into a drunken sleep. When I felt completely sure he slept soundly, I crept from the bed and slipped barefoot downstairs. I heard Russell's loud snores as I crept toward Sa'adoun's study. I turned on the light. On the bench beside his desk I saw his open briefcase. I glanced through a number of documents of little value. Then I found one that made me gasp, so I memorized it.

Memo: March 15. 1300 hours.

I have authorized Special Forces to test chemical missiles in specified northern

Regions. Target one. Town of Halabja.

Testing will be conducted March 18th between the hours of 0700 and 0900. All military personnel are instructed to remain clear of the target area for 48 hours after impact. These missiles contain substances that may result in serious injury or death. Signed Saddam Hussein.

Shaken, I crumpled into a chair. Halabja! Oh my God! I did not expect this development so soon after the chemicals had been purchased to get rid of the Kurds from the region just as they had discussed it.

I felt horrified as I read the words. They were typewritten on a sheet of paper. So cold. So simple an instruction concerning the deaths of so many innocents. A memory surged from my childhood, of bodies yellowed and bloated, disfigured and decomposing. The yellow fluids mixed with blood oozing from facial orifices the entire village smelling of death. It was a memory I could never put behind me. I regained my composure. March 18 was the day after tomorrow. I realized I was probably the only person outside of the highest government officials and leading military men in the Halabja area that had seen this document. I carefully replaced the papers in the briefcase. I knew I had to do something, but what?

I heard a sound from outside the door. In fear of my life I turned out the light and stood behind the door barely daring to breathe. I heard the door handle turn. I stood motionless. The door burst open. The pale light from the window showed the figure of a man holding a raised club or some such weapon. He stepped inside swinging the club wildly. As he ventured further into the room I made a dash around the open door. An arm grabbed me and hurled me to the floor with a loud crash. As the intruder tried to pin me down, he felt the roundness of my stomach.

"Najat?" He exclaimed. It was Russell's voice. He loosened his grip on me and I struggled to rise. "Good God, Najat, I almost killed you! I thought you were an intruder. Are you all right?"

"Yes, Russell. But I have to get out of here. Go! Go!" I fled for the living room and hurled myself on the couch and curled up into the fetal position. I heard Sa'adoun bounding down the stairs. Then he entered the room holding a handgun.

"What's going on down here? Is it the baby? Are you ok, Najat?" I nodded vigorously. "Then I will call a doctor."

"Please don't leave me right now, Sa'adoun Stay with me. I really don't need a doctor." In a rare move of compassion for the baby he came to the couch and knelt down. Frankly I did not want his attentions, but I knew that Russell had not left the study.

"So what is the matter, Najat? Is the baby coming already?" He looked at me expecting an answer but his eyes indicated he was likely too drunk or in a state of hangover to understand what he was trying to do or say.

"Did the phone wake you, Sa'adoun? It was a message from home. My father is very ill. the news made me feel ill and I stumbled and made a noise."

"Your father? What happened, an accident?"

"I don't know, Sa'adoun. I don't know. They didn't say but I have to go to his side as soon as I can before he dies." Changing his tone from compassion to one of authority he said,

"You are not going anywhere! There is my child to consider. The only place you are going to is back to bed." I felt nauseated as a result of my narrow escape from being discovered spying. I forced myself to go back upstairs unaided, for I didn't want to take the chance of not being allowed to leave in the morning. Lying in bed, with Sa'adoun sitting on the edge, he said,

"I will send the maid to accompany you if you feel up to traveling." I was able to convince him that Fawzia would be horrified to go on the road to Sulaymania, and that I would be alright traveling unaccompanied.

"Najat, you must be very careful. I have no wish to

chance losing my child over your visit to your father."
Sa'adoun dropped off to sleep, and I lay awake with my
mind churning about how I could stop the planned mass
slaughter. I only prayed that there would be enough time
for me to warn the people of Halabja and for all the Kurds
to run from certain death, but where could they run?
My mind raced for a solution as my heart beat wildly. I
questioned myself knowing that night travel was
forbidden this left me in a state of anxiety.

I realized that my quick thinking response about my
father's imminent death was not the wisest statement I
could have made. It would be so easy for my husband to
check up on the situation himself. I wondered too, if
Sa'adoun had become suspicious of me. After all he had
basically given me permission to travel into an area close
to where the bombing would occur. Halabja was only a
hundred kilometers from Sulaymania. He must have
known that. Also he knew what chemicals were involved
in the planned attack. I could not help but wonder if he
thought I was expendable. Perhaps he considered his
wife and child to be cheap Kurdish blood.

Morning arrived, Sa'adoun awoke.

"Do you still intend to visit your father, Najat?" he
said rubbing his eyes of sleep.

"Yes. I love my father and I must go, for it may be the
last chance I have to be with him."

"Then I shall arrange for a taxi to take you. How long
will you stay at your parent's house?"

"I can't say at the moment, it depends on my father's
health." I went down to the kitchen while Sa'adoun took
a shower. Russell stepped into the kitchen and
whispered,

"I have put all the documents back where they belong,
Najat. He will suspect nothing, no damage has been
done." Fawzia walked in from the garden and placed
fresh flowers on the table where breakfast had already

been prepared preventing any further conversation between Russell and me. Then Sa'adoun strode into the kitchen.

"Good morning, Sa'adoun. I thought that you would be at work by now."

"Good morning to you, Russell. I trust you slept through the noise last night?"

"Noise? What noise? I slept like a log." I was astounded at Russell's quick response in order to protect me and my activities. I wondered how much he had guessed about me. Who was he really, and why he was even here in Iraq working for the government? Was he a Western spy who had wangled his way into an incredible source of information? Certain things seemed to point to it, but I could not be sure.

"I'm afraid we made some noise in the night. Najat had a phone call saying her father was dying and she tumbled making a noise. In fact it woke me and I came down to investigate."

"I thought I heard the phone ring but you know how it is when you are overtired and have had a few drinks." Russell had covered for me again but why? Could I trust him with my safety?

chapter sixteen

"I'm sorry to hear about your father, Najat. I hope everything turns out for the best. I have tons of work to do, my dear friends. Thank you for your hospitality."

"Oh, by the way, Russell, I need to get the rest of the tapes and pictures from you. I will see you soon." Within minutes of Russell's leaving I was ready to go. Sa'adoun came from his study to wish me a safe journey as my taxi waited outside.

"You had better be sure that this journey does not harm my child. Call to let me know when you will be coming home." Without a further word he turned and went back into his study.

My taxi traveled through the streets of the city. When I got out at the Nahza bus station a sudden cramping gripped my stomach and I doubled over in pain. I thought, For the love of God not now, not this day when

I have lives to save. The pain eased and a taxi had stopped by the curb.

"Driver, I wish you to take me to find a telephone? It is urgent. After I have made a phone call I want you to take me to Sulaymania."

"I will drive you around until we find one." We found a place with telephones but I could not reach Shwan or anyone closer to Halabja to pass on the message.

The taxi was stopped and checked at each checkpoint on the road. I was questioned each time but my high profile identification and my pregnancy caused suspicion. At one checkpoint I was instructed to drop my dress to see if the pregnancy was real or if I were hiding something. I refused and told them to contact my husband for permission. They laughed at me and so in order to proceed I had to obey the guard. At any other time I would have insisted the guard contact my husband, Sa'adoun Alwan. But because of the dire emergency of my journey, I complied with his demand. I felt embarrassed and cheap. My face flushed as he looked at my bare belly. Through a mouthful of bad teeth he told me to, "Pick up my dress and cover my ugly body."

I had always been respectful for the feelings of others but after the long delay, the urgency of my journey caused me to forget, and I'm afraid I chastised the driver for not going fast enough.

"Sister, I have driven this route for over twenty years. I know what I am doing." By the time I had arrived at the Sulaymania telegraph station, the time had reached four thirty p.m. and time was quickly running out. I looked around me trying not to arouse any suspicion, for one never knew whether one was being watched. I made my way inside to find lines of people waiting to use the telephones. I could not wait, so I asked each person in one line if I could go ahead of them since I had an emergency. One glance at my middle and they gladly granted permission. My pregnancy had served me well this time. Now at the front of the line I recognized the woman behind the counter. We had worked together in the underground. Leaning over the counter I whispered,

"Ronak, get me a line to Halabja as quickly as you can." She understood the urgency in my voice but her eyes sent me a different message.

"We have trouble reaching anywhere today, Najat. But I will try my best." By five p.m. she had not been able to get a reply from Halabja. I could tell from Ronak's face she felt under stress. She began to sweat while sitting in her enclosed cubicle. She kept trying to get through but kept shaking her head in defeat. The line of people behind me was incredibly calm and understanding, but I'm sure Ronak sensed there was a terrible urgency in me that she could not help with. I was unable to tell the whole Kurdish nation that they were in danger.

My anger rose to unsafe levels considering my condition. I felt anger with Saddam Hussein, fury at my husband, and this insane country. I was mad at Shwan for not being here to help me. I even felt more anger with Russell for not finding a way to get back to America pleading with his nation to wake the world up. I felt even more anger at the telephone system, and the people waiting in the office made the place hot and odorous. I needed fresh air and I felt the most frustration at myself for being so helpless and not acting sooner. In short I was terrified. I felt ten times heavier than usual; my body was sticking to the stained plastic chair in the cubicle. Spasmodic pains shot up my spine. I could take no more. I looked at Ronak for the last time and left. I entered the street and mingled with the crowds and traffic. The sounds of voices, honking horns, smoke belching, and roaring engines filled the air. Coupled by fear for my countrymen, my own life and feelings of futility, I began to lose the will to do anything but crumple to the street. I knew not what I should do next, nor where to go.

Even though I was armed with the facts written down in black and white, this broken down country that I claimed as my own, did not have even the most simple communications system in working order. In a matter of hours the military would launch a guided missile to accurately hit a target many miles away, but my nation had no operating telegraph or telephone system for me to send a message to Halabja.

I wandered in a mild stupor until I came to the bus depot. A man stepped out of a taxi. I do not know how or why, but seeing it jolted me back to reality. In a flash I stepped into the same taxi ordering the driver to take me to Sarshakam. I gave him the directions to Shwan's family's house. His mother came to the door and stared at me.

"My God, child, what is it? What has happened to you?"

"Shwan told me to ask you for shelter. I need a place to stay until early tomorrow morning." His mother welcomed me and offered me her hospitality. I told her I had to get to Halabja early the next day and that I would be traveling alone.

"But it is not proper for a woman to travel alone, Najat. Some one must accompany you, surely you know that."

"Khaje-Khan! I exclaimed. I have become accustomed to breaking the rules of our society, I must travel alone." In the morning I took a taxi and left on my errand of mercy.

On the way, people in the villages carried on with their normal business. I kept watching the horizon for smoke or fires. The driver concentrated upon his driving. We passed through farmland with huge fields of green sunflower plants. There were farms with row after row of newly planted vegetables. I wondered who I should try to contact first. In my utter mental and physical exhaustion, I dropped off to sleep and awoke to the driver shouting out loud,

"Oh my God! Something is terribly wrong!" He stopped the taxi as many people swept down the road toward us. As they approached I could make out individual faces with contorted features, eyes staring in wild shock and fear. Human zombies were running in terror from Halabja. Some were dragging family members behind them who from my vantage point were obviously dead. The appalling smell of burnt bodies enveloped the taxi as they moved around it. Trucks loaded with people and bodies moved painfully and slowly, unable to pass the walking wounded. Some of the casualties, unable to continue, fell by the roadside and died. I did not understand. It appeared as though the attack had already happened. I could make no sense of it, for it was not supposed to happen until tomorrow at seven in the morning.

Our taxi could go no further against the human tide so I pulled my headscarf over my face and climbed out. I stepped into the field beside the road to check the bodies lying there. All were dead. A pond in the field stood filled to overflowing with the dead who had tried in vain to escape the gas just as Shwan and I had done so many years before. This tragedy was of a much larger scale and much worse. I looked with horror at the dead. Some had eyes burned clear out of the sockets. Others had smoke still drifting out of open mouths from scorched lungs. Some had skin lifting clean from the bone, others with hair burned down to the skull. Families clinging together for protection were fused together in charred lumps. Those still alive screamed in agony and pleaded for water to ease the burning. But there was no water. There was no help. Death would be their only relief.

In 1988, 5,000 people were exterminated in the town of Halabja by Saddam's chemical weapons along with 24 other communities.

جدول الهجمات الكيمياوية للقوات العراقية ضد المناطق السكنية
والعسكرية في إيران من آذار ١٩٨٤ حتى شباط ١٩٨٦

حجم الخسائر	وسيلة الهجوم	مراحل الهجوم	المكان	تاريخ الهجوم	التسلسل
٢٠ شخص	—	مرحلة واحدة	آبادان	١٩٨٤/٤/١٠	١
٣٠٠ شخص	قصف جوي	٤ مراحل	جزيرة مجنون	١٩٨٥/٣/١٣	٢
٦٠٠ شخص	قصف جوي	٤ مراحل	منطقة خور الهوزة	١٩٨٥/٣/١٤	٣
٩٥٠ شخص	قصف جوي	٢٠ مرحلة	جزيري مجنون	١٩٨٥/٣/١٥	٤
٩٨٠ شخص	قصف جوي	١٣ مرحلة	جزيري مجنون	١٩٨٥/٣/١٦	٥
١٣٠ شخص	قذائف مدفعية	مرحلتين	منطقة خور الهوزة	١٩٨٥/٣/١٧	٦
٢١٥ شخص	قذائف مدفعية	مرحلتين	جزيري مجنون	١٩٨٥/٣/١٨	٧
٤٥ شخص	قصف طائرات	—	معسكر جديد	١٩٨٥/٤/٢٥	٨
—	قذائف مدفعية	مرحلة واحدة	منطقة جفير	١٩٨٥/٤/٢٩	٩
٤١ شخص	قذائف مدفعية	مرحلة واحدة	منطقة الرقابية	١٩٨٥/٤/٣٠	١٠
١١ شخص	قذائف مدفعية	مرحلة واحدة	منطقة جفير	١٩٨٥/٤/٣٠	١١
١٥ شخص	قذائف مدفعية	مرحلة واحدة	منطقة جفير	١٩٨٥/٤/٣١	١٢
٣ أشخاص	قذائف طائرات	مرحلة واحدة	منطقة جبل غوش	١٩٨٥/٥/١٨	١٣
٨ أشخاص	قذائف مدفعية	مرحلة واحدة	منطقة جفير	١٩٨٥/٥/١٩	١٤
٤٠ شخص	قذائف مدفعية	مرحلة واحدة	منطقة خرمشهر	١٩٨٥/١٢/٢	١٥
٥ أشخاص	قذائف طائرات	مرحلة واحدة	منطقة خرمشهر	١٩٨٥/٢/٢٠	١٦
٤٥ شخص	قذائف مدفعية	مرحلة واحدة	منطقة جيلانه	١٩٨٥/٢/٢٠	١٧
—	قصف جوي	مرحلة واحدة	جزيري مجنون	١٩٨٤/٣/٦	٤٥
٥١٤ شخص	—	مرحلة واحدة	جزيري مجنون	١٩٨٤/٣/٨	٤٦
٤٠ شخص	—	مرحلة واحدة	عربي مجنون	١٩٨٤/٣/١٠	٤٨
٢٥٣ شخص	—	مرحلة واحدة	منطقة البيضاء	١٩٨٤/٣/١٣	٤٩
—	—	مرحلة واحدة	خنادق جزيري مجنون	١٩٨٤/٣/١٥	٥٠
—	قذيفة حارقة	مرحلة واحدة	منطقة الحسينية	١٩٨٤/٣/١٥	٥١
٤٠ شخص	قصف جوي	مرحلة واحدة	منطقة نفر	١٩٨٤/٣/١٥	٥٢
—	قصف جوي	مرحلة واحدة	منطقة البيضاء	١٩٨٤/٣/١٧	٥٣
٥٥ شخص	قصف جوي	مرحلة واحدة	منطقة كارل	١٩٨٤/٣/١٩	٦١
٣٧٠ شخص	قصف جوي	مرحلة واحدة	منطقة خور الهوزة	١٩٨٤/٣/٢٠	٦٢
—	قصف جوي	مرحلة واحدة	منطقة حاج عمران	١٩٨٣/٨/٥	٣٦
١٢ شخص	قصف جوي	مرحلة واحدة	منطقة بيراشتبو	١٩٨٣/٨/٩	٣٧
٢٩ شخص	قصف جوي	مرحلتين	منطقة الزجين	١٩٨٣/٨/٩	٣٨
٢٤٠ شخص	قصف جوي	مرحلة واحدة	قرية بيراشتبو	١٩٨٣/٨/٩	٣٩
٢٠٠ شخص	قذيفة مدفعية	مرحلة واحدة	مرعشمده النقرة	١٩٨٣/٨/٢٣	٤٠
—	قذيفة مدفعية	مرحلة واحدة	منطقة سايمي	١٩٨٣/٨/٢٤	٤١
—	قذيفة مدفعية	مرحلة واحدة	منطقة مرباشت	١٩٨٣/٩/٢٥	٤٢
—	قذيفة مدفعية	مرحلة واحدة	منطقة سايمه	١٩٨٣/٩/١	٤٣
٤ أشخاص	قذيفة مدفعية	مرحلة واحدة	مرعشمده بازي مراد	١٩٨٣/٩/٢٥	٤٤
—	قذيفة مدفعية	مرحلة واحدة	منطقة مراغية	١٩٨٣/١٠/٢٣	٣٥
—	قذيفة طائرات	مرحلة واحدة	منطقة ديوالة	١٩٨٣/١٠/٢٦	٣٦
٤ أشخاص	قذيفة مدفعية	مرحلة واحدة	منطقة مرعش	١٩٨٣/١٠/٢٦	٣٧
—	قذيفة مدفعية	مرحلة واحدة	قرية سايمو	١٩٨٣/١٠/٢٦	٣٨
—	قذيفة مدفعية	مرحلتين	منطقة مرعش	١٩٨٣/١٠/٢٧	٣٩
٣٠ شخص	قصف جوي	مرحلة واحدة	قرية بلندلان	١٩٨٣/١٠/٢٣	٥٠
٨ أشخاص	قصف جوي	مرحلة واحدة	منطقة بانه	١٩٨٣/١٠/٢٥	٥١
٤٦ شخص	قذيفة مدفعية	مرحلة واحدة	المنطقة الشمالية لرجوان	١٩٨٣/١٠/٢٦	٥٢
—	ثلاث مراحل	قرية بايمنك	١٩٨٣/١٠/٢٥	٥٣	
٤١ شخص	قصف جوي	مرحلة واحدة	منطقة كرماب	١٩٨٣/١٢/١٥	٥٤
٧٧ شخص	قصف جوي	مرحلة واحدة	منطقة حسينون	١٩٨٣/١٢/١٥	٥٥
—	قذيفة مدفعية	مرحلة واحدة	منطقة بانه	١٩٨٣/١٢/١٥	٥٦
—	قذيفة حاوي	مرحلة واحدة	منطقة رصيف آبادان رقم ١٢	١٩٨٣/١٢/٢٩	٥٧
شخص واحد	قذيفة حاوي	مرحلة واحدة	منطقة حسينيه	١٩٨٤/١/٥	٥٨
—	قذيفة حاوي	مرحلة واحدة	قرية ديوديده	١٩٨٤/٢/١٤	٥٩
—	—	مرحلة واحدة	منطقة الحرم	١٩٨٤/٢/٢٦	٦٠
—	ثلاث مراحل	منطقة شط علي	١٩٨٤/٢/٢٦	٦١	
١١٠٠ الخص	قصف جوي	مرحلة واحدة	ضفة خور الهوزة	١٩٨٤/٢/٢٧	٦٢
—	قصف جوي	مرحلة واحدة	منطقة خور الهوزة	١٩٨٤/٢/٢٨	٦٣
٤٠ أشخاص	قذيفة مدفعية	مرحلة واحدة	منطقة خلاب	١٩٨٤/٢/٢٩	٦٤
—	قذيفة مدفعية	مرحلة واحدة	منطقة خلاب	١٩٨٤/٣/٢	٦٥

Name and time of places where they used experimental chemicals that the Iraqi government used.

Large numbers of the still living were showing the effects of severe nerve damage. (I learned at a later date this was a consequence of gas bombing)I found a woman sitting dazed and exhausted by theroad edge who could still talk."Tell me what happened? What did you see?" I beggedof her."It happened at sunrise. Either yesterday or the daybefore, I'm confused I can't remember. There was anexplosion in the air above the city. A smell like freshgreen apples drifted through the town. The peoplestared at the sky wondering what had just occurred.Within a short time the screaming began. Many of thechildren fell to the ground writhing and flailing theirlimbs; they never arose. Parents rushed out throughopen doors and they too were stricken. Some terribleplague has come to Halabja. God must be punishing usfor something.""

There was nothing I could do to help the woman andso I left her. As I walked through the dead and dyingtoward the town, holding up my dress away from theground, I felt thorns pricking my legs and ankles.Looking down I saw that a rash was forming, no doubtfrom the gas residue coating the surface of the plantsand ground contaminating my skin. I made it into thetown center. Silence prevailed. Within this unholynightmare my two legs were the only things moving asthey stepped over the dead scattered in profusion onthe streets, doorways, sidewalks, and draped overthresholds in grotesque positions.The scene overwhelmed me. The smell of roasted fleshnauseated me. I vomited and then I must have fainted. Ihave a pale memory of looking at the cloudless sky astwo men carried me in a blanket. I prayed that they knewthat I lived and was not just one more corpse to bedisposed of. I returned to consciousness with the sound of running feet passing my head. I discovered I lay on the floor of a hospital corridor. Doctors, nurses, and volunteers raced up and down attempting to care for the neediest. Around me were people who appeared to be Western journalists assisting all the while asking questions of the victims whose mouths and lungs were not sufficiently burned and thus could still speak. Those suffering nerve damage had no control over bodily functions and the putrid smell of burned flesh, feces, and urine must have challenged the most seasoned of war correspondents among them. I noticed Iranian soldiers and hearing the Persian language. I was in shock and panic and was unsure if I was in a state of coma or had been drugged when a nurse came and briefly held my hand,

"You are one of the lucky ones. You have been in and out of consciousness for a couple of days. This place has been an utter nightmare since the attack.

"Is my baby all right?"

"Yes, so far as we know, your baby is still alive."

I sat up and discovered I lay alongside a little boy whimpering for his mother. His entire right side was an open wound; the flesh had burned completely away showing the white of his bones. I stared at the child. The remains of his eyes were bloodied empty holes in his head. I could do nothing and a feeling of hollowness and inadequacy swept over me. I staggered to my feet. I could no longer tolerate my surroundings. A doctor spoke to a nurse close by.

"Did you explain to the man lying next to the boy?"

"No," she replied and so the doctor bent down to speak with him and I overheard the doctor say,

"No one must say a word to any of the journalists, at least not yet." Then I heard him say,

"After the gas bomb the explosive bombings by the Iraqis will continue just as it has continued since the sixteenth when it began." It struck me he had said the sixteenth. The document from Saddam read the eighteenth. My understanding of the extreme security measures the government took caused me to realize that the document had been encoded. The act had already been committed shortly after I left Sulaymania. I heard many talking out of anger. I also heard them tell of what had really happened in Halabja.

On the day Saddam Hussein ordered the missile attack to take place on the town, the Iranian army had marched in and Halabja fell into their hands. Not only did they lose a lot of their own personnel in the attack, but it gave the Iranians the opportunity to fly in foreign journalist to report on Saddam's gas attack on his own people. While the two governments played at propaganda jousting, over five thousand Kurds perished in horrific circumstances. Another seven thousand in surrounding areas suffered critical injuries. Medical treatment services were totally inadequate to deal with such a massive amount of desperate patients. Nor were there sufficient medical supplies. Out on the streets of Halabja the dead rotted where they had fallen. There existed no manpower to bury them The death toll mounted daily as survivors succumbed to their injuries. As good as it was for Iran to invade Halabja it was equally good for the Ba'ath to blame the chemical experiment on Iranian aircraft and military attack.

I thought I might be able to slip out of the hospital before any of the journalists approached with a T.V. camera. The last thing I needed to happen would be to have my face plastered across the world's television screens in Baghdad. I would certainly be recognized on the secret service T.V. screens. I walked down the corridor between the rows of patients with appalling burns, now beginning to fester with an intolerable smell. Having underestimated my strength, I found myself sinking to the floor. Then my mind went blank.

I came around lying in the same place as I had been before. The child alongside me had mercifully died. His body lay awaiting someone to drag it outside. My throat and tongue were parched. I had no idea when I had last had any water. A nurse passed down the hall and I begged for a drink.

"Sorry. There is no uncontaminated water left in the hospital. We have to wait for clean water to arrive before any of us can have a drink."

I had a definite feeling that unless I found a way to get back to my family in Sulaymania I would die here on the floor, either from thirst or disease from the rotting flesh surrounding me. My hopes for my life and my quest to help my people were fast fading. I heard a voice from down the hall. The sound snapped my brain back from melancholy to hope.

"Najat." My eyes opened to see my brother Rebwar standing over me. "Najat, thank God I have found you." His strong arms reached down and lifted me from the floor and he carried me down the hall into clean, cool, fresh air.

"Thank God you found me, Rebwar. I think I would have died in there had you not come to rescue me." Rebwar lifted me into the back seat of a taxi.

"You have to thank the taxi driver for your rescue, Najat. He discovered you had left your suitcase in the rear seat when you left, began walking, and didn't return. He loaded the taxi with as many injured as he could carry, then took them to the hospital in Sulaymania. Assuming you had probably died; he returned to Shwan's family and brought his mother to our house. I asked the taxi driver if he would bring me back to help find you." The driver turned in his seat and smiled at me.

"Thank you. It's good that most of us stick together," I said in a weak voice." Rebar leaned close to my face and whispered,

"May God bless you, my dear sister, whatever you are up to." I whispered back,

"Go to Shanna's father. He must deliver the message of what is about to happen to the Kurdish nation." The welcome of my family could not comfort my emotions while my family and the entire north suffered under the same sadness.

I telephoned Sa'adoun and informed him I would be coming home the next day as my father had recovered.

chapter seventeen

The memories of Halabja haunted me. They were visions that were etched into my brain. Even though I tried to force my mind to take me past those memories, they kept recurring so I was more or less wide awake when the sound of boots rang down the passage and stopped at my door. My heart skipped a few beats. Was this my last day to live? The door swung open and two guards grabbed my arms and pulled me from the cell and dragged me down the hall to a room I had not been in before. They forced me to stand against the wall and watch as five men were shot in the head. I knew this was part of the torture designed to break me.

"You next, unless you tell us what we need to know," they said as they dragged me back to my cell. Somehow I managed to put all the evil out of mind and continued to recall my life before this Hell I found myself in.

Two weeks after the gas attack, I sat on a bench in the university grounds. The horror of my experience in Halabja would not leave me. The thousands of dead, the suffering of the survivors, the small boy who died at my side, the smells all had a stupefying effect upon me. I could not concentrate on my studies. I had been coming back to the university daily just to escape the house of evil that my home had become. My baby's expected arrival just thirty or so days from now added to my misery. After hearing what Zead Ibrahim had said about the side effects of the chemical ingredients they had purchased while sitting in my house, I worried about how my contact with the noxious substances at Halabja might affect the child's health. And I felt a greater worry of bringing an innocent to the feet of my murderous husband for him to perhaps twist and mold into a clone of himself. My university work had begun to suffer as a result of missing so many classes. Most days I sat in the warm spring sun breathing clean, fresh, air and staring at the flower beds with unseeing eyes. Many moments I wished I had died on the hospital floor like so many others, but I hadn't. I sat here alive but inside I felt dead. Nothing could lift my shattered spirits and my eyes were reddened from weeping.

"Najat, there is someone waiting to see you in the reception hall. I told them I would bring you along." The professor's voice awakened me from my melancholy. I stood up wondering who would want to see me. Could Sa'adoun have discovered the truth about my actions during my absence from home? I waddled behind the professor as fast as my extended belly would allow and entered the hall.

I found myself face to face with Russell MacMillan.

"Russell, what are you doing here?" I motioned him to follow me outside into the gardens where we could be away from prying ears.

"Are you feeling O.K., Najat? I can tell you have been crying."

"I'm fine now, Russell. Thank you. This is the first chance I have had to thank you again." I could tell I had confused him for a moment, but then he caught on.

"Yes. Right. You are quite welcome, but tell me what that was all about?" I acted instinctively to protect you. However, now I believe I have the right to know what you have involved me in. I could have killed you, Najat; I thought you were a burglar, a thief in the night."

"You did protect me, Russell. I would be dead now if you hadn't. You took a huge risk and now you are asking me questions I don't know how to answer. How do I know that you will believe me? Trust me? Protect me. It is unfortunate that caution and mistrust have become vital components for survival, for you also, Russell. You work for my husband. How dare I trust you and indeed as Sa'adoun's wife, how dare you trust me?" I waited for his response.

"You're right I guess, Najat. But I am your friend regardless of whether I agree or disagree with whatever it is you are involved in. I would never bring harm to you; I come from a culture with great differences from yours. I would ask you to try to understand the values I was raised with are all I have and I would expect you to reciprocate. Please understand I am not involved in your country's war or the country's black market in any way nor do I have any desire to be. So I am simply a journalist, Najat. I write about what I see. Right now I am seeking to find a way I can leave Iraq and what your husband has got me involved in. But as you already know I would be found and liquidated wherever I might go, for this regime seems to know everything. I have nothing to gain by hurting you. Surely you can understand that. When I first came here I was simply a reporter, a misguided foreigner. Now I don't know what I am anymore. Give me some credit, Najat. Of course, it's your choice whether you confide in me or not. As hard as it may be to believe, you can trust me so don't hold back your trust back unless we still have to pretend we do not have feelings for each other."

Russell took my arm, then remembering my culture dropped it. "Come with me, Najat. There are things I need to show you; then perhaps you can trust me."

I glanced at the hall window, and saw the professor watching every move we made, no doubt hoping to gain favor by reporting on my activities. With my arms folded, Russell and I walked toward the campus gates. Desperate to unload my weighty feelings I blurted out,

"The night you discovered me in Sa'adoun's study I found a directive from Saddam Hussein advising that a chemical bomb was to be deployed over Halabja, a medium sized town in the north. I saw the memo. I held it in my hand then I tried..." I remember breaking down in deep sobs. Russell had me sit down on the grass while the eyes at the window kept vigil. When I recovered I began again. "I...I... I... tried so hard to get there to warn them. The phones were all out. So many dead, so many burned beyond recognition, and choked with poisonous gas. I should have left earlier. I failed my people, Russell, I arrived too late. You should have done something Russell. You were in the room. You defended America, saying this would not happen, but the Kurdish Nation will indeed be erased from the planet."

"It is not going to happen, Najat. Besides how could you take such a risk? Had I known you intended to do that I would have prevented you. It's a bloody miracle that you managed to get there at all and an even greater one that you got back home alive. You are lucky it happened before you got there." Instant anger rose in my chest. I climbed to my feet and exclaimed,

"You knew it was going to happen and went there to

cover the aftermath story and you are telling me it is not going to happen? Who are you?" Who are you really working for Russell?"

"No! No! No! I didn't know about it. But the whole world knows about it now."

Russell kept speaking but I blocked out his voice and overrode it with my own.

"You come to my house for company and enjoyment! You laugh, eat and, drink at my table with my husband knowing everything and you pretend that nothing is going to happen!"

"Shush, shush, Najat. How could I tell you what I know about anything at all. We never were alone. I must tell you, when you are in pain or in terrible fear there is no difference between tears or laughter. And I have never laughed so much in my life as I have since coming to this country. Isn't it how every Iraqi lives his or her life in order to survive? If you learn to trust me, perhaps you will get to know the real Russell MacMillan. By the way, I cannot read sufficient Arabic to completely understand what was in those papers. But I'm telling you I wouldn't have helped you had I known you were planning to take such a stupid and dangerous risk. I'm sorry, Najat. I know you feel I am I angry with you. That's because I am. But please understand I do realize you did a noble thing. It was brave and selfless and the anger comes from the thought of you being in such danger. Just look at the state you are in. No, my dear friend I did not go there, but I have been informed."

I, too, am appalled, but in all honesty, Najat. Halabja is not the worst of the things I have seen on film taken in this country. I have trouble even imagining you were there. No damn wonder you are so emotional! You are in shock, Najat, just like some of the soldiers in your country's war, although I don't expect the military here in Iraq recognizes it. I wholeheartedly wish there was something I could do. Maybe I can help you."

Russell opened his bag and handed me several books, "Here, read these. They are about pregnancy, the ones I brought from America for you. I just received them this morning. Remember I said I had something to show you? We are going to my apartment. I will make you a strong cup of hot tea, and we can talk privately without some busybody professor gaping at us through the window. All right?"

"Don't be ridiculous, Russell. It would be suicide for the pair of us. There are many more eyes you don't even see. The one at the window would be on the phone to Sa'adoun before we had even left through the gates." Frankly, I began to wonder if Russell would ever grasp all the restrictions that guided my life. It was my experience that Westerners rarely ever understood our culture completely.

"That's right, Najat. I tend to forget that we live the Western lifestyle at night and in the daytime we live in some kind of Mecca where everything is prohibited, even breathing it would seem. This city has worse things happening than anywhere else in the world, and we cannot even walk out of a damn gate together. So fine! We won't leave together. I will go in my car and you can follow on later in a taxi. Please, Najat, I beg you. We need to talk." Russell left me and strode angrily out of the gate.

Despite the volatility of our conversation I felt better, and I began to leaf through the books he had left me. A shadow fell across my page. I looked up and saw my course supervisor.

"You haven't been attending classes, Najat. I'm worried about you falling behind. Your grades are not what they should be. She smiled at me and I felt that she showed a genuine interest in my welfare. I closed my book and returned her smile.

"I'm having a difficult pregnancy. I am tired and I just want to have some peace and quiet. It is hard to have that when my husband's employees constantly interrupt and watch me at all times. Some days I feel like I am living in a cage."

"Do you mean the foreign gentleman?"

"All of them."

"My dear, Najat, you never own your own life when you are married to the government. There are always watching eyes, mostly for your own protection." I placed my hands on my swollen belly,

"I'm just not ready for all of this. I wish I had been born somewhere else. All I want is to go to my classes and to have some enjoyment and peace in my life." My supervisor smiled knowingly at me and turned to leave. I leafed through my books again for ten minutes then quietly left through the side gate and hopped into a taxi. My nervous tension returned. I looked around me to see if I was being observed, then changed into a different taxi.

"Drop me here!" I said to the driver, and then I walked around the corner to Russell's apartment block and his room on the second floor. He must have heard my footsteps in the hall for he opened the door the moment I reached it. Russell grinned when he saw the look on my face.

"I'm sure we will be just fine, Najat. It must be terrible to have to be so suspicious of everything." With a tone of admonishment in my voice I said,

"You know that's not it, Russell. You must realize it is most improper of me to be in the home of an unrelated man, unescorted. Surely you realize that we are both being watched." I looked around the apartment before choosing a chair. Since there were only two I sat away from the window. From a woman's point of view the apartment was an untidy mess. Papers and manila envelopes were strewn about, film canisters were heaped in a corner, books sat in small stacks against the walls and everything had a coat of fine dust on it. Russell ducked around the corner into his kitchen.

"I was afraid that you wouldn't come. I'm glad you couldn't resist my hospitality. I'll have cup of tea for you in a second."

"You had better make this visit worth the risk, Russell. It's time you told me more about yourself, your background, and how you came to meet my husband. What brought you here to this country when you could be living peacefully back in America?" He stuck his head around the corner.

"You call this risk? You actually consider being here a risk? My dear, Najat, you have a strange concept of risk. You enter active war zones and God only know what else you get up to, and you consider coming for tea in my apartment risky?" He pulled his head back into the kitchen to respond to the whistling kettle. Momentarily alone, I looked around at the chaos in the apartment again.

"Is this the way all journalists live? It seems you need a wife and a maid to take care of you. How do you find anything in this disorder?"

"My dear, Najat, now you know why I enjoyed staying in your house whenever I was invited, but sad as it may seem, I always had to return to this." He placed the tea tray on a stack of old newspapers beside my chair then poured and handed me my tea.

"Where shall I begin, Najat? My birth, parents, school? O.K. I'll try to tell you what you wish to know. But please understand, Najat, there are also answers I want from you."

I sipped the hot, strong tea gratefully as Russell began to speak. My eyes carefully scanned the room not really knowing what I expected to find, after all, Russell

MacMillan worked for my husband and my caution exceeded my trust.

"My parents divorced when I was about ten years of age. Even at that tender age I knew they had an acrimonious relationship and conflict was a part of my daily life. My father left the family home and I have not seen or heard from him again, which tells me how little he thought of me or my mother. She worked at a bakery and spent a lot of time away from the house. I learned how to function by myself and, I suppose, this is where I became an independent person. After high school I went to college in the U.S. and studied crime scene investigation. I had a yen for travel, and so I packed a couple of bags, went to England and studied there. I felt a need to travel the world. With a pack on my back I traveled from country to country and continent to continent. After three years on the road I ended up in Africa.

I had been almost everywhere, I had seen much of the world and experienced many different cultures, and my eyes had seen some wonderful things. I began to think I should perhaps settle down and put some stability into my life. One afternoon in Tangiers I met Rosemary and we discovered that we both were becoming tired of rambling aimlessly in exotic places and shared a yearning for a more stable lifestyle. I suppose you could say we fell in love. And so we returned to her home country of England and began living together. Shortly afterwards I received word that my mother had passed away. The news disturbed me greatly for now I had no connections to my early life. Apart from Rosemary I had no one.

Each of us had traveled the Middle East extensively but at different times. I worked for a while in Lebanon, teaching Criminal Investigations and Photography. Although I had discovered that there was little interest in investigating crime there, I developed my own interest in photography, having done some decent work in my travels, and I seriously thought about it as a career. The Middle East as a whole fascinated me and with one conflict after another, it provided me with a continuous supply of material for my photography work.

As Rosemary and I made new friends in England it seemed perfectly natural that we would gravitate toward that culture and its people. My passion for the camera led me into a full time job. But the bland and dreary happenings in Britain failed to excite me. I became friends with a man named Musadek Badawe whom I first met in Switzerland. Badawe was the nephew of one of the Ba'ath party regional commanders."

"I became quite well connected through this relationship. Badawe introduced me to important members of the Iraqi government of the day. At that particular time Sa'adoun Alwan did not occupy the position he does now. And I understand that he reported to Badawe. I found myself socializing with powerful men like the ones you have already met. In hindsight, Najat, I was young, naïve, and terribly impressed by these powerful men. I let them lead me down the path of deception. My judgment became distorted and I believed the propaganda they fed me. My close friend, Badawe, had a high education and never even once did I question or doubt his information. Blind-eyed, I reported what he told me, adopting his perspective on any topic as my own. I never questioned facts nor even why a man in his lofty position would choose a mediocre American born reporter for his friend. Again, in retrospect, I was so incredibly naïve I actually believed I was enhancing my international career."

Russell paused to take a sip of his tea, and so I took the opportunity to break into his narration.

"This is obviously making you feel uncomfortable,

Russell. I do want to hear your story. After all I did ask you. But tell me only if you really want to."

"But of course, Najat. Why do you ask?"

"Simply because I feel that you are somewhat uncomfortable, perhaps even hesitant."

"How perceptive of you, Najat. Yes, I am. I have never before admitted my naivety to anyone, nor ever have I made this type of confession regarding my lack of sophistication, but let me continue what I have begun. There was one request to which I did not immediately respond. It is one that I will have to live with for the rest of my life. My friend, Badawe, was most persistent in the suggestion I should work within the Arab community. He knew I had a reasonable knowledge of the area's geography and customs. Badawe manipulated this knowledge into claiming I was an expert on the area's affairs. For the first time I became slightly suspicious. I sort of knew what he was doing, but not why he spent so much energy into recruiting me. He offered me money, more than I had ever dreamed I could make. He promised to arrange for the cost of my tuition to study Journalism at the University of Baghdad or even in England. The choice would be mine.

Many times I declined his offer. I had come to realize that I was involved in intrigues I didn't understand. I had no real desire to be in Iraq while I sorted out the facts. I wished to remain in safety in England. Badawe simply could not understand my reluctance and accused me of trying to make a better deal for myself. Between you and me, Najat, I really wasn't that smart. The last thing I heard him say on the subject was, "I think I offer you as my friend too much for nothing. You do not know how to accept my offer because you are just an ordinary man and this is not your dream."

Not long after this exchange Badawe, his English wife Margaret; and Rosemary and I were taking a late afternoon stroll in London's Regent Park. Margaret asked Rosemary if she was free to go shopping with her on the Saturday of the following weekend. Rosemary suggested she would prefer to take a drive up to Oxford. They agreed it would be an exclusively ladies' trip. Margaret leaned over to Badawe and whispered something Rosemary and I didn't hear.

The girls drove to Oxford. Badawe and I had lunch and then met some other men in a club for a few drinks. The time had turned to early evening by the time we left to go to his elegant house to await the girls arrival. A police car stood in front of the house. The attending officers informed us that the girl's car had been in an accident as they were leaving London that morning. Both had lost their lives."

For a few seconds Russell turned quiet. He took several deep breaths, and I knew he struggled to choke back emotions. Instantly I realized that Russell, unlike my husband, was human. He had feelings. Having caught himself, he continued.

"At first the tragedy brought Badawe and I closer together. In my grief and loneliness I spent more time with him. He proclaimed his grief loudly while I suffered my anguish in quiet privacy. Reading the accident report, something seemed to be terribly wrong. It did not add up in my mind. I became suspicious that it was no real accident. The more I thought about it, I became convinced that Badawe had in some way been responsible for the deaths. As the days passed, I made friends with some Kurdish refugees that had settled in London. They told me their side of the story and spoke of the Ba'ath regime. I knew little of the Kurdish people and began to learn more about them. Badawe had told me, they are a parasite; a warlike people living on the backs of the Iraqis. They live in the mountains like wild animals and have no pride in themselves as a people and are, for the most part, uneducated about anything but the local area.' Of course, everything they told me was the exact opposite of Badawe's side of the story. They were survivors of many years of conflict from all sides. I learned that at times they never knew if the breath they had taken would be the last. They did have pride, education and a thirst for knowledge. The Kurds were a brave people willing to fight for their rights and to destroy the Ba'ath regime and those who were trying to undermine them in the name of religion. I learned the Ba'ath regime judged the Kurds on their place of birth and not upon their character."

Russell's words brought a smile to my face. It pleased me to know what he knew. He looked up and noticed the smile.

"What a pleasant thing to see you smile, Najat. It is so rare. Anyway, I could go on forever, but I will get to the point. The Kurds advised me about my suspicions. Perhaps Margaret knew too much and had become a liability to the Ba'ath party members in Britain. I asked why they might target Rosemary and they told me that she was probably Margaret's only friend and may have confided her secrets to her. So in the Ba'ath party's methods of operation both had to be liquidated. It turned out, as I discovered later, that Margaret was a paid prostitute hired to play Badawe's game.

Despite certain misgivings I still went out from time to time with Badawe and his friends even though I knew it might be a dangerous journey. But I had to see the end of Badawe's story. I felt passionately that I had to do it. One particular night we drank far too much while drowning our sorrows. I surprised him by accusing him of being directly linked to Rosemary's death. Fueled by excessive alcohol, I attacked him in a violent anger. I punched him, tore at his clothes hit him with anything I could lay my hands on. He yelled out that the accident was caused by Kurdish guerrillas living in London. Of course, I didn't believe him, but it did indicate that he did indeed know more than he had previously admitted. I didn't stop until I had bloodied his nose. Strange as it seems he did not try to stop me, and when I thought about it the next morning, it seemed odd that he had not called upon his bodyguard in the next room to stop the fight.

After the fighting incident, Badawe never trusted me to hold back on what I thought. He knew I had courage, but he also knew I was naïve to his real work in London. Eight months later, after almost no contact, he came unannounced to my apartment. He handed me a package containing first class flight tickets to Baghdad via Syria, a confirmed five star hotel reservation, and a wad of British pound notes.

"This is for you. Have a first class vacation at my government's expense to help you get over your grief and anger. I value your friendship, Russell, and I wish to renew it. Come with me to Baghdad and I will ensure you have a great time"

Although I missed Rosemary, I had begun to get over her death and move on, so I took the chance by taking the trip. I can still remember the rush I felt riding from the airport to the hotel in an orange and white taxi into the hot, humid core of Baghdad, the proclaimed root of civilization. Brilliant sunshine bore down, a sharp contrast from the cool and dismal weather of London. Badawe and I checked into the opulent Sheraton Baghdad hotel. Inside the temperature and ambiance spoke of a different world from the outside. An ocean of calm amid streets teeming with people, indoor gardens filled the cool air with the fragrance of tropical flowers. It was an oasis amid a concrete desert.

I found myself quite delighted to be in the Middle East again and especially here in Baghdad. As we enjoyed a cool drink, I reminded Badawe that we had promised to bring Margaret and Rosemary here one day. For the first week he introduced me to a multitude of family and friends. All appeared well educated and since the majority of them spoke English I had no trouble communicating, and, for the most part, I found them interesting. Almost every night we were invited to dinner in a different home and rarely arrived back at the hotel before three or four in the morning.

Badawe showed me around a very different Baghdad than I had seen on my first visit here. He encouraged me to take lots of photographs suggesting that my interest would be considered a compliment to the city. With him as my guide I took pictures all over Baghdad city. The military jails interested me greatly, especially the facilities around Abukreb in the city's southern region. The compounds were enormous and the soldier guards threatened us until they recognized Badawe and then they backed off. I asked him why was this happening I wanted to know who it really was that I was friends with. He replied, "I'm the man you want to be friends with Russell"

That evening he took me to the notorious al-Alvia Bar situated behind the Sheraton Hotel. I wanted to see this so-called foreigner's club for myself. The al-Alvia Bar boasted the most beautiful prostitutes in all of Baghdad, and, as I found out at a later date, the bar was where much of Iraq's dirty political business was conducted. We sat at a table, and I spread out a number of my photographs for Badawe to look at. A man came over and looked at them then spread out more of them without asking me. He offered his comments on each shot in the language of a man who understood the process. He asked if I were a professional photographer and where I was from.

In my culture, Najat, such intrusions would be

considered as rude and so I hesitated. I felt unwilling to disclose my personal life to a stranger who had come to the table without any introduction. He did eventually introduce himself and he and Badawe spoke together as if they had known each other for years. The man ordered drinks for the three of us. I felt reluctant to accept his gesture at first. Badawe expressed annoyance with me. He said, 'Get used to this Russell, my people are open, friendly, and generous. Just relax and enjoy the hospitality.' The man, Najat, was your husband, Sa'adoun Alwan."

"Sa'adoun turned the conversation back to my photos. To my complete surprise he offered me a job as his personal photographer. Although frankly he made it abundantly clear that he didn't hold the profession in high regard. He flattered me into believing I had a great deal to offer his country. Also he could arrange for me to document the most exciting war zones that no other journalist could even hope to get close to. The job offer included this apartment or a permanent room at the Sheraton; the choice was mine."

"How could I turn down such an incredible employment offer? I knew it could never be equaled, and so I accepted Sa'adoun's proposal on the spot. Several years passed before my original suspicions were confirmed. Badawe had set me up. He had caused the deaths of two English women in order to convince me to eventually come to Iraq. Now my position here in Iraq became clear. I was no longer free to make my own choices. I had become a paid employee of the Ba'ath regime. My job? Make Saddam Hussein's point of view clear to the Iraqi people. They required me to document every event, every meeting, inspecting the guards ...whatever! Everything was documented."

Russell ceased talking and went to the kitchen. He returned holding a video tape.

"I need you to translate this for me, Najat. I have watched it a hundred times but I understand only some of it."

"So where is Badawe now? It's a name I haven't heard before. Is he part of the regime? Is he Mukhabarat (intelligence service)?"

"I don't know, Najat. I haven't seen him since that night. He did not return to the hotel. I was told he had left for England after completing his mission, but I dare not ask. I'm sure you understand. Will you watch the tape with me and tell me what it is about? Whatever is in it, I am sure I am in great danger just by having it in my possession."

"Russell, I don't think you have a clue how deep you are involved and how much danger your life is in; therefore, I will watch and translate the tape." I know I spoke my words with a tone of anger and Russell picked up on it. "Tell me about the nights you were filming what you actually saw through the zoom lens, Russell. Were you dead to what was really happing in front of you? I saw you filming that night in Fazil, detachedly operating your camera as people were pulled from their homes and beaten on the street. Helpless old people were kicked into military vehicles"

"You may think this has nothing to do with you, Russell, but it has everything to do with you. Has it never occurred to you why only foreigners are behind the cameras in this country? Why the regime does not hire domestics to do what you and your compatriots are doing? I'll tell you why! No one here would take such a risk. You and your kind, Russell, are perpetuating the cause. You are assisting Saddam Hussein and his gang of butchers' to be the monster that he is. Sa'adoun is using you to further his career and hoping you will turn against your own country."

Russell remained silent. I was right and he knew it.

With a pained expression on his face, he inserted the tape and pressed play. This is what I remember of the tape.

Sa'adoun, with a group of familiar faces, sat around a table all dressed in spotless military uniforms. Saddam Hussein took the head of the table position puffing on a big cigar clouding the room with smoke. He sat firm and confident while the faces around him showed an element of fear. Eyes shifted in anxious motions, fists above the table clenched nervously.

"I've seen it before," I exclaimed.

"The tape ? You've seen it?"

"No not the tape. I have seen that look. See the faces? They are terrified. They suspect that they will soon die."

Saddam sent a puff of smoke across the table. 'So you know why you are all here?' The men gave silent nods. Sa'adoun tried to speak but Saddam said, 'No not you! The man next to you. The man opened his mouth, but Saddam said, 'Perhaps you are too nervous to speak. He then pointed back to Sa'adoun. Your husband responded, 'The whole purpose of foreigners involved in our work is to build a bridge of communication and friendship to deliver our needs. We want to establish ourselves among them, to master their language and culture, to let them train us and trust us, to prepare us against them, and to never let them master us,' Saddam replied, 'Enough with the lecture! I am aware of the accomplishments of each of you, but what makes you so sure that your private foreign employees will be different from theirs?'

Hearing the question, I became even more concerned for Russell's life. I tried to stay calm. As I translated my voice tone changed, and I felt that the meaning of my translation had not been lost on him.

"Saddam continued 'Make him perfectly aware of his situation. His death can be just as easily arranged as his hiring. After all, we have mutual goals. Journalists want their story and we want ours." Russell stopped the tape and ran his fingers through his hair.

"When I first came here I took pictures of Baghdad City, the children, markets, agriculture, and then Saddam's life here in Baghdad, as if the war had no effect upon the citizenry and everyday living. I took photos of the trials of soldiers, the line of the war zone. I saw so much that less than a year later, I found it difficult to keep my camera straight, my hands shook so much. I couldn't think or breathe properly. I vomited at the things I witnessed. I felt the pain that the young victims felt. At times I felt even more dead than they were. I couldn't eat or sleep. I just kept on filming without question. Each time I saw an atrocity I knew I had seen worse. The torture and crime are endless in this goddamn country." For the first time I saw deep emotion in Russell's face and heard a resigned sadness in his voice. He pressed the play button. Sa'adoun spoke,

'To begin with my employee was not mine. He was the former friend of Badawe Musadek. MacMillan knew a little too much, so I took no chances in clearing up Musadek's mess in England as you ordered so I brought him in. Not only does he not know anything but he has made a great contribution to our regime,' Russell exclaimed.

"Did I! I haven't done anything to aid this regime. He is covering his own butt!"

Russell stopped the tape again.

"They are talking about the Koran!" His statement confused me so I asked him to explain.

"You know the Koran. Remember that night in your home? He showed it to me. It is not the real Koran, the religious one. This one was the Ba'ath government Koran. Saddam told me that only fifteen important Tikriti men in the regime have one. One of them is missing and Sa'adoun told me he has it. One of the

Tikriti men has lost it and is desperately trying to find where it has gone before Saddam discovers the loss. The Koran is an instructional book for the Iraq future military plans designed by Khayrula Tufa, Saddam's uncle. He shaped the Ba'ath regime and all Tikriti. He is the head of the snake. He was a soldier. In 1941 when he moved against King Hashem Phasile, he was kicked out of the military. He raised his generation by street fighting, guns, murder. It is hard to believe he is a military designer. This Koran is the master plan of the Ba'ath regime. Its purpose is to raise every child in future generations to be Ba'ath soldiers for Iraq in order for Iraq to invade the world. That means building and feeding forms of terrorism. These children will be indoctrinated with terrorist ideals, willing to sacrifice themselves. Lastly they will have no human feeling for the enemy. I believe they were even to be trained as cannibals. This program has already begun Najat. These children live among us even now. You have heard about Fidai. They are true follower warriors and give their lives to their lord, Saddam Hussein."

"I don't really understand what you are saying about the Koran, Russell."

"There is a lot more than you think. Let me refill your tea and see more of the tape." Russell sat on the floor with his back to the wall as the tape re-started. It showed Saddam rising from his chair and without giving the men at the table a chance to speak to defend themselves, pulled his handgun from the holster. They sat immobile, too terrified to move as he shot them in the head one by one, stopping when he got to Sa'adoun.

You make sure you show this tape to the Fidai students. Show them this is what happens if they do not follow orders to the letter."

The vision shocked me even though I had witnessed multiple murders such as this in my neighborhood of

Goyza. Russell saw my distress and stopped the tape.

"I have seen enough, Russell. Saddam kept my husband alive. That means you are in good hands. You would be wise to keep things just the way they are."

"You must find me that Koran, Najat."

"Then what?"

" I can send it out to the West. America, England, anywhere."

"Why? Sa'adoun has already explained to you all about this war: the chemical bombs, cleaning up the Kurdish nation, and weapons acquisition. American support and involvement, they wouldn't care. Remember, Russell, they eat and drink, talk and make deals all at the same table. It is all very civilized."

"You have the ears of a wolf, Najat. Perhaps I shouldn't trust you when you smile. Think about it. The Americans may not be aware of this secret document. Perhaps all of the deals were made by individuals. We too have criminals, murder, and crime in the West. Our society has masters in crime but that does not mean the government is criminal like the Ba'ath regime. This Koran is of concern to everyone, not just Iraq and Iran. It could mean a terrorist war in any country. Trust me, if the Americans knew this war would travel into their country, they would do anything to stop it and make sure the war stays right here."

"Maybe you are right, Russell. But perhaps it's a little too late for us to keep America safe." I think he felt I was being sarcastic. He stood up and came and held both of my hands. At another time I would have welcomed his touch, but not on this day. There existed far too much emotion in the air for the move to touch my heart.

"Listen, Najat. You have risked your life to save others. A thousand people a day get tortured or killed for absolutely nothing. If I die trying to get this particular Koran to the West, it will have been worth it, don't you think?" I answered Russell with deep sincerity,

"It was my genuine concern when I said save America, I was not trying to protest. Please give me more credit than that. Anyway… I will do what I can to get it to you to help Iraqi citizens, Kurds, Arabs, and Shias all of us, if you promise to deliver it into American hands and get them to help us get rid of this regime. Where shall I start to look for it? I have already looked since that night when he showed it to you, but all I found was the real Koran in my wardrobe."

"Perhaps it is in the little room with the store of gold and stacks of American money?" This surprised me. Gold? Money? "You obviously know my house better than I do, Russell MacMillan."

"Perhaps. It is behind the book case in Sa'adoun's library. A door takes you into a small room half the size of my kitchen. It contains more bullion and cash than a London bank. It also contains tapes and photographs. You name it."

"Name what?"

"It's just an expression. Anyway that's where I got this tape. I also picked up an envelope with pictures that I took in England five years ago. Then I went through Sa'adoun's paper files. Here, this one is important. Maybe it's not too late for you to do you some good. I recognized a few words in it like Halabja." I grabbed it from Russell's hand. I began reading it at the same time I was apologizing for my rudeness.

"This is disappointing, Russell. We are just about a year too late." I read out the names of villages and towns: Sardush, Khormal, Dohjailey. Twenty four in all. In late 1987, Ba'ath regime warplanes bombed and used chemical weapons on the populations of these towns in twenty four hours. Only ash and residue remained after the intense fires died out. It seemed unlikely that the bombing of these towns would be the last time they would be used and the recent attack in Halabja was positive proof. "You did hear them, Russell, when they said they will turn us all to ash. It's not going to stop here."

"Yes, it will. The world has been alerted by Halabja. Iraq got caught red handed. They wouldn't dare do it again. The world would not stand for it and those involved would stop the killing."

"I hope that one day a much larger attack will not make the Halabja bombing look miniscule in comparison." I saw that he was quite agitated and worried, but I did not want to pry.

"I'm sure you are much more involved than you are telling me, Russell. I don't care if you are. You must know that your life is in much more danger than mine. I have a feeling you will be able to find your way to the north with Sa'adoun's help. From there I will have my contacts help you cross the border into Turkey, and I will find a way to send the Koran to you later." A smile came to his face and his fingers gently brushed my cheeks and moved a lock of hair from my face.

"I love the way you care, Najat, but I could never let you risk your life, for that matter anyone's life for mine." As I closed my eyes, he moved his hand away as though he were afraid to show his affection. He began to advise me, sarcastically at first.

"Your husband, my employer and friend, is not a man to take a chance with. Now we both know we are not who and what we appear to be. You know who I am. I know who you are. But you had best learn to be more cautious. I don't want to have to tell you who your husband really is. You have no idea who he is." Russell's voice began to choke up. I knew he was recalled the horrors he had seen.

"Najat, I've seen more than you will ever. Your husband has been taken in by Saddam's power like many others. If anyone was to have that power it would be Sa'adoun. Why am I saying this? He told me once he has a mission to complete and if anyone were to get in his way they would be brutally killed, including his own mother, his own flesh and blood.

That night in your house when I surprised you and then Sa'adoun came running downstairs. When you had both gone back to bed I waited a while. Then I returned to his study. Among other things, I found a number of video tapes. I knew they were not mine, they did not have my tag on them. I brought them here the next day to study them. I was appalled at the images appearing on the screen. They were tapes witnessing the most horrific torture, it was evident that the acts were not carried out to obtain information. They were deigned to kill by creating so much pain that the victim eventually died. Of all the atrocities I have witnessed since coming to this country, nothing had prepared me for what I saw. I forced myself to watch despite my churning stomach. Young men were beaten to death with black electrical cable. Another tied to a contraption like a ceiling fan with his head beaten during each revolution. Blood hurled out, coating the walls and the uniforms of his torturers much worse than any slaughter house. Among the most horrifying was to see naked children." I placed my hand on my stomach. Russell saw me and stopped and said no more about the children's torture. Then he stopped the tape.

"I could have described a lot more of the torture methods so you may understand better who and what we are dealing with."

Russell looked at his watch.

"Do you have to be somewhere?"

"Not yet, Najat, but I have to meet Sa'adoun at your house at three thirty, something about going to Kuwait. I'm not sure what for." I became much more uncomfortable.

"I have to go. Ever since I have been here I have been expecting the Mukabarat to come crashing through the door. Having learned what I have today, I feel even more threatened by the fact that I am almost always followed, and I'm sure you are too. I feel ill at ease being here and feel the same about leaving. I suppose you know what will happen if we get caught." Russell put his two hands on my shoulders.

"Relax, Najat! Calm down, take a deep breath. Just because you have learned things today, doesn't mean anyone else knows. Do you know what I admire about you? You are always in control. Never in a million years would I believe that a beautiful, innocent and lady-like young woman would be doing what you are doing to save the lives of others. Since you are nervous, I will go down and take a walk around the block to see if the building is being observed."

As he reached for his shoes he pulled out an abaya from the closet and handed it to me. I smiled,

"What's this for? Are you using it to go to the market?" He looked at me with an uncomfortable look on his face.

"No. There are times when a young lady might be here with me and the abaya is for security." I didn't expect such an honest answer from Russell and instantly my feelings for him were dampened.

"I mean long before I had the pleasure of meeting you, Najat." I placed the abaya over my head and adjusted the face cover. While such garments were not required by law, some women used it by choice, while others conveniently used them to hide indiscretions. Russell realized that dressed in the abaya, I once again felt comfortable. He walked me toward the door with his hand on my back. I turned and extended my hand and gripped his in a gesture suggesting I had entered his culture for a moment. We shared a mischievous grin.

"Thank you for your gracious hospitality, Russell."
He lifted down the veil to cover my face and at the door
he whispered,
"You are very welcome. Please be extremely careful."

chapter eighteen

As I walked a few blocks from Russell's apartment I smiled under the protection of my veil. It had been pleasant to have spent some time with him despite the seriousness of the conversation. But the fear of watching eyes soon overcame me. I hailed a taxi to take me home, for I had decided to skip my evening class at the university. Feeling somewhat nauseous, I left the taxi to walk the last block in the fresh air. I made my way up the driveway to my residence, the palace at Azamiya, where to all appearances I lived a lifestyle of privilege. The fact is that being there gave me a sense of constant fear, of being surrounded by increasing numbers of secret service people.

I went to unlock the door but my maid, Fawzia, was already there and opened it for me. Fawzia carried out her job as maid dutifully but I never trusted her. Yet I always treated her with kindness and respect. She reached for my bag of books,

"You are home early today, Najat," she said in an unusually nervous tone. "I was not expecting you at this time. You look quite tired today. Let me run you a warm bath." Oddly she tried steering me toward the kitchen. "Perhaps a cup of tea would revive you instead." My sensitive ears picked up a sound coming from upstairs. I walked to the bottom step with Fawzia tugging on my arm to go instead to the kitchen, and then I heard the sounds again.

"I'm sorry, Najat. I answered the door at one p. m. The woman's name is Roza Bykofski. Your husband was expecting her. I recall him saying he was disappointed at her late arrival. She told him she had been delayed getting the information from a Mr. Brown." I knew Fawzia to be illiterate so I said,

"You understand English?"

"No, madam, she spoke perfect Arabic. I don't know how to say this delicately, Madam, but she threw herself at him. I think your husband has brought shame on your marriage. They have been in your bedroom since her arrival. Please, Najat, I beg you. Do not go up there or..."

I knew, of course, that my husband was a philanderer, but never before to my knowledge had he brought his whores to our home. Looking back on it now, I suppose after hearing even more about his depravity from Russell and knowing that at this moment he lay with the whore upstairs was the straw that broke the camel's back. With a burst of energy I bounded up the stairs, flung open the bedroom door, and saw my husband's bare back and buttocks as he rode the naked woman under him. Roza Bykofski, the woman who had flirted with Russell at the bar, saw me over his shoulder but made no move to stop the activity. I shrieked,

"You are a whore just like all the others!" Realizing they were no longer alone, Sa'adoun pushed her away. Despite all of his great power and influence I knew he felt this was not something that should be seen. I'm sure he realized that if this got out it would bring shame not only to the marriage, but to the household and extended family. In the Ba'ath society war, murder, and torture, do not bring shame to the family. On the other hand, a woman of infidelity or rape victims are considered to be bigger criminals than murderers and torturers.

Freed of her embrace he grabbed for his bathrobe as I turned and ran back downstairs. Sa'adoun raced after me and grabbed my arm. He pulled me close to his body and looked me directly in the face. I tried to wiggle free of his grip and I screamed at him,

"I love you, Sa'adoun! How can you bring such shame upon us?" My rage came from the things I had seen and heard earlier in the day about cleaning up the Kurd nation. At this moment my anger superseded common sense and I spit right into his eyes. "You disgust me!" He brought up his hand and slapped my face so hard I could feel my blood rushing to the surface. Before I had a chance to utter another word, both his hands were at my throat choking me.

"How dare you spit in my face! You are more of a whore than all the others!" It revealed to me that although I carried his child, in his opinion, he saw me as no better than a prostitute.

Fawzia, at great risk to her own safety, tried to pull his hands away from my throat. Then Roza too, wrapped in a bed sheet, tried also. I thought he would not stop until he had killed me. I struggled to remind him of the baby but no sound came from my blocked throat.

"Get away! Both of you!" he yelled at Fawzia and Roza. Suddenly Russell appeared for his appointment and pulled everyone apart. I crumpled to the floor.

"What the hell do you think you are doing, Sa'adoun!" Russell yelled. "If nothing else she is pregnant! Think of the baby. Are you crazy?" At the mention of the baby Sa'adoun slumped down on the bottom step and leaned against the banister railing. Russell motioned the two women to leave, and then knelt down beside Sa'adoun. No one moved. The two women just stood and stared. After a few seconds Roza offered a hand to help me get up but I swatted it away. I found my own way to my feet and limped off to the garden. A glass wall separated my heavy breathing from the loud tones going on inside as I sat on the garden seat with my hands holding my belly.

Despite the pain in my throat, I smiled. Proudly I congratulated myself. I had showed my concern to protect my marriage, my husband, my unborn child, and this family. I had re-established my trust even though I was afraid of the punishment I might suffer later for spitting in the face of the husband I had sworn to obey. I hoped that I had not ruined everything by my actions. I placed my hands on my stomach again, for I knew this child would be the only one to save me from Sa'adoun.

I heard Russell speaking with Sa'adoun.

"Don't explain anything, Sa'adoun. Just calm down. You were seriously out of order and control. She is your wife; she is carrying your baby. Think for a moment how she must feel. Out of love for her husband, of course she would be angry and shocked. If she were not, you would have reason to be concerned." Russell spoke in a lower soothing voice and calmed the lion.

"Cancel the meeting, Russell. I can't deal with it at the moment."

"Take a nap, Sa'adoun, and try to relax. I will call you later." There was silence for a short while. My mind and body calmed down as I gazed at the brilliant green vines with a multitude of orange blossoms spread evenly along the fence leading to the front entrance of the house.

The delicate fragrance of the flowers relaxed me even more, and my bare feet were soothed by the cool carpet of freshly cut grass.

The sound of high heels clicking on the marble passage to the main entrance brought to an end the momentary peace. I turned to look and saw Russell propelling Roza to the front entrance. I forced my heavy body to my feet and followed them until I could grab Roza's other arm.

"Don't you ever show your face in my house again, Roza, or be in my presence anywhere in this city. Women like you belong in the trash can. You are a recipe for disaster." Roza responded,

"You know that Arab men like to go with white women. Just like my friend here has his preferences." Recognizing my anger, Russell pulled her even more violently to the waiting taxi and pushed her inside.

"You are completely out of line, Roza." he snarled. Roza stuck her head out of the taxi window.

"If you were to give a polite and interested response when I acknowledge you, then perhaps I would spend more time with you and your crowd."

"You don't need me, Roza. You fit into the crowd just fine,"

"Why, don't you?" she said acidly.

He banged the taxi roof as a signal for it to leave. My anger was reflected in his face as he came back to the doorway, shadowing his permanent smile.

"Remember, Najat, I told you to be careful. I will see you soon."

I stood on the front step and watched his car leave our block. Then I returned to the bench in the garden of the devil.

Relative peace existed in the Alwan household as the days counted down to the birth of the baby. Sa'adoun spent long periods away from the house which in itself was not unusual, and I studied hard for my university examinations. When we were in the house together we actively avoided each other. We were polite and civil but conversing only when necessary. I had never experienced physical violence within my own family and Sa'adoun's rage had frightened me. I needed time to learn how to manage it. I had no intention of allowing any situation to bring his rage on again. I knew I had to resolve the problem before the child's birth.

My faith and belief were much stronger than my hatred for Sa'adoun. The fact is I really had no choice. I decided the best course of action would be to apologize for breaking the rules and disobeying his orders. I played the part of the naïve wife and told him of my embarrassment at spitting at him. I asked him for forgiveness and reminded him how he had put his own position in jeopardy by coming to the north and choosing a Kurdish wife. I told him of my gratitude for the life he had provided for me. My words certainly piqued his attention.

"Najat," he said in a kind way. "I know things happen. I am aware that it was out of concern for our marriage and the protection of our soon-to-be family. You are lucky that I did not kill you in my anger thanks to the child. That is behind us now and hopefully you have learned from your mistake. In the meantime I need to have a word with Fawzia."

"Fawzia!" he shouted and there came no response, so I went out and found her cutting herbs in the garden.

"Do you think he will fire me for witnessing his shameful act with another woman?"

"I don't think so. But if he does I will make sure you are taken care of." In the living room Sa'adoun addressed her.

"Fawzia, I will be out of town a good while in the near future. I need you to stay with Najat as her due date grows closer. Here is a list of phone numbers. If you need groceries call the chauffeur to deliver them to you. Also here is the number of the doctor who will attend to her. But remember, the doctor is not to be allowed into this house without my family being present. When you call him also call my mother. If neither is available, no one under any circumstances is to be allowed in except the two of you, even if it means the child's life.

Without waiting for Fawzia's agreement he continued, "For this service you will receive double wages starting today. You may be excused now. Oh, by the way, Najat, Russell may stop by to drop off some work for me. I will leave my library key for you. Do not open the work he brings but put it on my library book case and relock the room."

I wasn't sure if Sa'adoun had plans to test my honesty, or if he had learned I had been in Russell's apartment. Sa'adoun packed a bag and left after saying,

"I could be gone for up to a week. Remember the contact phone numbers." Hearing him go, Fawzia came to see me

"Najat, does he want me to stay with you twenty four hours a day? I will gladly do that. But I really should let my family know or they will think something terrible has happened to me. Please, may I go to tell them?"

"Yes, of course, Fawzia, but I don't think for a minute he expects you to be away from your family at night. Once your duties are done I shall be just fine until the morning. Besides if I feel the baby is coming I can telephone you to come right away."

In truth I felt glad that Fawzia would be away from the house. It gave me time alone in the evenings to look in the library for the Koran Russell had mentioned.

During the final period of my pregnancy I felt weak and heavy. I had little energy and I struggled to move the heavy bookcase each evening. An inch at a time I moved the heavy book case giving me sufficient room to squeeze my body past it and enter the vault. Russell had not lied. Stacks of gold bullion blocks filled the lower shelves and neat heaps of American dollars and dinar bulged out of a metal cabinet. The upper shelves held hundreds of video tapes and documents in manila folders. I searched the contents carefully but I did not find the Koran. As I sat behind Sa'adoun's desk I felt I had his power without his crimes. Knowing the contents of each file I read only elevated my fears. I put back each item exactly as I had found it, assuming that Sa'adoun had possibly laid a trap and would know if I had touched anything.

I wondered why my husband kept all this information. What were his plans? Now I understood why no one was allowed in the house without his presence. I made sure everything was as I had found it and struggled to replace the bookcase.

After three days with no one but Fawzia for company, I decided I would visit and take a basket of fresh fruit to Fazilla Hanm at the university women's residence. Our chauffeur delivered me there agreeing to wait for me to take me home again later. I found her sitting on her little wooden stool behind the door fingering her worry beads. She seemed far away, taking a moment or two to recognize me.

"What a joy to see you, Najat." She said kissing both my cheeks. She offered me her stool to sit on while she sat cross-legged on the floor.

"Are you all right?" I asked noticing a tear in her eye. She nodded and began to empty the fruit basket into her lap.

"Are you happy in your marriage, Najat?" I had no wish to burden this sweet old woman with my problems so I just nodded.

"Then you are lucky. To be honest, Najat, I thought it

might not be too long before something awful would happen to you." Fazilla began to weep.

"What is it? Can you tell me?"

"I waited here in this spot for two days and nights, my old body and mind have no strength left to pray so intensely for her return. Finally at four a.m. on the third night I saw Sahira, your old roommate, drag herself to the door. She was barefoot, her clothes ripped to shreds. Her hair had been cut off, her skin covered in cuts and bruises, and blood ran down her legs so she could barely stand on her feet. I did my best to take her to her room to protect her reputation from the eyes of others. The new girl woke up and I made her promise that she saw nothing and for her to tell the university I had been taken ill and had gone home for a couple of days. Sahira begged me to get her out of here, out of Baghdad if possible, and so I took her to my sister's house to recover. She shook and shivered no matter how many blankets we placed on her and her eyes were wide open staring at a blank wall. At first she could not tell us anything saying 'Don't ask, it's beyond this world.' But eventually she broke down and revealed what had happened."

"Please, tell me, Fazilla, what happened then?"

"She and her sister Salma had been at the al-Alvia and al-Said Bars and afterwards intended going to a private party. She found herself having to accompany Uday Hussein to one of his parties. Knowing of his reputation she refused. He became infuriated and threw his weight around stating that she lived the high life because of his father's benevolence. How dare they refuse the invitation of the President's son?"

"I too have heard of Uday's reputation for gambling, alcohol, and violent sex, but I thought they were just rumors and a form of warning."

"Sahira called Hashm Nasry Nailas to accompany them to the party, feeling that by being escorted by one of the Ba'ath men, they would no longer be under a threat. I saw the sisters the night of the party. They were dressed conservatively and expressed some nervousness and showed no excitement about going. Arriving at the party there was loud music, food, alcohol. Uday was already inebriated but he welcomed them and joked around saying they needn't have brought a guard with them. He said he didn't blame them for being nervous at a private party for the President's son. Sahira told me that his eyes fixed upon her as he got steadily drunker. Uday put his arm around Hashm as though Sahira and Salma didn't exist. Soon Muajed Fadel, who carried out rapes on Uday's orders with no hesitation, took Hashm out of the house. In no time Salma was thrown onto Uday's bed. He forcibly raped her as she struggled and screamed while Sahira pounded on the door to save her sister while the partying continued downstairs.

Uday strangled Salma. It is said of him that violence and sex go together and the violence is the thing that excites him. Not content with the strangulation, he slashed her with a razor while she screamed in agony. Sahira was helpless as she heard her sister's dying shrieks. Uday flung open the door grabbed her hair and flung her at Muajed Fadel.

"Here, it's your turn!" he yelled, and Sahira was raped over and over again while the party continued. She found herself locked in a room until the next night when she was thrown into the trunk of one of Uday's shiny cars with her dead sister's body. She was forced to witness it being thrown into the Tigris River. Uday told her,

"I don't need two women like her. One is enough. If you ever breathe a word of this, I will have your entire family murdered." He tore at her hair pulling out a large handful. "This river is filled with the bodies of women I have had sex with. You are no more special than they were. But Muajed likes you. You are going to be my gift to him."

I began to cry, along with Fazilla.

"I need to know if she survived."

"I got hold of her parents, Najat. Her father went crazy with anger, vowing that one day he would bring justice to this country, and her mother fell to pieces. We all did."

I took a deep breath and asked myself why was Uday doing this? What makes him so sick? Then I had a memory of overhearing how Saddam had showed him torture in order to toughen him up. Fazilla must have heard the stories too for she said,

"The boy is sick, Najat. Apparently when he was young his father took him to the prison and forced him to watch how they tortured and killed the inmates. If Uday cried or complained, Saddam would hit him with a cable and threatened to hang him. Of course, that's all the boy knows. I know when Saddam was only twelve years old he killed a man in Tikrit. Two hours later when the police called at his house, Saddam was in such a deep sleep they had a struggle to wake him, so, of course they discounted him as a suspect yet the gun was still warm under his pillow. So now you know. Father like son. Son like father."

"Baghdad is not the paradise it once was, Fazilla. The country and the city belong to Saddam's family and his officers and everyone suffers. I feel blessed that I was chosen to be a wife rather than a one night rape and torture victim, finally to be fed to the Tigris River fish."

I sat with Fazilla until I could be sure she felt better. I excused myself as the chauffeur sat waiting to take me home. I stared out of the car window at the people on the street. It amazed me to see them act as if nothing was wrong, and I wondered what it would be like to live our lives without fear. Or is this the only way we know.

It occurred to me that there is a texture to life but my people have not yet tasted it. I wondered if they ever would.

By the time I met Shwan again, the story of Halabja was no longer news, but the documents and the special Koran that Russell had spoken of were still secret to the outside world. They had no idea what to expect. The documents were so scary they were almost unbelievable. Some of the Western powers might consider them a joke. According to the ones I had read, Iraq believes it could take over the world. Once Shwan knew of the existence of this Koran, he became desperate for me to locate it and Russell said to me,

"If we get the Koran it will validate every document that exists in Iraq. Life without Saddam Hussein would be a reminder what life was like before him."

chapter nineteen

While deep in my thoughts and memories, I must have moved out of habit to lie on my back. The pain and shock of the move brought me rapidly back to conscious thought. Searing pain entered my shoulders and buttocks where they came in contact with the mattress. A moan came from down deep in my lungs as I returned to lying on my front, causing a rat to scurry away into the drain hole in the floor. Although it was of a different nature, the pain brought me quickly to re-live memories of the back pain I had experienced just before childbirth.

Fawzia had gone home several hours before the first pain shot up my back. Unable to rest, I wandered throughout the house pausing to hang on to something until the next clutching cramp subsided. I had an insatiable need to keep moving. Despite my limited knowledge of what I would soon experience, I felt remarkably calm. I had only on rare occasions held a baby in my arms and other than the doctor's clinical advice on the matter, no one had ever discussed with me the details of giving birth. Now that the moment had arrived, my mind went blank about the procedure. I telephoned for Fawzia to come to the house feeling that very soon I would need her assistance. Not long after her arrival my water broke. I screamed, not in pain but in panic at the loss of control over my body. I ordered Fawzia to call Oum Sa'adoun as my husband had ordered. But there was no answer at her home. In mild panic I said,

"Call my husband from the list of numbers he gave us." But Fawzia could make no contact.

"I cannot reach anyone. What can I do now? Break your husband's rule and call the doctor? Shall I go and wake the neighbors and have them drive us to the hospital? What else can I do?" It was quite plain that Fawzia had begun to panic.

"Certainly not, I don't even know them! Besides we have to do what my husband instructed us to do. Try Oum Sa'adoun again." As Fawzia struggled with the telephone I had my own struggles with the increasing frequency and intensity of the contractions.

"Haven't you got hold of anyone yet?" I yelled. "Get someone! Anyone!" Moments later Fawzia came to my side,

"I have called the American, your husband's friend. Mr. MacMillan is the only one with your husband's permission to enter this house when he is not here. I said Najat - baby - hospital. I think he understood, for he said 'ok'"

"What! Who did you call? You might just as well have called in the security people patrolling the street."

"But we need help. I didn't know what else to do. I do not know if you have any other friends, and Mr.

MacMillan was the only one to answer to telephone. He is coming to take you to the hospital."

I tried not to be angry with her. I knew that she had been embarrassed to speak with a male about female matters, for in my culture the subjects of childbirth, labor, and pregnancy are strictly the domain of women. Russell arrived looking disheveled, having rushed to my house straight from his bed. He tried calling emergency services for an ambulance not knowing that ambulance services for civilians had been discontinued for that particular night. He discovered to his horror that emergency service vehicles were controlled by the military and not even available for the wife of Sa'adoun. He and Fawzia managed to get me into the back of his car.

He drove as fast as he dared. A dense layer of unseasonable fog shrouded the city. Over and above the fog hazard, fast driving tended to attract the attention of the ever-present military and might possibly force us to stop and undergo lengthy questioning. Until this moment I had never appreciated the strength required to be a mother. My back ached and each contraction left me sweating and weak. My brain told me I should scream to ease my mental anguish, but with Russell in the driver's seat, I withheld the urge and whimpered. Every slight bump in the street transferred a shooting pain throughout my body.

Fawzia's voice annoyed me. She knelt on the front passenger seat facing me trying to offer words of comfort in Arabic as I lay across the rear seat. Then she turned to Russell who understood only a little of it and spoke to him in the same language.

"Mr. MacMillan. You do realize that this is quite comical. Only women are permitted to accompany a woman through labor. Men are not allowed, especially a man from outside our country. So what is happening is not proper. When we get to the hospital just drop us off and I will see to Najat." From my position in the back seat I saw Russell nodding as though he understood, all the while concentrating on his driving in order to get us there without delay.

"Ya Allah." Russell exclaimed. "When will this bloody war end? There must have been another major attack. What else will slow us down?" The hospital driveway, clogged with military vehicles, prevented him from driving up to the entrance doors. The scene was bedlam. Soldiers and civilians alike hobbled or were carried through the doors. White bandages and scarlet blood abounded. Unable to proceed further, Russell stopped the car and came to help me to get out, assisted by Fawzia.

"I will return as soon as I can. Help her to get inside the hospital, Fawzia." With Fawzia assisting me, we managed to get inside the doors. The mayhem inside was worse than outside. Injured bodies lay on the floor, every cot and seat taken up by wounded soldiers, some screaming in pain, others with their life's blood slowly draining into inadequate first aid dressings. Doctors and nurses unable to cope with such numbers flitted around trying to deal with the worst cases, pressuring each other to work faster. One nurse with a loud voice yelled over the din of the reception area,

"We have no room left for any more patients! Please get them out of here and take them to a military hospital." A wounded soldier yelled back at her,

"They sent us here! There is no room there either!" Having parked his car away from the military vehicles, Russell reappeared and grabbed my arm and between him and Fawzia, they managed to get me moving down the hall.

Russell and Fawzia clutched my arm and began dragging me down the hall with Fawzia all the while protesting in Arabic,

"Mr. MacMillan. you must leave now! I will take care of her." I wished that Fawzia would stop babbling to Russell in her native tongue. I'm sure she felt he understood her. Ignoring her he took me by my arm leaving Fawzia to follow. Perhaps I had been wrong and he understood more of the language than he led us to believe.

"I don't give a damn how improper it may seem to you! I'm not just going to leave you here! You will never get any attention if someone doesn't make a big fuss. He managed to get the attention of a nurse. In a state bordering upon panic she said,

"Get her up to the second floor." Then she shouted at someone, "Jassm go get a stretcher." Russell demanded that I receive help right away. Hearing his Arabic with an American accent, the nurse looked at him as though he was a no account foreigner but she relented. He and the nurse, Jassm, put me onto a stretcher and took me on a gurney to a much quieter room on the second floor. Russell asked Jassm, who spoke broken English,

"What the hell happened tonight? Why so many wounded?"

"A fight broke out at the city centre between the wounded soldiers brought down from the war zone and the regular troops stationed here. We don't know who or why it started, but over sixty soldiers are dead. Many more are wounded plus a high number of civilians who were caught in the crossfire."

"Since this war began all the doctors and nurses have become strangers to their families. We now live inside the hospital. This is not a life we are living here in this country, mister, but we have no choice. What are you doing here when you could be somewhere else?" The harried Jassm left to go about her work. Fawzia had left to bring a maternity nurse or a doctor to me. A few minutes later a nurse appeared followed by a doctor. After a cursory look at me he said to the nurse,

"Let's go." Then they wheeled me away down a long hall and through a door with Russell and Fawzia following. From my position on the gurney I saw the doctor look Russell in the face and heard him say,

"This is not the night I need to be dealing with a prostitute! There are men dying downstairs. I have lives to save." He showed no concern for the extent of my labor and I was embarrassed at his comments. Fawzia shocked at hearing his words, began shouting and swearing.

"Did you hear what the doctor said? I must find Sa'adoun and have him deal with this man." Russell was clearly disturbed by her outburst, but I don't think he really understood what had just taken place. Fawzia rushed out of the room.

"I think she is going to try to find Sa'adoun's family. Don't worry, Najat. You will get through this." A different nurse entered the room. She spoke to Russell in Arabic,

"Is this woman your servant?" Russell looked at me and I translated. His eyes suggested instant annoyance and he answered her curtly,

"No! She is not my servant!"

"Then are you married?" Again I translated and Russell this time spoke angrily,

"No we are not married. I brought her here because we cannot contact her family." The nurse left. After hearing words spoken in the hall, a doctor came in saying,

"I speak a little English."

"Does this woman have a family? Did you pick her up at a malha (bar)?"

The look on Russell's face was one of utter disgust. It was obvious that he realized that this idiot doctor had no idea who I was and had assumed that since a foreigner had brought me here I must be a prostitute. In frustration

Russell grabbed the doctor's shirt and drew him forward until they were face to face. His voice exploded in anger,

"Idiot! You are a doctor. No matter who is on the hospital bed you have an obligation to care for them and in answer to your equally idiotic question, No! She is not a prostitute, you goddamn fool. She is the wife of one of the most powerful secret service commanders. I, as his personal friend, have stepped in to assist his wife since he is away on duty. But I promise you this; he will be informed of your appalling behavior toward his wife in the absence of his mother and family." I looked at the doctor's face to see his reaction. It paled instantly. He began to stammer and I felt sure he knew just what might happen to him

"My... m.... my apologies. I.... I... did not know." At that moment a different nurse stepped into the room.

"You must come downstairs at once, doctor. You are needed there!" his demeanor changed instantly. He had obviously heeded the warning.

"This patient is as important as any other. Stay here, nurse, while I examine the patient. When I have completed the examination stay with the patient and see to her every need or you will come to rue it." To Russell he said, "You may leave us now, sir, and again I apologize for the misunderstanding." As he left, Russell passed Fawzia coming through the door.

"I haven't managed to get through to Oum Sa'adoun's house, madam. But I will try again." She left the room and the examination proceeded. The doctor left after again admonishing the nurse to stay at my side and to call him when the time for delivery arrived. Fawzia returned in an upset state. It worried me. I had never seen her behave this way before. She proceeded to tell me the source of her distress.

"I'm tired of being treated like a low life maid. Most of the time I feel like I don't exist."

I knew I had to calm her despite my own discomfort so I said,

"I know you exist, Fawzia, and I appreciate you."

"I'm so grateful you see me that way, Najat hanm. (Madam) You always treat me with respect equal to all levels of society."

"So what is really bothering you right now?"

"I finally got Oum Sa'adoun to come to the telephone. I told her I had been calling all night and that her grandchild was soon to be born. Her response was as cold as ice. She said I was crazy to even think of asking her to come here to the hospital at this time of night especially since the city was being turned upside down with the fighting. She had no questions about your welfare. But she said she might come down here after her breakfast since her son had requested she assist at the labor and birth."

I reached out to touch her hand to let her know I understood how she felt, and then I closed my eyes as the next pain enveloped my body. When I opened them Russell stepped back into the room.

"Are they taking care of you properly now, Najat?" I nodded. I saw a blotch of blood on his shirt. Then I closed my eyes again. I heard Fawzia saying,

"Mr. MacMillan, you are a good man. You have helped so much."

"Well, I certainly hope so, Fawzia. Did you talk to Oum Sa'adoun?'

"Yes, but she and Hayfa refused to leave the comfort of their home to come here. Besides, they do not care much for Najat. They hired me to become her maid and to spy on her. But Najat would not hurt a soul. Our trust and moral integrity has been badly betrayed, Mr. MacMillan. It is an awful shame." I lay on the bed listening and it occurred to me how well they were communicating despite the language barrier.

"I hope, Mr. MacMillan, I haven't said too much so it will get me into trouble."

"Fawzia, you can talk to me anytime. You have nothing to fear from me." I heard him get up and leave the room. Several hours passed. Fawzia stayed with me holding my hand as each contraction gripped me. I drifted in and out of consciousness thought until at last a merciful easing of my struggle culminated with the placing of my child upon my chest.

"It is a beautiful baby boy, Najat hanm," Fawzia exclaimed with relief and joy in her voice. I opened my eyes to get my first glimpse of my son. My heart swelled with pride at my achievement. Love so long denied to me sprang forth from deep within my soul. I marveled at the perfection of his tiny fingers and toes and miniature grasping hands. Wisps of wet hair lay streaked across his well shaped head. I felt absolute pride at the wonderful new life my body had produced and then joy of joys, I heard his insistent voice. That second. That sound created a bond that nothing could ever break, the timeless bond between a mother and her child. I raised my gaze from my child to Fawzia. I knew she must have been exhausted, but the sight of the baby had given her a burst of happy energy. Her smile stretched from ear to ear and her eyes sparkled as never before. The fact that we were master and servant no longer had any meaning. We were together like sisters. We had shared this magnificent moment.

Russell came to the door.

"It's a boy!" Fawzia said in an excited tone.

"A boy? How is Najat doing?" The doctor hearing him, turned to Russell and said,

"She is a strong woman, quite strong. I do have some concerns, however. Is her husband here yet? I must speak to him."

"No. Not yet. I have tried to contact him but have been

unable to get through; however I am his close friend. You can tell me."

"I'm sorry I must speak with the husband. Although you may see Najat hanm for a few minutes she must rest after her ordeal." Russell gazed in wonder at my son as Fawzia sat erect and proud by the bed, with a grin that suggested she was the one who had produced the child. Russell spoke in a soft, reassuring voice,

"I want you to know that I think you are quite amazing. May I be the first to offer congratulations?"

"He is beautiful, Russell." I said stroking the baby's head with my fingertips. "So soft, so pure. I just want to hold him forever."

"Yes, Najat, he is beautiful and he will grow up strong just like his mother."

"It has been a long night for you, Russell. Go home and rest. Fawzia will stay with me until Sa'adoun gets back. I am so grateful to you. Thank you."

"See you sometime, Najat." Then he left. Fawzia smiled at me,

"I think the American likes you a lot, Najat."

"No, Fawzia. It is his culture. He shows respect to all others." I smiled to myself. If she had noticed then perhaps it was true. Oum Sa'adoun, Hayfa and, Russell must have passed each other in the hall. For Oum Sa'adoun stepped haughtily into the room. She did not acknowledge me. Instead she went directly to the crib and picked up my baby.

"Oooooh. Sa'adoun will be so happy he has a son. He looks just like my boy doesn't he, Hayfa? My joy at his birth now became tempered with anger at Oum Sa'adoun.

"Please put him back in the crib! He has only been born. I don't think he should be handled so much so soon. It has been a long arduous battle." She stepped back in shock with my having spoken to her in a commanding tone. And for the first time since her arrival she looked at me. I watched her face as she sought to come up with a remark to cut me down. With eyes like thunder she placed the child in my arms. At the same moment, my husband dashed into the room. He saw me cradling the child and began to come to my side. His uniform appeared torn and dirty and his hands and face were streaked with dirt.

"How are you? Let me see my son." After a brief greeting the joy of our newborn son was shared between Sa'adoun and his family.

The attending doctor entered and broke into their moment so Oum Sa'adoun and Hayfa excused themselves from the visit. I'm sure the doctor was intent on making a good impression on my husband, fully aware of his precarious position.

"May I offer my most sincere congratulations, Mr. Sa'adoun?" The doctor signaled Sa'adoun over to the window out of my earshot and whispered something to him. Then in an audible voice I heard him say,

"It was a difficult birth, sir, and so it is essential they both stay here in the hospital a little longer." Exhausted, I had to force myself to stay awake for I had a feeling that something was amiss. The voices were almost dreamlike. I heard Sa'adoun say.

"I would prefer to bring my family home with me."

"Mr. Sa'adoun, they must stay at least one more day. It is not advisable to move them so soon after such an exhausting experience. As I said it has been a difficult birth, equally hard on the infant."

"I would have a doctor look after her at home. Can we not find her some better accommodation?"

"A man in your position, sir, can have anything but not in these circumstances. Moving her anywhere at this time would amount to the same thing; otherwise, I would care for Najat hanm at home personally. I give you my word that she will be well cared for and safe here under my care." The doctor dismissed himself and Sa'adoun came once again to my side.

"The doctor wants you to remain here for a few days, Najat. I know this is not the most comfortable place for my son, but he says it is for the best. You will just have to get well quickly." Sa'adoun leaned over and gently kissed our son, "Your name is Jamal. Jamal Sa'adoun Alwan. He looked at me and announced. "His name is Jamal Sa'adoun Alwan." I did not answer for I knew he would name the child without consulting me. Frankly I didn't care what his name would be. I was just ecstatic to have and hold him. Sa'adoun brushed my forehead with his lips.

"Would you like me to send you any special foods? I will return as soon as I can. Fawzia, stay with Najat until she is ready to leave!" he ordered. I noticed he never offered any thanks to Fawzia for her Herculean efforts on my behalf. I could stay awake no longer. Some time later the nurse woke me to breast feed Jamal. Afterwards I fell asleep again. When I woke the second time, the daylight had begun to fade. A different doctor entered the room. I looked up and saw him, and then I glanced at the crib, my baby had been taken away. I immediately became frantic. The doctor tried to calm me suggesting that nothing terrible had happened.

"You know we have been running this hospital like a mad house, but in your case I have taken the time to study both you and the child with great care. I tried speaking with the doctor who was supposed to be looking after you, but the man seemed quite ignorant, either not knowing or not wanting to become involved."

"Please tell me what is going on. You are frightening me. Is my child going to die?"

"No, no. Najat hanm. But tell me, have you ever accompanied your husband into a war zone?"

"No. Why on earth would I?"

"You are from the north, Najat. I do not know much about the north. But I do know that Iran attacked Halabja with chemical weapons. When did you move to Baghdad?"

I did not understand what the doctor was implying with his unfinished question. Having been aware for most of my life to be wary of questions from those you were unsure of, I responded in a rather rude manner.

"I have just had a baby. That's how long I've been living in Baghdad. Besides the Halabja tragedy occurred just recently."

"Forgive me, Najat. But I don't think you know much about chemical weapons and the results of their affect on humans. I hope you are not blind to your surroundings. Jamal has been undergoing some tests and examinations while you have been sleeping. He shows the symptoms previously only observed in children who had suffered the effects of chemical warfare. In this country it is no longer unusual. In fact it is quite common even here in the city of Baghdad."

"It's my fault my child is damaged, isn't it?" I said with the tears beginning to roll down my cheeks.

"No. In this prolonged war I'm sure other chemicals have been used and, believe me, you are not alone. Many of the military personnel have been affected and as fathers they also can cause birth defects in their children. A lot of research has been conducted by us and with foreign specialists. The closer to an area of warfare they are, pregnant women have a massive increase in still-births, deformities, brain damage, spina-bifida and cancer. Even children who survive, rarely live past the age of ten years. Those who do are still subject to all manner of complications. I must tell you that to some degree we are all affected. I am truly sorry for Jamal. There will be further tests, of course, but I have to tell you that our suspicions have been confirmed."

"Have you explained any of this to my husband?"

"No. Not yet. He has not returned to the hospital. I would appreciate it if you would allow me to do the explaining. I must go now. It is still a nightmare in the surgical department."

"Which part of our country were you born and raised, Doctor?" He told me he was from Najaf in the south of Iraq where ninety percent of the people are Shia Muslim and also against the regime. Fawzia was not present. I thought she had probably gone to eat. Now completely alone, I felt overwhelmed by my own guilt. I had jeopardized my baby's welfare. The elation I had felt this morning degenerated into mourning and self loathing. I hated myself for going to Halabja and jeopardizing the life of my son. I had failed in my mission there, just as I had failed to warn the Iranian residents of Baghdad of the assault upon their community. Now I had failed my own flesh and blood. At that moment I wished the earth would open and swallow me up.

Darkness had descended upon Baghdad when a nurse brought baby Jamal back to my room. She proceeded to place him back in his crib but I demanded she hand him to me. After unwrapping him I examined every inch of his body looking for blemishes or irregular birthmarks, often a sign of chemical effect but I really didn't know what to look for. There were none.

Sa'adoun came to the room later in the evening dressed in a clean pressed uniform.

"Did the doctor talk to you?" I asked. He did not answer but nodded. Instead of his head being held erect and confident as usual, he held it down in a suggestion of sorrow. His eyes normally alert and sparkling looked dull and despondent.

"Are you feeling better now, Najat?" I did not understand the context of his question, did he mean in the physical sense or was he suggesting something else?

"The doctor says you have to continue staying here for a few more days. I will come for you when he releases you." He kissed my forehead, stood over the crib looking at Jamal, and then he left without uttering a single word. I wondered, did my husband have a heart after all? Did he feel guilt for the atrocities exacted upon the people of the North or the war zone now that it had a direct effect upon him? A week later I still had not gone home; my baby was taken away each day for tests while I gained strength. Sa'adoun had not returned to see me and his son, nor had Oum Sa'adoun or Hayfa. While I had no desire to have his mother and her attitude come to visit, it reinforced my feelings of rejection by her.

I sent Fawzia home each evening so that she could be with her family. She was my only company in the daytime and without her life would have been more difficult. I did not have the sensation of loneliness but a great sadness filled my heart. I had thought until this point in my life that I knew what sadness felt like. But this feeling consumed me. I had brought a beautiful child into my life, and I knew that he would one day be taken from me, and I would have to cope with his loss alone. With each passing day the pit of sadness became deeper and the more I stayed in the room my feelings of hate for the things I could not change grew like a cancer.

I took to wandering the halls when Jamal slept peacefully. The second floor held civilian patients while the first and third contained wounded military men. I found the moans and cries coming out of open doors distressing. There must have been an insufficient supply of anesthetics, for the cries often went unabated until the unfortunates died and were taken away. One evening I made my way down the halls listening to the sounds of a functioning hospital. My curiosity led me to a flight of stairs leading to the basement floor. There I heard the muffled voices of children behind closed doors.

I opened one of them slightly to peek inside. A number of children looked up at the opening door. I saw that they were not playing children's games but stared at me with no emotion on their faces. It became immediately apparent that they were suffering from mental disabilities. One girl child ran to the door in what appeared to be an attempt to escape. I closed the door and went down the hall opening about six others, each held fifteen or so children all appearing to be suffering from brain or physical disorders. Some were asleep held by distraught mothers, others just sat rocking back and forth moaning. All of the children were malnourished and underweight, starving for milk and nutrition. I walked further down the hall trying to ignore the inhumanity, trying to ignore the fact that we live in a land of great wealth and our children were dying of starvation.

I staggered to the end of the hall to a set of steel double doors. I heard adult voices through the gap between them. The voices became louder and I knew someone was approaching the doors intent oncoming through. Instinctively I knew I should not be here, so I hid in an alcove until two smock clad workers passed and went up the stairs. I went back to the doors and looked through the gap. An appalling stench greeted my nose.

My eyes saw a hallway wider than the one I stood in. The walls were bare and filthy. The conditions unfit for any hospital. Scared of being discovered, I pushed on the doors and entered the hall. It led to some concrete steps going down below the basement level. The stench increased as I stepped down to the lower floor to another set of double doors. One side hung twisted; the gap between them giving me a plain view of the inside of a large room. Eight white smock clad workers brought groups of six children of varying ages into the room. To my horror, I was witnessing a production line. Some of the children had no strength to struggle as their little bodies were put onto narrow tables. Two of the workers injected the children with large hypodermic syringes. Off to one side, some were opened up and organs removed. The balance died quickly, and the bodies were then hurled into a huge metal container as new children were brought in. I stood mesmerized. I felt sick and appalled. I saw two grinning soldiers come in pushing an empty container and then wheeling out the one filled with dead children. I could take no more.

I think my mind forced itself from the awful scene. I rushed back to my room to hold Jamal in my arms with the intent to escape from the hospital before the doctors placed my son in one of those appalling rooms to be slaughtered. He no longer lay in his crib and Sa'adoun sat on a chair in the corner. I panicked,

"Where is my son? Where is he?"

"He is alright; he is with the doctor. You don't look well, Najat."

I tried to tell him. Help me to get Jamal out of this awful place! They will kill him here! Right here in this hospital "They are killing babies in there behind the basement doors. They will kill Jamal if we don't get him out of here. Hurry!"

"Stop it Najat. Calm down. You mean you left Jamal alone in your room and now you think someone will kill him?" I told him everything I had seen, but he did not seem terribly concerned.

"This is a military operation, Najat. We live in a military country and harsh decisions have to be made." Sa'adoun sat me on my bed and looked into my face showing no emotion. "They are sick children, Najat. Our regime cannot waste medicine on children damaged by chemicals. They are going to die anyway, with or without treatment. We do not have the resources to help them anymore. Hell, we don't even have the milk to feed them. If we did, it would take food from the mouths of healthy children who are already undernourished and dying."

"Who are those children? Where are their parents? Do they know about it?

I turned again to look at the empty crib. At that moment a nurse came in with Jamal in her arms.

"He has just had his bath, Najat hanm. I think you should feed him now."

With my mind in chaos, I grabbed Jamal and clutched him to my breast. I didn't know what was happening. How could the father of my baby live with himself knowing that night after night, babies and young children were being exterminated like rats. Would he send my son to die there also? I didn't know what or how to feel, or how to process this awful information, how to think, and how to act. Did he not know that our son's existence had been threatened by chemicals? Did the doctor gloss over the facts?

"Sa'adoun," I said, "Those were not only babies I saw in there. Children of up to seven years old were being euthanized. Perhaps mass murdered would be a better term." He just stared at me. "Why do you feel this awful place is safer for Jamal and me than being at home?"

"I don't think that, Najat. I too understand." My husband's voice for the first time since I had met him sounded contrite. I wanted to hate him. I wanted to hate the ground he stood on, but the moment of rare tenderness moved me. The eggshell of his cruel unfeeling self had developed a small crack. He touched our son's head with his fingers and drew them down his cheek.

"I am not afraid to explain what you saw tonight, Najat. The reports I received on this operation made no mention that other than newborns were involved. The murders of older children were never mentioned. The euthanasia of newborns made sense to me at the time for we did not have the resources to care for babies who would die anyway. Besides, the country is filled with lunatics, and we couldn't afford to have more of them than healthy sane ones."

I forced myself to look into his evil face.

"I want you to take me away from this place right now, Sa'adoun. Jamal and I are going home tonight. You will take us right now! Or he and I will get there by ourselves!"

An instant change occurred in his demeanor. No longer contrite, he became the old Sa'adoun, authoritarian, dictatorial and loud.

"Don't you dare give orders to me! I know what is best for my family. Jamal will be fine. He is different from those other babies. Their problems are caused by chemicals and Jamal has not been exposed to those things." His voice calmed once again. "Come, I'll take you both home." Carrying Jamal, we walked out of the hospital to Sa'adoun's waiting car and driver. It was blessed relief to get out of that awful building. The fresh night air filled my lungs, banishing the putrid smells they had become accustomed to. The coolness bathed my face, hands and legs. I covered Jamal's face with his blanket to be sure he didn't get chilled. On the ride back to the house, Sa'adoun held our child on his knee with the crook of his arm supporting his small body. On the outside a scene of parental bliss, but I knew different. Behind us in that wretched building, children were systematically being murdered at the behest of the man holding my baby.

chapter twenty

Cool spring days turned into summer days burdened with the unrelenting heat. Jamal had gained weight on a steady diet of my own milk. I played with him every moment he did not sleep. A happy child, Jamal cried only when hunger demanded my attention. Jamal felt soft and sweet in my hands. He held a power over me in that his presence transformed my life. Even my marriage had become more palatable. That is not to say I had come to love Sa'adoun, for I never could. But there were times when Jamal created moments of tenderness between us which made our union seem normal.

Sa'adoun spent a lot of time away from home during Jamal's early months. He never shared the details of the reasons for the absences. However, through my contacts in the underground I had a few clues. Russell MacMillan continued his friendship with Sa'adoun and often came to visit. Russell doted on my son and played little games with him. I liked to see them together and I would sit and watch, all the time thinking that Russell was a more caring father to my son than Sa'adoun.

Oum Sa'adoun had invited us to dinner at her home. While I did not look forward to an evening of rude indifference from her and Hayfa, I was, however, obliged to attend. Sa'adoun opted to drive himself rather than have our chauffeur take us. It seemed odd and in fact he appeared to be worried and nervous. He kept glancing in the rear view mirror suggesting he thought someone may be following him.

His mother had organized a beautiful traditional dinner for the family. Apparently she had hired a new chef who it was whispered thrived on his employer's abusive tongue. She must have given him a huge tongue lashing earlier that day for the meal was superb.

"Oum Sa'adoun asked,

"Did you not invite your friend, Sa'adoun? That Russell Macmillan fellow, is he coming?"

"No Mother, I didn't ask him. It would not be appropriate for him to be here for what we have to talk about tonight."

I sat alongside my husband at the elegantly appointed table. As usual I spoke very little and then only when spoken to. Jamal had been removed from my arms immediately upon arrival, effectively commandeered by Oum Sa'adoun. She fussed and cooed over him repeatedly, "Oooh, you do look like your father." The entire dinner conversation centered on Sa'adoun.

I suffered Oum Sa'adoun's mindless babbling, at the same time wondering why Hayfa had not joined the group. It amused me to think that possibly she was on a date with a man as insufferable as herself and perhaps she would marry and produce a flock of equally intolerable children. Suddenly I realized that Oum

Sa'adoun was actually speaking to me,

"It is time for him to relax. My son looks tired; he has given enough, and he doesn't have to work." Sa'adoun spoke for me,

"Mother! You know better. There is no such thing as quiet retirement; there is no way out when you are part of this regime. Besides, I am pleased and content with what I have been able to or will accomplish."

"Then, my son, why don't you tell us the complete story?"

"Everybody knows. This regime is no secret to the Iraqi people. But we will not be secret to our neighboring countries. This must stop before the West learns of it."

My husband's statement made little sense to any of us so Oum Sa'adoun said,

"You seem very restless tonight, Sa'adoun. Tell us exactly what is going on?" My husband looked around the room as if he thought someone besides the family was listening. Then he blurted out,

"Saddam Hussein and his family are in crisis. It can't be controlled by anyone, not even Saddam himself. Father like son! Son like father! Can you remember Mother when I told you that most of us start our day with a strong cup of coffee? Saddam has to kill three or five men to begin a relaxing day and to help him think clearly. Now he is killing his own Tikriti family. Saddam isn't stopping there. He has a mistress whom everyone knows he is madly in love with and intends to bring her to live in his household. His wife, Sajeda, will walk out and Uday is becoming more of a madman, so he will turn against his father even more. Khayrula is threatening Saddam's actions for turning against the Tikriti. On the other hand, Saddam's son's mess of rapes and murders has to be cleaned up by others. The Hussein family has become a public joke among the Ba'ath party members. Even the guards and the soldiers on the corners are laughing. Somebody has to take over and control this war. The Koran's plans for the war of the future involve the West far too much. There is too much going on that is a threat to us." Oum Sa'adoun spoke, "What are you thinking? What are you doing to prevent it? Besides, it will all end including the bloody war. By the way, I thought Barzan al-Tikriti had been dealing with the U.N. to end the war with Iran?"

"It may never come to an end, Mother."

I sat with my eyes closed and wondered if Oum Sa'adoun had any idea of the things her son was involved in. If she knew as much about him as I did, would she still be the proud mother? Would she be disappointed or horrified at the son she had raised? Sa'adoun sat with his head bowed and his eyes closed. Then he raised his head and began to speak.

"If we don't do something about Saddam soon, the West will find out more than they already know. They will assassinate him and then we will all go down. So before we go down....," He paused in mid sentence. I could not help but smile with joy at what I had just heard. My husband saw me and yelled so loud that Jamal began crying.

"What are you smiling at? Is it because our country is going downhill?"

"No, husband. I am smiling because my husband is smart enough to think ahead and try to prevent this country from committing itself to another war." Oum Sa'adoun for the first time ever spoke in my favor,

"Sa'adoun, she is your wife and the mother of your son. You should trust her by now. If Khayrula Tufa is threatening Saddam, isn't Saddam afraid of him? After all the future of our country is in Saddam's hands."

Sa'adoun rose from the table. With a tired expression on his face and weariness in his step, he went to the liquor cabinet and poured a medium sized Spanish cognac. With the appearance of an exhausted man he returned to the table. Our eyes were upon him as he took a cigar and put a flame to it. He drew the smoke in, then let it out as he said,

"There is no way to approach Saddam. He will not listen to reason; the man is losing touch with reality. A lot of the time we can't even find him. He is so paranoid about assassination attempts that he frequently moves from palace to palace. He stays in a different one every night. The staff in each must prepare three meals per day for him even if he is not staying there on that day. He has doubles riding around the city in expensive sedans to confuse everyone. The West thought they had assassinated all his doubles since 1984 but they haven't yet. Host families throughout the city are required to move out for part the night, as Saddam stays in their homes haunted by paranoia, addled by dreams of martyrdom.

My last meeting with him and others of the secret service went badly. We offered to coordinate the different factions working within the regime, but he screamed at us,"

'I am the president and only I will decide how this country is governed! I will direct the military, and I will give orders to the secret service, not any of you!'

"We told him. That if he didn't allow us to help, he would virtually guarantee you own assassination. Doesn't he see that he is gambling with his life, the Ba'ath party, and indirectly, our country?" Saddam laughed.

"Assassination? This is not the first time I've been reminded. There is only one ruler of Iraq and it is certainly none of you! You are dismissed! Go while you are still alive and before I change my mind!" I once admired Saddam. He called me a good soldier, and we called him the god of all Arabs. He has lost control and cannot keep track of those who would take it from him.

"Iraq is filled with the usual turmoil. Saddam continues to order chemical weapons testing on the northern Kurds and inflicts limitless punishment on all the citizens of our country. Doctor Rahib Taha, who recently returned from university in England, creates unspeakably potent and toxic weapons for use by our military. Meanwhile, the underground resistance movements continue to make progress undermining the authority of the Ba'ath regime. In order to help them to further their cause, foreign powers are turning up the heat on Saddam Hussein. Assassination is seriously considered by certain Western leaders as an option to stop the lion in his tracks. Do we also have to worry about Saddam's personal and family life? The women he is in love with, and who will betray him? My God!" Sa'adoun let out a huge sigh, the only sound in a room of complete silence. Then he spoke again,

"As a member of one of the highest levels, should the situation happen to change I would expect to have more influence over the Ba'ath party. Many things must change if we are to hold on to power in this country. Too many factions exist with no central core. We need focus. There is too much going on in Saddam's palaces' a as well as within his family."

Oum Sa'adoun looked lovingly at her son while I rejoiced in silence at what I had just heard.

"You deserve everything my son. But what do Saddam's family problems have to do with you or the power of this regime?"

"I'm not worried for Saddam or Tikriti in losing power. Half of Iraq's population is military and Ba'ath membership. If the Ba'ath goes down, this half, our half, will end up on the streets with no employment. There will be endless civilian crime. Our soldiers only know how to be soldiers. I'm not worried about me; I will simply spend more time with my son. He is growing, isn't he? Besides, I'm not getting any younger." He took Jamal and set him on his lap, and Oum Sa'adoun leaned over to kiss the baby while he grabbed for her long shiny earring. Sa'adoun looked at me,

"It's time we went home, Najat."

Another month crept up on me by surprise. I spent a lot of time in the nursery with Jamal. While I was with, him all the pain and horror of the outside world seemed like a faraway dream. I played with him, rocked him. I sang the lullabies I could remember from my own childhood, and I held him close to my breast, each giving love to the other.

Soon, however, every night became the longest night as it brought changes in Jamal. It began with an insistent fever. His tiny body was often soaked by own sweat. He could not sleep and cried in misery. No matter what I did for him, he could not be comforted. I noticed his hands were always tightly clenched. Even when in the warm bath which he had always enjoyed, they stayed rigid. By the following month his skin took on a different tone and his lips became swollen and blue. By mid month his skin became transparent and his veins were visible. His eyes turned red and were constantly leaking fluid. No one, not my husband, nor I, nor the doctors could change the creature now in my arms back into the son he had been at birth.

Despite my personal rejection of organized religion, I prayed at length that my child's suffering would come to an end. I wanted him to lie down, say goodbye, and have peace come to his tortured body. By the same token, I did not want to let him go. I heard his troubled breathing and would rest his head upon my breast so he could listen to the music of my heartbeat. During that time the outside world did not exist for me. All had been forgotten. I had no concept of time. Day, night, light, dark it was one and the same. Eating and sleeping were no longer a part of my regular day. Had it not been for my loyal maid, Fawzia, I think I would have starved to death. She was the only person who understood my personal agony.

The father of my son felt that he had the Ba'ath regime to save, and our dear friend, Russell came to visit whenever he could. He told me that he didn't know who saddened him more me or Jamal. I would reply to him that the guilt was mine alone because I had gone to Halabja, and I was born into a land of chemical experimentation. I knew I had been ignorant of the results and had delivered my son into a brutal world of silent torture.

My own family had never looked into the face of my innocent child. Perhaps gratefully they never witnessed the devastated being that I had become on Jamal's last day of life, leaving me shattered into a thousand pieces like broken glass. I remember screaming, "My baby, my beautiful baby." I sounded like a demented animal, as my screams echoed throughout the palace with no one to hear me but Fawzia.

I could not put Jamal down. Instead I held him tight to my body. Perhaps in a moment of dementia, wanting to place him back inside me where he had been safe. I kissed his swollen face and brushed his soft curls with my lips. The creamy silk of his nightgown became discolored with a dark liquid oozing through his skin. On this final day he didn't even cry. I rocked him back and forth as though he were asleep as in former times. I could not put him down and break the symbolic bond between us until Fawzia forced my arms apart and took his little body away. She bathed and wrapped Jamal in a sheet and placed him back into his crib while I prayed that I could join him on his journey.

Later in the afternoon, having been told the news, Sa'adoun arrived bringing his family with him. He immediately ran upstairs to the nursery. After a few minutes he came back down and sat on the bottom step crying, while Oum Sa'adoun tried to comfort him. Soon silence filled the room, and I felt hopeless and full of hatred.

In the Iraqi tradition Jamal was buried the next day. For three days thereafter Sa'adoun's circle of friends came to offer their condolences. Oum Sa'adoun who just took over my house served as hostess. Only occasionally was I acknowledged. Sa'adoun Alwan had lost a son that he really didn't know, and yet the condolences were mainly for his ears.

After the three day mourning period, Sa'adoun went about his business saving the Ba'ath regime. For me every second seemed like an hour. Emotionally I had turned to granite. I could not face the world feeling the way I did, so each day I made the journey to Jamal's grave to sit and talk to him. I should have been going to the university, but I had lost my will to learn along with my will to serve my countrymen. This situation continued for several weeks until one morning I overheard some words from a child which brought me back to reality. Several children were following me on the road to the cemetery. One said,

"There goes that woman everybody says is crazy. She always goes to the cemetery and talks out loud. My mother said she was strange to begin with and now she is completely crazy."

From the mouth of a child had come an honest truth, and it jolted my thoughts back into perspective. I said a final goodbye to Jamal that morning and never returned to his grave again. I hailed a taxi outside the cemetery and had the driver take me towards a lesser wealthy part of the city, an area of wide streets, bustling traffic, and shoppers. No prominent soldier guards stood on the corners and no security people followed me. I felt almost free and for the first time in weeks, a smile crossed my face. I wandered in and out of the shops only occasionally feeling uncomfortable. Then I thought I heard someone call out my name. Then I heard it again. Shwan rushed up to me,

"What are you doing in this part of town, Najat?"

"I have just escaped from my part of town," I answered him.

"I haven't seen you for ages, Najat. I spoke with Rebwar and he told me of your loss. I'm truly sorry." I offered him a smile of thanks as we were pushed around by the surging shoppers. "Please come and have lunch with me. I often eat at this small restaurant. You look like you could use a good meal. What have you been doing to yourself?" Shwan led me to a table for two. The waiter placed a jug of cold water and two glasses before us. "Waiter, I will have the usual, but today make it for two." You will love the food, Najat. He will bring us lamb stew on rice with Arabian smoked fish." As a tantalizing aroma drifted to our table from the kitchen, I asked him about himself and how things were going. Shwan was right. It was the best meal I had enjoyed in a long time. After we had eaten he looked into my eyes and said,

"Najat, you know now that nothing has changed; everything is the same. I am disappointed that you have not been to visit your family. Will you find a way to resume your university training? I know you are living in a circle of fire but these things seem unacceptable to me." I thought about what Shwan had just said. I replied,

"Shwan, I know I'm a mess. I am ashamed to present myself to anyone and I am well aware I have to pull myself together. I have just this day accepted that Jamal is not the only child to suffer such agony, nor am I the only mother to lose a son."

"What of Sa'adoun?"

"His trips get longer. Most of the time am unaware if

he is alive or dead. Sometimes however does inform me if he will be coming home, like tonight for instance."

"From where? The war zone, Europe?"

"I couldn't tell you. He does not tell me where he is, where he is going, or where he has been. But when he does return, he only reminds me of my worst nightmare. I feel a pain deep in my chest that doesn't go away. I feel so weighted down that I cannot climb up again. But when Russell comes to visit him, it eases my troubles."

"You are in love with him, Najat. Is he in?...."

"The joy of seeing him has changed lately. Losing Jamal has taught me about losing someone you love so much. I'm learning to bury my feelings for Russell."

"My dear, Najat, true love can never be buried. You feel culture bound to put him out of your mind. Your marriage to Sa'adoun is a wall you cannot climb over. One day Russell will leave this country far behind unless the regime kills this crazy American."

"I will resume my quest in life, Shwan. In the meantime, I will go to visit my parents in Sulaymania. Where are you staying?"

"I am staying in Fazil with Amear and his family. You know where it is if you need me."

We left the restaurant and went our separate ways. I walked for a long time, considering how the words of a child had changed my day, and how they would change my future. Despite my raised hopes and feelings, I felt that as I entered the front door to my palace I was inside a cold prison. I was the sole prisoner and in charge of my own incarceration.

Sa'adoun sat at his desk, papers heaped up around him. He glanced up as I entered, and we greeted each other as if we were two strangers. I made a comment on his appearance,

"You look like you have just come through a storm in the desert."

"I have. So where have you been? Moping around in the cemetery, I suppose." With a sudden change in the tone of his voice he asked, "Why did I find my office unlocked? How could you be so stupid as to forget such a thing?"

"How could I? I have had a lot on my mind lately. You know that."

"Once I thought you had talent and courage and you would look good on my arm. Was I ever wrong! Someone to help me, work with me! What a joke! You would have destroyed me before you had even begun! You can't even handle one simple responsibility. You are distracted you say? As if no one else has ever lost a son before!"

"Certainly not you, Sa'adoun, but I have." He slapped my face as hard as he could. The side of my face felt hot as the blood surfaced. Our actions were that of two people discussing a different child.

"Now! Prepare a hot bath for me and I also want some fresh fruit that is if you have bothered to tell Fawzia to bring some home." Later, after his bath and having made several phone calls he grabbed the plate of fruit I had prepared for him as I watched an American movie on the television. Angrily he switched the channel to the local news. "These American shows have poisoned your mind with the Devil of America, Najat. Where is Fawzia? I have told you I don't want you alone in this house. Do you think you are living in dreamland? From now on she is to stay here at all times and, by the way, tell her to make a special dinner for tomorrow night for I have a special guest coming."

"For how many people?'

"Just two, Russell MacMillan, and a foreign man. Remember I said to prepare a special meal, for it just might be Russell's last." His words hit me like a brick. My mask of indifference dropped. I could not hide the fear I suddenly felt. "What's the matter with you?" It took a few moments to gather my wits about me. "I said, what is the matter with you now? I asked you a question." Thinking as fast as I could, I blurted out,

"He hasn't betrayed you.... I mean us, has he? After all you have done for him. If it wasn't for you, he would still be a nobody. You treated him as if he was your brother and I treated him as if he were a part of our family."

"Enough is enough. I have to get some rest. I haven't had a good nights sleep for some time."

Sa'adoun went to bed and slept like a rock, but I could not rest. My mind dragged me slowly over my life's journey and would not let me forget what Sa'adoun had told me earlier. I left the bed and went to Jamal's room. I touched his crib and the pillow he had used, trying to recapture his fragrance of him. I suppose I relived the final days of his life remembering I sat by him praying for a miracle. But now I found myself praying for Russell's life.

At one time I had thought that when I married Sa'adoun I would be able to deliver lots of documents and information, and that I would be able to save the lives of many more people. But I had been mistaken. I had simply become a spectator. I saw and felt everything happening in my country but I could do nothing.

The sounds of dawn from the city mosques tore me from my forlorn thoughts. I felt exhausted and went to my bed taking a couple of sleeping pills and slept until eleven. I woke up in a panic. Too much time had been wasted. Sa'adoun had gone and Fawzia had left my breakfast on the table. I felt ill. I had become accustomed to thinking too much and doing too little. I racked my brain to think of some way to warn Russell but I didn't want to scare him. I was well aware that he had taken some of Sa'adoun's tapes, and I thought Sa'adoun must have found out. I searched the house like a burglar and

I found one of Sa'adoun's handguns in the back of a kitchen cabinet.

I didn't hear Fawzia enter the kitchen as I examined the pistol. She let out a shriek and grabbed the gun from my hand.

"What are you doing with this? Have you gone mad? If you have I don't blame you but he is not worth it, Najat." I had to explain to her that it had not been my intention to kill my husband or myself. I had come to know Fawzia's character remarkably well and so I decided to take a chance and put my trust in her.

"My friend Russell's life is in great danger."

"I'm not surprised. I think he has seen and heard too much in this house."

"Fawzia, I am going to place my trust in you and ask that you help me out by warning Russell. I want you to take a taxi to Fazil, deliver this gun, and contact Shwan at the address I will give you. Give him the gun and ask him to get Russell out of the city. If you can't find Shwan there, give the message to the family he is staying with, and then come back here as quickly as you can."

"You can trust me, Najat. I am on your side." Fawzia hurried away and I went to work cleaning and chopping the vegetables for the dinner. I became worried after an hour had passed and she had not returned. Eventually she rushed into the kitchen. "I found Shwan and gave him the gun and message. He said he would notify his friends, and they would try to locate Russell. He said that they should be able to find him unless he happened to be in a prohibited zone." Noticing the vegetables had been prepared; Fawzia jokingly declared that I was not the kitchen maid.

Later in the day Fawzia said,

"Let me make you a cup of tea"

We took our tea out to the garden and we began to talk. Now that there was mutual trust, Fawzia felt free to air her views and tell me of her family. She was as tired of the regime as much as the rest of Iraq was. She had not had an easy life and had cared for her siblings while she was still quite young and had sent all of them through school.

"So you see, Najat, I have never had a life of my own. Yours is no different than mine."

"What happened to your parents?" I asked. But I could tell that the subject was too painful for her, and she changed the subject. She began telling me jokes and soon she had me laughing out loud. I realized that I had not laughed at anything for a long time, and I felt gratitude toward her for allowing me to escape from my mental prison if only for a short while. Before we knew it the sun had begun to sink, coloring the sky a brilliant red as the sounds of the call to evening prayer echoed across the city from the multitude of mosques. We returned to the kitchen to prepare for the dinner.

At eight o clock Sa'adoun stepped into the house followed by a tall, blonde haired man with green eyes. Fawzia, who had been sat speaking with me, abruptly left as Sa'adoun gave me a look suggesting he was not impressed to see me conversing with a low-life maid in front of his foreign guest.

"This is Orjan. He is from Sweden. He will be dining with us. Go bring two glasses of Arak and some appetizers."

I welcomed Orjan to our home, but I wondered what was going on. Was Sa'adoun playing some kind of macabre game? Perhaps the Swede would be the one to replace Russell's position after his death.

"Russell has been delayed. He will be joining us later. I need you to socialize with us tonight but know your limits. Do not embarrass me." I served the drinks and snacks and then Russell arrived. My heart sank. Shwan had obviously not been able to give him the warning.

After introductions Fawzia served the meal. It began formally enough but my husband had consumed at least four glasses of Arak. The more he loosened up the more I began to relax. As my husband drank more, the topic of conversation was mainly of a cultural nature no doubt for the benefit of our guest.

Both Orjan and Russell had visited many countries, so Russell asked,

"So, Orjan, what impresses you most about Iraq so far?"

"The women. They are liberated; they are more liberated than in most other Middle Eastern countries. They are well educated, hard working, yet remain feminine. I wouldn't say they are subdued but definitely culturally humble."

"Since I have been here, I realize we Westerners are woefully ignorant about this part of the world. For the most part we do not take interest in what the societies are really about and the journalists who control the bridge of communications are scaring the Western world."

"I agree, Russell. I too am guilty of it. Our newspapers like to print tragedy and chaos. We send photographs and tell most horrific stories. We make foreigners look less tolerant and less capable than we are." Russell responded with words that I knew were not from his heart,

"Our world has a more comfortable life but it is a life of speed that is too easily put aside. We may have what some would consider everything but we will never have what the people have here. These people haven't lost the most important thing, valuing each other. People here certainly will not die lonely as many of ours do. They may lead shorter lives but their lives are fulfilling. But don't worry, Orjan. You will get plenty of tragic pictures."

"You must really like living here then, Russell?"

"I would never leave. This place has become my home. Besides, look at me. I have become an Iraqi, I even look like an Arab. No one knows I'm an American until I speak."

I listened to the conversation in silence, mentally noting that Russell knew how to play the game. I realized he was giving a subtle warning to Orjan rather than his real opinions. Orion obviously was not yet accustomed to living here in this Hell we call Iraq. Neither he nor I understood why Russell expressed such sympathy for the Iraqi people. Was it because he had seen too much, or did he know things I didn't?" Orjan looked at Sa'adoun,

"It seems you and your wife have been a great influence on Russell."

"No. Russell is a smart man; he does not need influence. Living here he has every freedom to do as he wishes."

Orjan asked me about my level of interest in politics, about my career, and had I ever been out of the country. I answered politely and succinctly knowing the limits I had to stay within. Sa'adoun took over the conversation and the men got into a friendly argument over politics and business. Fawzia came to clear off the table and replenished it with fresh fruits and pastries. As usual she made our table look inviting, but the men who were busy drinking and talking failed to notice. I excused myself and left the table and indicated with my eyes for Russell to follow. After a few minutes he came to the kitchen,

"What is it, Najat? Is something wrong? You haven't looked well since I got here. It was as though you couldn't see me."

"You must leave, Russell. Did you talk with Shwan or his friends? Did you get my message?"

"Slow down, Najat. What message? Talk to me, Najat.

You are scaring me." I could not hold back the tear, that fought to surface.

"You are in danger! My husband said this might be your last meal here. I don't feel right about the situation. I have just buried my son and now this. Please leave while you can." Russell smiled and brushed away the escaped tear with his finger.

"He told me the same thing, Najat, but it is not what you think." His fingers went to my hair and I felt them move a curl from my forehead. His eyes fixed on mine and I could feel the warmth of his breath caress my face. The intimate moment was disturbed by Fawzia entering the kitchen with an empty garbage can. I laughed until I shook, now released from my paranoia. I said to Fawzia,

"He is going to be alright." She smiled without commenting. So I pulled myself together and went back to join our guests. My face was flushed at Russell's display of affection but he was busy in conversation and did not look at me. I felt he wore a mask over his feelings, and I wondered if he had borrowed mine. Orjan thanked us for our hospitality and indicated he had to leave. Sa'adoun and Russell walked him to the door. When they returned Sa'adoun ordered me to remain in their company. It occurred to me that this was unusual and perhaps he had imbibed a little too much, but it was never enough to stop him having his say.

"Russell! I'm touched by your appreciation of our culture and our people. Furthermore, I am glad you like living here as much as we like having you."

"So Orjan will be working with me? Does that mean some time off for me?"

"No, no. I wanted you to meet him because there is a project as I mentioned earlier. The project people need your previous expertise in crime lab work. Here we call it the chemical lab."

"But I have never worked in that field. Crime lab is

about the human body from the minute they have come into contact with something until death takes them. Then they study the effects of what the body has been exposed to."

"This is not much different. You have been asked to work with Dr. Rahib Taha to do some analyzing work. You will learn from her and also Orjan. He is a specialist in the field but we call him a journalist."

"So what is expected of me?"

"You will be joining others at the Biological Warfare Center. You are a smart man, Russell. You will learn about different strains of cholera, pulmonary anthrax, and typhoid, and their side effects. Like you say, the minute you use them, the minute you get results."

"So you don't want to make the same mistakes you made in the Majoon Marshes Operation?"

"Yes. But that was weather conditions. They were adverse on that day and the mustard gas was blown back onto our own forces. We also learned that rain and humidity dilute the effects of mustard gas and that temperatures in the south make operations with it there impossible."

"Sa'adoun, my friend, you are talking to me of things I know nothing about."

"I am telling you these things because if we can learn about them, then so can you."

I became quite shocked to hear my husband speaking so freely about the regime's secret plans in front of me, his wife, whom he did not trust or respect, and I wondered what kind of position he was putting me in. He excused himself and left the room and Russell and I looked at each other. We both were now as involved as Sa'adoun. Russell saw the worried look on my face.

"Just let's wait and see what else he has to say." And so we both worried in silence. Sa'adoun entered the room carrying the Koran, the one we had looked so hard to find ever since my visit to Russell's apartment. Sitting back down he said,

"Now I'm about to give you the most secret information of this country, the regime's military plans."

"Are you sure about this, Sa'adoun? Maybe you should do this another time when you haven't had a couple of drinks."

"I'm more sober than you think." He laughed, passing the Koran across the table to Russell. "One day the world will be desperate to get their hands on this. In a few days this regime will be gone. Saddam Hussein will be gone. We are about to stage a coup."

"A coup! How many coups have been tried? None has ever succeeded. What makes you so sure you can?"

"I'm not the one leading it. I'm just one of the hundred men."

"In the past these one hundred men have been shot or hung."

"You are right, Russell. As you say, if we get caught we are dead men. If we do not succeed, my wife will take you to her city of Sulaymania and you can hand the Koran to the Kurdish revolutionary to do with whatever they wish. That will be my revenge on the Ba'ath party. If they take my life I will sleep in peace. Then you can stay there or go back to America, although I wouldn't suggest that. On the other hand don't get any strange ideas. If we succeed you will return the Koran and my wife to me." Russell began to laugh.

"How long have you been planning this coup? Wait! What am I asking you this for? It's since you got me into this and since you married Najat." Now Sa'adoun began to laugh and shouted,

"Bravo, my friend! See you are a smart man, but I have no regrets. You have made me a fine friend and a good worker and Najat turned out to be a good wife after all."

"Like I have a choice? Do I have any choice?"

"No. Don't try to be a hero and take this book back to America. Read it with Najat's help. Then you will understand why you shouldn't try to be a hero."

"I have no wish to be anyone's hero, but why don't you tell me what is in the Koran?"

"Because my friend, no other country gives a damn about what is going on in Iraq unless it directly affects them. Besides 95% of Saddam's arsenal of weapons of mass destruction was imported from France, the U.S.A., West Germany, Britain, the Soviet Union, and believe it or not, from South American countries like Brazil and Chile. Iraq has massive financial credit generously extended by Western banks, so we not only purchased large numbers of sophisticated aircraft and weapons, we established our own arms industry including nuclear weapons and a very complex military;" Russell responded,

"Now I'm really impressed. No one could imagine the Iraq military's capabilities and so advanced too. We could never fill your shoes."

"You gave it to us, Russell."

"But Sa'adoun, you don't have to wear the shoes and what about the Iraqi people and the safety of their country?"

"So you see Russell, you do have a choice. Two days from now you report at six a.m. to the research center to work on the West Nile virus that we purchased from Atlanta, Georgia in 1985, just as we purchased the Rabbit Fever Virus Tularhemia."

"Don't put the blame on America! You told me yourself you bought it for medical research."

"These viruses cause fever, nausea, and death, and you don't think they know what they are selling to us? They are politicians and businessmen just like us. Besides, that is not my point."

Having heard my husband's speech, for the very first time since marrying him, I felt free. I had great confidence that the coup would not succeed. I knew I would never return here, I would find a place of safety for myself and for Russell. For a few seconds I went into my imaginary world as I thought about the comfort of Russell's arms, to safe place he would take me to taste and touch freedom there. Finally, I would have the escape from tyranny I had dreamed about since I was a child.

"What if I do not want to become involved?"

"You are already involved. Besides, Russell, you must be a fool just as you were the first time I met you. The Iraqi people have a death sentence over them the day they are born, so do you and my wife." I could hold my tongue no longer so I broke into the conversation,

"You should listen to him, Russell. Either way I am going to stand by my husband. I can do this on my own." Russell looked at me and I felt he had read between the lines.

"Then perhaps we have no choice, but, my friend, I could kill you with my bare hands for what you are making me do. Oh well, what are friends for?" Russell joked.

"So, Russell, tomorrow you and Najat grab a taxi at the end of the block at separate times and go to a different part of the city. Change taxis mid journey and go to the bus station." I interjected,

"Sa'adoun, what are the societal implications for me, your wife, traveling unescorted with a foreign man and what about my marriage vows?"

"I told you once before, Najat, that you knew nothing. Yes, you did see a document, a fake one saying we were married. I had thought you would have become a useful tool to use against whomever I wished, that I could redirect you in whichever direction I desired. But you turned out to be useless. Despite that I did like you a great deal. You know how to carry yourself in any situation and you did make me look good."

Sa'adoun, having become a little tipsier, excused himself again and left the room. I smiled at Russell and whispered,

"I will break free, Russell. I am going to be free." He returned the smile and said in a quiet voice,

"No, Najat, you are in more danger now than ever. Remember Saddam gave birth to Sa'adoun and every other Ba'ath member. No matter which side wins in this coup, the situation is not going to get better; it will become much worse."

"What a fool I have been, Russell. He has made a fool of all of us but you. I would never have thought of the reason behind my marriage. Sa'adoun was right. I knew nothing."

"Perhaps you are both as guilty as each other for your own reasons for marrying. The problem now, Najat, is that now you know too much. Sometimes not knowing is much safer. Anyway, none of this matters right now. But with this Koran in our hands we can do more than you even dreamed of." Sa'adoun re-entered the room carrying the same briefcase with which he had attempted to buy me from my parents. He placed the case in front of Russell and opened it, revealing it still was filled with American currency.

"This will get you out of here if you have to, but remember no silly ideas. If the coup succeeds, I will find you even if you are under the sea." As usual Russell expressed his anger by laughing. Pointing at the cash he said,

"Well, getting out of Baghdad with the Koran, the money, and your wife won't be a problem, will it? If I have had a death sentence hanging over me since I got here, how safe will I be tomorrow?"

"I have here two letters written officially and signed

by Saddam himself. It is a safe conduct letter issued to all spies and intelligence personnel. You will be able to travel safely. Not only will you not have to answer any questions, you will be saluted at every checkpoint. Remember the coup does not take place for another two days."

Fawzia's services were no longer needed and she came to the door to ask if we needed anything further.

"Perhaps Najat has forgotten to tell you that you are required to stay overnight like everything else she forgets." As usual he did not wait for a reply but ordered her to bring in some strong coffee. After his coffee, he said "I'm getting tired." He excused himself and left the room again.

"Ya Alla! Now what is he going to bring back?" Russell held his head in his hands in mock grief. "I can't believe that just a short time ago I was desperate to find this Koran and now I have it in my possession it seems like the most poisonous of species. We must leave tonight, Najat. The failure of most coups is because they don't run through the operation beforehand."

Fawzia walked in,

"Sa'adoun is already snoring like an army tank on the hall couch. Should I wake him to go to his bed?"

"No, Fawzia. I want you to get your abaya and put this book and briefcase under it and take Mr. MacMillan to Shwan at the same house in Fazil, but change taxis half way there to lose the trail." Russell appeared as if he did not want to leave without me. He argued for my safety and I argued for his, as though one life was no less valuable than the other. But I felt his life was worth more than mine in this circumstance. He could do more with the Koran. His word would be much more readily heard in the Western countries than my own.

"Najat, you don't have to be here any longer. You have put your life in danger for this moment. If you do not take it, you will have thrown all your work away. You are afraid of nothing but still you are afraid of him."

"Yes, I am. You know my husband. If I were to leave without his last order and permission, he may think we had just taken off with the Koran. He knows where we are going and he has the power to stop us. Then we would be left with nothing. If I don't make it to the first bus at six a.m. you and Shwan must leave without me. You know only too well, Russell, if the Ba'ath find out about this there will be a countrywide curfew to get the Koran back. You will be described as an American spy. To him you are the one stealing the Koran. It's important for you to take it. You might just be able to save this country from itself."

I took my birth mother's coin necklace and placed it in his hand,

"This is my life, Russell. It is all that I have ever had of value. You must return it to me." Russell's arms embraced me. I felt his hand slide up my back. I felt his fingers grasp my hair and he kissed my forehead. I knew it was not a kiss of passion but one of desperation. Then just before he left with Fawzia he said,

"If you don't show up I will find you even if you are under the sea." As he walked out of the house every fiber of my body felt hollow. I had the emotions of love found, and love lost, and the real fear of death for both of us.

I went to my bed but it afforded me no rest. I counted down the hours on the chime clock as I struggled with my thoughts and fears. I heard the clock strike four. It still was not the time to begin my dash to freedom. I heard a noise downstairs. Could it be Sa'adoun moving around? So far as I knew he was still asleep on the couch. Then I heard a louder noise so I sat up in bed. I had a feeling that something might be amiss so I rushed down the stairs, abandoning all caution for self preservation. I saw that some lights were on in Sa'adoun's study and library. All I remember after that was feeling a violent blow to my head, then hitting the floor and sliding to the base of the couch. I looked up and saw that Sa'adoun no longer lay upon it.

chapter twenty one

I must have been stunned for a few moments for when I next opened my eyes everything was blurred yet I had no sensation of pain. Shiny shoes kept crossing the floor in front of me. I remember nothing more until a rough hand seized my arm and pulled me to my feet. In the next second I was flying through the air and landed on the couch. I felt the rough hands slap my face from side to side. A voice yelled,

"Where is he? Where is your husband?" I heard my own weak and dazed voice saying,

"I don't know. Perhaps he is in bed." The voice yelled again,

"Where did he go?" I closed my eyes and I could hear voices and feet running, I tried to concentrate. When I opened them I could see more clearly. The office door was open. The men inside turned it into a sea of white paper. Drawers were flung on the floor, the contents of the filing cabinets were strewn about and all the books were being pulled from the shelves. The vault behind the book case was open but the men appeared to have no interest in the bullion or the stacks of banknotes. They were ripped all the video tapes apart. There were eight men, none of whom I recognized. One man yelled,

"I found it!" The others crowded round him. One of them shouted,

"It's a false alarm, that's not the Koran. It's gone!"

Now I understood what was happening and I silently prayed for Russell and Shwan. They had less than a seven hour head start to reach a safe place. The man who appeared to be in charge of the operation said,

"Now that you are completely awake, tell me where your husband is?" I replied,

"I never know where he is or whether he is coming or going. He is often in the war zone. Last night he said if he didn't return in three days, he would be in Europe. He never discusses his work or his travel plans with me. I hope if you find him you will allow me the honor of shooting him." He yelled at the men,

"Let's go. Get moving but try not to alert the neighborhood as you go. Act as if nothing is wrong." He grabbed my arm and pulled me toward the door, I pleaded,

"If you are taking me away at least let me get dressed." I wore only my nightgown and had no shoes on. He did not respond but dragged me out of the house along the wall through the shrubbery and out to a waiting car. I asked no further questions realizing it would be a waste of breath. I was pushed into the back seat and sat between the leader and another man. The car and two others sped away into the darkened streets. Since I had not been blindfolded it seemed certain they were taking me away from the house to be killed. The two cars ahead of ours swerved off in the direction of the airport. I did not intend to go meekly to my death. Somehow I would fight against it. But I also realized that even if I were lucky enough to escape, I had no place to hide. I knew only too well what the regime would do. They would announce that I had committed adultery with the American man, or that he had raped me. I would be branded a fallen woman. I would be humiliated. In our culture, death was preferable to the humiliation and shame.

I began to struggle and fight the men in an attempt to get to the car door. They were much too powerful for me so I yelled at them,

"Don't be cowards like my husband, shoot me now!"

"A bullet could end up being less painful than staying alive! Do exactly as you are told or you might just get your wish. Maybe I will shoot you!"

He grabbed my hair and slammed my head into the head of the other man so hard that I felt my eyes popping out and the blurred vision returned. Then I remember nothing until I awoke in total darkness lying on a cold stone floor. I had no idea what time it was or even how long I had been there. But I had a feeling I had been there at least a full day. I did not know what would become of me, but I guessed it would be torture since they would have had ample time to have killed me.

I heard the sound of approaching footsteps and a key turning in a lock. Light suddenly flooded my cell, revealing it to be small with no furnishings of any kind. A man entered. He seemed to be a secret service man rather than a uniformed guard or soldier. He shone a light into my eyes temporarily blinding me.

"It's a Kurdish slut, isn't it?" he mocked. "A good looking one at that." He looked me up and down. I resisted the urge to kick him. The gag in my mouth prevented me from spitting at him as he ordered me,

"Up! Follow me. Maybe we'll get a chance to get together later, huh?" My hands were tied with a coarse, rope and I struggled to rise as he watched me with a look of amusement on his face. I followed him down a corridor with many closed doors on each side. We arrived at a small room where he pushed me inside. It contained a desk with a chair at each end. A man in military clothing sat at the far side with his back to me. I took a step forward and the soldier's chair wheeled around. I found myself face to face with Saddam Hussein. It surprised me that he considered me important enough to conduct the interview personally. Due to fear of the man and the knowledge of the acts he was capable, of sent a shudder down my spine, and my skin tightened all over my body. At that moment I wondered was it really him or was he a double?

"Sit down!" He commanded. I was too scared to move. I just stared into his face feeling like a block of granite. "I said sit down!" He walked around the desk and removed the gag from my mouth. He brushed his fingers across my cheek causing me to give an involuntary shudder. He replaced the thin strap of my nightgown back on my shoulder. I summoned up all the courage I could muster as he held my face between his hands and spoke with a controlled voice,

"Your husband. Where has he gone? Where has he disappeared to?" He took his hands from my face and thumped the desktop. "I want answers! I want the plans of your destination? Where were you and Sa'adoun planning to run to? I am warning you not to waste my time." He grabbed my hair and whipped my head back." Besides killing me what were his plans. Sa'adoun was a traitor but he is no fool. Did he really think my people would follow him? I think not. His hand gripped my hair even tighter. "And you, Najat? Who are you trying to fool? Your husband or the rest of us?" Where is the

Koran?" He snapped my head back again waiting for my response.

"Firstly, I don't know. I told the men who brought me here that Sa'adoun told me if he hadn't returned in three days he would be somewhere in Europe."

"Then perhaps we can bring in your friend, Shwan. Maybe he has the Koran and the tapes of the documentary system? If not him, then who might have them?"

My mind reeled. How much did Saddam know? Was he just testing me? Iraqi intelligence would already have the answers. Of course, he was testing me.

"You are the wife of Sa'adoun and you tell me you don't know anything? Did you never question or were you naïve or blind? How about the guests that come and go from your house? Are you saying he never got drunk and talked? Perhaps your friend, Russell, will tell me about him?"

"Even if you kill or torture me it won't change anything. For truly I know nothing of the things you ask about."

"I warned you not to waste my time, Najat Alwan." He raised his hands in readiness to strike me, but abruptly turned away and called the guard in. "Get her out of here!" The guard manhandled me out the door as Saddam called out, "We have not finished our discussion! Perhaps you will feel more cooperative after a few days of our special hospitality."

The cell door slammed behind me and I was in darkness once again. Sitting on the cold floor, leaning against the wall, the flesh of my back and buttocks molded to the uneven surfaces. My legs hurt. They felt thick and dead and my stomach had long since ceased to growl. It must have been days since I had eaten or had a drink of water. My body had by now become accustomed to the cold, but there were times when I shook and trembled with fear. Nothing interrupted the darkness and real life seemed so far away. In my solitude I thought about my family: my mother who had always believed in me, my father who had great hopes for me and Shilan and Rebwar. I felt great fear for them. I thought about Sa'adoun and Russell, my life at the university, my daily routines. The memories did not seem to be mine. I dreamed the dreams of others. Mostly I thought about Jamal, my beautiful child. I would fold my arms and pretend he was still here, alive and well with me. I would rock to give him comfort and by doing so I comforted myself. I thought about my lifelong friend, Shwan. I wondered if he was safe and if he had helped Russell to reach the border and ultimate safety. I remembered my real mother and father back in Zalan and I wondered if I had failed them in my quest to help bring peace and justice to all of the victims of Iraq. It occurred to me that perhaps all of them had been killed, and soon I would join them.

My cell door burst open. There was the expected glare of the flashlight. I stiffened as the man stepped over me and lifted me by the hair, then shoved me out the door and down the hallway. My legs did not want to support me. He growled,

"You had better talk this time or I will be back to have a good time with you." I tried to move away. He pinned me against the wall, his hands were everywhere. I tried fighting him off but he held me even tighter. His breath was fetid and he almost overpowered me. I managed to wiggle free. Then he pushed me into the same room where I had seen Saddam before. I was forced onto the table and he was preparing to have his way with me. Then I heard a voice yelling,

"Nasr! Nasr! Out!" I sat up on the table. The guard tied my wrists behind my back as if I had sufficient power to react without it, then he left. In the doorway stood the officer who had saved me, at least for the moment. I knew it was not for my own sake. His assault would be no less invasive. He appeared large and well fed, about the age of my father. With a salute, Nasr, the guard left the room.

"I am General Tark. Why do you put yourself through this? You can save yourself from such humiliation by telling us what we want to know." His voice was gentle and persuasive. "Tell us what you know. The Koran doesn't mean anything to anyone except to the government."

"I have nothing to say; simply because I do not know about anything you are asking." Tark looked at me as if I were stupid.

"Say anything of course, protect yourself from harm." I wondered how this man could pretend to give me advice.

"Do you really expect me to believe that once someone is brought to this intolerable place they would be permitted to leave?" The General smiled before answering.

"No. Exactly. It is your choice, however, whether you hold on to your life. No one would choose to die here. You appear to be an intelligent woman, choose to live."

He walked around me and untied the rope binding my wrists. I had begun to deduce where I might be from the direction the cars bringing me here, and the noises from somewhere up above I guessed I was under the Revolutionary Court.

I massaged my wrists now that my hands were freed. "Some prisoners do manage to get out of here. Some choose to cooperate and work with us. We set them up very well, Najat. We reward them with a good life. There is no harm and you too could do this. Save yourself." He stared at me waiting for a response but I had nothing to say, I would give them nothing. I sensed the officer had no respect for martyrdom, for he turned and left the room. Then I was returned to my cell.

The Revolutionary Court located in Kark not far from our home was specifically for suspected political revolutionaries against the government. The lawyers were all members of Iraqi intelligence. Once apprehended, there would be no deliberation regarding the accused prisoner's innocence or guilt. The decision had already been arrived at. The only decision made was if the accused was worth the attempt to recruit for intelligence purposes. If not, the death could be brought about by a staggering selection of methods, so we have court without existing law.

Alone again in the dark, I tried rubbing my skin to aid circulation. I was so intent upon my task I failed to notice my cell door had opened and that someone stood watching me.

"Feeling a little numb, are we?" I knew who owned the voice. "I hope you are feeling more talkative today." Four men stepped in and marched me stiffly down the hall to the interview room. "Are you going to take your seat today or do I have to make you?" I sat on the seat edge ignoring Saddam's eyes. But I could not ignore the gun on the table under his hand. "Good, you learned how to do that. Let's see if you have learned anything else." He asked me the same questions as before and I responded the same as I had earlier. "It would appear, Najat, that you haven't learned anything yet. Perhaps you need to be persuaded. Saddam signaled to the men who grabbed me and lay me face down on the table, one holding my wrists while the other my feet.

"Now, Najat, this will make you feel uncomfortable but you can stop it when you give me the answers I want."

I saw him lift a bat from under the desk, He stepped up to me and I expected my head to be smashed hoping that he would take my life before I sold my soul to the system. Instead he hit the wall. He yelled,

"Where is the Koran, Najat?" Fear overpowered my shaky voice.

"I don't know." He hit the wall again.

"I said, where is the Koran?" he yelled. Before I could answer two bullets whizzed by me killing two of the men holding me. Then he left while the two remaining men began beating me until eventually the pain became too much for me to bear and I must have passed out. I had a vague recollection of being dragged back to my cell. In utter exhaustion I fell into a troubled sleep and a nightmare came to me. I remember every detail. I saw myself rushing through an endless field of death turning over one body after another, unaware for whom I searched. I came across the faces of everyone I loved then I came to Russell's body. I awoke with a scream, shaking violently. Once again I found myself alone in the dark.

Many hours later the same two men came to my cell, blindfolded me, and led me out into the fresh air. Then I felt myself being hurled through the air. My fingertips told me I had landed on wooden boards. I heard an engine start and the boards began moving under me. I realized that I was in the back of a truck and I felt certain I was being taken to be killed. I had come to accept the inevitability of my unnatural death. It was simply a matter of how and when, and how much I would have to endure before my life ended. Over the last period of time since my arrest, I had begged for death more than once. Now that it was at hand I felt relief that it would soon happen. I managed to partially remove the blindfold from my eyes by scraping my head against the metal benches on each side of the truck bed. I saw that no guards were there with me and I was thankful to be alone.

I reflected on what my life would have been had I

not married Sa'adoun. I may have been able to do a better job for my country than I had. Sa'adoun had taken everything from me. Yet the part of me that would never give up caused me to believe there had to be a reason, a purpose for all this and for my life. Another thought found its way into my brain. Perhaps they had found Russell and Shwan with the Koran and no longer needed my confession. I felt a sudden sickness wondering if they had been captured, and what kind of appalling torture they would undergo. I wondered too if my family in Sulaymania had been arrested. The thought of my dear mother, father, and sister undergoing torture on my behalf caused me to cry dry tears for them. I welcomed the fresh air coursing through the canvas-sided truck. It helped alleviate the foul human smells from the seats and floor.

I knew that prisoners were often taken to open fields to be shot, then dumped in wide trenches which became mass graves. Others were taken to the chambers of Kirkuk where they would endure days of debilitating torture. I had learned from listening to Sa'adoun that the guards there were totally devoid of mercy and were considered the elite of the corps. The assignment there was their reward.

The truck stopped moving. The guards dragged me into a building Echoing sounds indicated it must be a large structure, likely a prison. They prodded me with rifle butts until they stopped me and tore off the blindfold. I stood before a man whose face was the most evil looking I have ever encountered. He stepped behind me. I expected a bullet to end it all but instead he removed the rope from my wrists. I took a brief glance at my new surroundings. I discovered we were in a small concrete cell with a high barred window, the only source of light. There was an appalling smell of rotting human flesh and waste. A crack in the wall revealed a steady stream of roaches moving around the floor. My ears discerned the moans of other unseen prisoners somewhere within the building, unable to keep their suffering to themselves.

I realized instantly that I would be imprisoned here. The cell had a filthy threadbare mattress atop a wooden cot stained with blood and excretement. A hole in the floor acted as a toilet. By it stood a pot of dirty water for ablutions. While this place was appalling, it was an improvement on the last place. At least I could assuage my parched lips and mouth with water, dirty or not. I watched a rat disappear into the crack carrying a crust of bread.

"I am Abdula Jamshiry. I'm sure you have heard my name from your husband. I am the supervisor of this prison, I'm also sure you have heard of the Kirkuk jail." He watched my face for a reaction. "If you make things difficult I promise to keep you alive. I will do everything in my power to make the balance of your life a total misery, not that you will be alive that long." He spoke to me with the practiced resonance of a stage performer. "Perhaps you know some of our former guests? Possibly you have a brother, a cousin, or even a friend who came to Kirkuk."

At this point I realized that Saddam had no further use for me. Perhaps they had already found Sa'adoun and there was no need for further interrogation. "You look so clean and fresh," Jamshiry said sarcastically. I still wore only my stained nightgown and my hair was matted from lack of grooming. My exposed skin was dirty with dried blood and filth from the floor of the last cell. "Obviously, you have been handled with great care." He reached for my hand. He held it in a gentle manner as if he were about to offer fatherly advice. "I'm sure you will want to cooperate with me, Najat. You don't want to be hurt any more, do you?" Before I had a chance to answer he whipped my arm around, arching my body so violently that my back was turned to him. He lowered his voice to a soothing whisper as he twisted my arm up my back even higher, "You need only answer my questions. You can do that for me can't you, Najat?"

I held my breath ignoring his question, trying to stifle a scream.

"Did your husband give the Koran to you, Najat? Or did you take it yourself? Sa'adoun is careless with his possessions is he not?" With a final wrench of my arm he pushed me towards the two guards entering the cell. They pulled me into a larger room with Abdula following behind. Several other guards joined us and bound my wrists.

The men picked me up, placed my tied wrists over a hook in the cell roof, and left me hanging there. My arms were pulling out of their sockets. Already raw, I felt the rope slicing right through my wrists and blood dribbled down my arms from the cuts. Abdula signaled a guard to stop me from swinging. Then he stepped up to me, grabbed the hem of my nightgown, and tore it off my body. I suffered the humiliation, but screamed inwardly and foolishly struggled to pull myself free and cover my nakedness. The soldiers touched me anywhere they wanted as if they had never seen a female before, making crude comments about me like little boys trying to impress each other.

Abdula ordered the men to administer the truth treatment; whereupon, the men stood around me and displayed their cowardice by overpowering a woman who was already half dead. They slid their military belts fitted with metal buckles from their waists as though it was their intent to rape me, but instead they began whipping me with their belts. They worked in rhythm, increasing the tempo until I could no longer contain the screams I had held within me since Jamal had died.

Throughout the beating the questions continued.

"With which Kurdish groups are you affiliated" We know that you have a plan for connections to the West. Perhaps you made your plans with your contacts using the many foreign guests you entertained at your house? Did Sa'adoun leave you for us to enjoy? Your friend, Shwan, has told us a great deal about you ,Najat. He is not so stupid as to suffer for his people like you are."

My screams whirled around in my head. Abdula's words hurt me almost as much as the whipping. I knew that informers were a source of great pain to the Kurdish underground workers, and I wondered how we could ever win when our own workers were bought off with the promise of survival. It meant that all trust within the community became undermined and rather than uniting in our misfortunes, the people were irrevocably divided. But I could not permit myself to believe that Shwan had been cowardly.

Looking directly at Abdula I spoke to him for the first time,

"If you kill me now or tomorrow, it will make no difference. I know nothing therefore, I have nothing to tell you." He ordered the soldiers to stop. He rose from his chair and stepped up to me. He ran his hands over my wounds and smeared the blood over my breasts. With his calm soothing voice he said, "It pains me to see such beautiful flesh defiled." He ordered the guards to continue but said, "be sure to leave some life in her" and then he left. I screamed with every strike of the lash until mercifully I lost consciousness. Some time later that day they dragged me down the passage, then threw me into my cell. I crawled on hands and knees on the filthy infested floor to my mattress while the guards stood laughing. Every part of my body hurt, the rips in my flesh burned with an unquenchable fire. It occurred to me that if I went to sleep I might never wake again. I could hear the sounds of prayer from the mosques outside the building. It soothed my mind to hear the sounds of normality beyond these walls. Occasionally I discerned the sounds of the Koran played within the jail. At other times the silence of death covered the residents like a blanket. Later that day the guards came for me again. I fell to my knees and begged "Please, not again." But they dragged me down the filthy hallway and out to the prison yard to witness the hanging or shooting of several men. Abdul stood before me.

"Until you begin to talk, many men will be hung or shot. So it is up to you when I stop doing this." I begged for their lives. One of the young men about to die shouted at me, "My sister, don't let them break you down. We will all be killed anyway." Then they hanged him. I watched until he stopped struggling for breath. This became part of the routine. I had to witness the deaths, or they had to watch my torture in order to break them down. When they took his body down, the soldiers placed it with the others in a vat of chemicals they called Tezab, which dissolved their remains before our eyes.

I realized now that each time we heard a recording of the Koran, one more inmate would be freed from his torture and hanged. Three times each day I received a piece of bread and some warm drinking water intended to keep me alive. The walls of my abode were covered with writings and the poems of hundreds of victims. Written mostly in their own blood, the writings framed their pain and last thoughts. Torture had driven them to labor to write their last hopes, and to try to remember a reason to live. One poem in particular held my attention. It had been scribed on the wall by a seventeen year old boy. His words gave me strength to endure as he had endured.

Long past, my families protection.
Violence has broken all connection

A childhood missed. So much not known.
The nightmare ends when comes the dawn.
My life will end with so little done,
In this my land ruled by the gun.

For the next ten days I was subjected to the whippings. My endurance had been tested. I would never have believed that I could withstand such treatment. My body was deadened and blue with cuts and bruises. Nothing mattered any more. I could not comprehend how I had come to be able to ignore the pain. I had been issued a rough prison robe and it had stiffened with dried blood rubbing against my newest wounds. I had virtually no energy for thought. I tried to recall the religious teachings of my mother but the childish comfort of those days was gone. The only comfort left to me was my desperation for life. Fear taught me to pray and pray. As unreligious as I have been I found no comfort there either. Although I must admit I felt that someone, somewhere, watched over me, and I asked God what had I done that my punishment was so severe.

Open sores now covered my body. The open wounds and the unsanitary conditions were making sleep impossible. I did eat the meager food they brought me each day. Life in Goyza and Baghdad receded from memory. Lying face down I heard the key turn in my cell door lock. I lay there trembling. It would begin again, but Abdula stepped inside and closed the door. He undid his belt and unzipped his pants.

"Don't bother to scream. No one will come to help you." He bound my wrists, turned me over and like an animal. He mounted me. He was heavy. His body forced the air from my lungs. His breath was foul and his presence was appallingly abhorrent. When he had satisfied his primal urges he stood up. Then he called me all manner of names until he had prepared himself to rape me a second time. This time the ordeal lasted much longer with him pinching and biting me. Then he rose and adjusted his clothing.

"I trust I have given you pleasure." As he left he said to a soldier by the door, "Your turn!" That night I suffered the act of rape from three different soldiers. It is impossible to describe how I felt. I spent the rest of the night shaking. There was never enough water in the bowl to properly clean myself of the constant assaults. The smell of the rapists could not be washed away. Abdula had been right. No one would come to my rescue.

A prison doctor visited me daily. His purpose was simply to keep me alive. I did not know that there were doctors that came to the prisons and I didn't trust him. He was a haggard man with mournful sunken eyes surrounded by yellow smudges. I wondered if he too was imprisoned here and had been put to work using his skills to keep the inmates alive. I asked him if this was so and he responded,

"I am often asked the same question but I am not about to tell you my troubles while you are in the middle of your worst nightmare. Don't let them bury you in this cemetery. You know too much to be buried under rocks and mud. There are people trying to help you, Najat."

I did not trust him or believe him, but I needed the comfort he gave me while ministering to my wounds. So far as I knew he might be dispensing his kindness to elicit information to pass on to Abdula. Like other's had before me, I began to express my thoughts and feelings by scratching them on the walls of my cell with a small sharp stone. I had no real objective other than a need to communicate. To whom I did not know. I did not sleep long enough to recall the faces of my family and close friends. My dreams were restricted to nightmares of a slow death and most of my thoughts resulted from hallucinations.

One day when the doctor came to tend me, he said in

a soft voice words that shocked me,

"He will find you even if you are under the sea." They were Sa'adoun's words and Russell had echoed them. How did he know? Was the doctor a connection to the outside world? On subsequent visits he continued to encourage me with the promise that there were people willing to take risks for me. "I am doing what I can to keep you alive, Najat. Don't let the sand wash away what you know. Don't let the knowledge you possess be lost in the sand of the desert, the knowledge which might save us all one day."

I marked the passing days by scratching them on the wall. My captors refused to let me bathe and there was insufficient water in the bowl to be of any value. My own body smells made me nauseous, my matted body hair felt strange. I lay on the bunk thinking of Russell and Shwan. I imagined them being safe in a mountain village and as I did my fingers strayed to my itchy and burning underarms. The hair felt like soft bees. I plucked at it and something came out. I looked at it and screamed in horror. It was a maggot. I felt at my pubic area It was the same there they were coming out from under my skin. I picked at them frantically, hurling them to the floor. I was being eaten alive. I could not distinguish if it was real, or if I was going out of my mind. A guard came to my cell in response to my screams. He banged his rifle butt against the door,

"Shut up! I said. Shut up, that's enough!"

"Look! Look at these! I need to shower I need to wash myself." He left but returned after a few minutes and opened the door. Abdul accompanied him. He pushed me to the ground.

"Eat them!" I didn't move so he picked up the maggots and stuffed them into my mouth. "If you want a shower eat them." He held my nose closed and I had no option but to swallow. At least Abdul kept his word. They dragged me to a room with shower heads. I threw my prison dress under the shower intending to try to clean it as I bathed. I could hardly wait. Opening the faucet full force I scrubbed and soaped my skin, my mouth, and hair. I could not get clean enough to satisfy myself. I sat down on the floor and let the water spray on me as I found momentary peace. A woman stared at me from under another shower. I had not noticed her before.

"Would you like me to wash your back?" she asked in Kurdish. I nodded and she gently scrubbed my back between the welts. "You could make yourself comfortable here. I have been here three years."

"Three years!" I said without looking at her.

"Yes, three years. I was a student at a Kurdistan school at Sarkaritz. One day I listened to my teacher tell of Archimedes philosophy. It was an interesting lecture. I quietly repeated the words after my teacher to be sure I had the correct pronunciation. Two army mulazem entered the room and began to lecture us about education and studying.

"They left when the class ended and I and two others were ordered to report to the school supervisor's office. The supervisor told us that the visitors today were very impressed by our work records. They would like to take us to the student center to honor us with their gift. One of the girls said she would prefer to be honored right here at the school. I suspected something was not right and I said, 'but we have not been top students.' The supervisor said 'you should be grateful that top grades were not the only consideration for this honor, so do not embarrass me.'

The voice of the woman scrubbing my back became stiff and angry and she scrubbed harder than she should.

"I had trust in my supervisor. How could she let it happen?" She threw the soap against the wall and burst into tears.

"Tell me what happened?"

"I was a virgin. They brought me here and I was raped every night by a different officer. They played poker on my naked body and bet for the winners turn at me. They raped me in front of other prisoners to make them talk. I couldn't eat the piece of bread they gave me, or sleep for days. Once I weighed sixty kilos. I became so sick I dropped to thirty. I had to learn to live with my situation for I had nowhere I could go. I knew that my own people would not take me back. One of the girls that came here with me got out after a year and informed my family where I was. She could not deal with the accusations against her from the community so she committed suicide by pouring gasoline over herself and lighting it. After sixteen months my family was allowed to come to see me. My father sold our house to pay the jail supervisor to authorize the visit. I kept apologizing and my father held my hand. He told me the school supervisor had been killed by the revolutionaries. I cannot ever go home again for I will be labeled a government whore, spy, and betrayer. My parents cannot tell anyone where I am for they too will be shamed. In the eyes of society I'm dead, but to my family I am alive and a pain in their hearts."

The woman broke down again and wept. Then she raised her head and spoke again,

"Please don't allow them to do to you what they did to me. Six pregnancies! Six abortions! When I came here I was fifteen and pretty. Now I'm eighteen and I look like I'm a fifty year old. I have experienced so little of the world, yet know more than any young girl should." A pounding on the washroom door disrupted our conversation.

"What are you doing? Your time is up!" I have no doubt that the guards were trying to listen, but I wanted to hear more and to talk, I put on my dripping dress and we parted without even exchanging names. Back in my cell, feeling relatively clean, I could not lie on the filthy bed. Instead I paced on the cleanest section of floor as my dress slowly dried. I thought about the girl in the shower wondering how she could have survived in Kirkuk for three years. The girl still functioned as a human being, feeling concern for my own and other people's lives. I wondered how many other women shared her history.

During the long night I must have slipped into unconsciousness. The first thing I remember, the guards were forcing my head into a bucket of water. The sensation of water entering my nose and mouth, choking me, brought me around.

The guards bound my hands and feet and beat the soles of my feet with short clubs. After a few minutes Abdula stepped in to the cell and watched as he smoked a cigar. Eventually he called a halt to the beating and in a sarcastic voice he said,

"You are trying my patience." My feet felt as though every bone had been smashed. He took his cigar, drew on it until the end glowed red and placed it on the arch of my right foot holding it as it burned into my skin. I squirmed and screamed and then he repeated it on my left foot with sufficient pressure to extinguish the cigar. I fainted with the pain. After once again being roused with the water bucket, Abdula announced,

"We have a lovely afternoon planned for you, Najat," To his men he said, "Take her and follow me." It was impossible for me to walk so they dragged me to a room and left. The doctor came to attend to my latest wounds. The sadness in his eyes as he tended to my feet made me want to climb into his arms and cry. He held my hand as long as time would allow to give me comfort. Just before he left he put his hand in his pocket then returned it to mine. I felt something cold in my palm.

He leaned close to my face and whispered in my ear. As he spoke I glanced and saw my mother's coin necklace laying in my hand.

"Your family is safe and Russell and Shwan are alive. They are staying in a village supported by the Yakete (Revolutionary). They have been formulating a plan to save you. None of us have the luxury of a single mistake. That includes you. Tomorrow you are to be taken to Mussal to be hanged. Do not panic! They will be waiting for you at Valley Gwear which is located between here and Mussal on the way to Sulaymania. You need to know in case something goes wrong."

"Why Mussal? Why not here?"

"This is apart of their process to mentally break you down. Najat, death is easy. Waiting for death is another form of torture. Besides there is not much burial land here in Kirkuk."

Ironically with the news of my death, my heart brimmed over with joy at the news they were safe. For the first time I couldn't distinguish between joy and fear. "You don't only need to listen, you need to trust me. Trust is a fragile thing our people have little of. My name is Aref Failley. I'm from Kannaken. I was badly burned but the scars on my face only reflect the scars in my heart. But today is about you, not me. He will find you even if you are under the sea. Now I must get the coin necklace back to Russell.

chapter twenty two

I lay down, standing was no longer an option for me. For the rest of the morning I slipped in and out of consciousness. In my lucid moments I thought about Sa'adoun. I wondered if he too had been captured and suffered as I had. My captors wanted me to believe he was in their custody perhaps even here in Kirkuk, but they had not convinced me of it. I felt that as smart as he was, Sa'adoun would be safe and sound in some faraway European land. With his ability to think far ahead of others I felt sure of it. I realized how naïve I had been. Were I able to turn back the clock now, I knew I would rather keep my pride as a Kurdish woman than to masquerade as a military wife. Not that I had any choice in the matter at the time.

I thought too of the possibility of my freedom. What would Russell say if we were to meet again with me looking like I did? How would he greet me? Would he take me in his arms and hold me despite my appalling appearance? I thought of the consequences if my attempted rescue went terribly wrong. Would I be hanged tomorrow as the doctor had said, or would I be brought back here?

All too soon the afternoon arrived. The guards dragged me to a room where Abdula waited. In his hand he held a well used straight razor while alongside him a table held an array of surgical instruments.

"Tie her to the metal chair!" He ordered. He tested the edge of the razor, "Not sharp enough, get me another." He stepped up to me and lifted a handful of my hair then he dropped it. Wiping his hand on his pant leg he declared, "Your hair was beautiful once, Najat. You haven't kept it clean, have you? Such a shame for a woman not to look after her hair and keep it clean." Taking a different razor from the guard he said, "I'll help you, shall I." He lifted a second handful and scraped the dry blade across my scalp. I watched my hair drift down to the floor. The next handful he took a thin slice of my scalp also with it with it and hot blood spurted out and ran down my face and neck. I struggled. "Don't be melodramatic, Najat. You have endured worse pain than this. Must I tie your head down?"

I knew that prisoners due to be hanged always had their heads shaved. Therefore, I knew the doctor had spoken the absolute truth. When he had finished, Abdula ran his hands over my shaven and bleeding head. "Tomorrow we are going to hang you up again." Rigidly tied, I could only imagine striking him. "Ghaza!" He called out and a soldier handed him a small clay jar. Abdula pried the lid off and put his finger into the contents. I saw him taste it, then he poured the contents over my shorn head. Honey dribbled down my face and neck, it entered my ears and I closed my eyes to prevent it blinding me. I could no longer see what would come next. I began to panic. I heard feet approach my chair, then I heard laughing.

"Perhaps we can give you something to enjoy with your honey?" The strange sensation began at the top of my head. I did not understand. Then suddenly I realized they had poured an ant's nest on my head. I felt hundreds of tiny bodies dashing all over me. They were on my chest, my arms, and back. They crawled between my lips and teeth and into my ears. I jumped around hysterically trying to escape this appalling nightmare but the chair held me fast. I could not get the ants away from me. He released the rope binding my wrists. I thrashed around hysterically trying to brush them off. My screams filled the room while my torturers laughed like madmen.

"What do you think, Najat? Should we continue? There is no longer a need for you to tell me what I need to know. Everyone involved with the Koran has been captured. Your family will be killed one by one in front of you, and then tomorrow you will be hung." His face was mere inches from mine and I could smell his foul breath as I struggled to inhale through the dense liquid clogging my nostrils. I knew now that Abdul lied and expected me to break down and tell him what he wanted to hear. Despite my frantic attempts to rid my body of the ants I remembered the doctor's words. If I remained strong and survived until tomorrow, I stood a slim chance of freedom from this hellhole and its sadistic leader.

"Filthy whore!" Abdul hit the side of my head with a powerful blow as he yelled at me. It was obvious to me that he had failed in his quest. The veins on his forehead stood out in blue lines and he wiped the spittle from his lips onto his sleeve. "Take this whore back to her cell and do whatever you like with her. She is no longer fresh enough for me. Besides she will hang tomorrow and I don't want to see her anymore." After being dragged to the shower room, I attempted the painful effort to clean myself of the honey and ants.

Within these walls I had become a stranger to myself. One moment I felt strong, another weak. One minute I loved life, in another I would welcome death. The soldiers came to my cell later and one by one they raped me for the final time. I awoke to the sound of the same piece of the Koran that was always played when someone's life was taken from them. I silently sang the familiar piece word by word and then it stopped and the sound of boots came to my door. I told myself the plan must have been changed. I would be hanged while other prisoners watched. I felt an odd kind of peace knowing that my family was safe and that Russell and Shwan had the Koran. But this day I was neither the victim nor the audience.

They hauled me outside. I saw the high wall topped with barbed wire surrounding the Kirkuk prison. The soldiers pushed me into the back of a military jeep as the cowardly Abdul watched from the door.

"Take off," he yelled, and the jeep with two others, one following and one ahead, left the prison yard. I asked myself if freedom would come to me before my appointment with the hangman.

I feared only for the living. I feared that Sa'adoun's Koran, now in Russell's care might disappear along with my flesh, blood, and bones. I feared that in that event nothing would change between East and West. I feared that many, perhaps tens of thousands of my people's lives would remain hidden in darkness forever. I feared that their life stories would be written only in the sand awaiting a desert storm to sweep and hide them for all time. I feared that the trials of my country would go unnoticed and the many thousands who have died under this regime would all have been for naught. I feared that

America, Britain, and the other countries around the world would turn a blind eye to our pleas for help.

I ceased to fear for my own life, but I found myself in a high state of nervousness as the jeep gained speed on the winding road. I tried to stay still as the jeep bounced on the rough pavement. One hand had been tied to prevent me from jumping out and escaping. It had a kind of macabre humor to it, I could not walk let alone run, nor had I the strength or energy. The only part of me able to function was my brain and out here in fresh clean air it became sharp and ready for what might occur. I had to keep adjusting my dirty rag of a garment for the wind kept blowing it open, although the wind on my damaged skin felt good.

"Hey back there, are you watching?" the soldiers laughed, "You may as well enjoy the beautiful scenery. We are taking this trip just for you, besides you will be the big attraction in Mussal today." The driver looked back. "So you are awake then?" His partner said to him,

"Why do we risk our lives delivering her from prison to be hung in Mussal when we could deal with her right here on the road?"

"Don't be stupid. The longer they keep them under torture the more it plays with their minds. This is all to break her down. Some end up talking and some end up dead."

This was just what the doctor had told me. He turned around to look at me and asked, "So what's your story?" The driver responded,

"Leave the poor woman alone. She has had enough already." Suddenly his partner yelled,

"Watch out!" Trying to avoid the large newly excavated holes in the road, the driver swerved, losing control of the jeep. It almost tipped over but it regained its wheels and left the road. I hung on to the seat as best I could but the action hurled me around during the wild

ride. The familiar sound of flying bullets reached my
ears. I knew this would be the time I would be freed or
die in the attempt. I saw the other vehicles now behind
us explode under a hail of gunfire; dust from stray
ammunition flew up from the earth around them. A
grenade put one of them out of action in a volcano of
metal shards, dust, and bodies. The other returned fire
to my rescuers. The vehicle I rode in had left the road
and rolled down an incline stopping at a rocky outcrop
with a bone shaking crash. The sound of gunfire filled
my head as the two men in my jeep were annihilated
before my eyes. Hands grabbed me and tore me from
the vehicle. Part of me wanted to sleep at my relief and
part wanted and needed me to stay awake. I knew I had
fallen into Russell or Shwan's arms. Just as my mind
led me into unconsciousness I heard Russell shout,

"Go! Go! Get moving! What the hell have they done
to her?" Shwan shouted,

"Cover us! We have to carry her to the truck. The
weight of my body in their arms caused excruciating pain
to my injuries. My friends placed me carefully onto the
bed of the truck and climbed in with me. The gunfire
had ended and the brilliant sun forced me to close my
eyes. I felt Shwan pillow my head on his thigh and his
hand on my cheek. Feeling safe at last, exhaustion
overtook me. It was as if a tornado had come and gone
leaving an eerie silence.

I struggled to open my eyes when I emerged from
my coma-like sleep. I tried to pay attention to the sounds
around me. I heard Russell's voice. He must have been
sitting at my side. I heard Shwan's, sat at the other. I lay
between the two people I loved more than life and felt
calmer than I had in months. As I became more conscious
of my surroundings, I heard the Peshmarga proudly
discussing the raid that had saved me. They spoke of
the life long fight against oppression with no fear in their

voices. My heart brimmed over with joy. For a moment all my pain and degradation were forgotten, and a smile came to my lips. I heard Russell's voice breaking in emotion,

"She is smiling; she is going to be okay. She knows we are here." As I became more awake and aware, I knew I must look awful. Beaten, bruised, and shorn and in my appalling prison dress, I began to feel ashamed to be seen this way and to have them see what I had become. I felt in my heart that no man, certainly not Russell, deserves to have the love of a woman whose purity had been stolen away from her. I had nothing left with which to honor him. The truck stopped and I felt myself being carried into a house.

I heard the men planning what they termed the second part of the operation but before I heard it all I was taken to another room by a group of women. They bathed me cautiously, then covered my open sores with an herb poultice to encourage healing and prevent scarring. They spoon fed me some kind of medication through my cracked lips and administered a special tea to help dull my pain. I heard one of the women say,

"No wonder her brother is so devastated. He hasn't rested since we met him." I realized that Shwan claimed me as his sister to protect my reputation.

The women left me alone and Shwan and Russell came to advise me of phase two of the operation which they said could not be postponed. With great care to avoid hurting me, they placed me in a coffin.

"Don't worry, Najat. You know the coffin has ventilation holes, it will be dark and constricted, but you will be able to breathe. Whatever you do make no noise until we reach our destination or until I remove the cover. You will be riding in the back of a military truck and the coffin will be draped with the Iraqi flag along with a big picture of Saddam Hussein. Our

Peshmarga will be dressed in army uniforms lining the benches on each side with Russell and I back in the farthest and darkest recess."

I had been bounced around within the confines of the coffin for quite a long time before I heard our arrival at the first check station. I heard the soldier ask,

"Identification?" I heard the faint sound of rustling papers. "What cargo are you carrying driver?"

"Casualty of war, Sir." I felt the truck begin to move again and I breathed in. After we had been mobile for a few minutes I heard Russell let out a whoop of elation.

"Shwan! It was great that you had that document. You never told me where you got it." Shwan replied,

"It's just a part of my collection from before they began using mass gravesites. The body of a neighbor was shipped back from the war zone. I obtained the document from the family since they didn't need it. I just changed the date."

I heard an exchange between Shwan and a young protégé of his.

"We do what we have to do, right, Ratha? But my friend Russell had everything to do with this mission. Pretty smart for a foreigner, don't you think?" Shwan lifted off the lid and smiled down at me, but my eyes looked for Russell.

The peshmarga men were in high spirits as we continued on the journey. Russell's involvement and closeness was well accepted for whatever story had been told to them. Phase two had gone without a flaw. Laying back I saw the light of a brilliant sunset through the ventilation holes. As darkness closed in, I saw stars dotted all over the heavens like diamonds. Every few minutes Shwan would check on me and whisper,

"Are you alright, Najat? Don't worry, you are safe now." The men kept their voices low joking among themselves. I felt the truck slow down, then change directions. From the bouncing I realized we were no longer on main road but on a gravel trail. Eventually the engine stopped, we had arrived. The men lifted out my coffin and carried me to a small dwelling house. A knock at the door brought an old man.

"Yadlla Kher (God bless you.) What's the problem now?" Shwan answered him,

"Is Na-Na Hapsa at home?" He nodded and Shwan and Russell carried me inside. A heavy set woman with long braids and dressed in traditional Kurdish clothing emerged from another room.

"Shwan! Is that you? You have brought me another customer? Why is it all your friends get hurt?'

"They are not customers, Na-Na. How many times must I tell you?" She looked down at me and her eyes darkened at what she saw.

"Just bring her in, Shwan. Bring her in." They set the coffin down on the floor and Na-Na went to bring water. The Peshmarga roared off in the truck. With Shwan and Russell's help she placed me on a bed.

"Go!" She said to my friends, but Russell did not move. "What are you doing?" She asked in Kurdish. Russell not understanding said nothing. Shwan returned carrying a box of medical supplies. "Thank you, Shwan. I'm afraid my medical stock is badly depleted. I haven't even got any rubbing alcohol but I have some herb medications I can use on the poor lamb." Shwan tried to pull Russell out of the room.

"I don't understand what is going on, Shwan, She needs a doctor!" Na-Na spoke,

"You are a foreigner. What kind of trouble are you in?" Shwan broke in,

"I know she needs a doctor, but we can't get one to come here. We have to wait until one of ours becomes available. I can try in the morning."

"She could be dead by then, Shwan. I thought you said

you had a doctor standing by. So! This is the doctor?"

"Look we can't trust anyone here, but this old woman is good. She has been helping the underground for seventeen years. You have to trust her at least for now." Na-Na ministered to me through the night, her tender words eased my whimpering as I slept through nightmares of my incarceration. I awoke into light. A new day had dawned.

"You have been sleeping since last night, Najat. You look a little better this morning. You must have been fighting someone in your dreams. Just look at the bedclothes, you have tied them in knots." Na-Na lifted me higher and put a pillow under my shoulders, then straightened the bedcovers. "I have cooked rice, lamb, and eggplant stew just for you. You have to eat in order to get well." She placed the meal on a table at my bedside. But I sank back down into my pillow. "Perhaps you will eat when your brother returns; he won't be much longer. Your family is in good hands hidden in the mountains in the valley of Balkeh, and the American is staying here as ordered. It's much too dangerous for him to venture beyond the door of my house. I have been told that Fawzia, whoever she is, so far has not been arrested and is fine"

Na-Na's voice seemed to drift away. I heard only the sound of the wall clock ticking. Whatever medication she had given me sent me back into blessed sleep. Again the nightmares came.

I woke screaming and Russell rushed to my side despite having been warned by Na-Na not to enter my room. I saw him standing over me and I returned to healing sleep. I have no recollection of how many nights I stayed in Na-Na's house, but I do remember that each time I awoke either Shwan, Russell, or Na-Na sat at my bedside to comfort me after each terrifying dream. Na-Na would shoo the men from the room while she attended to all my needs. As the dawn light filtered into my room, I opened my eyes and saw Russell watching over me. I wanted to reach out and touch his lips with my fingers and give him a smile of love and hope.

"What have they done to you? I am deeply sickened by your pain, Najat." He took my hand and gently pried it open placing my mother's coin necklace in my palm. "It has been my magic coin all through our separation; it gave me hope." I squeezed his hand. Then Shwan's voice broke our special moment.

"Is she ok? It's my turn." I watched Russell's face. He cleared his choked throat and said,

"Yeh, Yeh. She will be fine. Go back to sleep." His fingers brushed my face then he kissed my forehead. Having him by my side did more good for me than Na-Na's medicine. I fell into a deep, dreamless, healing sleep as Russell watched over me.

They tell me it was two weeks later when I regained some sense of time. I no longer felt lost or needed to sleep around the clock. I began feeling sensations other than pain. My wounds were healed well enough for me to sit up, but I still could not stand on my feet. They were much too swollen. The mirror had become my enemy, my reflection frightened me. It terrified me to think that the scars on my body would remain forever, capturing my memory like a trap ready to spring each time I viewed myself. My ego was much too fragile to handle it, but Russell's tender words helped to un-spring the trap. His affection and promises sheltered me from my fears. Often he would read to me in his soft sweet voice, at others he would tell me about America and England, his childhood, and his travels. I never for one second tired of hearing him. Shwan, too, would come and sit by me. He would tell me encouraging news about my family and his. Along with Na-Na's nursing and motherly care they all helped to bring a genuine sense of life back to me, and the horrors and nightmares began receding.

At times I talked with Norie, Na-Na's husband. He was typical of the old men of my country. For generations the men hung around the neighborhood. They were not privy to the information and wisdom of our time. They boasted about their ages and were respected, but their focus was on the safety and secrets of everyone's life. We heard that the military were searching every town and city looking for us and the Koran, and so we were still fearful all the time. We knew that things could change in a heart beat, putting us right back where we had started. Pressure had begun to build. We had been trapped within NA-Na's four walls for almost a month. Gratefully we had plenty of food and stimulating conversation but still at times it tired me. By now I had grown a scrubby stubble of hair on my head and I found I could stand without my feet feeling like they were on fire. I had re-learned how to smile and have opinions, which cheered up my companions no end. I believed it was close to the time to move on.

Na-Na's husband entered the room,

"Shwan! He cried excitedly," I have good news! The intense checking on the roads has ended. The military are giving up so you are all safe. You will be picked up early in the morning and taken to Balakh!" Shwan translated the news to Russell.

A big grin came to his face and he looked directly into my eyes,

"I will not leave without you this time. I couldn't handle the guilt and blame and accusations from Shwan which I deserved, by the way. Besides you people are so stubborn and do not take direction." Shwan interjected,

"How can you direct the life of others when you are not a part of it?"

"You're damn right; I'm a part of it! I am part of your world as much as mine! My values, my appreciation, my defenses, my religion are all divided between the two worlds! You may have one world, Shwan, but I have both."

Na-Na walked in with the last meal of her hospitality to us. She must have heard the verbal sparring between Russell and Shwan.

"What are you two arguing about? I enjoy the love story of Mamu Zine. There is nothing more nourishing to the heart than two men fighting over the love of a woman."

She put the tray down and left the room. Russell looked at me.

"What is she saying?" I did not answer out of embarrassment but Shwan told Russell,

"She thinks we are fighting while expressing our love for Najat."

"Then I agree with her. Nothing is greater than a man fighting for the love of a woman."

"No, you don't want to agree!"

"Shwan, why are you so afraid of what you feel?"

"Russell, you can't even begin to understand!" The argument continued with both of them so intent on proving their point they must have forgotten I sat there listening. Before me was the clash of two cultures, neither entirely right nor entirely wrong.

Russell! You can't give her what I want for her, and I can't ever give her what you would."

"You are losing me. What can you possibly give her that I cannot?"

"Russell, my friend, you do not understand. Najat is my whole life. I love her differently than you. She is my dearest sister and I will not give her up!" Russell's next statement in my opinion was rude and out of line.

"But you did give her up! You gave her up for Sa'adoun, to help further your cause and I'm telling you, Shwan,

I'm a much better man than he."

"Perhaps one day, Russell, she will tell you everything. Have you ever asked why that coin necklace is so precious to her?"

"I don't need to. I have seen enough!" Hearing this debate I wondered if there had been similar conversations while I languished in prison. Despite my feeling that talking about it in front of me was disrespectful, I felt gratitude to both of them for their love and caring. I felt I had to stop the discussion.

"Enough is enough! Sa'adoun is no longer a part of my life. From now on I wish to speak for myself. Besides look at me. Yes, have a good look." The argument stopped. I think they both realized they had said too much. They both apologized for their behavior. They blamed each other for putting me into Sa'adoun's life and for leaving me behind when I had a chance for freedom.

"No one is to blame. I made choices and decisions on my own. They may not have been the cleverest ones I ever made, but because of my actions I found the Koran and I found.... Never mind I was about to say love, but enough has already been said. Speaking of the Koran. Where is it?" Shwan answered,

"It is hidden in the same village as your family. Now let's eat, I'm hungry."

After dinner we played dominoes as if nothing had occurred between us. I took to my bed early to prepare for the early start. I lay thinking with some nervousness about tomorrow and realizing how much I was loved, a warm glow flowed over me. I heard my two friend's laughter in the next room, and I knew that everything would be all right.

chapter twenty three

At five thirty a.m. filled with the confidence of fortune, we three were ready to begin a new adventure. Russell expressed self-assurance dressed in a traditional Kurdish outfit as he posed for us with a flourish. He looked like a handsome young Kurd with his turban and mustache. No longer did he look like a healthy American man. Russell behaved in an agitated manner eager to get started but unsure of himself in his unusual dress.

"I can't go out into the world looking like this." He pulled one jacket sleeve down over his hand letting it dangle. Then he began walking with an exaggerated limp while twisting the sleeve round and stuck it in his mouth. His humor in his excitement flowed like water and despite the early hour he had us all laughing, but it was not humor that caused the levity. Rather it was the nervousness of our journey of life or death.

Na-Na kissed both men's cheeks and wished them a safe journey and thanked Russell for his financial support. She kissed both my cheeks and covered my head with her scarf

"I wish you joy and good fortune in your life. You are young and beautiful, Najat, go become involved in your life again. You can't hide from life, you have already proven yourself. You must go and do what you can. Seek adventure, take the consequences and keep your secrets to yourself. There is too much ugliness to face." Na-Na's husband stepped in,

"Time to go. The taxi is here. It will be crowded.

The taxi driver's wife had claimed a place in the back seat. She was holding a six month old child in her arms. Shwan sat next to the driver while Russell and I joined the woman in the back. Our hosts waved and we were on our way. Within my heart came a great sadness. I knew I would never see the city I loved again. My childhood, my parents, and all the friends I had made crossed my mind. I took with me the memories of green meadows, the wildflowers, the little love-filled houses and my people.

"This is Nazaniny, the driver's wife." Shwan said turning in his seat. She will act as my wife. Najat, you will carry her daughter in your arms but say nothing unless asked. They will honor you as a lady anyway. We have a few check points to pass before we get to the back country. Russell sit there looking dumb and suck on your sleeve as though you haven't eaten for a day." When we arrived at the first checkpoint I already held the baby in my arms. I ignored the fresh baby smile and her little dimpled feet kicking as she giggled. Russell secretly brushed his hand on my lap to reassure me he knew of my sensitivity.

"Get out!" The soldier ordered. The men were

thoroughly checked for weapons or contraband. I kept my eyes on Russell. I didn't know whether to be afraid or laugh at his antics. He was hilarious. He jumped up and down on his toes, pulled on his sleeve and even poked the soldier's gun. The soldier pushed him away. The driver spoke up,

"He is blessed by God's cause. He is mute, deaf, and crazy. He does not know what he is doing. Have God's mercy on him."

"Let these crazy valley farmers go!" He shouted at the barrier guard. We got back in the taxi and left the checkpoint behind,

"Russell! You are a crazy man. You should be an actor, not a politician."

"I guess, Shwan, living in Iraq you pretty much become anything."

"Welcome to life in Hell," the driver commented. Nazaniny spoke only when spoken to; otherwise, she quietly crooned to her baby. I watched Russell's eyes as he took in the scenery. It seemed as if he did not wish to miss anything from the green fields to the distant mountains.

"Get ready for the next checkpoint!" The driver announced. Russell said,

"Don't worry they are not going to stop us to ask any questions or interrogate us." Shwan contradicted him,

"They have no mercy just like on the road to Baghdad, but they will go through everything quickly because they are nervous. They are fully aware they are in revolutionary territory and on the alert for attacks."

"But not after the way I acted. They already have our taxi license number and who they believe we are. They are not going to move their lazy asses for us."

Russell had been right. We passed through several checkpoints with only a cursory look in the taxi trunk. The driver, obviously an astute man, said to Russell,

"Perhaps you have been in this country long enough to have learned how to survive?" Driving through the back country we were stopped occasionally by the Peshmarga with a quick hello and where are you heading. Shwan and the driver were deep in their own conversation concerning complaints and politics and I enviously watched Nazaniny peacefully holding her baby and trying to sleep. I looked away, for seeing them brought back vivid memories of myself and Jamal. Russell had his gaze fixed on the passing scenery.

"I'm quite taken with this part of the country, Najat. I'm amazed that after all the years of war there is this much left untouched. He reached out to hold my hand, and I realized I had paid no attention to it.

"Are you ok, Najat? You seem nervous."

"I am. The closer we get the more nervous I become."

"I understand. But you have nothing to worry about."

"Russell, think about it. My family gave me everything; in turn I have given them nothing but grief. I became a great disappointment to them. I wonder if secretly they are apart from me and have disowned me. I left them with no choice. I'm the worst fortune they found."

"Found?" Russell appeared to be puzzled by my statement. "You are so full of surprises, Najat."

"You, Russell, are a very smart man. You do exactly as my mother taught me to do which is to listen; suck in people's wisdom, think, and talk less."

"Here we are in Balakeh!" The driver called out

We entered the high mountain village. Fruit trees abounded along the narrow streets, Peaches, apples and others I could not recognize. Vines with grapes clung to the walls of the low mud and rock dwellings so reminiscent of the houses of Zalan where my life began. On the hillsides hundreds of sheep grazed, while a flock walked through the street with a shepherd cajoling them to let our car get by. Shwan turned to look at me and for the first time since meeting him I saw tears in his eyes. Nothing needed to be said, for some things are never forgotten.

The taxi stopped. The steep, narrow, muddy dirt street made further travel to get to the small houses higher up the hill impossible. With Russell's assistance Nazaniny and I exited the taxi. I saw all four members of my family anxiously waiting for me at the bottom of the hill. I posed difficulties for them but their sprits were still alive. Mother approached me first,

"My daughter, you look so thin, so fragile. What have they done to you?" We soundlessly offered our love and we both began to cry. Father joined us,

"My daughter, I prayed. You know the old man never prays, but I did pray for a miracle for you." Shilan and Rebwar rushed in and we all hugged together. I saw my father bend to kiss Russell's hand. But Russell had learned our customs so he bent and kissed my father's hand.

"Your daughter is a very brave woman." Then my mother kissed Russell's forehead.

"My dear son, I cannot return the favor of life. You saved us all." Then Rebwar gripped his hand in a powerful handshake,

"Thank you for bringing my sister home!" Shilan hugged Russell and said. "I knew you would rescue my sister. When Shwan told me about you I had no worries. Thank you for not letting me live my life without her." We gathered together to walk up the hill. I could not walk far so Rebwar picked me up like a baby and carried me. Then he transferred me into Shwan's arms. The tiny house offered my family nothing except safety and peace. The floor was carpeted in dishes and their meager belongings. I told my father,

"I will get everything back that you have worked so

hard for Father. I promise."

"I have it already. I have you back." It had reached four o clock and Shilan laid down the leather dining cloth. We all sat down to eat the welcoming festive dinner my mother had worked so hard to prepare. I could tell that Russell felt nervous in my parent's home, especially being an honored guest, but still he relaxed and accepted the hospitality and returned his respect well. After the meal, Shwan along with Nazaniny and her husband, left for a different house. They would be staying with his family who had fled the danger in Sulaymania. His final advice to all of us, "Say nothing to anyone." As night covered the valley extinguishing a long day a cool mountain breeze began to rustle the leaves. The perfume of ripening fruit wandered through the village. Candles flickered in dimly lit houses. Coyotes wailed their mournful howl in the rim rocks above as we sat outside, bathed in the tranquility of a star filled sky. Many questions were asked of Russell about America but almost none to me. Everyone knew what happened to people having a taste of the Ba'ath Regime's prisons. I took the opportunity to ask my family if they knew how my old friend Shanna was, or if they had heard any news of her. Rebwar said.

"I heard that she got married to a fellow university student and left the country. We have not heard a word since, so I don't know if she made it out."

My family and Russell stayed out in the cool air, but I had become terribly tired and retired to the bed Mother had prepared for me.

The sound of Shwan returning to the house with two men aroused me from my sleep so I went outside and saw Russell standing with them. Shwan was telling Russell,

"These two men are brothers. They are smugglers and they will take you to the border crossing point.

Everything has been arranged. You will easily smuggle the Koran and yourselves even out of Iran. Then, Russell, you can fly back home. There is no need for you to stay and suffer." In an angry voice Russell shouted,

"You're darn right I have a reason to stay! You are as bad as Sa'adoun Alwan for kicking me out of here!"

"It's not what you think, Russell. You have no time. Your life and our lives are on the run. Don't kid yourself for too long, this place may not even exist in a few months."

"I don't care, Shwan. I'm not leaving here without her and I'm not going to risk her life. Not now. Not ever." Knowing Russell's determination, Shwan gave up and handed him two passports.

"You must leave now. Look at the passports. They are perfect Iraqi passports and your name is Khalid. You will not be stuck.

"Shwan! I'm sorry I called you Sa'adoun. Why didn't you explain to me what you were up to and when did you take my picture without asking me?"

"Time is valuable, I've been working on this since before we kidnapped Najat, and I couldn't ask you to take her unless you truly wanted to. I needed to hear it from you. That's why I made two passports. Just one has your picture and information, the second one has both of your pictures, for as you know women cannot travel alone and must be accompanied. You are no longer an American. Also remember you are deaf and mute as a result of God's cause or Saddam's cause, as you prefer, my friend." Both of them laughed. "I trust you know you cannot leave or enter into Iran with a woman unless"....I interrupted Shwan.

"I'm not going anywhere! You two must leave, not me!" Russell stepped up to me,

"What did you say? What is it you are afraid of?"

"The fear of the memories I carry will never let me

be free." With emotion breaking free, looking deep into my eyes, he said,

"I love you, Najat. I have loved you since the first moment I saw you. On that first night I envied everyone who knew you. I envied Sa'adoun more than anyone, and I felt saddened that you were on his arm and not mine."

"Dear Russell, your love saved me then and it will save me for every second I breathe. But my faith and my purity have been stolen from me. I'm left with nothing with which to honor you."

"But, Najat, you honor me with your love." My sister Shilan having heard us, stuck her head through the little window. Never having been one to hesitate in speaking her mind she said,

"I never knew American men are so....how do you say it?" Appearing annoyed, Russell replied,

"Ever since I have been here you have interrupted our most intimate moments. Are you sure you are Najat's sister? You don't seem like you have been brought up in the same culture. Go and quietly wake up your mother and father." We went into the house while the two smugglers waited outside. Rising from his bed on the floor father said,

"I'm not young anymore. Don't you get tired? Why are you still awake?" Obviously feeling shy and nervous, Russell nodded at Shilan,

"You first."

"No, you first. I'm not going to marry my sister. You are!"

"I know I should give the honor to Rebwar, but his English is limited so tell your father exactly what you heard me say, repeat it to your father; nothing added, nothing deducted." Under Russell's watchful eye she translated his words to Father. I saw a smile come to Father's face at the goings on in his house. Summoning up his courage, Russell began,

"I know you don't know me well, I am a stranger to you all and to this culture, but I have shared a great deal of your daughter's pain. I have shared her loss and I understand her fear. I also know she will never be safe here." Shilan stopped him,

"Not so fast Russell. If you want me to translate speak slower."

"Look at me, Najat. Is it proper if you translate this yourself? I'm stuck. All I want to say is that I am deeply in love with your daughter, please let me marry her" I told Father what Russell had said, but he did not respond and I wished I knew what he was thinking. Russell spoke again,

"I understand, sir, that Kurdish women are forbidden to marry foreigners or into different religions. But we all have the same God and we all cry and love the same way. I will do whatever it takes in order for me to marry Najat." Father moved to speak,

"You are a good man with a great heart. I have no wish to prevent the wishes of my daughter or yours. You do not know me either. I'm ignorant of nonsensical traditions and customs. But we value marriage differently than you Americans. In your culture you do not stand by your marriages."

"That is not exactly true."

"When I was a child, Russell, my grandfather was a soldier for the British army. Generals, officers, and common soldiers were all husbands and fathers, but they all broke their vows, faith, and promises, and apparently it was the same in their homeland. What you have today you do not throw away tomorrow. Humans are not like a pair of old shoes." I felt I had to break into this discussion.

"Sa'adoun threw me away Father when I was new and pure. Russell, through his love for me, is giving my honor and dignity back to me." Russell asked Shilan what I had said to my father but she did not respond.

"Russell you have already proven your love and caring for my daughter. But keep your faith and promises."

"And I expect the same from her," Russell responded. My sister Shilan said,

"Rebwar! Hurry down to Mullah Esmail and wake him. Tell him I want him here urgently."

"I'm so happy for you, Najat. No, I'm not; it will mean I never see you again." Russell confused at the language exchanges asked,

"Does that mean yes?" Shwan grabbed Russell's hand,

"Congratulations, my friend. Don't forget what you have to do." Russell kissed the hands of both my parents and they welcomed him into the family. In respect of my familys presence there was no display of romance or affection. It seemed as if we had not met before. Shwan was busy translating the lecture Father had given Russell, but I knew that Russell knew almost as much about our culture as we did. Rebwar appeared at the door with Mullah Esmail. Still looking sleepy, the Mullah dressed in his long black robe with his belt tied around his waist and his white turban resting squarely on his head, stepped into the house. He held his Koran in his hand draped under a green cloth, a symbol of respect.

"Ya Allah Khear, I was just heading for the mosque!" My father made the Mullah swear on the Koran that he would never repeat what was to be done here. I knew the Mullah could not make a promise with God and then lie. He must always tell the truth. So he did promise.

"Are you ready to be a Muslim, my son?" He asked Russell.

"I thought I was to be married, not change my religion?" Shwan answered him,

"You know none of us believe this rubbish. Just repeat

the words after him to get your bride." So he did word by word as the mullah dictated them to him.

"Ash hadu lae laha elalla wa ashhadue ana Mohamed rasullalla."

I believe in God, I believe in spirit, I believe in Mohammed. Russell spoke out after repeating the word Mohammed, gratefully only I, Shilan and Shwan understood his outburst.

"What an example! He was a warmonger with over eighty wives!" We started laughing. Mother, Father, and the Mullah looked at us bewildered.

"Is he making fun of the Koran?" Father asked, Shwan quickly jumped in to save the solemnity of the moment,

"No, no, he is cleaning himself of his old religion." Mother took her own thin almost weightless wedding band from her finger and passed it to me.

"It's your turn, my daughter," the mullah said in a tired voice. I stepped closer to the mullah and I repeated my vows turning to look at Russell. His virtually permanent smile returned to his face, the smile that had always enchanted me. The mullah handed him a paper to sign.

"What am I signing, Shwan?

"If you divorce her you must pay five hundred Turkish gold liras. It is left over from the Turkish Ottoman Empire. The mullah can't even read it himself."

"Then as far as I'm concerned he can make it a thousand," the Mullah said,

"He must be rich. I should have married him to my daughter!" Father answered him,

"He is just showing his love for her and confidence in his promise." The Mullah signed the document. Shwan made it clear to the Mullah he should leave right away for the mosque. Turning to Russell he whispered,

"By the way, any one of us could have made this document. It was done this way to give peace of mind to

Najat's parents."

"Have you brought the "you know what", back here, Shwan?"

"No. But I will be back with it in a few minutes." He returned with a sack containing Sa'adoun's Koran and a second sack with money in it. Russell handed the money sack to my father and told him,

"When we arrive in America there is sufficient money in this sack to get you out of here, or hopefully things will change and you can go back to Sulaymania and live your life in peace." The moment had arrived when I would leave my parent's behind again. My past would soon not belong to me anymore, my family would once again become a memory. In return I had been given Russell's love and the freedom I had often dreamed.

We had to hurry for our guides were waiting. We gathered a few essentials for the journey and my parents gave me some warm clothes and food. Then together we walked down the rocky hill with me walking much slower than the others, but it gave me a little extra precious moment with my mother. At the hill bottom the same taxi we had used yesterday waited for us.

As we hugged goodbye, the emotions in our hearts kept us silent. We expressed our love with our tears. It felt as though part of me was being torn away. But I only had to look at Russell to know his love mesmerized me with his feelings toward me and his heroic journey to save my life. It gave me hope and promises of every tomorrow together and closing page after page of the life I was leaving behind me, a life that offered me nothing anymore.

We drove off with one of the smugglers driving, the other sitting next to him and Shwan, Russell, and I sat in the back. We drove ever higher into the mountains through cloud and fog. I laid my head on Russell's chest. In such peaceful comfort I fell into fearless sleep. I remember the taxi stopping. A light covering of snow hid the ground; we were in a valley between two high peaks wearing caps of ice.

Cold, clean air swirled around us as we alighted the taxi. The only sound was the soft moan of the wind and the snorting of some horses tethered close by. They were being tended by two additional smugglers. They soon had our belongings loaded onto the horses, but Russell held on tight to the bag containing the Koran and the money. One of the men placed me on a horse and Russell climbed on behind me. We all got a quick lesson in handling our animals and received a stern warning not to deviate from the trail.

"There are mines everywhere so follow the horse in front of you. If you do wander from the trail and set off a mine, the army will be immediately alerted. Then it is game over for all of us. There is a military presence on the mountain over there in the distance where they would send a missile." Shwan joked with Russell,

"This is the best honeymoon you could ask for. Are you ready to walk through fire?"

"It is the worst, Shwan." Russell laughed, "How often does a man get to walk through a minefield on his honeymoon." Three of the smuggler guards rode ahead with constant security reminders to us. I heard them all, but for the first time I had no fear and nothing fazed me. Russell's love and his arms around me holding the reins allayed all my concerns. Sometimes he would squeeze my waist with his elbows, at others his lips would brush my neck and he would whisper,

"I would walk through fire to keep your love." I remembered my mother's words from long ago when she advised that love was complicated. But my love had freed me from complications, nothing like what mother had said. We rode for hours, uphill and down. At one point the sun came out, and we sat to eat and rest the horses. The smugglers said we were relatively safe now and they broke into song. A lone Peshmarga heard them and came to visit; it appeared he knew the smugglers well. By evening we had descended the mountains on the far side finding ourselves in a grove of walnut trees close to Karmak village. We were instructed that we must stay here until after dark and then we would walk in the moonlight.

We tied the horses to the trees while Shwan already lay on the gravelly ground fast asleep. The smugglers positioned themselves close to the horses. Russell and I sat away from the others with our backs up against a tree trunk. He pulled out the forbidden Koran and handed it to me to read and translate into English. We covered the first thirty pages but at that point there were no real surprises. Everything we read about was already happening. The war, the Kurdish genocide, the map drawn for every Iraqi child's future, to create the Ba'ath Regime's most complex military organization. The next few pages were no surprise to Russell and I. It was to bring shock and disaster to Kuwait and blackmail other countries named in the document. Every detail about the weapons of mass destruction was listed.

"Look at the next page, Najat! Look at all these codes written in English. I can't make sense of this; I wonder what it could be." By the time we had read the thirty pages it was getting dark and I could no longer see. The smugglers broke their conversation. In panic one of them lay down with his ear to the ground.

"Shh! They are not just one or two and they are loud." Two others joined him to listen. "We must leave in a hurry." With the sounds getting closer by the minute, Russell put the Koran back in the sack. Soon we could see figures on horseback in the gloom. They were other smugglers and escapees, seven of them. Their horses were out of breath and the escapees could scarcely put two words together. They told us they were traveling along the border from north to south and the military are traveling from south to north. Russell said,

"This is strange. If this is a border attack why haven't we heard a single shot or explosion;" He grabbed Shwan's arm. "Tell them we must leave as fast as we can." Before Shwan had finished translating, the smugglers were already directing the horses to the peak of the mountain. We too climbed on as fast as we could to run from death.

In the urgency of the moment I felt no pain. My energy and strength rose to levels not felt in many months. We climbed part way up the mountain, hid the horses and ourselves behind some high rocks and, surveyed the scene below us. The military vehicles crept along the base of the mountain. Some stopping and some continuing, the only thing to be heard was the sound of vehicle engines.

"It is not a usual raid or attack that I am familiar with," Russell whispered. A cloud drifted away from under the moon allowing it to illuminate the valley floor. We saw soldiers hurrying like ants, transferring the load from the vehicles into a cave. "Let's pray they leave before daylight. Otherwise they may see us and we will all be shot. My God I have just realized what is happening down there. Remember, Najat, when Sa'adoun spoke about the critical temperature for the toxic gas? Well, those are gas canisters, I have seen them before. They are storing them in the cave because this side of the mountain receives a lot less sunlight; therefore, it is in a much cooler and safer place."

We watched in silence almost afraid to breathe as the soldiers completed their work and began laying mines in a fan shaped configuration around the entrance. We had witnessed the hiding of weapons of mass destruction. Russell remarked,

"I thought this was Peshmarga territory? My God, everybody is involved." I answered,

"Yes, Russell, everybody."

"It takes only a few bad men, Najat. Where is Shwan? Where is that crazy man? He was here just a minute ago?" We stayed in hiding lying on the rough ground until after the sun had risen watching the proceedings below us. One by one the trucks left and headed south leaving the area bathed in silence and peace, but in the bowels of the mountain they left behind packaged terror and death. Shwan returned, we had been worried about him but could do nothing.

"My God, Russell, did you see what they were doing?" He said after catching his breath. "They are hiding weapons of mass destruction. I heard every word they were saying."

"You didn't have to risk your life, Shwan. For that matter all of our lives to figure out something we already know!" Shwan turned to me,

"My dear Najat, I realize this country, Iraqi, Kurd, or Arab cannot be saved by any number of people like you or I." Then he faced Russell, "So my American friend you had better stay alive to take back to America what you have witnessed and learned. Because you are the one with the Koran and the message, stay at the back of the group. If someone has to die by a mine it had better be one of us. One less Kurd, what does it matter?"

The smugglers were annoyed at the long delay and cautioned us again about not wandering off the trail. In fear of a possible mine we started off again. We had been a long time without sleep but safe in Russell's arms, I believe I slept sitting on the horse as we walked. The sun had almost completed its journey across the sky when the head smuggler shouted,

"This is the village of Tawela." We had arrived at a place with hundreds of small rock built houses situated on the side of a steep mountain. Farms of walnut trees stretched all along the valley but few people were to be seen except for a group of boys who appeared to be waiting anxiously for some excitement.

Leading us into a paddock with precious little grass for the horses, the smugglers helped us off the horses and handed us our belongings.

"You go with this boy Kulla" Kulla reminded me of a miniature Shwan about eleven or twelve years of age. "You are staying overnight in his house. I will be here to meet you at dawn." The smuggler divided our group of escapers among the eagerly awaiting boys. We followed Kulla up an extremely narrow road paved with large rough rocks. The boy, completely sure of himself and obviously used to the street and its individual rocks, bounded ahead of us while we stumbled and tripped as we tried to follow him. We reached a house part way up the hill and Kulla offered the three of us some rubber shoes then led us into the house and into a tiny bedroom. The floor was carpeted and felt warm and comfortable with an array of blankets and cushions.

Kulla's mother entered and offered us clean, but threadbare towels. Then she showed us a small room built from piled rocks with many holes and gaps. The room was for bathing with a large tub of hot water boiling on a fire. Close by sat a barrel of cold water and a plastic container. The men allowed me to wash first and a little girl of five or so years came to assist me. She tried to ladle the water for me with her small hand having little strength. The steamy room made her gasp for breath and yet she refused to leave, having been taught responsibility and hospitality. When she could no longer tolerate the heat she poured cold water over herself with a grin and a sigh of relief.

Russell and Shwan went to the washroom next aided by Kulla. Through the thin wall I could hear every word they were saying,

"I don't understand this culture, Shwan. Grown men bathing together, a man holding another man's hand, women too as they walk down the street, but not a man and woman before they are married."

"Don't be fooled by the Islamic world and everything that is going on here, Russell. We just don't talk about it. I heard the small girl giggle as she peeped through a crack with her face to the wall. Kulla's voice rent the quiet as he yelled,

"Zearin! I can hear you giggling. How many times have I told you not to peek! It's not polite. Wait until Mother finds out, she will punish you." Then I heard the men laughing. When we were all bathed, the mother served a meal of rice, fried tomatoes, and bread. From time to time the children would put their heads around the corner to watch us and giggle. Despite his eleven years Kulla was the man of the house. He had younger brothers and sisters and his smuggler father had been killed with a land mine. Kulla had taken over his father's position smuggling goods and refugees over the border with the two horses his father had left behind. Russell asked him

"How long have you been doing this, Kulla? What kind of goods to you smuggle?"

"Since I was nine years. Most times I don't know what I am taking. It depends on what the boss hides in the sacks of walnuts or rice. Some of my friends got caught taking alcohol into Iran. The Iranian Pasdar caught them, so they were put in jail for a few months, then they came home." Russell spoke to Shwan,

"Don't tell me this young boy will be responsible for leading us across the border into Iran?" I translated the boy's answer.

"Yes, you are my customer. Every day, all day, I wait at the horse paddock to hear the boss call my name. After four days with no work, today he called me. Don't worry,

I am a responsible guide. For the last two years I have never got a customer in trouble and besides my mother has almost run out of food and money."

"How much does the boss smuggler pay you for each trip, Kulla?"

"I get fifteen dinar or one dollar fifty."

"How much did we have to pay the smuggler, Shwan? Five hundred dollars American wasn't it?" Shwan nodded, "Goddamn!" Russell exploded. The Iraqi people live in one of the most oil rich countries in the world, yet children have to live like this! In my country most children of eleven years do not know how to make a meal for themselves, but here a child has to be a man at that age." Kulla looked at Shwan,

"I think I have upset him. I did not mean to beg you to come with me."

"Don't worry, Kulla, he did not mean anything. We are coming with you. He is just mad at your boss for not paying you enough." Russell asked the boy,

"Do you have any sacks of rice here?"

"No, sir. Early in the morning the boss will bring the goods to my horses in the paddock."

"Listen Kulla. Find me four sacks of rice and two of walnuts, also a knife or small saw, and I will give you five hundred dinar. And if you swear on your father's grave you will never tell anyone, I will give you five hundred more when you get us over the border." Kulla, the young businessman, remained cool and accepted Russell's offer like a gentleman. After some weak tea, Kulla and Shwan retired to one room for the night while the mother and her other children went to another, leaving Russell and I to sleep in the main room.

Roosters sitting atop the village walls announced that the dawn had come. The sounds of crowing mingled with the sound of a horse banging its food bucket while other's whinnied in anticipation of a morning feed, wakened us. Cooking smells drifted in the window from houses along the street. We rose from our beds to find that Kulla, accompanied by Shwan, had been up long before the dawn and had rented a spare horse, and it stood loaded and ready tethered by the door. Shwan told us the Koran was hidden deep inside a sack of rice on the right side of the horse. Kulla handed Russell a butcher knife, proudly stating,

"This is the biggest knife I could find!" This started our morning with a laugh, after all Kulla was just a pure innocent child. Russell pulled a coin from his pocket and placed it in the boy's palm telling him it was an American tradition showing that the knife would not cut the friendship or the trust to the promise you made to keep our secret. Russell turned to me and said,

"With a knife this big, I had to do the coin thing."

We made our way down the bottom of the street. We passed flocks of sheep and groups of farmers on their way to work in the fields. Young girls walked up the hill with their long dresses flapping in the morning wind. They carried clay pots of fresh cow or sheep's milk. We were offered some warm milk to drink which we gratefully accepted.

We mounted our horses as the names of the boys who would lead us were called. The disappointed ones leaned resignedly against the paddock wall with the hope that their turn would come soon. Kulla took a rope and tied it around each horse's neck and handed the ends one to both Russell and Shwan. In total thirteen horses and escapers left the paddock. These boys leading us without the smuggler's advice or direction were the masters of the road. The terrain soon became rough and rocky with only an extremely narrow trail sufficient only for one horse at a time. Kulla indicated we should dismount and lead the horses.

"Najat stays on. Her feet cannot handle this rough

ground," Russell stated in a firm voice. The mountain side became extremely steep and the men and the boys struggled to climb while leading the horses. Sweat poured from their brows and dripped down faces and they fought for breath along with the laboring animals. We climbed ever higher and, while I had it relatively easy, my adrenaline pumped through me to break free one more step from the life that had abandoned us all.

This first mountain turned out to be a training ground for the next one. The grade seemed like it was almost vertical. The horses had to be pushed and pulled as hooves slipped on the shale like slippery rocks. Sometimes pieces of the rock broke loose and plunged down the mountain, and we could hear the echo of the falling rock from the mountain beyond, along with our cries of struggle. This mountain had no mercy as the thirteen horses in pairs climbed the track. The adult smugglers led the way with the boys and the other refugees following while Russell, Shwan, and I were the third pair from the rear. The footing was treacherous and both man and beast slipped constantly. A shout came from behind us. We quickly turned to see one of the horses directly behind us had gone down with all four feet sliding backwards knocking the legs out from under the horses behind. They struggled to regain their footing while the horse that had gone down first slid over the edge of the trail, taking the boy handler with it. The terrain was so steep that the boy and horse rolled over and over down a hundred feet or more coming to rest against a rock outcrop. Our caravan stopped and all the men quickly slid down the rock face to help. While the rest of the boys did their best to control the horses still on the trail where they trembled in panic and fear.

The child lay under the horse's body. He had been crushed to death by the sheer weight of the beast. I saw the men try to extricate his small frame but there was

SHANNA AHMAD

insufficient manpower to move the heavy horse who moaned in pain. A piece of white bone poked through the skin of a foreleg. There was nothing they could do for either of them. The head smuggler cut the horse's throat to end its misery. After the men had fought their way back up to the trail, the head smuggler said in a commanding voice,

"The journey must continue!" One of the two bachelor refugees who had been with us since the start of the journey elected to go back to Tawela village taking the news to the boy's family. The journey to the peak took every ounce of energy the men, boys and horses had. It became a somber procession. While losing the horse would affect all of us indirectly, we all felt the loss of the boy deeply. Being forced by circumstances to do this kind of work was in my opinion another striking condemnation of the Iraqi Ba'ath regime. We rested before beginning the descent to the valley below, traveling in silence, contemplating the death of the smuggler boy. As the trail became easier the jagged mountain blended into rolling hills.

"We used to take a different route." Kulla advised us. "It was much easier and faster but too many mines exploded killing many of my friends. That's how my father died. One boy did not know he carried explosives in his rice bags and when he stepped on a mine it caused a huge explosion killing everyone with him. The boy's father admitted he had sent his son off with such a cargo. He said he needed the money. Anyway, it slowed down our business for a while until the boss decided we should take this route."

"Does what has just happened to your young friend not seem so bad to you?" Shwan asked,

"Of course it's not okay with me. I mean winter will soon be here with blizzards and surprise snowstorms; we freeze every step of the way, both ways. If we don't

360

go, the boss gets upset with us. The mountain we have just crossed is often ice coated and we lose horses or they cannot get a foothold. There are many more accidents in the winter."

"Do any boys die in the winter, Kulla?"

"Yes, that's what I'm saying. But we are lucky we have this route, or we would have no business."

Now that travel was easier for the horses, Russell and I rode together again and as he held me around my waist, I translated what Kulla had been saying. I remember telling him,

"Children enter the world to be protected and to be raised with the love of parents who value their needs. Here the children feel blessed that they have a route to take and to be frozen by the storms of winter. Where is God if there is one? Why would God allow such things to happen to the children down below the mountain? And what religion would give a life like this to a boy like Kulla? What of the Muslims that create and order gas and biological weapons and of Christians who blindly support this kind of religion and wars?" Russell held me even tighter and kissed the back of my head and whispered in my ear,

"This journey has taken too much out of every one of us; rest your head on my shoulder." Shwan must have heard snatches of our conversation and asked Russell,

"What do you think of religion?"

"Right now I have no religion and I don't feel any less good and decent than anyone else who does have one."

"It is nearly the end of our trip, Russell, and I must know what my American friend thinks about religion. I have learned everything else about you."

"Shwan! If you believe in good and God, it doesn't matter through which religion. Muslim, Christian, Catholic, Buddhist, whatever. It makes no difference, it is still the same God. It's just a choice you make. If your belief made a significant difference then it would be well received. If we use religion as a tool to cover evil and war propaganda, what would that religion be? It is how and what you think that matters." Shwan replied,

"Perhaps we all need something to believe in to give us a healthy direction in life. It could be religion, family, a good foundation and tradition, or even education. For that matter it could be your circle of intellectual friends or politicians." I entered the conversation,

"Perhaps all of this war has to happen to accumulate wealth and power. Also it is possible that it is a way of cleaning up our planet. But right now my mind is giving up on me. I am so tired I can't keep my eyes open any longer." With a soothing movement of his hand Russell pulled my head back onto his shoulder, and I fell into sleep interspersed with moments of wakefulness when I could hear the horse's hooves on the rocks. Then I fell once more into deep sleep despite the fact I sat astride a moving horse. I awoke to hear a voice saying my name. For a few moments I was confused about where I was. I had expected to arrive at a checkpoint. I thought I would see an Iranian military presence but there was none. We were crossing into Iranian Kurdish territory which was controlled by Kurdish Peshmarga.

When we were about two miles across the border we stopped to rest. It was a moment of jubilation severely dampened by the knowledge that this was a parting of the ways. Russell and Shwan gave each other a farewell hug. Russell said,

"If I had known what it takes for every refugee to enter my country, I would have had a different attitude. Don't stick around for long my trusted friend. Be safe on your return journey. I haven't told you this before but I have left you a sum of money with Shilan, you will need it. If you ever decide to leave this country, I will find a way for you."

"Remember, Russell, you are still in Kurdish territory. Don't trust anyone. Put on your act as the crazy Khaled, this is the name on your fake passport. Also remember that to be an American in Iran is a death sentence."

The men exchanged a trusting hug. The parting was a difficult emotional moment for each of us. As we hugged for the first time in our lives, Shwan spoke to me with a faltering voice and slipped a small piece of paper into my hand,

"Here are the names of Kurdish contacts in England, Germany, France, and Sweden. Najat, I have loved you as though you were my own sister since we were children in Zalan and I will love you as long as I draw breath. I am glad your heart belongs to a good man like Russell. Now go! Don't make this any harder for me. I pray that one day you may feel as though none of this had happened."

"But it did happen, Shwan. There will always be a place in my heart for you." I turned my back to him and began walking to Russell who was holding onto a fresh horse loaded with our sacks of walnuts and rice. I stepped toward the man I loved, with my heart feeling that I had betrayed my life long friend. I could not help feeling that Shwan's eyes hid a deeper meaning of love than I comprehended.

We had a new guide. He led us through more mountain passes but they were not nearly as steep as the ones behind us and the trails were wider and riding was easier. Our new guides had been told that Russell was a deaf mute and had been driven crazy under torture in Iraq because of his fanatical Shia religious beliefs. The guides, as well as the other refugees in our group never questioned the story and left Russell well alone. I, of course, could not speak to him except in whispers when we were completely separate from our guides. At one of these moments as we rode at the end of the stream of horses, Russell asked,

"If we are still in Kurdish territory and no one checked us at the border, why do we have to hide our story?" I told him,

"Because we can trust no one. Children are the innocent victims of grown men. If the smugglers know what you are carrying and that you have money in one of your sacks we would likely be robbed and killed and left to rot in a mountain pass and would never be found. Many young refugees carrying valuables have been murdered by the smugglers leaving their families to believe they had reached safety in a new land."

"So we are to be more concerned about the men leading us than the passdar, the Iranian military?"

"Yes, Russell. They expect that we have money in order to escape with, but passports whether real or fake are no concern of theirs."

"What about the Koran?"

"At the first opportunity you should get it out still wrapped in the green cloth and hold it close to your chest. That way the smugglers will be convinced you are a religious fanatic." The trail seemed endless. We traveled in all four different directions to maintain our safety, but eventually we came close to place called Sinneh. We could see farms, vehicles, and tractors off in the distance. This development brought to Russell the a fear of being seen, so he took his knife and slit open the bags of rice allowing the grains to fall to the ground as we walked along. From one, he handed me the money to hide under my clothing and from the second bag he took out the Koran. Blowing the rice dust off the cloth cover, he took a letter from under the wrapping and handed it to me, He whispered,

"When we get there this will introduce us as Shia Moslems. The doctor who helped you in the prison helped us all. He got us a letter written by an Ayatollah

Al-Baker Sader follower saying I had been tortured and brain damaged inside the Ba'ath prison. The doctor also gave me some contacts."

"So Russell, you planned all this a long time ago?"

"Yes, I realized this was the only way out, the day I realized just how many chemicals were being used and learned of their side effects, especially the brain damage. It was so neglected by the medical community. They abandoned the victims with no respect for human dignity. The victims became invisible members of society. There was nothing left for them but sympathy. I began to plan to find a way out and waited for the opportunity."

We reached Sinneh. The smugglers gave us no time to rest or even look at the surroundings. A truck waited for us, we and our baggage were hustled aboard and the truck left in a hurry. As the vehicle sped toward Sanandaz, the first place where we would be interrogated, the letter we held gave us some comfort. However, the fear of not speaking the language and not knowing what to expect, overrode it. The truck slowed at the checkpoint which was the first official entry into the country. Both fear of what lay ahead and regret entered my feelings. Regret at leaving behind the land of my birth and all I was familiar with. Despite the appalling memories of my recent past, I would try always to remember the good times and the good people.

Soldiers were everywhere. They carried guns and the sound of their boots reminded me of similar sounds on the road to Baghdad. Our driver handed over all our passports to the guards. I felt nervous but not afraid. We were not the first refugees coming this way and I'm sure the soldiers were familiar with the desperation we felt, having seen it all too often. We were ordered out of the truck, the women to be interrogated by women soldiers and the men were separated to be interviewed by males.

Quickly, I pointed to Russell, handed over the doctor's letter and said in the Pharsy language,

"Please take care of him, he is not well." Russell played his part brilliantly, clutching the Koran tightly to his chest and raising his eyes to the heavens in silent but mouthed prayer. An hour later a Passdar led Russell back to the truck and pointed for him to get back in. He winked at me as he sat down. A bang on the side of the truck signaled it was alright for us to leave. We were bound for Humadan, a town about half way to Tehran, the capital of Iran.

Russell laid his head on my shoulder pretending to sleep but he whispered in my ear,

"If we keep going this way we will be out of this country in no time." I wish I could have shared his confidence, but I harbored the fear of what would become of him should he get caught. What would this Muslim ruled country make of him other than an American spy? In their eyes he would be considered a man of evil. The truck stopped in Humadan long enough only for fuel and a short rest stop. We tried to sleep as the truck raced through the night to Tehran.

chapter twenty four

The city of Tehran had always been known as the heart of beauty in the Middle East. The city of glamour and style under the influence of the French culture enjoyed the flavor of elegant living and trends along with the freedoms of America. Modern day Tehran was different. All of that had been taken away by the force and power of one religion. In the eyes of the strict ruling religious government, the freedoms had become a threat to God. The religion became a propaganda tool. Women and girl children had to be covered from head to foot in order to cleanse the society from the drug of freedom. The abaya was the only garment women were permitted to wear. Tehran became a city cloaked in black.

The bitter disappointment and desperation could be seen in the eyes of the populace. They spoke of the last day of their freedom and the lives they had led before.

Our truck took us through the city center and stopped at a big building. Then we were driven to Park Ehram which held the resort called Carag. In the days of the King Raza Shah, Park Ehram had catered to the wealthy from around the world. Now it was no longer a place of sophistication, it had been turned into a gigantic refugee camp. It was so noisy I thought a riot must be occurring. Men were shouting and complaining. I heard one say,

"It's my turn, I have been here for months." I heard another shout, "How come he gets to fly out ?" He has only been here a month, I have been here eight." I looked at Russell and we both understood there were bigger challenges to be overcome than we had anticipated. Our passports were taken from us, and the Passdar climbed on the truck and directed the driver where to go. He took us to the resort building. There were beds all over the lobby floor. We were to discover that they belonged to single men while the married couples had rooms on the higher floors. I held on to Russell's hand and dragged him. The Passdar took us to a room and opened the door for us. Russell, of course, was continuing in his mute act and the Passdar seemed to be sympathetic toward him, he touched Russell's head and said,

"Do you like your room?" I answered for him in the affirmative and he closed the door as he left. I locked the door immediately after he had gone and Russell checked for listening devices. At last alone for the first time since our betrothal ceremony many days ago we embraced as never before. We were now in the hands of the enemy of Iraq and the Ba'ath regime, but we did not take much comfort from it. In Russell's case, he could be counted as an enemy of Iran. He kissed me on my lips for the first time. He could not know how often I had longed for this moment. His fingertips found my cheek when the kiss ended and he said,

"Everything will be all right." We looked around this

once opulent room. It offered little but a well worn carpet, a mattress and faded bedcovers. We had a private bathroom with a shower but both of us were too exhausted from our journey to shower. Feeling somewhat safe for the moment we fell into sleep even though it was still midday. I awoke in darkness with my heart beating rapidly as there came a pounding upon our door. I turned over and felt for Russell and panicked because I could not feel his presence but was quickly comforted when I heard the water running in the bathroom shower. I hesitated in fear of who might be on the other side but I opened it. One of the men who had come on the journey with us had brought a meal for Russell and me. He informed me,

"I told the soldier that because your husband is ill, I would pick up your dinner since only men are allowed in the lineup. He understood and seemed agreeable. By the way, I am Bestwn. Please come visit my wife tomorrow? I will be bringing your breakfast in the morning."

I thanked him and placed the meal down. Russell quietly opened the bathroom door fully dressed in his clean clothes.

"Did you sleep well, my love?" he asked putting his open hand on my cheeks. I blushed as a result of his tender words and caress. I went to the bathroom to bathe and standing under the stream of warm water I cleansed my skin of accumulated dust and grime of many days.

I knew that on this first night we would be completely alone and I knew nothing else could matter that this was our night and only ours. I knew that I loved Russell deeply and that he felt the same way. I had great unspoken fears, not of the act of love, but of the possible consequences. As I dried myself, I anticipated Russell's expectations of me and I felt my hand begin to shake. I wrapped a towel around my short new hair, one around my waist and a third around my shoulders. As I opened the bathroom door Russell greeted me with his smile, then he took the towel from my head and gently dried my dripping hair. I could feel his warm breath on my neck. It felt like a summer breeze when I was a child and the world was still innocent.

With my eyes closed enjoying his attentions, I did not feel the towel come loose until it dropped revealing my scarred back to him. I turned abruptly in a desperate attempt to hide my recently healed wounds. I looked up and his hands came and cupped my face. As his hands relaxed I could see no shame in Russell's face, only compassion and love. The warmth of his hand soothed my phantom guilt and we embraced. He took me to our bed and disrobed me. I felt trust in him that I had never felt in anyone. He knew my history and he had heard me express my misgivings about not being perfect for him and he had allayed my fears. Russell loved me and wanted me for who I was. He kissed and caressed every scar on my body and I felt as though a heavy burden had been lifted from me with every touch of his lips. It was as though every violation and every sin inflicted upon my body had been forgiven with each stroke of his fingertips. I felt my body flush with the heat of desire. I could want no other as much as I wanted Russell.

I ceased to hear the distant sound of marching soldiers, the monotone prayers from the mosques singing out over the city faded out. There was no such thing as Muslim or Catholic, no punishable by death acts of love. There was only Russell and I, our embrace, our touch, our love. We had become one entity. As our eyes glazed over I entered a new world where nothing seemed real. In this new and wondrous world there was no sound other than two hearts beating as one. When the heat of our passion subsided, I lay still feeling safe and warm in Russell's embrace. I understood now, how beautiful love can be. A feeling of utter peace came over me and I slept within the security of his arms.

In one sense being virtual prisoners in the refugee camp overnight helped us overcome the dogged tiredness from our journey. But as dawn lit the sky we prepared mentally for whatever challenges we might face. Russell said,

"I'm going out there to find out why we haven't got our documents back." I told him,

"Russell, you are supposed to be mute and deaf. How on earth do you think you will fight your way through the crowds we saw at the administration building?"

"Good, then I will fit into the crowd. Nobody else speaks the language. Don't worry Najat, I will be right back." He left his charm and smile with me and put on his crazy man act as he walked down the hall to the stairs. Before I could close the door a voice said,

"Hello, I'm Sheareen. Bestwn, my husband, has gone to get our breakfast." I welcomed her in and we began to get to know each other. She seemed genuine enough but I told her very little about Russell since I had no trust for anyone. She had been in the room for about a half hour and I began to feel nervous, for Russell had not returned.

"Don't worry everything here takes a long time. Beastwn waited an hour for our meals last night." The constant noise from outside the building suddenly erupted into the sounds of a riot. In a few moments the sounds were coming from the hall outside the room. I did not understand and I feared that perhaps Russell had revealed by accident his real identity. Perhaps he hadn't figured how a deaf mute could demand his documents back and had made a serious error.

The room door crashed open. A soldier rushed in yelling,

"Let's go! Let's go! He grabbed my bag and yelled at

me to get our belongings. I began to panic. I wondered if Russell had got the Koran. I gave a quick glance to be sure I had everything, then the soldier pushed me out into the hall leaving Sheareen behind.

The hall was filled with women and children. Soldiers were herding then downstairs like cattle onto four buses parked outside. I ran to the crowd in front of the office. I forced my way in shouting both in English and Persian.

"Khaled. Khaled. Khaled." Just like a mad woman. "Please, someone tell this soldier my husband is not well. I must find him." A soldier prevented me from going any further with the tip of his gun. "Please have mercy my husband cannot survive without my care. He gave his life for your beliefs. Where is the reward?" The soldier replied,

"God will reward him." I struggled to get free of him and began yelling again,

"Khaled. Khaled. Khaled." A voice from the crowd answered me in the Kurdish language,

"He is here. Over here. I forced my way through the crowd and grabbed Russell's hand.

"Please take a look at him. Wherever you are taking us it will destroy him if I cannot take care of him." The soldier reluctantly allowed me to lead Russell to the bus and we climbed aboard followed by armed guards. "Our passports, where are our passports? We must get them back," I yelled. A soldier pointed to the bus driver and he went through them and showed me that he indeed had ours. We got the last two seats and had learned a valuable lesson not to be apart not even for a short time. A couple sat across from us and the man leaned over the aisle and told me,

"We are being transferred to Jahrom. Tehran is overpopulated by refugees from Iraq so they will keep us there until some of us can get out to a different countries leaving room for others." I said to him,

"We just arrived here yesterday. We didn't get a chance to apply."

"It's not that simple. Your turn to apply will come with luck, not with time. Some of the refugees are placed in transfer camps near the borders of Turkey, Afghanistan, and Pakistan."

The bus drove non-stop for twelve hours save for a short break for fuel and rest under the eyes of our guards. Russell and I sat the entire way like strangers not daring to exchange a single word. Fourteen hours later another new day had dawned. Nothing could be seen on the long stretches of the highway. Often the paved road merged into dry bleached loose gravel, splitting the golden desert from horizon to horizon. Not a single living plant broke the harshness of the landscape. Soon the sun began to bake the desert and the heat became unbearable. The open windows fanned us with hot wind and caked us with fine dust as it flowed like a wave on each side of the speeding vehicle. The only sound to be heard was the desert wind and the broken muffler on the bus.

When I thought I could not stand the heat and dust any longer, we could see the camp in the distance. Row after row of black tents stretched over a large fenced area with a guarded gate. Once inside, the driver stopped the bus and we were ordered out. As our names were called our passports were handed back, but we did not get the letter written for us by the Shia Muslim.

"Follow me!" A soldier shouted and we followed him along a line of hundreds of the black tents. I began to feel as if our situation had become hopeless, we had escaped one nightmare to land right in the middle of another. Families suffered in the intolerable heat with little comfort. Those who had come before us looked at us with pity and sorrow. Just like ours, their dreams of freedom and a better life were stalled in this God forsaken desert coated with black canvas and multiple laundry lines. I looked into the faces of the people watching us as we walked by. They looked old, haggard and tired as if they had been here forever. In the utter boredom of the desert our arrival created the only excitement of the day. Their eyes scanned each one of the newcomers possibly with the faint hope they might recognize a friend or relative.

Russell and I were allotted a concrete block room amid a number of others on the outer edge of the camp with a lockable steel door and containing a bed consisting of a thin mattress on the concrete floor, dishes for two and a small stove for cooking. We stepped inside. Russell yawned and stretched his body, unwinding from the excruciating bus ride.

"Thank God they gave us this block house instead of one of those tents, Najat. The heat in them must be unbearable. Those living conditions are out of the dark ages. How come we have ended up here? This is a jail without bars. Why the hell are we here, Najat?" Just as quickly as he had been negative he became positive, probably for both of our benefit. "We just need a little time to get familiar with things, we will find a way out." A knock came upon our door. A couple introduced themselves,

"Welcome! I am Sarhang and this is my wife, Ashty, we arrived last week. Just in case you don't know exactly where you are, this camp is at the southernmost point of the country. It is very close to the Persian Gulf, right across from Saudi Arabia. At the north and south ends of the camp there are large washrooms and showers. Once each week you report to the office where they distribute dry foods. You will get rice, beans, tomato paste, bread, and feta cheese. Remember to always lock your door. Did you notice the envy on the faces of the people you passed? Those are the Iranians that Saddam

Hussein threw out of Iraq some time ago, being homeless they have become permanent residents here. Apparently they envy us because we are supposedly temporary. We have money and resources to get out of the country at some point and we have better accommodations. I will leave you now, so try to get some rest." As they left us a new ray of hope brightened our room.

The days became a week and the weeks became three. The haves and the have nots lived day by day in the scorching heat. We breathed the same hot air, ate the same foods and generally kept one another from going insane, and we tried to retain some semblance of hope. Families with young children bore an extra burden. The heat overpowered some of the younger ones and regular deaths occurred. As we eventually earned the trust of the guards, some of the temporary residents got permission to be taken to the market at Jahrom to shop. While the women scoured the market for bargains, the men took the opportunity to enquire about escape routes. We discovered that a man named Akhy Muntazime appeared to be in charge of escape plans to cross the Gulf to Saudi Arabia. We sent our information to him. He said he would come for us when it was our turn but we heard nothing. We learned that putting the camp so close to the Gulf had been a political decision. The Iranian politicians had ordered the camps be placed near the borders of other countries so that it would appear that Iran had not expelled the human tide, but that they were escapees. The Saudi's across the gulf would have to shoulder the cost of taking care of the flood of refugees fleeing Iran, as would Turkey, Pakistan, and Afghanistan. It was all a big political game with human lives having little value. For Russell and I the clock was ticking. Every second we waited here a life might be lost.

We waited in utter frustration surrounded by golden sand. In the evenings I would translate from the Koran and we worked hard at memorizing its' contents in the event it might be lost. Russell and I would cross examine each other to ensure we had memorized and understood all the codes and dates. We learned from the Koran that it was the view and belief of the Ba'ath regime that they would build the most complex military nation the world had ever seen. Every child born in Iraq must be born a soldier and trained from an early age to be brutal and to obey the most atrocious orders. Both Russell and I had heard from Sa'adoun's own mouth his plans for my child, Jamal, had he lived.

As Russell and I had lived under the rule of the Ba'ath regime not a single page or plan surprised us. The worst of the plans drawn up for Iraqi citizens had already taken place yet with them not knowing the worst was yet to come. The invasion of Iran was only a training exercise for war. The Ba'ath regime was preparing them for the upcoming attack upon Kuwait and the Saudis until they controlled the entire Arab nation. United world wide terrorists under the guise of one leader, sought to overpower nations bigger than themselves.

Annihilating the Kurdish nation using chemical weapons was only a training exercise training to wipe out the populations of other nations. All the plans were numbered. They included all the countries involved which were printed in code while the terrorists were printed in letters. From time to time I would become lost. It seemed as though no one could stand in the Ba'ath's way. It also seemed that every country named was guilty of some kind of support for the regime. Russell spoke up,

"Now everything is hush, hush. The West stages everything and the battle in the Middle East is in our military equipment and our economy's favor. But one day this will all go against us and you will control and unite the Middle East by war or religion."

"Russell. Whatever has been done or who is guilty of what or who made mistakes is of no consequence now. All we are doing is reaching out to America for assistance and asking why they helped Saddam to power even though it was with good intentions. It wouldn't really help to assassinate him, all of the Ba'ath members work together. We need America to give life to our people, save the Middle East, and stop Saddam's worst intentions toward others."

"I don't think it is that simple, Najat. America still has not been forgiven for their war in Viet-Nam. Do you think that if they attack Iraq it wouldn't be worse? Then the whole world would be against America, and Saddam Hussein would not look like such a bad guy after all."

"I'm not talking about an attack and another war. We don't want American soldiers to give up their lives for us. They are all someone's husband or father. No, I'm not suggesting that."

"I know you're not. But it is the only way it can be done."

"You take this Koran to America, Russell. Tell them to do their homework. Besides, America is the only country with the guts to do so. They have ousted dictatorships in a number of other countries. For a number of years many foreign Islamic terrorists have been coming from the countries neighboring Iraq. Their aim is to try to maintain the instability caused by years of Saddam's brutal regime and to create fear and terror among the people. As the years pass, Russell, this situation will only get worse. Their abilities and dedication will not only be Iraq's problem. They will operate everywhere in the world. That is what they mean by uniting the terrorists."

We went through some more of the pages of the Koran one by one, for the most part remaining calm as we absorbed its contents. I came to the last few pages

and as I read, my heart stopped for a moment A huge
lump came to my throat and I had to remind myself to
breathe. My mouth dried up. The words on the page
seemed to have come from the depths of hell. I began to
shake. I felt if I kept on reading the devil would come
into the light of day to take us all.

"What is it, Najat? You look frightened. You are
shaking, tell me what is it?"

"I feel there is nothing left to tell you. There is no
hope. This Koran is worth nothing. If you take it with
you to America, Iraq will become a bloodbath."

"What the hell does it say, Najat?"

"If all the plans of the Ba'ath military come to fruition,
no country would ever be able to attack Iraq. The
weapons of mass destruction would be used against any
country that turned against the Ba'ath regime. Every
chemical and biological weapon ever built and placed
all over the country would be deployed to annihilate any
foreign power and the ground under them, including the
citizens of Iraq who would then be reduced to ash."

"America can't even save America itself in that
situation. Najat, if we come to try to save Iraq, your
people might judge us no better than Saddam Hussein.
Yet in American eyes, you might be a nation of terrorists."

"After the life that has been given us and all the
fighting and struggling we have done, often trying to
reach out to America for help over the years, would we
not in the eyes of the American public be no less than
Saddam Hussein? Could we become the enemy of
America and the whole world for that matter?"

" But darling, Najat, the American people do not really
know anything about Iraq and its people. Remember
the unknown can create fear. It can frighten us all. But
if Americans know what the Iraqi people are about, they
will understand you; they will not fear you. But it doesn't
mean they still won't be suspicious of you or trust you."

"Russell, you must go with or without me to deliver this document. You must not fail America and you cannot fail the Iraqi people. Besides I was under the impression America was unbreakable. I know they will find a way to save us all."

"I have not lived in my country for a while, Najat, but I do know America is breakable. It would take only a few ounces of the Iraqi chemical bombs and New York City could become another Halabja. America is a land of great freedoms and we do not have an elaborate security system. It would only be too easy for such weapons to enter the country."

Russell's voice wavered as he tried to speak. It became abundantly clear to me how much he loved his country and his fellow Americans. I had a feeling Russell was about to spill his guts about something giving him great emotional pain.

"Since I have been here in this country I have wished over and over for each of us to walk in the shoes of an Iraqi. For us to understand what it is like to be an Iraqi living in fear, smelling death on a daily basis and waiting to be killed or be broken by torture. This country reminds me of a haunted house with no doors or windows, just walls. Walls that have been haunted by death. Screams with no one to hear. I walk, I sleep, I cry. I am in love with a wonderful strong woman, but inside I'm screaming with no one ever knowing what I feel. I must tell you, Najat, since we arrived here; this desert haunts me. I cannot escape the thoughts torturing me with a picture of what I have witnessed in a desert just like this one. What I saw was unforgettable and unforgivable, the images are burned into my mind." Russell paused and gave a deep sigh. It was clear he had no desire to continue.

"But you must tell me Russell. Empty your heart. Let me be the one to understand your inner pain." With a hesitating voice he began to speak,

"I was out one night out with the men, Sa'adoun's friends. I assumed it would be just a fun night such as would be enjoyed in my culture. No, they informed me, we would be going hunting in the desert. The men seemed to be really excited about the trip and so we all met at the soldier training camp at Rashed. Ali Hassan Majid was there along with a troop of his soldiers. We headed for the desert in the southwest of Iraq. We drove right through the night in a short military convoy with the soldiers joking back and forth breaking the formality. At dawn the rising sun turned the desert to gold stretching endlessly to the horizon. It was a similar sensation to being at sea, but it was a sea of sand. As I scanned the horizon with my zoom lens I suddenly reeled back in shock. No longer was the golden desert a paradise, we had come to a killing field. A massive hole dug out by earth moving equipment was rimmed by bound, gagged and blindfolded citizens. I was so shocked at what I saw that I dropped my camera.

Ali Majid broke into laughter, followed by the soldiers in our vehicle. The sand all around us was littered with sun bleached human bones and skulls. Shreds of clothing and shoes, scattered by the wind, littered the rocks for a mile beyond the hole. The convoy came to a stop when we were close to the unfortunates. I could smell their fear and their silent anger screamed at my sensibilities. Fists were clenched within the confines of their bindings. My eyes fixed upon a woman with unbound hands holding her children, a boy on one side, a little girl wearing a yellow dress in the Kurdish tradition on the other. I saw only a few other children. I wanted to break into a scream and cry but I controlled myself and stood like a man and not like the coward I felt myself to be. This is what the Ba'ath teaches you death, torture. It makes a man out of you to become immune to death and torture. The Ba'ath takes part of your humanity in order to make you a stronger man."

He broke down but did not cry on my shoulder as I wanted him to. Instead he entered into some kind of shock. His eyes glazed over, he was unable to speak or release his tortuous pain. He gripped my hands and his eyes could no longer disguise his loss of hope.

I knew that at this moment he reviled himself. It was my turn to offer him the comfort he had given to me at the lowest part of my life. I wanted to hold him in my arms, but he had become hardened to emotion like most of us. After a few minutes he began again.

"The only sound was the buzzing of countless flies feeding on the corpses in the pit. This and the hum of the desert wind passing my ears and the silent sound of imminent death. Ali Majid gave the order and machine guns sprayed thousands of bullets into the living flesh of the victims until none stood or moved. The desert became silent save for the moans of those with life still not yet quenched. More than a hundred Kurdish lives had been cut short within a few minutes. Those bodies still lying on the brink were kicked into the pit. The sadistic soldiers no longer laughed or joked as a tractor covered the victims with a layer of sand and I knew that some were buried while still alive. I heard one man scream for mercy and Ali Majid was the only one still roaring with laughter. I turned my back on the appalling scene and saw a pack of wild dogs feeding on corpses who had not been buried in the pit. It was as if I had stood in the eye of a desert storm where nothing could touch me. I could not have saved a single life and I felt as though I were the world's biggest coward. I was all alone amid total mayhem; there was nothing I could do. Nothing!"

Russell tried not to break down. I waited until he was ready to continue.

"Everyone got back into the vehicles but they remained still and silent as we gazed into the pit. After a few moments some of the wounded who had not died began to move, probably assuming we had all left. I saw a man push his way up through the layer of sand. He rose to his feet, clambered over the bodies, climbed out of the pit and began to run into the desert. Without warning a pack of wild dogs set upon the man and began tearing him to pieces. Another pack leapt into the pit seeking out the still living and began tearing flesh from arms and legs. A huge flock of circling buzzards, smelling the stench of fresh death, descended into the pit and joined the dogs as the soldiers watched the proceedings in macabre delight. The vision of those dogs will never leave me, Najat. They were utterly ferocious. I saw one run out of the pit carrying the arm of the same little girl with the yellow dress who had met her death holding onto her mother's hand.

The melee caused other still living victims to gather inner strength to get up and run. This was when the hunting they had spoken of began. The soldiers started up the vehicles and began chasing down the survivors and driving over them. This explained why human remains were scattered in such a wide area. A young boy I had not noticed before ran for his life. Without thinking I jumped from the truck to try to save him but in his terror he outran me. Suddenly bullets were flying all around me and I fell flat on my face. Then I felt a gun barrel on the back of my head. Sa'adoun saved me from his bloodthirsty comrade. He yelled, 'Don't you dare kill the foreigner!' I'm sure the men enjoyed scaring me almost as much as the hunt, for they threw me bodily into the truck. When I regained my seat I saw the boy running like a gazelle far off in the desert. He was the only one to escape the massacre.

Al Majid said, 'You are a crazy man! What were you

thinking? That you were hunting a deer or a lion? One day I was captured by the Kurds, they almost hung me and I swore that day I would hunt Kurds forever. I would never let them rest and would turn their healthy children into Fidai Iraqi militia while the affected ones would be brought here.' Turning to Sa'adoun he said, 'Have you taken your friend, Russell to the Fidai School yet?' Immediately the thought crossed my mind that I had learned the truth about the children I had witnessed in the hospital. The survivors of the genocide attempt were brought to the hospital to be checked for fitness to be sent to the Fidai. The ones chemically affected were to be killed. No longer was it a mystery where the children's parents were. Russell continued his story,

"Then Al Majid laughed, 'You know just the other day the Western newspapers were talking about human rights. They said that Iraq has the highest number of people missing. The United Nations has a group investigating the disappearance of 16,500 detainees mainly Kurds, Shia Muslims, and suspected political opponents.' He laughed again, '16,500, my friend, try doubling or tripling that figure. They will never prove anything. You know why? Come along with us in a couple of days. At that time we won't be using bullets. By using just one ounce of liquid we will turn our next guests to nothing but sand."

"I heard the sound of approaching vehicles. Five buses loaded with new victims arrived and the appalling scene was repeated. This time I could not control myself, I vomited and heard the jibes of the soldiers, Al Majid and Sa'adoun. When the day's slaughter had ended we left the killing field to the dogs and vultures. A short drive later we passed by a fortress-like structure sticking up from the desert like a massive wart on the landscape. Its walls held captive a large crowd of detainees unknowingly awaiting their turn to be taken to the killing fields. I watched them as we drove by. They stood or lay in the merciless sun, weakened by dehydration or sunstroke. My stomach was in turmoil and on our way back to Baghdad I threw up one too many times and it produced jokes from the soldiers about foreigners lacking the guts to do an Iraqi man's job, while the whole appalling scene was about to be repeated out in the desert. Since that evening, on our arrival in the city, in my mind Baghdad had turned into Hell. There has been no peace in my soul since that day, Najat. There have been nightmares, sweats, and a racing heart at the agonizing memory of those innocent victims and the many others I have seen since. Until now I have kept a bitter silence."

That night for the first time Russell heard the story of my childhood in the village of Zalan and of my real mother's coin necklace that I prized so highly. Well into the night I held and comforted him and he did the same for me and we felt blessed and fortunate that we had found each other in this crazy world gone mad.

chapter twenty five

We had been in this camp for three weeks. When the sun finally set each day, the cool air made the camp habitable at least for the following hours of darkness. We talked, made love, and slept, each comforting the other. Over time we had become good friends with our neighbors Sarhang, and Ashty, with a level trust built between us. In the company of Sarhang, Russell had gone to collect our food ration. Both he and Sarhang returned with excited grins,

"Guess what!" he shouted as he approached. "We have been given permission to go to the market at Jahrom." My heart was instantly filled with joy. I grabbed my bag and scarf elated at not having to look at a sea of black tents. Sarhang, Ashty, and three other couples joined us in the back of an army truck.

The market stalls, set up with long boards and shaded

from the sun with off-white sheets, were loaded with fruits, vegetables, an array of color such as I hadn't seen for months. The sounds of bargaining filled the air and the smell of the fruits and vegetables were a treat for the senses. I noticed a man who kept staring at me, making me feel nervous. I pointed him out to Ashty. She whispered to me,

"He is Akhy Muntazime, our smuggler. He needs to know who we are and for us to become familiar with our surroundings. Our driver is his contact. Keep shopping; the guard is coming our way. We pretended to shop for fresh clothing and foods while Russell distracted the guard with his mute act. Acting on our behalf, Sarhang handed an envelope to Akhy Muntazime as we purchased our goodies.

At the time both Russell and I had thought the visit to the market to be a promising moment but as it turned out not promising enough. Four more miserable months passed in this even more miserable camp. We suffered through numerous desert storms, freezing nights, an unvaried diet, and sadness for the lives of children who often did not survive the camp environment. We worried also about the new babies born in these harsh conditions. Night after night we lay together warding off the cold and telling our complete life stories to each other. I remember our conversations well,

"There was a time, Najat, when I couldn't imagine living in your world and surviving."

"And I can't imagine living in your world of freedom in America."

"In spite of all the things I have told you about life in America, it is not perfect. We too have some problems. American citizens are controlled also by the power of law, not by religion or violence. After all, populations have to be controlled for we are not smart enough for our own good. So if it wasn't for violence, there wouldn't be peace. If it wasn't for law, there wouldn't be crime"

"Yes, Russell, but you have freedom. The rest are choices you make for yourself."

"Freedom, yes! But perhaps we have too much freedom and that has possibly taught us that we think we know it all. We have come to think that the world revolves around America."

"But you do know it all!"

"Then if we do, Najat, half of America judges other cultures by their old fashioned values and customs, also by the clothes they wear and not by their talents, abilities, and individuality."

"Then so do half of Iraqis who judge American culture by what we see in American movies. They suggest you are a people who are strangers to each other with no faith, integrity or family values. You live in a selfish world. You heard my father, Russell. He lives in Hell, but he still thinks his culture is better than yours because of your dress code and sex without the bonds of marriage."

"Well, I thought the same until I discovered that all the things you are talking about are happening secretly in this culture also. Remember, Najat, I was brought up to be Catholic and basically the religion holds the same beliefs as yours. Not being intimate before marriage and no divorce. It is not necessarily bad. It saves you from confusion, broken hearts, improper desires, and mistakes. On the other hand not allowing sex before a later age creates a situation where rape and other crimes are sometimes committed."

"So religion and culture judge other religions and cultures from a distance?"

"True! In the West there are different religions and cultures within the same city and they judge each other. On the other hand we have our own war. We live a speedy lifestyle with selfishness aggravation and the complications which come along with it. We may come across as nice and kind within our own surroundings, but if anyone affects us directly, we retaliate, and therefore, do not appear to be kind and generous to those who do not know or understand us."

"Russell, I know you have traveled in many countries. Which of them do you like best?"

"Yes, I have been to many places and I am often asked the same question. I always have the same answer. Each country and culture has honored me with something different and significant that have made changes in me. It made me a better and happier person. But this country and knowing you has completed me."

Our conversation ended with a gentle rap upon our door. Answering it I found Jaffir, the driver, who we had been told was our contact. He whispered,

"It is your turn. In three days from now it is the Muharam celebration. Jahrom and the country will be distracted. I will pick you up in the same way to take you to the market. Try to lose the guard and follow Muntazime. Bring your passports and $10,000 each. Nothing else except perhaps some food. He will hand you over to a ship and they will smuggle you across the gulf." Then he left. The third day came with the sun high in the sky and the singing of the Koran rose from the tent city. The Shia Iranians were already celebrating. The men were stripped to the waist flailing themselves with ropes and chains, apparently feeling no pain being lost in their prayers. The women were entertained standing around watching them and gave gifts of meat, rice and olives from tent to tent. Jaffir, the driver, personally delivered a share to Russell and I. As he handed over the gift of food he whispered to us,

"There is no trip to the market today. Usually this is the best day of the year for smuggling. The military fighting no longer exists and we are not in danger of being hit by a missile." That night we realized that the war between Iraq and Iran had ended. But we were trapped in this camp and nothing appeared different than before to us.

"You are telling me there is no trip to the market today! If not now when is the next chance?"

"There is some politicking going on between the smugglers. There is also some suspicion. I'm not sure what it is, but today will be the last attempt for a while." In desperation I said to Jaffir,

"Take us. If this is the last chance we want to take it. If you take us I will double your price." I wondered if Jaffir was playing games to get extra money out of us, but I didn't care at that point. We had to get away. Jaffir smiled.

"I'm off duty today at ten o clock, so find a way to get in the back of the truck and hide. Otherwise I have no permission to take you. You must excuse me now. I have to deliver the rest of the foods. Jaffir left and Russell. said to me,

"Maybe it would be better to wait, Najat. Did you even ask if the market is open today and if Muntazime is available?"

"Russell, I'm not going to take a chance on waiting around for another four months. Anything could happen in that time. Besides he is a smuggler hoping for more money."

"I have an idea, Najat!" he grabbed the money belt I had made, put some money in it and fastened it round my waist. Then he put money and the passports in his pants pocket and removed his shirt and placed the Koran in his hand. He told me a telephone number.

"Memorize it, Najat! I was hoping it would never come down to this moment; but if we become separated, call this number. It belongs to a friend with whom I can trust our lives. We used to work together in a crime lab.

I was in touch with him before I came to Iraq. Whenever you want to send your address to me, send it backwards with the letters as numbers and the numbers as letters of the English alphabet. It is a means whereby you may be able to reach me in the event that we become separated. Bring me a towel. I'm going to act as crazy as I can, so don't take your eyes off me for even a second. I am going to fake passing out at some point. As Russell limped out into the crowd a man handed him a length of rough rope and Russell began beating himself with it just like the Shia men. I joined the women keeping my eye on Russell as he followed the men through the camp. Jaffir followed eager to collect his prize.

When we were close to the gates Russell went into his fainting act. He lay on the ground ignored by the praying men. Jaffir and another guard tried reviving him by splashing water on him but Russell did not respond. Jaffir shouted,

"I think he has sunstroke or beat himself in the wrong spot. We have to take him to the hospital!" They threw Russell into the back of the truck and I got in with him carrying the Koran. The guard also climbed in but Jaffir told him, "You do not need to come along, I'm off duty. Besides he needs his wife to speak for him and if he has to remain in the hospital I will stay overnight in the mosque and return to duty in the morning." The guard climbed back out of the truck and we left the camp without a single good bye. I said to Jaffir,

"There is no need to go to the hospital. He usually gets a minor seizure and wakes up after a while."

"God has his way of looking after us, you two were meant to escape." Russell opened his eyes and winked at me. I pretended to take care of him and helped him to get dressed as I admired his talent and courage. Jaffir turned to speak,

"We have a long way to go. I will pick up Muntazime

half way there and will drive straight to the Gulf; we are very tight for time." I had knots in my stomach and I shook. While I had lost my belief in religion I prayed that we would be safe and cheat death for I sensed it coming our way.

We arrived in the village of Shiraz. I paid Jaffir his blood money and he departed for Jahrom in a cloud of dust. Muntazime drove us in a different vehicle to Bushire on the Persian Gulf. The day had ended and darkness cloaked the shore. It was beautiful. Moist air kissed our faces and for the first time in my life I saw sea waves, bringing with them the smell of salt and fish. It was a flat, endless horizon much like the desert, but beyond this undulating horizon freedom beckoned us.

A ship awaited us with smoke pouring from the stack darkening the already dark sky. The engine noisily vibrated throughout the vessel. We were hustled below along with about forty others. The clanging of metal doors and pipes brought back memories of prison doors and I felt highly nervous. The smell of fuel, fish, and foul breath permeated the vessel. Muntazime wished us farewell.

"I wish you a safe journey. There is nothing for you to worry about, but remember once you reach the other shore there is no coming back. The ship will leave in a few minutes and then you will be free." A large metal door clanged shut and we were locked in the hold for the journey over the gulf. We counted down the minutes and the ship had not departed. Then I heard a sound, a sound I was familiar with. It was the sound I had heard in my nightmares. It was the sound of the times in the prison when I had been raped and tortured. It was the sound of boots becoming louder. Russell said,

"There is something not right!" For the first time I heard him speaking profanity in my presence.

"We have been tricked!" I remember telling him.

SHANNA AHMAD

"If we are to be taken back to a camp, Russell, find a way to run. In no circumstances turn around to look back. This is not about us. They will take us to a camp much more strict than the one we have just left and there will be no way out. Eventually someone will find out you are American and the Iranians will hang you."

"Do you even think for one minute I would leave you behind, Najat?"

"Russell, think about it. You have no choice, just go. I will find you again for I know where you will be." I grabbed his face with both hands. "Promise me?"

The door opened and we stared into gun barrels. The soldiers ordered us out but there were more of us than there was of them. As we left the ship the refugees began running in different directions. Russell gripped my hand and would not let go. I tore my hand from his and told him,

"You must go. I can't run as fast as you. Please, Russell, run!" I knew I had to force the issue so I turned and began to run the other way. Russell had to obey my wishes and he vanished into the darkness. A soldier caught me and took me back to where most of the women and children were being held. We were lined up on our knees and I begged God to let Russell escape, while I was quite prepared to die. The ship's spotlights came on illuminating the beach. I looked around me to see if Russell was being held with the captured men. I did not see him, but Muntazime stood with the guards and he gave me a sign. I had no idea what it meant or if it meant anything at all.

We were ordered to get up and march. My feet sank into the wet sand with each step. I spotted a piece of paper and then another as they blew along in the wind. While I couldn't see clearly, I assumed they were the pages of the Koran. Some flew up into the air and others landed among the incoming waves. Some paper pages

392

lay on the wet beach softening the inks and the words were now lost in the sand. Could this have been the Koran that Russell had torn up? My concerns were torn between the loss of the Koran and the man I loved more than life itself. I wanted to break free of my captors and collect up all the pages I could find, but the shouts of soldiers chasing down the men escapees in the dark made my concerns for the Koran become much less than my concerns for Russell. When the shooting stopped and the male escapees were assembled I could not see Russell among them. I wondered, had he escaped or had he been shot?

We were loaded onto military trucks and driven away into the night. Despite my knowledge that he was a fighter and a strategist, I wept for Russell. My feelings alternated between visualizing him in an Iranian jail awaiting execution and stepping off an airplane in America, safe and well. We were driven back to the Jahrom camp with no questions about the disappearance of my husband; they were obviously used to people disappearing without a trace. I have thought long and hard about that fateful day. It had been my decision to try to escape while Russell had been cautious. I blamed myself for my situation, but the driver Jaffir also bore a lot of the responsibility.

I remained two more months in this abomination of a camp spending every lonely night hoping for Russell to come and get me. I did not venture far from my room. I wanted to be here in case there any news came. I talked to myself of my childhood, my family, and the friends who had helped me along the way. I thought about my life in Baghdad that was a mystery to everyone. But the memories of Russell were what really sustained me at the moments when insanity threatened. The faith that he was alive and had made it to America with the contents of the Koran locked safely in his mind, helped get me through each agonizing lonely day.

Despite the fact that I reviled him for his treachery, Jaffir became my immediate messenger. It mattered not how many times he swore on the life of his children, when he told me that Muntazime said he had seen many soldiers chasing Russell but he had escaped and made his way across the gulf in the same boat that we had been on.

"Besides that, your husband was no longer limping and acting like a crazy man."

"He is long out of the country and I have spent half of the money you gave me to find out that he is not in any Iranian jail."

I obtained a child's exercise book and a pen and began to rewrite the Koran from memory, for I remembered Russell telling me that America would do nothing without documentation of the facts. I remember telling myself if 30,000 deaths from genocide were not enough to act upon, when would they? When every plan of the Ba'ath Regime will shadow the world? When we all turn to nothing and blend into the earth by the use of chemicals? Or would it be when America finds its young soldiers cleaned from the face of the earth just like the Kurds? In my months in this place I lived with hope. Jaffir came to my door and told me he felt remorse for his actions and felt that he owed me. He invited himself in to speak with me,

"I have already arranged for a passport for you with a young Kurdish refugee in Tehran. He is willing to take you out of the country acting as his wife."

"I can't leave this country. What if Russell is still out there?"

"I told you he is gone. Don't wait around. You are lucky you are still here. You have no idea how many lies I have told to try to help you. Go! Put my mind to rest and don't throw your young life away waiting for your man. He has left the country I tell you. All I want is a photograph for your passport."

"How much money do you want this time Jaffir?"

"None. I am grateful for what you have already paid me." A few days went by but I did not have the same anticipation of escaping or even of leaving Iran. I felt a great hollowness for I was torn between leaving or staying and still unconvinced that Russell had left the country. But although I felt sure that he had managed to escape, I still had no closure. I could not betray his love but we had made promises to each other to take the information in the Koran to America to save us all from a sea of death and a river of blood. I knew the journey must go on.

The day arrived when Jaffir came to take people to the market He collected the chosen ones and we left. At the market Jaffir held me back as the others went to the stalls he handed me over to a local family of five. He waved goodbye and we left on the long journey to Tehran. On the way to the airport we passed the camp I had been in with Russell. At the airport I was introduced to a young Kurdish man of about twenty four years of age by the name of Ary. He had my passport in his possession perfectly done with my photograph convincingly placed inside. Ary spoke for the both of us at the exit customs and at the airline desk. We boarded the aircraft and I could not help but remember being tricked aboard the ship. I buckled my seat belt and waited, filled with nervous tension which did not leave me until the plane was airborne. I looked through the window at the city of Tehran below. I began to cry as I thought that Russell might still be down there somewhere. But then I began to laugh, I had escaped. Russell was right; there was very little difference between tears and laughter. I turned to speak to Ary,

"As difficult and as complicated as my journey has

been, suddenly everything seems simple. There were no questions at the airport and now I'm far beyond this country."

"It wasn't as simple for my brother. He was trapped here for two years and one week. Three months ago he found his way out and I got here five months ago. I took over his contact and route. I paid everyone and I mean everyone but I forgot to pay our pilot." He laughed.

We had a long flight to Damascus in Syria and we got to know each other, He offered me the telephone number of his contact in England. We transferred at Damascus to a flight to Warsaw in Poland and from there we flew to London on a different plane. As we neared London, Ary excused himself and went to the toilet and tore our passports into miniscule pieces and flushed them. He said,

"By destroying the passports there will be no way they can send us back when we claim refugee status." Soon the city of London peeked through the clouds. A shiver of utter joy ran through my body, but I reminded myself that hope had disappointed me many times before and the joy and the fear fought within me. The plane emptied and we followed the other passengers through the terminal to customs and immigration. Ary and I hung back until we were the last ones. The uniformed officer looked at us and said,

"Passports?" while holding his hand out expectantly. With my voice faltering I spoke.

"My name is Banaz and I claim refugee status." Ary did the same. The officer pressed a button in his booth and a male and female officer came and took us to two separate rooms to hear our stories. I told only the worst scenario and I was terrified I would be returned to Iraq. For a few minutes I lived in great fear, but the lady was kind and I felt safe and protected with her.

"Our government policy requires that we check every

refugee entering our country." I stood with legs apart as she felt my body for concealed weapons. "Please take off your top." I removed my clothing and money belt and she saw the scars on my back. I saw a look of sadness come to her face and her voice took on an even gentler tone, "You can get dressed now and take a seat while I ask you some questions." I answered every question about my life in Iraq but even though I had promised to be truthful, I could not tell her anything about my real mission. "I have interviewed hundreds, maybe thousands of Kurdish Iraqis. You all have similar stories, but I want to hear yours. What made you come here to Britain?" Her question made me feel nervous.

"I was put in jail for no crime. I was tortured and repeatedly raped. Everything was taken away from me, the man I love, the child I gave birth to." I began to cry as the memories surfaced and the woman exuded sympathy. I knew she could never understand the depths of my anguish, but I also knew if I spoke loudly with conviction she would understand how our lives and spirits had been broken with the harshness of our existence.

"What are your expectations of this country, Banaz?"

"I have no expectations other than to receive human rights and be able to live freely so I can give back what is expected of me." The officer smiled and began filling out legal forms. Then she took them and left me alone in the room. About three hours later she returned.

"For the moment, welcome to England, Banaz. It will take some time to process your legal papers. Meanwhile you will be taken to an immigration building where most of the Kurdish refugees are housed. We will contact you there where you will be asked some final questions to qualify for Refugee status." The officer had no clue how I had longed to hear those words. She led me out of the terminal and placed me aboard a small bus.

chapter twenty six

Although I had been instructed not to go to live anywhere else until my status came through, the Immigration housing did not feel like a prison. I found myself among my countrymen, eager to share the stories of escape from the tyranny of Iraq. No longer had I to hide behind dangerous secrets that held endless grief, secrets that haunted me, bringing me close to madness. I finally tasted and felt the texture of freedom such as I had never known until today. I walked from one street to another never having to look behind me. I cannot describe the feeling of euphoria of finally walking free and I thought of myself as walking the streets in the English movies I had seen. I stared, I touched, and I smelled the aroma of freedom. As I walked entranced, I remembered Sa'adoun telling me I had been influenced and poisoned by Western culture through their movies.

I walked aimlessly for hours embracing the city of London. When I was not out enjoying my walks I began to write the story of my life. I had always kept journals before being imprisoned, but, of course, they had been left behind when I fled. I wrote everything I could remember about my youth, and my marriage to Sa'adoun. I wrote down all the facts and my feelings, right up to the present day.

I found the contact that Shwan had given me. Although I was cautious and hesitant, I spoke freely of my thoughts and opinions. They were well received and I felt a note of admiration in the contact's voice.

"I have left the country of Iraq mired in its own misery." I told the contact.

Before I began my life of freedom in London I knew I must search for news of Sa'adoun's disappearance to prevent any dangerous attention before attempting to find Russell in America. I started the search among the Kurdish community as the Ba'ath Regime continued to wage war on one of the four sections of Kurdistan which was controlled by the Ba'ath regime, while other Kurdish regions were controlled by Arabs, Persians, and Turks. We refugees took our culture with us to countries around the world. It mattered not whether we were in London, Paris, Berlin, or Stockholm. We all had a contact somewhere in the Western world but not in our own native country.

Under Saddam's law any citizen escaping Iraq automatically lost their identity, the identity we had never owned. The only news reaching our ears came from the most recent escapees. There was no way any of us could contact our families to let them know we were safe for there was no mail or telephone service in or out of Iraq. However, since the Iran-Iraq war had ended there was a sporadic phone service. I could never get through.

I attended a Kurdish gathering with a couple who were the contact Shwan had given me. As I spoke with them I heard a voice behind me. A shiver ran down my spine for it was a voice I remembered from my distant past. I could not place exactly who the voice belonged to but feared it might be someone who could cause me problems. I turned to look. I glanced at the face before me, looking intently into the eyes of the woman that stared into mine. We studied each other in disbelief. Instantly, we recognized each other. Both her eyes and mine glistened with tears of recognition and joy. Shanna, my friend since childhood, looked strong and healthy. It was obvious she had not suffered the way I had, leaving me looking older and tired. We both held out our arms and embraced. A small part of my past had come back to me and I wept unashamedly onto Shanna's shoulder. She too wept. Shanna gripped my hands and led me over to two chairs. We had so much to talk about. I explained to Shanna that since coming to England as a refugee I had been using the name Banaz, for reasons of my own security, but I did not elaborate. Shanna, had a passion and appetite for life, yet she was appropriately reserved and protective of herself. We had a lifetime trust of each other. While London was the destination for the exiles, the refugees were the welcome home group for all new arrivals.

My conscious awareness of the Ba'ath secret intelligence and my knowledge that they were everywhere, even in London, kept my contacts and visits limited.

As winter sneaked up on me, so did the news I had been desperately waiting for. A merciless fragment of light reflecting from the icy snow coated ground in front of the apartment building door caused my bleary eyes to blink as I scanned the horizon over the chimney pots of London. I stood on the front step feeling fear and vulnerability. I took in great gulps of the frosty air tinged with the smoke of the city. I heard the crunch of frozen snow underfoot as the middle aged man I expected approached. He wore no hat, but his hair, a dirty blonde color, was neatly trimmed. Even though his eyes were squinted against the reflection of the snow, I saw they were green in color. He looked tall and polished, wearing a long black overcoat with a pair of blue jeans protruding from under it. He had a look of serious intelligence about him. He shook my hand.

He didn't tell me his name, nor did he ask for mine. He pointed down the street and we began to walk. Speaking with a European accent he began to talk,

"The man you have been asking questions about, Sa'adoun?" I nodded. "I was in Gamlastan in Stockholm where we held an I.C.C. meeting every Monday night. We talk, write, and publish on behalf of those who have no voice and against those who are guilty of human rights injustices. Sa'adoun Alwan showed up one night with one of our members, Saman a Kurd from northern Iraq. Sa'adoun said he had wandered from Malmo to northern Stockholm under the name of Majied, claiming he was a Shia Muslim. Sa'adoun claimed refugee status saying he changed his hotel nightly, living the life of a fugitive while constantly on the lookout for secret agents from Iraq. It seemed ironic to us that Alwan sought refuge, help, and money from people who had been his enemy. He told the Kurdish community in Stockholm that his wife was being held prisoner in an Iraqi jail and that his son had been killed. He told our group everything he had been involved with as part of the Ba'ath Regime including his attempt at a coup. He said he knew he would be a dead man so he needed a complete new identity. He said he had nothing to lose by speaking out and didn't care if he had incriminated himself. But he could not escape from incriminating himself given the

LOST IN THE SAND

story he told. We were surprised by his information but not impressed by his exploits. So far as we were concerned it was a personal war for him.

The man told me everything he had learned about Sa'adoun in great detail including his wife and an American journalist but he had never once mentioned their names.

"Sa'adoun Majied breathed a sigh of relief after telling his story to our group; it was obvious to us that he had satisfied his drive for vengeance by taking advantage of our ability to expose the knowledge that he had drawn us to touch the devil. A week after our meeting Saman showed up with news that was no secret to the Kurdish community, for news travels fast.

Sa'adoun was selecting his hotel for the night. Just like in his old days, he had a beautiful Arab woman from Libya join him at the bar as he attempted to alleviate his feelings of loneliness and alienation. He had a number of drinks while she had but one. Then they staggered to his room. Soon after the woman left, four men rushed in. A few days later Sa'adoun's body was found in separate boxes without the head. Shortly afterwards Saman committed suicide by jumping from a building or so it was alleged. But we knew he was pushed because he had gotten a little too close to Sa'adoun to get the details of his life, costing him his own.

The two deaths became a mystery to Sweden. All of us who sat around the table at Gamlastan to listen to Sa'adoun's confession realized that he had put our group in a difficult position. We knew we would have to disperse to our respective countries knowing that our lives too were in danger from the Iraqi intelligence service. We had this most dangerous information in our hands and hoped that someone would act upon it. But who do we trust? Everyone is involved. Have I missed anything that you need to know?"

"No, thank you. Now I have my closure."

"So you do know what happened to the American journalist."

"Apparently he didn't make it out of the city of Baghdad." I answered. The man shook my hand and walked away.

I had an idea who the man was and how he had been able to contact me. He had been sent to me by the Musakafin group in Europe. However, it did make me feel nervous and no longer calm to know I could be found so easily. The placid life I had led since coming here began to melt. I had felt deceptively safe with my new identity and I realized that no longer was my life immune from intrusion. No longer could I be Najat or Banaz. I felt that death stalked me around every corner even here in London.

I did not run from my fears, I had to stay. I had to find Russell or he had to find me. I was struck by his love. I knew if he had lived I could not leave without giving him closure. I walked the streets both quickly and slowly. I tried to avoid bringing attention to myself. I sighed a sigh of weakness. I thought of the little girl in Zalan who fought for life and survival. I knew I must stay alive to complete the existence and purpose of my mission. Yet all eyes around me became spies, from the street vendors to pedestrians and even the mail man. I smelled danger in every scent drifting on the London air.

I had no memory of getting back to my apartment, but I stood in the middle of it suddenly realizing there was no safe place in the world for me. As long as there is a Ba'ath regime I would remain on their death list. No matter where I went they would find me. I knew that every minute I waited to act would be a chance to lose everything I believed in. I rushed through every page of the re-written Koran. Then I wrote a letter to Shanna without putting her name on it. I put together the Koran and all of my journals telling the story of my life. I was sure that at first my request would frighten her. I explained in the letter that my journals were not a literary compilation but a series of sparsely written notes and facts, documentation of discoveries and the things I had witnessed and encountered. I wrote, 'I'm not expecting to live. This is the evidence that will validate my existence written as though each day would be my last. These documents must get into the right hands, Shanna. It is no longer the property of the citizens of Iraq but the property of the entire Western world. These documents must be seen by America or they will become victims of every plan written in this Koran. I wrote secret directions on a scrap of paper to give Shanna in case of an emergency. The directions were 6-78-7126273-37884. This was just the way Russell had instructed me. It was my address written backwards in letters and numbers with instructions for her to do the same thing if she needed to. I sealed the package and ran like a woman possessed to the local post office. In fear I scanned the street and inside the post office, then stood in line to send them to Shanna anonymously.

As I handed the package over the counter it felt as if I were giving up a child for adoption not knowing what would become of it, but knowing it might be safer in the hands of a different mother. Feeling certain there was no time left for me I realized in a flash I could not do this, I grabbed the package from the counter, and ran from the building and hurried home.

Over the next few days it became impossible not to notice that something was going on. London had become like Baghdad in that I knew I was being followed by three different men. I had nowhere to go, no safe place to hide. Each time I ventured out into London's crowded streets I saw the men watching me. In blind panic I ran through the narrow alleyways and then I heard someone call my name, "Banaz, Banaz." As yet unaccustomed to my new name I did not respond,

"Banaz. It's Shanna! What's the hurry? Where are you going?"

I was frightened for my life and frightened for Shanna. It did not seem right for my innocent friend to be near me at a time like this. I looked around, but the men were no longer behind me.

"Shanna! I exclaimed. You must remember this phone number and extension. Repeat it after me and memorize it. It may save us all one day." I handed her the paper with the instructions I had written down.

"It is a number in America, Shiraz. Remember that."

"Whatever that means, Banaz." She replied. It didn't matter how well she knew me or of my activities, I knew she didn't understand. However, I felt that in time she would. Besides she was the only one who gave me sufficient trust and I had not much time left in my hands. Two days later as I had become accustomed to doing, I wrote another page in my daily journal. Then I wrote a farewell letter to Russell just in case he was still alive and ever showed up looking for me.

My dear Russell,

I will only think of you as being alive and well. I will only believe you are still out there watching for me. I so longed for the touch of your face as my last conscious act before leaving this world behind, but I fear of losing my grip on life and can only leave you with these last written words. You must know your love has sustained me through many cold desert nights in Jahrom. The sound of your heart has healed the hole in my soul left utterly empty without you. Often I close my eyes to see your face and your smile to shield me from the darkest night. I beg your forgiveness, Russell. Were it not for my need to be with you I could not face the guilt of being the one to separate us.

At times the selfishness of love overpowers me with regret and remorse. But the authenticity of the short life we did have pulls me from the momentary sadness that overshadows me. Giving me your love so completely causes me to realize for the first time how much I gave up by sacrificing our love for the lives of others. I know my destiny is not my own to choose. The reality of my past sobers me from loves intoxication. The lives of so many innocents weave their way past personal wants and so we must finish what we began.

Upon my arrival in London I made no attempt to contact you and for that I apologize. While in one sense I had reached a place of safety, in another I knew the Ba'ath forces were at work here. London, in essence, has become a death trap. Despite my immense need for your love and support, I could not endanger you by attempting to contact you and plunging your life back into horror. Not having your love to support me in my life has become the torture of which I have no experience.

So you see, Russell, my fears have not changed. I feel I have unwittingly walked into a cage and you are on the outside. Do not feel sad for us my love, most certainly not for me. Your love freed me and allowed me to see the colors of life and love in a darkened world. I can think of no better place to be. You carry with you a part of me and I will leave it with you. Wear my coin necklace but do not let it remind you of sadness instead let it bring to mind the vision of your smile reflected in my eyes. Let it be a reminder of my thanks to you for staying with the commitment of our promise so that I may sleep in peace. Thank you my only love for not letting the knowledge of the Koran be lost in the sand. I shall love you until the last breath has left my lungs.

From this point I shall leave you in the hands of my friend, Shanna, the young lady who will contact you the way you instructed me.

Yours for all eternity. Najat.

After placing my mother's coin necklace inside the envelope, I sealed it and put it in the package with a note saying, this could be my last page or there could be another tomorrow. My newly found courage forced me out of the house to mail the package to Shanna.

The clanging bell of a fire engine and the wail of a police siren rent the London air as the vehicles raced to a petrol station on the outskirts of the Kurdish refugee district. A distraught attendant waved the emergency vehicles in. A crumpled heap of humanity lay smoldering on the ground. Acrid smoke curled skywards as firemen dashed to extinguish the remaining fire. The body was barely recognizable as human; all of the skin was gone.

"What happened here?" The police asked the attendant.

"I don't know! There was an Iraqi lady who comes by here occasionally, hurrying past the pumps. Then a white van pulled in and I assumed they were here to fill up. I was restocking the cigarette racks and paid no attention to the outside and then I heard a whoosh of exploding petrol. I looked out and the van sped off leaving the woman on fire. I ran to turn off the power to the pumps as I have been trained to do. Then I called emergency services. That's all I can tell you."

The London evening papers picked up the story and listed it a probable suicide. They reported that the police could not identify the remains, but police indicated that the deceased may have been an Iraqi refugee. They suggested the woman had likely become despondent and ended her own life. No one knew who had died in the fire until Najat's disappearance from the Kurdish community was noted.

chapter twenty seven

The mail delivery man knocked upon my door. He handed me a package with my address on it but not my name, Shanna Amahd. I wondered if there had been a mistake and it perhaps belonged to someone else in the building. I placed the package on my coffee table and decided I should wait before opening it in case someone else claimed ownership.

Three days later my telephone rang. I sank to the floor as I heard the news. I went into shock and incredible pain. My stomach wanted to rid itself of its contents and I shivered violently. My mind would only allow me to think of the day we first met as she peeked around the door at me. The Kurdish community center informed me that they believed that the woman who had been immolated was my lifelong friend and confidant, Banaz, or as I had always known her, Najat. Instantly I felt that the package on my coffee table was from her. I hung up the telephone and could think of nothing else but the day we met again at the refugee centre. She was unlike all the other refugees; only I recognized that she seemed to carry the weight of the world on her shoulders. The tight bond of kinship we refugees felt did not seem to apply to her. To some she appeared stand-offish. I was the only one who saw through the veneer of her attitude. I felt instinctively that she was afraid. Banaz had deep secrets about things she could not share even with me. I tried numerous times to get her to speak of her secret life in Baghdad, but she would not respond. But instead she would speak to me as though she were lecturing and preparing me for some unknown task. I remember her saying to me,

"We are too little for a big world, Shanna, but when you learn something so big, so powerful, then you are not too little to think, act, and challenge big. You will know when time honors you with such a responsibility." I kept thinking of our last meeting on a London street. She was walking as if the world was chasing her and I wondered now what she had meant by giving me the phone numbers. I remembered the numbers and the directions she wrote down in case I needed them. I suspected danger and wondered why she would not speak of it. If her life was in danger why did she not go to the London police? Who was it she was running from? This is London after all, not Iraq.

I looked at the package on the table. Now I knew for sure it was from Najat. Carefully I opened it. I found a sealed letter to a man named Russell MacMillan and a sheaf of papers and documents. At the bottom of the pile was an exercise book titled, the Ba'ath Regime Koran. I put it to one side and began reading the hand written journals. As I read, I began to live in the story as a life other than my own.

Her fear moved me. Her fear touched me. The papers exuded the phantom smells of a thousand deaths. Najat's fears had never set her free, but her courage helped people like me to be free. Her descriptions of her love and passion for the man she called Russell caused me to have the greatest respect for him. With every page I was moved one step further away from my own life. Much of the time my heartbeat would increase with her words and I found myself feeling her emotions.

I felt Najat's pain and her loss, but her story nourished my courage and kindness. I considered it a gift that she had honored me with such a responsibility. I sat reading her story until late into the night. When I reached the last page I picked up the envelope addressed to Russell and felt the coin necklace she had always worn and had written about, tucked inside. I placed a kiss on the envelope to say good bye to my dearest friend, Najat. Now, fully realizing the responsibility she had placed upon me, I taped the letter to the underside of a biscuit tin (cookie tin) and placed the Koran and the journal inside then put it on the top shelf in my kitchen.

I could not sleep, so I arose early and checked outside my window realizing I had begun to carry Najat's fear. I made some tea and brought down the tin, took out the hand written Koran and began reading it. I read her writing over and over. I felt as though I watched the world through a glass that is cracked and ready to shatter without a single soul to know except the Ba'ath regime. I racked my brain trying to figure out why she had not approached the British police and sought their help and protection. I wondered if she hadn't, then should I, and whom should I trust that she didn't? Her life story read that she had the code but she had only memorized its importance.

I wondered how I could get in touch with the American C.I.A. Although I am still not a citizen of this

country I cannot leave England. I felt as though I were
swimming in a deep sea, much too dark to find my way.
All of this information left me in a state of confusion. I
had become a hostage in my own mind and body. I
replaced the Koran and her journal into two different
cooking pots and made myself some strong coffee. I
decided to seek help with the British police so I went to
the closest station. Outside I paced back and forth for a
long time unable to make a decision about how to begin
and what to say. In all likelihood they would consider
my story as that of a crazy woman.

I did not know how to handle the situation, it was
much too complicated. Najat's letter said that time will
honor me with the responsibility and that I must
challenge it. I returned to my apartment. I noticed the
door was slightly open and I remembered making sure
it was closed before leaving. Fear gripped me and I
stepped back with my heart pounding. I remembered
Najat's words about having courage so I stepped inside.

All my possessions were strewn about: papers,
clothing, everything had been taken off the kitchen
shelves. This was no ordinary robbery and it sent me a
sharp clear message about the danger to my life. All of
Najat's papers and the Koran were missing. With only
her story and the Koran being taken it was painfully
obvious that the thieves were the Iraqi Secret Service.
Somehow they had had missed the letter taped to the
bottom of the tin. I gathered a few of my personal things,
put the envelope in my bag and fled the apartment that
I shared with my best friend, Azad, the one who helped
me to escape from Iraq.

I did not stop in the apartment long enough to leave
Azad a note. Like Najat had been, I was afraid of leaving
a trail. I crossed the city of London changing taxis just
as she had in Baghdad. I did not return to the apartment
but stayed each night with a different friendly Kurdish

family. I dared not walk alone on the streets but sought the safety of crowds. Along with my fear of the secret service, I felt as if I had failed Najat by losing the Koran after having it in my possession for such a short time. After all she had gone through a living hell to keep it safe.

After a while I began to calm down and go about my business. But as I walked the streets, men always seemed to stand out as though they were watching me. I thought I had understood fear when I read Najat's story, but now the fear was real and powerful and overshadowed the peace I had found here.

I could only hope that the man, Russell, had made it to America with the original Koran. I knew I had waited too long to decide to get help from the British police. I had learned from reading Najat's handwritten Koran that the Iraqi Secret Service and its brother terrorists were everywhere in the Western nations and were most certainly active here in London. They had no fear and no mercy. They have dedicated their lives to take others and if I had gone to the police it would not have saved me.

I left London and moved to Liverpool in the north of England. I began sending messages to the White House in America and to the American media but perhaps they didn't know what to make of it. I received not a single response.

I wondered if perhaps America already had the Koran and was keeping the knowledge secret while they formulated plans to help our people. I began to feel uncomfortable in Liverpool; even here I did not feel secure. Fortunately, I received my refugee passport via Azad in London and fled to Europe across the channel. I wandered from country to country within Europe while continuing to send messages to America hoping to get a reply.

The citizens of Iraq had already witnessed the plans from the first pages of the Koran and were thinking the war was at an end since the turmoil between Iraq and Iran had ended. But today the world was witnessing the next page and the next after that. One hundred thousand Iraqi Ba'ath soldiers were moving to the borders of Kuwait, shaking the Arab world, and they were crying out to America to help. Saddam Hussein's voice was on every television and radio channel proclaiming to our citizens that the U.S.A. and Israel were planning to invade our country and take our land and pride from us. With no shame or thought for our people, he announced the Ba'ath power had no fear of either of them, bragging that Iraq had sufficient chemical weapons to destroy them even before they began. Not one single Iraqi civilian understood what his speeches had to do with invading Kuwait.

America was making decisions to send in troops with a promise to the Kurds that if they attacked from the north and the Shia attacked from the south, they would attack from Kuwait. Then together all would destroy the Ba'ath Regime and Iraq would be free. As a decision was about to be made between the U.S.A. and the Arab world, the oilfields of Kuwait erupted in a ball of flame so large it blocked out the desert sun as rolling thick black smoke filled the skies. There was no power available to extinguish the burning oil wells. Birds suffocated under thick black sludge and all types of wildlife succumbed to the rivers of oil spilling all the way to the Persian Gulf. Humans also succumbed to the smoke and their bodies absorbed the oil poisoning them. The pristine beauty of the Kuwaiti desert became a place of slow black death.

Under the supervision of Uday Hussein, Saddam's son, the city of Kuwait was rife with rape, torture, and robbery. Sa'adoun Alwan had made good his threat to

Abu Jamsher when he had said if Kuwait doesn't stop taking the oil, they would end up drinking it instead of the West taking delivery of it.

In the eyes of the world the actions were about the price of oil. They were unaware of the Koran, (the gift that the Ba'ath regime has for all of us). The plan was to defeat Kuwait and install Ali Hassan Majid as king of Kuwait. But American firepower drove the Iraqi forces out of Kuwait, protecting life and its investments. The Americans went home and Ali Hassan Majid did not become the king of Kuwait. The Ba'ath was betrayed by the Shia and the Kurds and they in turn were betrayed by America.

So the Ba'ath moved on to the Shia and used chemicals causing instant death, brain, damage and paralysis; then they moved against the Kurds.

By the millions the Kurdish men women and children fled to the mountains. They had no food or support, every border closed on them, and they froze and starved and died by the thousands.

Some journalists witnessed the appalling tragedy and reported it to the Western press and some letters delivered hand by hand outlining the suffering of our people finally reached London. One from Najat's sister, Shilan, reached Azad's hand, and he forwarded it on to me. Shilan could not possibly have learned of Najat's death and since Najat had entrusted me with her story, I opened the letter to see if there was any information I might use in furthering Najat's cause.

My beautiful sister Najat,

First let me tell you how much I miss you. I have no way of knowing if you will receive this letter and I am terribly afraid we may never see each other again. We found out through Shwan's contacts that you managed to reach London and now live there in peace. The following is what I can tell you about happenings in our country since you left.

The American army weakened the Ba'ath military in the south of our country giving the northern revolutionary the opportunity to move southwards. They were able to move the attack as far as Kirkuk. The fighting had shifted away from Sulaymania and so our family decided it would be safe enough to return home from the mountain village where we said goodbye to you. For a short while things were calm and we began to continue with our lives in peace and good health.

Obviously we here do not know how much of the truth arrives in the international news broadcasts and papers, but I'm sure you are aware that Iraq is in an awful mess. The Kurdish revolutionary did not get the support we expected and the Ba'ath army moved back into Sulaymania. The city became a slaughterhouse. There was no human tolerance left anywhere. I do know, however, that the entire city stood up for our human rights and every man, woman, and child turned on the soldiers who had come to butcher us.

People were using anything they could lay their hands on to fight the soldiers: axes, knives, saws, hammers, even bare hands. The women of Sulaymania knew it was a fight to the death and they pushed aside the men to get at the soldiers. The streets of our city were coated in blood, explosions rent the city. Gunfire, smoke, the stench of blood and death filled the air. People were determined to end this brutal regime forever, or die in the hand to hand combat.

Najat, my dear sister, I am sad to say that we were outnumbered and our primitive weapons were no match for the power of the Ba'ath soldiers and their armaments. During the struggle so many shocking things were discovered right within our city. Our people discovered *soundproof torture rooms with all gleaming modern equipment for inflicting pain. We discovered mass graves, kilometers of underground jails containing thousands of tiny concrete cells; women prisoners were found who had been inside them for a number of years. There were women with children who had no memory of daylight. They had become like bats. Sacks of documents were discovered and delivered to Yakete Barzany. The sacks also contained the death warrants for both present and future of thousands of our citizens. The named ones were to be delivered to Kirkuk, Mussel, or Baghdad.*

After a few weeks of mayhem, things quieted down but then there were rumors that we were to be gas bombed. We were all under a terrible strain and I worried for Mother and Father. Things in the city grew worse: food supplies, electricity, and water were almost non existent. Though it will be a long letter, Najat, I think you will want to know what happened next.

It began with a distant sound I am unable to properly describe. The whole city heard it and it drew closer. A massive swarm of bedraggled humans swept through the city streets. Some were burned and blistered with nothing but shreds of clothing hanging from their bodies. Many were dirty and blood spattered. Old people stumbled and fell and lost children wailed for their mothers. Some begged for water or a piece of bread, it was utterly grotesque. Those able to speak tried to warn us what was coming.

They had been traveling in any type of transportation available to them, attempting to warn as many as they could that military regiments were conducting a scorched earth policy and were just hours behind. They were unable to explain the use of flamethrowers on people and property. The mass of people moved through the city and many of our residents followed them.

The soldiers arrived. Doctors and nurses were hurled out of hospital windows. Teachers with classes of children were crushed to death in the schools with bulldozers, women were raped in their own homes, and men were tortured to death. Sulaymania was in utter chaos and thousands of us ran from the city carrying whatever we could. Meals were left cooking on stoves for the flight was so sudden and urgent. Cars, taxis and trucks were pressed into service. Our family joined the stream of despairing refugees in a stream that stretched for many miles in the direction of the mountains. I learned later that there were more than a million people on the trek towards the Iranian Border in order to escape. People joined the throng from the cities of the south all the way to the north with all the smaller communities in between and the Peshmarga marched in the opposite direction to help in the fighting

Death chased us. There was no stopping for rest. Families struggled to keep in sight of each other as we walked by starlight. In the morning we heard the drone of airplane engines, three passed over us. A million pairs of feet stopped to look up, the only sound were roaring engines but we did not know if they were Ba'ath or American. Many people panicked, fearing a gas or chemical attack. Some were hurt in the scramble to get away from the main column of refugees and children, lost sight of their parents. Two dropped bombs. One fell far from the column and the other killed a group who had been flanking the main line of refugees. A third plane nose dived into the mountainside. It seemed to many of us that he had elected to die in his aircraft rather than have the deaths of thousands of his countrymen on his conscience. I chose to believe that it was so.

I had lost contact with our parents. Rebwar was looking after them as best he could. I stood on the hill for a moment and looked back at the long stream of

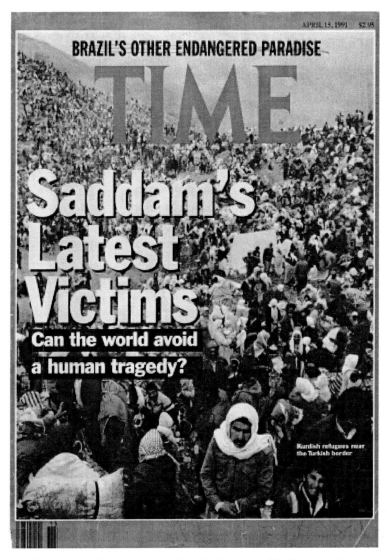

A million starved Kurds amassed at the borders of Turkey and Iran that were trapped by Saddam's military, feeling that America had abandoned them.

human misery. I heard nothing but the sound of feet. I began walking again alongside an old grandmother struggling with two children holding her hands and a baby in a pack on her back. I felt certain the baby had died some time ago but the woman had determined to keep going. I tapped on her shoulder and pointed to the child. The old woman took out the baby, sat it against a rock in soft wet mud and kept on walking as the two other children stared behind them at their abandoned sister. The old woman never once turned her head..

The old and weak fell by the wayside while the younger ones tried to help them. I found a little girl, Najat. She was barefoot and freezing, her cheeks pink with tears. Slivers of ice clung to her pajamas, the only clothing she had. Her parents were lost in the crowd and she screamed for them. I wrapped her in my jacket and began to carry her; the child fell into exhausted sleep. When she awoke she said her name was Soza and her mother was called Parwen. We never did find her mother and I fell in love with this helpless child. We had a harrowing crossing at a swollen river where some of the weaker refugees were swept away in the icy current. There was no escape from the cold, damp, and hunger. As the days passed, many children and old ones lay dying of pneumonia and dysentery.

Journalists and volunteers from the U.N. and the Red Cross began to appear. We welcomed them, expecting they would bring help to us from the outside world. Death and disease escalated with each day we waited for the food drops. The first plane to drop food packages arrived days later resulting in absolute mayhem; starving refugees fought like animals. Some managed to get several packages, others got none. Soza dove between the legs of the scrambling horde where she began picking up grains of rice from the mud and putting them her mouth. My anger gave me the strength to push

*my way through the struggling mass of men. I held on to
Soza with one hand and fought with the other until I
managed to grab some dry bread for us to share. Then
emergency supply trucks arrived from across the
Turkish-Iranian border. The clamor of so many hungry
people was just too much, so they threw the foods from
the trucks onto the ground for the multitude to fight
over.*

*Soza became ill. She coughed from deep in her lungs
and had a constant fever. Each day I stood in line for
hours for her to see the foreign doctor but he could not
help her. I kept promising I would find her mother where
she would be never be cold and hungry again. One day
she did not respond. She had become icy cold just before
she took her last breath .I walked far away from the
crowd crying and screaming, but I would not let anyone
take her from my arms. I laid Soza on my jacket and
found a sharp rock to dig a rudimentary grave. As heavy
rain poured from a dark sky, I covered her with thick
red mud until her beautiful black lashes and curly hair
disappeared under the heavy wet soil.*

*I don't presume to compare my loss to your loss of
Jamal. I just want you to know I understand your grief.
I am torn between my own grief and happiness knowing
you are safe and free. I would give my heart to see you
again.*

Your loving sister, Shilan.

Having read the letter I did not feel I had the right to
destroy it so I kept it with my papers. The war to save
Kuwait came and went. America took the blame for
betraying and abandoning the Kurds, disappointing the
ordinary citizens of Iraq. Anger rose against America
throughout the country. Many said that they and the rest
of the Western world were no better than the Ba'ath

Regime. But what the Iraqi citizens and the American public did not know was that in every mountain cave and in the ground and gravel, land mines and weapons of mass destruction were hidden. Some weapons were even hidden in the basement of houses in Baghdad and villages and towns throughout the country.

Iraqi people lived with the fear of chemical weapons while America's hands were tied, unsure where to begin, knowing they could possibly cause dreadful harm to our people. These facts were apparently forgotten by those in the West living in peace far away from the life of the people in Iraq and Kurdistan. It was my hope that the Gulf War and the abandoning of the Kurds was the answer to Najat's prayer and that the Koran had arrived safely in America.

I had contacts within each Kurdish community in all of the European countries, so I made my next temporary home in Paris. I made a promise to myself that I would send just one more message to America. I had exhausted all the addresses I could send the messages to.

The summer heat filled the busy streets of Paris and I sat at a sidewalk café sipping strong coffee, watching the passers by and taking in the sounds and smells of this cosmopolitan city. I began to study every moving object around me. I wondered what it would be like to live the lives of the people passing by, or the ones waiting for public transport and even the homeless men at the street corner. Each and every one enjoyed a freedom that I had known for such a short time, and I began to reflect on my feeling that everything had been taken from me. My personal ambitions and my desire for upgrading my university education had been abandoned. From the reflection came a mild anger that Najat had saddled me with such a responsibility. I turned the anger toward myself knowing I had failed her and perhaps in doing so, many innocents might perish.

My melancholy thoughts were disturbed by a loud noise. A man had bumped my chair with his and his coffee cup fell from the table. He apologized to me in English and reached for the napkin on my table. I stared at him in a state of confusion. In a mild fear I wasn't sure if I should run away from him.

"Have we met before, Miss?"

"No. But strangely you look familiar to me."

"Have you ever been to America?" I shook my head. "Then we haven't met. I just got here a couple of days ago from Virginia. Do you know where that is?" I answered,

"But of course. It is just to the north of France." He looked at me in amazement. I smiled at him. "It's a state in America located between Pennsylvania and North Carolina." He smiled back and said,

"I should have known better." He pulled his chair towards my table saying, "May I join you?" He didn't wait for an answer but sat down across from me.

"May I ask where you are from, now that you know about me? Let me guess, Morocco? Spain?" I did not answer but kept smiling suggesting my answer was no. "Iranian perhaps?" Suddenly I returned to reality. This man was asking too many questions. I looked at my watch, and informed him,

"I'm sorry I have to leave. I have to meet a friend in a few minutes." The man put his hand on mine and said in a firm voice,

"Please sit down. You can't run forever. I'm here to help you. I know you have been watched and chased since you left London. As I said I'm here to help you."

"Why now? You are a little late, aren't you?"

"You have managed to protect yourself, Shanna."

"Never mind that! Tell me something that I can trust that you are not working for the Ba'ath secret service and how do you know my name?"

"What would you like me to tell you? Do you want to know about my life in Baghdad, the Koran, or the woman I loved?"

"None of those things are secret anymore." The man remained silent for a few moments then he said,

"The coin necklace perhaps or perhaps the message you have been sending all over the place. No one except Najat knew it. She memorized the number. It is a crime lab with a connection to a C.I.A. insider's personal phone extension code and contact to find me or to get a hold of me."

"So you are Russell MacMillan and in a way I have met you."

"What do you mean, Shanna?"

"I have read Najat's entire life story. She wrote it all down after reaching London. I was supposed to deliver it to you along with her handwritten copy of the Koran."

In a voice exuding a great sadness Russell asked,

"Where is it now? I must have it."

"I feel ashamed, Russell. Najat made me responsible for the Koran and her story,. I did not protect it well enough and it was taken from my apartment, I believe by the Iraqi Secret Service. I apologize for losing the only thing she left for you."

"There is no need to apologize Shanna, Najat left me with much more."

"You managed to find me Russell, so I suppose you know what happened to Najat?" I saw Russell close his eyes and the darkest look came to his face. I could tell he felt the pain he carried in every bone in his body. "You still haven't told me why you have come to rescue me now?"

"Shanna I am telling you that you would not survive for long here. France is the worst country for international terrorists. They come through Morocco and Spain to France and from there throughout the rest of

Europe. Sooner or later they will figure you out. I know the Ba'ath regime will not give up on you. We don't have much time. I have an invitation to take you to a safer place in America under my personal supervision and you will be my responsibility. Your life is in greater danger, now more than ever." I believed him and decided to accept his generosity and go with him without argument, but I could not leave without going back to my friend's apartment to pick up the letter with the coin inside.

Having heard Russell say that I was in great danger I felt uneasy about going back but Russell and fortune was with me. Everything was just the same as when I left. I handed him the letter. He held it as though it were Najat herself in his hands. He placed it in an inside pocket over his heart. And with breaking voice he said,

"Let's go." At Orly airport, Russell received V.I.P. service, and we both went through the departure lounge and onto the plane with no questions asked. We took our seats and even before takeoff we were deep in conversation.

"What do you remember about Najat's journals? Do you remember everything in them?"

"Yes, I remember every word, every detail. I have been living with them since.... her thoughts have been mine, including knowing everything about you until the night you became separated." I told Russell about the day I met Najat as a child, and how I knew her again as Banaz, and all our meetings in between until she met her death. I asked,

"Russell, without wishing to pry, I would like to know the rest of your story after that night on the beach. Not so much for curiosity, but to put the pieces into the puzzle and have closure. Tell me please what good came of all this?"

"Najat and I made a promise. Actually she made me promise that in no circumstances would we put our love over and above delivering the Koran. That night she forced her hand from mine and ran, sacrificing her freedom to give me a chance to regain mine. I had a choice to make and a promise to keep. The soldiers followed her, giving me the opportunity to get close to a commercial fishing boat.

I knew if I were captured, I would be a dead man anyway so, I climbed aboard. One of the fishermen saw me but he did not give me away. Instead he pointed the soldiers in a different direction. I climbed into a bin of small fish and wiggled down with just my nose above the surface. The soldiers searched the boat, then left. I climbed out of the bin and saw that Najat was still safe when they put her into the military truck. The boat stayed docked overnight, and I learned that the captured escapees had been taken back to the camp at Jahrom. Leaving at daylight, I sat holding the Koran, weeping like a child feeling that Najat's life was no less important than those we were trying to save. I felt she should have been on the boat and not me, but knowing her strength and cleverness, kept me hoping that she would survive until I got back to her.

I reached Saudi Arabia without any complications and two days later I arrived in Washington, D.C. I made a deal with the C.I.A. in exchange for getting Najat safely to America, I would hand over the Koran. The C.I.A. kept me under protection while they interrogated me now that they understood there were terrorists among us. I had no passport and there was no way I could leave to act on my own. They took me seriously and kept their promise. But by the time they had made the right contacts with the Saudi Secret Police, the fishing boat crew, and Jaffir, and without jeopardizing Najat's safety, we discovered that she had already left Jahrom and Iran.

We learned that she was supposed to claim refugee status in one of the countries she was in transit through.

She apparently changed her plans, and it slowed down our investigation into her whereabouts. Her cleverness in changing her story and identification slowed the search even more. Her need to hide from the Ba'ath Secret Police also hindered our attempts to bring her to safety. I have to tell you Shanna, we were only hours away from reaching her but it was too late."

The stewardess brought a meal for us but our conversation was so intense we had no interest in eating.

"While I dealt with my grief and left with no closure, I returned to my old profession of crime lab work. I kept close contact with the friend whose number you had. He told me about a repeated phone call and a code, meaning your message kept appearing. It led me to believe that Najat was still alive, since no one but she had that particular code or away to get her message through. I began my own investigation into her death. Since she had only been in Britain a short time, there were no dental records to work from and I was told the information of her death had been sent back to Iraq."

"But Russell, that doesn't make sense. I received a letter from her sister Shilan and they didn't know about her death."

Perhaps the Ba'ath government kept her death a secret from the family?

With the assistance of the British Intelligence Service I met a number of Kurdish people around the community where Najat had lived. I heard a number of stories. Some made sense others didn't. Then I found out about you. I heard another young woman had disappeared, you. I realized that if I tracked you down via the code you were sending I would understand then and have my closure. But every time in all the countries you ran to another country, I would miss you and have to start searching again and wait for your next message. Two days ago when you sent the last code message, I was on a plane to Paris within hours. The moment you arrived here, Shanna, you have been followed by security people."

"I'm sure that the security people gave you my description as the only Kurdish spoken person on the plane, Russell. But it was not the description of the woman you loved, but still you came. Why?"

"I couldn't save Najat and I felt sure your life was in danger. I was convinced that if Najat had given you the code perhaps she had told you about the Koran. If the C.I.A. knew you had a second copy and that you were involved in the same mess, they would come to your rescue right away. But the fact is they knew nothing about you and the messages I had been getting. I didn't want to take any chances. I did not know if you would affect or jeopardize the security of the Koran since plans to act have already been prepared by the American government."

"Act! You mean some good will actually come of all this?"

"If you understood the Koran, Shanna, you would understand why the Kurdish people were abandoned."

"I figured it out but why don't you tell me?"

"What can I tell you, Shanna? I learned that every important government and military man sat around a long table watching the scene on a big-screen television. Kurdish people were running for their lives while Ba'ath aircraft were bombing them. Overhead American spy planes photographed the action. There was nothing that could be done while the refugees were streaming over the land surrounded by land mines and concealed chemical weapons. My country already had secret deal with the Kurds that we anonymously clean up the chemicals from the mountains. We had the assistance of some other nations covering us as a de-mining organization while they removed all the land mines they could find. Officially in the eyes of the world, the U.N. is communicating with the Ba'ath Regime and is investigating and looking for chemical and biological weapons in the south. How long this will take I do not know. But this I do know, Shanna. You will be living in the state of Utah in the city of Ogden. There is a home, school, and a job waiting for you there. No longer will you be Shanna Amahd. Your appearance must change: your hair color, the way you dress. You must put on or lose a few pounds. Your lifestyle too has to change and you must not engage in intellectual political discussions. At all costs avoid contact with Middle Eastern people."

"In the meantime, I am fairly close by, and I will be keeping an eye on you. The things I have just told you are important for the safety of your life and others. Understood?" I nodded and said,

"Once Najat's father said you were a good American man with a good heart and Najat called you her hero. I call you an angel that has come down to save us all. You are an incredible man, Russell Macmillan."

"You are a generous people. Don't put yourself down or doubt your own worth." The stewardess came and removed our uneaten meals, and now free to move my body, I placed my pillow against the window and put my blanket over my lap.

"It's too much for one day, rest your head." I recognized from her writing that these were the same words that he had spoken to Najat. I leaned back into the chair harboring no fear but wondering what tomorrow would bring. Resting with my eyes closed, I felt Russell moving to retrieve the letter from his pocket. He did not see me open my eyes to watch him and I feigned sleep, for I did not want to intrude on his most personal moment.

He put the letter to his lips for a few moments before he opened the envelope. When he did he held the coin in front of his face; he stared at it before pulling out the letter. As he read, I saw his lips tremble and his sniffle told me he wept. I could sense him screaming inside. Had we not been in an airplane, I think Russell would have struck out in his personal agony. He put the coin and the letter to his nose trying to discover Najat's scent, then he fastened the coin around his neck and placed the letter back into his pocket.

He leaned forward and adjusted the air flow to my face then drew the blanket up to my shoulders. Russell's kindness to others superseded his own feelings and emotions at this critical time during his grief.

I settled well in Ogden and the time passed in tranquility and peace. With Russell's guidance and support, I lived the life of those I used to envy. The longer I live here the more I shy away from the life I used to lead and my past identity is no longer a threat. Russell lived his life just as he had described it and he became both brother and family to me.

chapter twenty eight

Russell avoided speaking of his past life in Iraq or drawing any attention to it. Nor did he ever reminisce about Najat, at least never in front of me. It was my opinion that he grieved in silence. Political conversation became a less important part of our friendship that had developed and grown since the day in France when he rescued me.

The heat of the Ogden summer day had begun to cool with the approach of evening. Night scented plants sent out their perfumes to drift in the cooling air. I stood at Russell's front door, and as I waited for him to answer my knock, the delicate and sweet smell of honeysuckle reached my nostrils. When the door opened and he saw me standing there, Russell reached out and gave me his usual warm hug, the way he always welcomed my surprise visits.

"Come on in. Make yourself at home, I'm just on the phone. I will be with you in a minute." His call turned out to be longer than he had suggested, and so I browsed through the photographs mounted in rich brown frames. The glass protected many of his memories, but there was not a single picture of the most important person and part of his life among the others. The scenario screamed of emptiness, both on the wall and in my friend's heart. I brushed my fingers over the books in his book case as I gazed at the loose papers scattered over his desk in total confusion. I smiled, Russell had his own way of doing things and neatness was not one of them. He stepped into the room and saw me looking at the jumble of papers strewn over the desk.

"Najat told me once I needed a wife and a maid to keep me organized," Russell said with a grin.

"You don't look well, Russell. Are you alright? You look as white as a ghost."

"I have been feeling a bit under the weather lately." He coughed several times and over the course of the evening he had a number of coughing spasms. He seemed different somehow; he was in good spirits and no longer his usual, reserved self. Russell spoke freely on topics he normally might avoid.

"Shanna, it has been three years now. How are you really coping with life here in Ogden?"

"It sounds crazy, Russell. I came to live here from the most brutal place that offered nothing to its citizens but fear. And yet I crave the life I left behind, the sounds, the smiles, and the street I grew up on, but mostly I miss my family."

"It's normal to feel that way, Shanna. It is what you are familiar with and what you know best."

Russell began to cough again. It seemed as if he could only utter a few sentences before another spasm hit him.

"Hopefully time may heal the feelings of loss, Shanna."

"When Russell? Fifty years from now? I understand some action has taken place and Saddam is taking America as a joke because he believes they cannot touch him."

"Shanna, you know about the upcoming plans for Iraq. Don't let it leave you in confusion. Iraq will be free of Saddam Hussein and his regime. But you know that in the effort to bring peace to Iraq and to keep peace in the outside world, the American operation demands a much different approach and a change in the regular soldier's duty. America has to use its magical power, skill, and courage along with the most trusted Iraqis and Kurdish men. It will take trust and time. I hope not too much time. Najat's biggest fear was that America might wait too long before acting on it, allowing a bigger tragedy to take place. It might make the Halabja operation seem simple in comparison. Now it is becoming my fear."

"Why? What do you know?"

"War is mathematics, Shanna. It is a calculation and will always equate. As far as I am concerned, we know the reason behind everything that would happen from now on until the day Iraq is free. Our world will still be here and will remain safe." Russell had another coughing attack before he could continue speaking. From now on, Shanna, there will be other heroes and heroines, another story, another document to tell why America soldiers had to sacrifice themselves by going to Iraq. They will be there as long as it takes to bring peace to Iraq. America's attack will target the terrorists around the world. The Iraqi people will still be the victims. In the effort to save our borders and our people, America and the rest of the world will maintain the battle against those who stand against us until the world is completely safe from terrorism. It is not the fear of the Muslim religion taking over other religions; it is the fear of the terrorists using the Muslim religion as a tool of power.

We know that the Kurds in the north will support an American presence; the south will just be a guess. If the Western powers do not get control and the full support of all the ethnic groups in Iraq, we know that the Ba'ath supporters will continue to fight to regain control. The next war will be between the Shia and the Sunni and that will be the beginning of another conflict. That's when America will be tested. Will they really abandon the citizens or will they really free Iraq?"

"So this is the plan that has been made to free the people of Iraq?"

"No, Shanna, this is what I meant by saying war is a calculation. It is my theory that this is what would happen if America brings war to the Ba'ath regime. I understand the Iraqis and I hope that if America does attack, it will finish what it started. But as I said it would be a war between the Shia and the Sunni, and it wouldn't stop there. The Shia Hezbollah already have millions of followers. So the Hezbollah and other terrorists would not only be against America, one Middle East country would be against the other. If America were to abandon Iraq no country in the Middle East would have faith left in America." Russell began coughing again, his skin paled even more. He looked to me as though he were sicker than he was willing to admit. For the first time since I had known him his conversation turned to remembrances of Najat and his sojourn in Iraq. It seemed odd to me at the time that he should finally admit his deep love for Najat. He spoke of her in a soft voice brimming with emotion. I said nothing but allowed him to empty his heart of his memories and feelings. I did not think too much about his admissions, thinking that perhaps he was not feeling well brought on a sadness which overwhelmed his usually upbeat attitude.

We had a cup of tea together before I left him. We had no further communication until two weeks later when I received word that he had been admitted to the hospital after falling ill. I rushed over to see him, my anxiety spilling from me as I rushed down the halls to his room. I stopped at his room door to look at him before entering. He looked chalky white and had lost weight, but had no visible bandages. I gave him a cheery greeting. He forced himself to smile, but quickly told me he had cancer.

I felt the strength drain from my legs and I had to sit. My lips trembled as I took his hand in mine as it shook uncontrollably. His fingers were cold. I wanted to be strong for him and let him know he would never be alone.

"We will fight this together, Russell." He raised his hand and put his finger on my lips to silence me.

"Shanna, I have but a month at most." I struggled to not cry in front of him. I so desperately wanted to be his strength. But the tears overwhelmed me. Once again Russell relieved me of my burden saying, "Shanna it was to be expected that this would happen. I'm just like the Iraqi people and the many soldiers surviving the wars who came in contact with Saddam's chemicals. Frankly I'm amazed I have lasted this long."

His words were cold comfort for me. A week passed and I did not leave his side except to eat and sleep. He was able to carry on short conversations, but I could see the agitation in his eyes. The coughing had become constant, occasionally bringing blood to his mouth. I felt in awe of Russell's mute heroics when severe pain swept over him, and knowing that his end was near. In the second week his breathing became more labored and his body rapidly betrayed him. I stayed with him, gently wiping the beads of sweat that ran down his face in cold rivulets. I left him only when he slept, feeling grateful that at least for a little while he felt no pain. But when he was awake his kindness still reached out to me.

"Dear Russell," I asked him, "why is this your fate?

This curse is upon our heads to be born an Iraqi or a Kurd, but what crime have you committed to be punished this way?" He answered me in a weakening voice as he struggled to draw breath to his lungs. His hand reached for mine, and I felt him squeeze it without much strength. I felt the coolness of the coin necklace in my palm. His hand left mine and the coin remained in my hand.

"Shanna, I have lived with no regrets. I have served a purpose which has driven me." I waited as he struggled to continue. "What would have made me happy? A mansion, a yacht in the sea, blue sky, and clean air in between? To let the little Iraqi children with chemical burned lungs envy me for each breath of the fresh air that I took? No." Russell slipped back into a morphine induced sleep.

In the third week of his hospitalization the morphine shots were increased and gratefully he slipped longer and longer into unconsciousness, but on each awakening he bravely made an effort to smile at me. As I sat by his bedside, I pondered upon the bizarre circumstances that had brought us together. I wondered how this world can be so small and yet its people so alienated from each other. I remembered Russell saying that once he and Najat were strangers from opposite sides of the world. Two different cultures and religions, but from those differences came the most wonderful love, respect, and a total lack of fear of each other in the most dangerous part of the world. Russell stirred and I listened quietly to hear if he had anything else to say. I watched as his lips formed the words,

"I will find you, Najat, even if you are under the sea." Even though he slept, tears held back for so long fell from his closed eyes. With his final breath I discerned the words, "I'm sorry, Najat." I put my head down on his stilled chest and wept quietly. The extreme emotion of the moment, as painful as the day Najat left this life also caused me to sob again for her and the great love she and Russell had shared. I grieved until the nurses came and took his body away. I wasn't prepared for Russell's leaving and after the final arrangements were completed I felt all alone within the city of Ogden. I felt haunted by the thought of the two heroic people that had become a large part of my journey through this life, the two people who had given a purpose for my existence and who had taught me not to waste a precious moment I had been given.

I had thought that Russell's journey with the Koran had taken away my responsibility to Najat's request. But after knowing both Russell and Najat and now knowing the contents of the Koran, elevated my wish for the upcoming truth. While in my mind the two of them had in essence become the document, the Iraqi people had become the witness and victim of it. Now that both of them were gone and I was freed of Russell's restraining influence, I found the courage to travel back to Iraq. There was so much I wanted and needed to know. I knew the danger I would be putting myself in, especially that of a single woman traveling alone. I had to make a decision on which border I would cross to gain entry to my country. It really didn't make much difference, the soldiers had way too much power and I feared interrogation should I get caught.

The purpose of my journey was not to follow in Najat's footsteps or to become involved in the confusion of so many political views inside the country. I wanted to see for myself the forthcoming plans for the north and south of Iraq. I wanted to hear the voices of the Kurdish and Arab peoples telling me their stories in their own words, to hear the stories not heard in the outside world.

In late 1993 I booked a flight to Frankfurt in Germany with a connecting flight to Damascus in Syria where I had contact with a Kurdish family. Being familiar with the language and their generous hospitality eased my fear of being in a country so well connected with Iraq's Ba'ath regime, for I was unsure of what I would face. The day after my arrival in Damascus, Amear, the son of the family I stayed with, accompanied me on the train to the town of Al-Qamichlyel, the closest rail center to the Iraqi border.

Amear arranged a hotel room for each of us at a decent hotel situated on the main street of the town. Exhausted from traveling I fell asleep as soon as my head touched the pillow. When I awoke in the morning, Amear was involved in an altercation in the hotel lobby, having been accused of sharing my bed. It came as a sharp reminder of the strict society influenced by religion and the rules of an older generation. I found how easily a woman's reputation can be destroyed by the power of an unintelligent and uneducated male. Amear was in a state of confusion as he fought on my behalf with the intellectual mind of his enlightened generation with much less emotion than those around him. Amear hired a taxi to take us to the border crossing. We made the journey to the Iraqi border controlled by the Syrian military. The post was just a couple of buildings on the banks of the Tigris River close to the crossing point.

The soldiers did not interrogate me, but they did check my American passport carefully. There were no female guards so I was not subjected to a strip search; however, I had to stay overnight. I built a friendship with an officer, a family man with children who expressed displeasure at the work he had to do. I discovered there was an easier way to cross the Tigris, but it wouldn't take me to the safe part of Iraq. Amear stayed behind and a soldier handed me over to a man who ran a small boat to where the Tigris River met a tributary named Faysh Khabur, running from Syria to the north of Iraq.

I knew anything could happen but I ignored the facts. At our destination the boatman then handed me over to a Kurdish man with two truck inner tubes tied together. I sat on one in silent fear of slipping off, while the man sat along with my luggage sat on the other.

With a long pole he guided the craft through the current to the far bank where a man with a Toyota truck had agreed to drive me to Sulaymania. At one point in the journey we got caught in the crossfire between the Ba'ath military and the Barzany fighters from northern Iraq. We took shelter behind some semi-trailer supply trucks with the vehicle lights off. The sight and sound of tracer bullets lit up the dark sky. To the drivers calmly sitting around talking among themselves, this was just an ordinary night for them. Sitting with them I too began to relax and waited until the shooting stopped. We then proceeded, arriving in Sulaymania in the early evening of the next day.

I could scarcely recognize the city I had left behind a few years earlier. The house I grew up in was a pile of rubble. Since mail had not been able to move freely in or out of Iraq, I had no idea if my parents had survived. The signs of war littered the city; buildings were mounds of rubble with the occasional bullet-pocked wall left standing. Broken and burned tanks and trucks sat where they had been destroyed. Sadness emanated from the survivors. I searched the city looking for clues as to where my parents and sister were. I went to the school where my sister had been a teacher and through some kind of miracle the school had survived, and I did find my sister. She advised me that my parents had survived and they were all living together. It was such a joyous reunion that remembering it thrills me to this day. We traveled around the city visiting and looking for old friends only to find that many of them had already left this life.

As I moved on I discovered that everything that Najat had written about in the Koran and everything that Russell had told me had come to pass. I found out that Shwan Grewen had been taken by the military and his body had been discovered in a field about the same time as Sa'adoun and Najat lost their lives. I also discovered that Najat's family, along with Shwan's family, had been able to escape the country. I heard the story of the young man Russell had tried to save on the hunting expedition in the killing fields. He was saved by a family living in a desert tent and he now lives in the north. I heard from his lips the same story Russell had described to Najat. The boy is now a man who speaks the Arabic language.

As I traveled through this broken nation and met and spoke with as many Iraqi citizens as possible, often I was advised to put my fancy camera away and not to bother asking questions. 'We have spoken before and no one has listened to our voices.' I traveled through a land of tragedy, and I sensed a fear in the people that the worse was perhaps still to come. It is their story that I tell, not the voice of confusing political views or of one individual but of the Kurdish and Arab people. As I traveled through my city and the north of Iraq these are some of the things I saw and heard that truly didn't shock me.

After the Gulf War the better part of a million Kurds began returning from the mountains suffering the after effects of hunger, freezing cold, and the deaths of thousands of young children. They arrived in their cities and found that it wasn't the end of the suffering. It was just the beginning. Years of pumping out oil and delivering it to the West to pay for the wars, along with illegal oil smuggling to different countries, had depleted the resources while the moneys went into Saddam Hussein's pocket.

The program of food for oil became the desperation

of a broken country and yet the people were starving. Embargos were placed on the country despite the suffering of the people. The Ba'ath regime and their supporters lived their lives as if they were in paradise, but the children of the land had no milk or food. In order to buy food and have fuel to cook for their families, many children took to carrying pails of heating oil. They were caught repeatedly on the road from Kirkuk. Soldiers without mercy poured the oil on the children and set them on fire. This was supposed to send a message that the Kurds would be punished if they tried to survive. Fathers poisoned their families rather than watch them starve to death, but this did not ease their pain. The Kurds lived in a land rich in oil, and yet they starved and froze in the dark. Many humanitarian organizations moved into Kurdistan to try to help the victims of one of the world's largest acts of discrimination: one was I.N.G.O. the international non governmental organization.

The O.T.I. the official transition initiative;

The S.U.K. Save the Children United Kingdom.

C.M.O.C. Civil Military Operation Center.

Then there were the mine defusing teams:

N.D.A, Norwegian; M.A.G. England., K.O.M.A., Kurdish Organization Mine Advice; and the U.N. Although it was not generally known by the citizens at the time, people who assisted in the relief agencies knew that the U.S. Secret Services Weapon of Mass Destruction squads worked in the mountains and caves. They braved death to dismantle the weapons. They worked in the cold and heat braving minefields. It was the thought of the Kurds that not only were they bringing freedom to us but were fighting to destroy the one stirring madness in our world. Yet they were not alone even though Saddam Hussein was threatened both by the U.S. and Geneva for Human Rights violations.

However Saddam would not forget nor forgive the Kurds for siding with America. Genocide, embargos, hangings, and chemical attacks did not stop the Kurds fighting to free themselves from the Ba'ath Regime.

Saddam Hussein secretly sent two powerful terrorist groups to the north under the name of the Muslim religion: J'nud Islam; and Muslim groups consisting of Muslims, Nahza Islam, and Ansar Muslims. Ansar was led by Abu Eubeda Shaffef, who was Iraqi secret service trained, and Abu Yael, a demolition and suicide bomber trainer from Afghanistan, who was part of Al Qaeda.

They established themselves in the northern towns and valleys like a disease. The Kurds could not survive cut off from vital supplies, so the Muslin groups offered them welfare cash at a price to be paid. They were to return to the barbaric times by prohibiting television, education, and women's rights. The women were given cash to cover their bodies except for hands and faces along with extra cash if each girl child was also to be covered. Out of desperation many followed the edicts. Others did not for they did not want to lose their personal freedoms of dress code and education. It was the only thing left to them. The point of all this was to get the majority of the Kurds on their side to expel the foreigners living among them and to protect the weapons of mass destruction. The first mass slaughter occurred when twenty-five young men tried to cross the border. Unknowingly, they strayed into an area where weapons of mass destruction were stored. Every young man was bound hand and foot and shot in the head. The horror of this act of terrorism alerted the citizens of Northern Iraq to this new threat.

The two groups feared the Kurdish people and the mountain fighters, so the town of Kalle Hama became just one more brutal evidence of terrorism. They used their barbaric weapons of axes, saws, and butcher knives to behead all the men in the town. No children were left without the trauma that is still with them even today. I saw with my own eyes these abandoned children living in a world of weapons, dressed in rags, and discarded shoes, trying to make a living, by selling drinks or cigarettes or even old, hard cookies, anything to produce some food money.

I saw children who had been chemically affected whose spines had not joined and were therefore confined with leather straps. They were condemned to live out their lives unable to ever stand or sit unaided. Their mothers asked me, since weapons and war goods were able to enter our country so easily, why could not medicine and medical help also come?

Just before I left my family to continue my research, my sister handed me a shocking document. It was an official death warrant for me. My name was on the warrant as convicted of knowing the secrets of the Ba'ath Regime's Koran. I learned that during the Kuwaiti War when the Kurdish attack went as far as Kirkuk, tens of thousands of documents were captured and given to the Americans, including many death sentences which were secretly returned to the affected families. Mine was among them. The Kurdish fighters protected the citizens, and so my family did not have to pay the price for something I had really no part in.

I began my return journey to America via Syria, the same way I had come. I underestimated the Syrian military. This time I was searched and interrogated and I did not see the officer whom I had met on my entry. I began to worry about the documents I was carrying to support Russell and Najat's story, along with the many stories of others. I knew only too well it could cost me my life. Amazingly I found myself wearing the same mask that I had left behind when I left Iraq the first time. I discovered a renewed self-control as I tried to convince

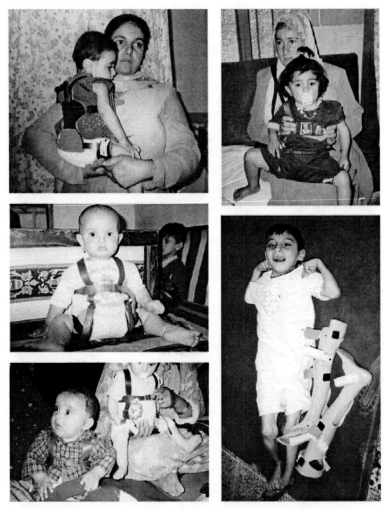

Even this present day, many chemically affected children born of chemically exposed parents are born with un-joined spines. They are confined with leather straps unable to ever sit or stand unaided.

the interrogator that I had no interest in politics except in the historical sense and in doing a biography on the Middle East. The interrogation continued until about four p.m. Then thankfully the officer who had befriended me on my entry to Iraq showed up.

He ordered a soldier to take me to his house where his family put me up for the night and fed me. The next morning he drove me to the railway station and put me on a train for Damascus. I traveled for many hours looking out of the window with a new awareness of my surroundings and situation. The fields seemed greener than I had ever seen them before, and I felt the rush of exhilaration from my new freedom. From there I went directly to the airport where once again I was questioned. Then they took me from the airport to an office in the city for further interrogation by their security people because I had planned to leave the country. I was terrified they would send me back to Iraq where most certainly I would meet my end.

Again I played my convincing game. I flattered Syria and the wonderful life they were giving to their citizens. It didn't change the expression on the interrogator's face. Whatever decision he made, there was nothing I could do to change it, and my mind toyed with the worst scenario. Finally he stamped my passport and explained,

"It is my duty to protect my country from spies or terrorists coming or going across the border. We may be on friendly terms with Iraq but we are not willing to let them steer our lives." Had it not been for the kindness of an officer that day, I possibly may never have regained my freedom.

I returned to Ogden and began to write the story of the Kurdish people surviving under the thumb of the Ba'ath Regime. I also wrote the story of Najat, Russell MacMillan, and their experiences living and escaping from Saddam Hussein's Iraq. During the process of documenting their stories I returned to Iraq three more times to gather further information. My route on these journeys ran through Iran and Turkey. Now that Kurdistan was protected by American support and controlled by my own Kurdish people, it made my return journey to northern Iraq and the lives of hundreds of thousands of Kurds much easier.

The organization, Save The Children of Kurdistan gave me a conducted tour of many towns and cities. Thousands of orphan children lived in the streets like wild animals, scraping an existence through all manner of crime and secret prostitution. Most of these young victims were between eight and twelve years of age. I discovered that approximately one thousand and two hundred children per day between the ages of one to ten in the city of Sulaymania were taken to the children's hospitals suffering the after effects of chemicals. The hospitals were not able to offer them a cure or even simple pain killers. The adults suffered and died from their complications. Like Russell had said, at some point in their lives they expected complications.

I spent a fair amount of time with hospital staff and doctors touring the wards seeing many chemically affected children born with major disabilities and facing death without experiencing any quality of life. I learned of large numbers of escapees paying the smugglers to get them out of the country, but who were murdered for their money, and their bodies were left to rot in the mountains.

Saddam's Iraq was a living hell for its people. While the 1980s were bad the 1990s were even worse. There was no humanity left. Many citizens wondered what the Americans were doing for them since they often disappeared from view. Some thought they were here as spies, others felt that they were studying us, but most hoped that they were trying to do something good and were not abandoning our people again. While years of fighting against the Ba'ath regime failed to bring us freedom by the year 2000 the north was already free of the Ba'ath military but not free of Saddam Hussein. Kurdistan was still in the process of cleaning the country of mines and chemical weapons. It was hoped that the cleaning, studying, and learning about the people of Iraq would lead to the safest possible way of taking down the Ba'ath Regime and that war would come to an end.

But it was the City of New York that woke up on September 11, 2001. The tragedy of New York shook America and sank it into the fear of terrorism. It reminded me of Najat's writings of the conversation between, Sa'adoun Alwan and Russell when Sa'adoun drunkenly used the words, "nine eleven" several times. Still an attack did not take place upon Iraq, but America sent ongoing threatening messages to the Ba'ath Regime. On the other hand, the United Nations firmly got into the Ba'ath regime's face to clear all the chemical weapons. This gave Saddam time to dispose of thousands of drums of chemicals by pouring the contents into the desert sand and dispose of the weapons of mass destruction by dumping them into the Indian Ocean. So the U.N. inspection teams came up with nothing. But perhaps all the countries around the Indian Ocean are in danger of a massive undersea explosion. Afraid that Saddam still hoarded chemicals, the Kurdish people sank into a new fear of attack when Saddam received his last warning from the American government.

Saddam brought all his forces together telling them and his followers that they would fight the American, or any other foreign troops. They would turn every soldier, vehicle, and weapon along with our country to gravel and ash exactly as it was written in the Koran. Despite their fears, this time the Kurds did not run having nowhere they could run to, but everyone's heartbeat increased with each tick of the clock. They wondered how much time they had left before they received the punishment Saddam would heap upon them. Many sat in barrels of water for hours to protect themselves from chemicals while others held onto their heavy gas masks and some found faith in God. Some families sat together through the night wondering if their lives would end on that night, and if they would re-unite in heaven because there was no real life in this world. Others took a shower, dressed in clean clothes and lay on their beds with the hope that the end would be fast and painless. Mothers gave their children their best last meal and comforted them in bed. They prayed that their children's lives would end before their own, knowing the consequences the orphaned children would face.

The dark, silent night of the devil Saddam was broken by the sounds of an explosion. American tanks and soldiers moved from the desert in the south and from the mountains of the north towards the centre of the country and the holy city of Babylon! In the intervening weeks the people of Kurdistan began celebrating and hanging banners thanking America and expressing gratitude to the soldiers who had come to save them. Often heard on the streets were the words, 'God bless you, young soldier, for sacrificing your life and giving up your family to save mine.' The Peshmarga took the lead, clearing the highway of mines as they went south.

Around the world, were ignorant of the fact that Iraq was a mass graveyard. Also they could not understand all the messages and warnings in the international news.

Chaos reigned throughout the country as the forces of the West moved towards and took over Baghdad. In the west the grisly stories of mass-murder, torture, terrorism, and genocide still did not stop the protests over the war.

Baghdad fell and Saddam was pulled out of a hole. It

Every day more ordinary citizens express gratidude to the American military in Iraq.

was achieved without fighting or shooting a single bullet. Ironically America saved him from his own people. Madness took over the population. Criminals were freed to roam the streets while banks and public buildings were looted. The history of the beginning of civilization was stolen from the museum and some of it destroyed. It was an insult to every citizen of Iraq. Documents of the Ba'ath regime tapes and C.D.s were carelessly passed from hand to hand as children yelled and waved C. D. s in everyone's faces. 'Saddam's crimes on tape for only a dollar.' The knowledge of the Koran, the master plan for Iraq became public knowledge. Documents were made freely available showing America's past help in bringing Saddam into power, its support of the Iran war, and the supply of chemicals to the regime.

President Bush announced he would fight terrorism and continue to fight for the freedom of the Iraqi people. Protesters around the world continued to protest, forgetting about the plight of the people America wanted to free. The protesters claimed the war against the Ba'ath regime was to aid the Western oil industry. Everyone's voice was heard except the voice of the ordinary law abiding citizen of Iraq. Even in America many protesters spoke out against the government, in effect saying to the Iraqi people. "This war is not about giving you freedom."

I wished most fervently that Najat were alive and here in America reading to the nation from the Koran. Then the protesters would perhaps understand that they may one day also be living under the threat of mass terrorism, and that clear thinking Iraqis should not see the Americans as an occupying force, but as a force risking the lives of its young people to bring liberation from the most brutal regime since Adolph Hitler

As much as the Kurds now felt free from Saddam Hussein, the past terror still haunts them today. This was shown plainly by the silence that gripped me as I stood on a long stretch of highway in May 2003. A stream of hundreds of cars, trucks, and taxis in solemn procession brought home thousands of unidentified skulls and bones bringing closure to families in the faint hope that at least some of these bones might belong to a family member. As I stood there I realized that we were all separated by death and escape. There were differing opinions among the Iraqi people. Some felt that President Bush should be tried along with Saddam Hussein for selling chemicals. But after America Sent its young men and women to help free the Iraqi citizens, America was forgiven.

In my travels to Kirkuk, I observed the unique and dangerous ways that orphaned children made a living. They worked scavenging the refuse dumps, selling alcohol, and cigarettes, and even working as money exchangers on the street corners; in effect they became the bankers in the absence of real banks. Heading back to Baghdad on a two narrow lane highway unlimited high speed was the norm, because Ba'ath supporters fired upon any suspect vehicle identified by insiders. Killing and kidnapping were carried out routinely. With the victims handed from one terrorism group to another to reach ransom demands.

Born with the gift of growing up in a war torn country, our people feel they are unbreakable in their effort to survive. Thus the madness of kidnapping was not a threat to me until I was directly affected along with a group of six media people. We were taking a tour of Baghdad streets interviewing all manner of citizens from the young to the old as well as the educated, using a video camera. We took an unfortunate turn onto a residential street where two cars ahead of us had stopped ahead of us The occupants were being interrogated by Ba'ath ex-fighters, now called terrorists. As Najat had often described it, the fear of the men brought a deathly silence to us. We knew we were the next to be interrogated and our lives were in grave danger. But luck was with us that day as an American tank roared around the corner stirring up the dust from the street. The terrorists fled in a matter of seconds without the young American soldiers knowing what had just occurred and how they had saved the lives of seven people.

During my few days in Baghdad, I faced the confusion of many street battles. It seemed that each corner displayed an American tank. Around them, young soldiers trusting no one, stood armed and ready for surprise encounters. They feared everyone around them since they did not know the facts of war not and were unable to separate the citizens from the terrorists or Saddam's supporters. Ironically I could see no difference between the American soldiers and the young people fighting under the influence of the terrorists. They were the same young people who cherished the day when Saddam's statue hit the ground in Baghdad City. Today they are patriotic followers. They believe what they are told without questioning and without knowing the facts of the war, leaving confusion on either side.

I asked them, "Why are you fighting the Americans? Do you still support Saddam?" They responded that they did not, but believed that the Americans had come as occupiers and not as liberators. I and others reminded them that they were in effect supporting the return of Saddam's brutal power and terrorism if they did not disarm.

The citizens of the South felt the same as the people of the North about the goodness of the American attack and their anger towards the ones who stood against America and us in their attempts to clean up our country. They told me, "We are not blind to the global news and documentation that American C.I.A ex-members were telling the world. This war is Dick Cheney's war. He convinced U.S Congress that they had documents of Iraq having chemical weapons of mass destruction and Cheney and his staff fabricated the entire war." The Iraqi citizens said, "Listen to our voice, America. Wake up! Do not test our faith in you. We have been the victims of chemical warfare for a number of years. We are the true document of this war. Do not allow your biased document to poison our minds; we need you to use your power, influence our young citizens who are followers of terrorist doctrine, to fight terror, and to clean up our country.

Overnight shooting within the city was endless. During the day soldiers and equipment roared endlessly on the ground, and helicopters chattered overhead. I had requested to be taken to Najaf City where the Shia Muslim ruled. Instead I was sent back north by three different taxis in an effort to ensure I did not fall into the terrorists hands. I felt we were being watched and suspicion was all around us.

Some Western and American politicians were saying Iraq was not their problem and that America should withdraw. Iraqis feel that because the West underestimated the resolve of the Ba'ath Regime before, they should not be abandoned again, or a parallel would be drawn stating that there really was not much difference between the two powers. Iraq had been a dangerous place if one spoke out against Saddam. Now it is an even more dangerous place. For those who stand by America they have now become the new targets of terrorism. We saw America trying to save Iraq, but the world is beginning to abandon America. This new opinion may convince America to abandon us.

It is now the year 2006. Nothing has happened that the Koran master plan did not foretell. Everything that Najat and Russell witnessed and sacrificed for, along with many other Iraqis, prevented the Middle East from being turned to dust and gravel. Most of Russell's predictions came true. Iraq became a slaughter house and much of the West is still ignorant of her situation because they have never walked in Iraqis shoes. The West doesn't know what it is like to live in constant fear as the Iraqis do.

The exceptions to this ignorance are the brave Iraqi citizen supporters and the courageous soldiers from many foreign lands who came to Iraq trying to bring us enduring freedom. Many volunteers have come to help the Iraqis in any way they can, despite cries from around the world to let the slaughter of innocents continue. Finally gratitude goes to the journalists who tell the truth about the atrocities still occurring in Iraq. These news investigators ensure that Iraq's story will not be swallowed, nor Lost In The Sand. Then to be blown away by the desert's constant wind.

***

Many people continue to question me an Iraqi, ask me since I am from Iraq, why the people of my country fight among themselves and other nations. It is my opinion, that young men whether they are from the Middle East or any other country can be brainwashed into fighting for a cause whether real or imagined. Those same young men, trying to be strong leaders in society can easily be brainwashed using their own constitution and laws. In the case of Iraq, no law or constitution exists, only religious dogma which turns these young people into unfeeling soldiers.

Lastly I believe that only those who truly understand war become wealthy. In contrast the naively innocent are often killed.

Glossary

Abaya	A Black cloak with arm slits that fall from the top of the head to the ankles. Worn by women in Middle Eastern countries.
Abu	Father. Arabic eg, Sa'adoun Abu Jamal. (father of Jamal.)
Amn-al Khass	Presidential security detail.
Amn-al-Amn	Ba'ath undercover domestic spy operation
Ba'ath Regime	Iraq socialist party.
Baba	Father (Kurdish)
Daya	Mother (Kurdish)
Estikhbarat	Military intelligence.

Kurd	Nationality. Ancient culture descended from Persia. The country of Kurdistan divided among Turkey Syria, Iraq and Iran.
Mukhabarat	Political intelligence service.
Musakafin	Non violent underground resistance movement consisting of Arab and Kurd. United by the ideologies of equal opportunity, non prejudice and education as a means for peaceful resolution.
Mullah	Muslim clergyman.
Oum	Mother (Arabic) Address Oum Sa'adoun. Mother of Sa'adoun
Peshmarga	Kurdish Guerilla fighters. Self sacrificing ones, or those who face death.
Rafeek	Comrade.
Sayidi	Honorific Arabic Address Like Sir but more respectful.
Sayid Rais	Mr. President.
Shiite	Orthodox Muslim sect.
Sunni	Muslim of the modern Sunni sect. Minority traditional source of ruling class.
Malha	Hostess in a gentleman's club provides companionship & sexual favors.

Author's note

Due to circumstances beyond her control, Shanna Ahmad's story has been delayed for a number of years.

Since the completion of the work, the United States and its allies invaded Iraq.

At the time the work goes to press, many of the things foretold in her story have come to pass. Saddam Hussein, Chemical al Majid, and some of his accomplices have been executed and civil war rages in Iraq between religious factions.

Bio

❋

Shanna Ahmad was born in Kurdistan in northern Iraq to a peace loving family, despite growing up under the brutality of Saddam Hussein's Ba'ath party.

During her time there, she spoke out against the atrocities that were being committed by the Ba'ath Party. Her outspokenness drew the attention of the Estikhbarat (Military Intelligence) and Shanna was forced to flee the country or risk torture and death.

She arranged for a sham marriage to a lifetime friend who had graduated from university. Together they fled over the mountains of Northern Iraq into Iran, the two spent time in an Iranian Military refugee camp before escaping to the West. Shanna resumed her education then traveled the Western countries extensively.

Shanna, despite being haunted by the existence of a death sentence in Iraq, has found the peace that many Iraqi citizens crave.

SHANNA AHMAD

General Security Administration
Sulaimanya Security Administration
No. 60
Date:

> To all of especially security apparatus
> Regarding\Arrested

We would like to inform you to arrest (................) and she is one of those against Iraqi government and she has information which concerns the Iraqi National Security and its sovereignty and its all about the future plans for the Iraqi intelligence against Iraqi nation and she has some special secret information about the president Saddam (God protects him), and these information would be dangerous on the future of Iraqi army and it would also be a damaging cause for Iraqi reputation outside

We ask you to send her to us immediately

With regards

Copy to:

بسم الله الرحمن الرحيم

العدد /س/ش/٥٤٨

التاريخ ■/ ■

جمهورية العراق

رئاسة الجمهورية

مديرية الامن العامة'

مديرية امن ممحافظة

سري للغاية

الى / معاونية الامن محافظة

م / القاء القبض

اشارة الى كتابنا المرقم (٥٨) في (■/■/■) نؤكد القاء القبض على المتهمة
(■■■■■■) من سكنة محافظة (السليمانية) علما ان المذكورة متعاون مع
الزمرة العميلة أي المعارضة العراقية وشارك في تنشير البيانات المعادية ضد الحزب
والثورة والقائد (حفظه الله ورعاه) وعند القاء القبض عليه نرجو ارساله البنا
مخفورا

((مع فائق التقدير))

نسخة منه الى :

مديرية الامن العامة

مديريةالاستخبارات العامة

مديرية الامن المنطقة الشمالية

مديرية شؤون السيطرات

مديرية الامن العامة
الامن محافظة ١٦)
السكرتير

466

By the name of God,
the Compassionate and Merciful

Republic of Iraq   No. 548
Presidency of the Iraq   Date:
General Security Administration

TOP SECRET
To the Governor
Regarding\Arrested

With regard to our letter (58). Dated (...........) We would like to confirm you that we have arrested (................) from Sulaimanya residence. We have been acknowledged that she has been cooperating with enemy of Iraq and participating on distribution of pamphlets against the party, the revolution and our great leader (God protects him).

With regards,

Copy to:

Acknowledgments

I would like to thank my dear friend, George James Thomas for helping me get this story from my handwritten pages into book format. For his understanding and passion for the language and cultural issues arising from the story.

I would also like to thank friends and supporters of this work for their assistance in the final editing. Their abilities have made the story sharper and even more compelling.

I would also like to thank the photographers and journalists from several countries, all of whom are unknown to me, for the pictures and articles circulated to the world's press for publication.

For the safety and security of some of the persons in the story, still living in Iraq, some dates, names, and places have been altered.